Samuel M. Smucker

A History of the Four Georges, Kings of England

Containing Personal Incidents of Their Lives, Public Events of their...

Samuel M. Smucker

A History of the Four Georges, Kings of England
Containing Personal Incidents of Their Lives, Public Events of their...

ISBN/EAN: 9783337099497

Printed in Europe, USA, Canada, Australia, Japan

Cover: Foto ©ninafisch / pixelio.de

More available books at **www.hansebooks.com**

A HISTORY

OF

THE FOUR GEORGES,

Kings of England;

CONTAINING

PERSONAL INCIDENTS OF THEIR LIVES, PUBLIC EVENTS
OF THEIR REIGNS,

AND

BIOGRAPHICAL NOTICES OF THEIR CHIEF MINISTERS, COURTIERS,
AND FAVORITES.

BY

SAMUEL M. SMUCKER, LL. D.

AUTHOR OF "COURT AND REIGN OF CATHERINE II.," "MEMORABLE SCENES IN FRENCH
HISTORY," "LIFE AND TIMES OF ALEXANDER HAMILTON," ETC.

NEW YORK:
D. APPLETON AND COMPANY,
346 & 348 BROADWAY.
LONDON: 16 LITTLE BRITAIN.
1860.

ENTERED, according to Act of Congress, in the year 1859, by
SAMUEL M. SMUCKER,
In the Clerk's Office of the District Court of the United States for the Eastern District of Pennsylvania.

PREFACE.

The period during which the Four Georges wielded the sceptre of the British empire, may justly be regarded as the Augustan era of British history. At no other period has the nation produced so many eminent statesmen, orators, generals, philosophers, poets, and savans; nor have public events of equal magnitude and interest occurred at any other epoch of the nation's progress. If there were few features of the personal character of those sovereigns which rendered them worthy of notice, there never existed rulers in any age or country who derived so brilliant a reflected lustre from the colossal minds by whom they were surrounded; from the thrilling transactions in which they were compelled to act a part; and from the imposing eminence on which the accident of birth had placed them.

Hitherto little knowledge of this era and of its events could be obtained by the general reader, except at very considerable expense, and by the perusal of many ponderous volumes. As this process does not comport with the convenience or the leisure of a large portion of the reading public, it seemed to the writer that a work which narrated the chief incidents of the public history and private lives of the Four Georges, in a compact and convenient compass, might be useful, by filling up an unoccupied niche in that department of our literature. The present writer has therefore attempted the task; and has endeavored to present, beside the matters just named, a survey of the causes and the consequences of events, historic portraits of the chief ministers, courtiers, and favorites of those sovereigns, with summary views of the nature and results of their measures.

In performing such a task within the prescribed limits, a prudent condensation of materials became an essential element of success, while at the same time the danger of being superficial and unsatisfactory would be imminent. The writer has carefully labored to attain the former, and to avoid the latter. His effort has been to select what was most important and noteworthy in the history of the men and the epoch under consideration, at the same time omitting whatever seemed trivial in itself, incidental in its occurrence, and insignificant in its consequences.

That the subject of this volume possesses an interest with American readers, cannot well be doubted. The era of which we have written was the formative period of the present time, both in England and in the United States. England then gave birth to the men and the institutions which were the predecessors of those which now exist among us; and though, by assuming the airs of a stepmother, she compelled her offspring to desert her bosom, and maintain an independent, and for a time, a hostile relation toward her, they feel an interest in her history and her fate. If this volume may diffuse information in reference to the past career and condition of the most important and influential nation of modern times, the writer will be happy to have contributed, in however humble a degree, to so desirable a result.

S. M. S.

PHILADELPHIA, *Sept.*, 1859.

CONTENTS.

INTRODUCTION.

EVENTS WHICH PRECEDED THE ACCESSION OF THE HOUSE OF HANOVER.

Colossal Power of Louis XIV. at the commencement of the Eighteenth Century—William of Orange—Accession of Queen Anne—The War of the Spanish Succession—Marlborough—Capture of Liege and Bonn—Events of 1704—Memorable Conflict of Blenheim—Its Results—Rejoicing throughout the Continent—Exultations in England—Events of 1705—Third Campaign of the War—Battle of Ramillies—Defeat of the French—Results of the Victory—Supremacy of the Duchess of Marlborough—Decline of her Influence—Battle of Oudenarde—Humiliation of Louis XIV.—His Appeal to the French Nation—Great Battle of Malplaquet—Defeat of the French—Influence of Mrs. Masham—Disgrace of Marlborough—Extraordinary Treaty with Louis XIV.—Death of Queen Anne, 1

PART I.
LIFE AND REIGN OF GEORGE THE FIRST.

CHAPTER I.

Origin of the House of Hanover—History of the Family of Zell—Birth of George I.—His Visit to England—His Accession to the Electorate of Hanover—His Marriage—Sophia Dorothea of Zell—Her Attachment to Koenigsmark—The Countess Von Platen—Her crafty and malicious Intrigues—Peculiar Qualities of her Family—The Imprudence of Koenigsmark and the Princess Sophia—They determine to elope—Discovery of the Plot—Violent and mysterious Death of Koenigsmark—Popular Rumors in reference to his Fate.   19

CHAPTER II.

Imprisonment of the Crown Princess—Her formal Separation from her Husband—Evidences of her Guilt—Her mode of life at Ahlden—Her Memoirs—Accession of her Husband to the British Throne—His indifference on the subject—His arrival in England—State of Parties at that time—Doctrines of the Whigs and Tories—The Government in the hands of the Whigs—Coronation of George I.—Proceedings in Parliament—Violence of Parties—The Royal Mistresses—First Visit of George I. to Hanover—Hostility between the King and Heir Apparent, 30

CHAPTER III.

The Jacobite Rebellion—The Pretender proclaimed in Scotland—The Victory at Preston—The Septennial Bill—Furious Debates in Parliament—History of the South Sea Bubble—Its Unparalleled Effects—National frenzy—Universal Bankruptcy—Judicious measures adopted by Sir Robert Walpole—Peculiar qualities of this Minister—His Personal and Political History—His Eminent Services to the House of Hanover 45

CHAPTER IV.

Movements of the Pretender—Apprehensions felt in England—Bishop Atterbury—His Trial for Treason, and Banishment—Theological Controversies—Doctrine of the Trinity—Spirit of Religious Toleration—The Earl of Nottingham's Bill of Pains and Penalties—Bigotry and Intolerance of the Bishops—Persecution of the Roman Catholics—Relations of England with the Continental Powers . . . 57

CHAPTER V.

Treaty formed between England and the Continental Powers—Horace Walpole—Dissatisfaction with the Treaty—Trial and Punishment of the Earl of Macclesfield—Return of Bolingbroke to England—He unites with Pulteney and Windham in opposition—Character of William Pulteney—His remarkable Attainments—Character of Windham—Description of Bolingbroke—His Early History—His Physical Advantages—His Prodigious Talents—His Political Career—Death of the Wife of George I. at Ahlden 65

CHAPTER VI.

Meeting of Parliament—The Royal Speech—Loyal Address of the Legislature—The Restoration of Gibraltar—Threatened Hostilities with France—Sudden Establishment of Peace—Domestic and Foreign Prosperity—Last Visit of George I. to Hanover—His Illness and Death—Character of this Monarch—His neglect of Literature—Survey of his Reign—Joseph Addison—Dean Swift—His Genius and Irreligion—Writings of Alexander Pope—John Gay—Sir Isaac Newton—John Flamsteed—State of Morals and Religion in England during the Reign of George I. 76

PART II.
LIFE AND REIGN OF GEORGE THE SECOND.

CHAPTER I.

Birth of George II.—His Removal to England—His Marriage—His Court in Leicester House—Commanding Talents of his Wife—Her Female Favorites—Prince Frederic—Hostility between him and his Parents—The Accession of George II.—He destroys his Father's Will—His Cabinet—He retains Robert Walpole—Duke of Newcastle—Earl of Chesterfield—Lord Carteret—His Remarkable Talents 91

CHAPTER II.

Revenues and Expenses of the Government—Spanish Aggressions on British Commerce—The Treaty of Vienna—Walpole's Law of Excise—Marriage of the Prin-

CONTENTS. vii

PAGE

cess Anne to the Prince of Orange—Incidents connected with the Marriage—Mortifying conduct of Frederic, Prince of Wales—He leads the Opposition against Walpole—Motion to repeal the Septennial Parliament Act—Increase of the National Forces by Land and Sea 100

CHAPTER III.

Domestic Life of George II.—Quarrels with Prince Frederic—The King's Visit to Hanover—Singular Correspondence between the King and Queen—The Monarch's Contempt for the Bishops—Marriage of Prince Frederic proposed—First Speech of William Pitt in Parliament—The Princess Augusta of Saxe-Coburg—Her Marriage to the Heir Apparent—Her Arrival in England—Visit of George II. to Hanover—His Intrigue with Madame Walmoden—Popular Satires and Caricatures of the Monarch at Home 108

CHAPTER IV.

George II. embarks for England—A Storm arises—Apprehensions for his Fate—He narrowly escapes Shipwreck—Congratulations of the Royal Family and of Parliament—Revenues of Prince Frederic—Coarseness and Vulgarity of the King and Queen—Confinement of the Princess of Wales—Disgraceful feuds in the Royal Family—Declining health of the Queen—Domestic Scenes—The Queen's last Illness—Her Death—Ridiculous Conduct of the Bereaved Monarch . . 117

CHAPTER V.

Fate of the Queen's Favorites—Lord Hervey—Intellectual and Moral Character of the defunct Queen—Spanish Aggressions—The National Forces Augmented—War Declared against Spain—Events of the War—Cabal in Parliament against Walpole—Its Failure—Hostility of the Prince of Wales to the Minister—Walpole compelled at last to Resign—His Services to the Monarch 123

CHAPTER VI.

The Members of the New Cabinet—The Pension Bill—Lord Carteret Prime Minister—The Seven Years' War—George II. present at the Battle of Dettingen—Events of 1745—Battle of Fontenoy—Movements of the Pretender in Scotland—His Successor—His Defeat at Culloden—Success of British Arms at Home and Abroad—Treaty of Aix-la-Chapelle 133

CHAPTER VII.

Death of Frederic, Prince of Wales—Peculiar Conduct of the King on the Occasion—Decline of the opposition in Parliament—Increasing Eminence of William Pitt—Character of his Eloquence—Mr. Murray—Henry Fox—Acts of Parliament—Death of Henry Pelham—Duke of Newcastle Prime Minister—War between the English and French Colonies in North America—The King's Address to Parliament in November, 1755—Furious Debates which Ensued—War with France—Cowardice of Admiral Byng—The Disappointment and Rage of the Nation—The Trial, Conviction, and Execution of the Admiral 143

CHAPTER VIII.

England without a Ministry—New Cabinet formed—William Pitt becomes Premier—His Extraordinary Character—The Vigor and Energy of his Government—Success of the British Arms by Land and Sea—National Exultation—The British

Empire in India—Its History and Vicissitudes—The French Power in India—Conflicts between the two Nations—Brilliant Victories of Clive—Surajah Doulah—Horrors of the Black Hole—Popularity of Pitt's Administration at Home—Death of George II.—His Intellectual and Moral Character—Eminent Men of Letters during his Reign—State of Religion and of the Established Church—Cardinal Principle of the Government of George II 159

PART III.
LIFE AND REIGN OF GEORGE THE THIRD.

CHAPTER I.
Birth of George III.—His Connection with Hannah Lightfoot—Lady Sarah Lennox—Proposals for his Marriage—Researches of Colonel Graeme—The Prince's Marriage to Charlotte of Mecklenburg Strelitz—Her Character—Accession of George III.—His Mental Qualities—His Personal Appearance—Administration of William Pitt—Lord Bute—His Relation to the Princess Dowager—A New Ministry—Meeting of Parliament—War declared against Spain—Incidents of the Conflict 175

CHAPTER II.
Birth of the Prince of Wales—Policy of the Bute Cabinet—Treaty of Peace with Spain—Dissatisfaction of the Nation—Eloquence of Pitt and Fox—Resignation of Lord Bute—His Great Unpopularity—George Grenville becomes Premier—John Wilkes—His Singular Character—His Wit—His Contest with the Court—His Expulsion from Parliament—His Arrest for Libel—His "Essay on Woman"—His Intrepidity—His ultimate Triumph over the Ministers 189

CHAPTER III.
Financial Affairs of the Nation—Resolution to impose Stamp Duties on the American Colonies—A Council of Regency Appointed—Death of the Duke of Cumberland—The Rockingham Ministry—Inefficiency of this Cabinet—First appearance of Burke in Parliament—Dispute with the American Colonies—Discussions in reference to their Taxation—Arguments advanced on both sides of the Question—Return of William Pitt to Power 203

CHAPTER IV.
Lord Chatham's Inefficiency—His Illness—His Absurd Conduct—His Singular Seclusion—Inflexibility of George III.—Resignation of Lord Chatham—The Parliamentary Election of 1768—Renewal of the Contest with Wilkes—His Repeated Election to, and Expulsion from, Parliament—His Ultimate Defeat—Charter of the British East India Company—The Letters of Junius—Intense Excitement produced by their Appearance 211

CHAPTER V.
Lord North becomes Premier—Renewal of Wilkes's Case—The Stamp Act—Wilkes elected an Alderman of London—His Contest with the Court—Growing Troubles with the American Colonies—Benjamin Franklin in England—First Conven-

CONTENTS.   ix

                                                                    PAGE
tion of the American Congress—Petition presented to George III. by Wilkes as Mayor of London—Commencement of the Revolutionary War—Hostilities between England and France—Disturbances in Ireland—Death of Lord Chatham 223

CHAPTER VI.
Domestic Life of George III.—His Public and Private Cares—Repeal of the Laws against Roman Catholics—First Appearance of the second William Pitt in Parliament—Affairs of the British East India Company—The Rise and Progress of that vast Empire—Outrages and Tyranny which disgraced its history—Administration of Warren Hastings—Incidents of the War in America—Second Administration of Lord Rockingham—Proposals of Peace with the Colonies in America—Provisional Articles—Final Adjustment of the Treaty 230

CHAPTER VII.
Joint Ministry of Lord North and Mr. Fox—Renewed Insanity of George III.—Mr. Fox's East India Bill—Dismissal of the Coalition Cabinet—The younger Pitt becomes Premier—The Quality and Effects of his Oratory—Splendid Era of British Eloquence—Mr. Pitt's East India Bill—Troubles in Ireland—Influence of Flood and Grattan—Pitt's Financial Measures—Affairs of India—Administration of Warren Hastings—His Life, Character, and Genius—His Trial before the House of Peers—Unrivalled Displays of Forensic Eloquence—Hastings' final Triumph and Acquittal 239

CHAPTER VIII.
Attempt to assassinate the King—State of his Mind—Disgraceful Conduct of the Prince of Wales—The King's Insanity returns—The peculiarities of his Disease—His Successive Attacks—Regency Bill—The King's sudden Recovery—Important Events in France—Their Influence on the Popular Mind in England—Debates in Parliament in reference to these Events—Riots—Recall of the British Ambassador at Paris—Expulsion of the French Ambassador from England—Dangerous Excitement pervading the Nation—The French Republic declares War against the King of England and the Dutch Stadtholder 249

CHAPTER IX.
Events of the War with France—Increased Unpopularity of the King—He is assailed by the Populace—He is fired at in the Theatre—The Roman Catholic Bill—Demand of Bonaparte that the French Princes be expelled from England—Incidents of the Hostilities which ensued—Conspiracy of Robert Emmet in Ireland—Its Suppression—Decline of the Addington Ministry—Hostilities with France—Triumph of Nelson at Trafalgar—Exultation of the Nation—Death of William Pitt—He is succeeded by Charles James Fox—His short Administration and Death—Lord Howick—Mr. Canning becomes Foreign Secretary—British Victories in Spain and Portugal—Prodigious Power of Napoleon Bonaparte . . 261

CHAPTER X.
Renewed and Hopeless Insanity of George III.—Details respecting the Origin, Nature, and Effects of his Mental Disease—His Physicians—His Treatment—His Condition officially communicated to Parliament—A Regency permanently

1*

PAGE

appointed—Gradual Decline of the Health of George III.—War with the United States of America—Growth of the Power and Supremacy of Napoleon—His Overthrow by the European Coalition—His Retirement at Elba . . 273

CHAPTER XI.

Napoleon's Escape from Elba—His Arrival at Paris—Combination of the Great Powers of Europe against him—His Prodigious Efforts to Confront them—Immense Resources of the Allies—Conflict at Charleroi—At Ligny—At Quatre Bras—Preparation for a Decisive Battle—The Field of Waterloo—Incidents of this Memorable Battle—Heroism of the Combatants—Defeat of Napoleon—Gratitude of the British Nation to the British Generals and Soldiers—Pacification of the Continent—State of the Finances—Commotions in Ireland—Domestic Legislation—The Regency—Death of George III.—State of the British Empire at this Period 279

CHAPTER XII.

Importance of the Era of George III.—Historic Portraits of its most Distinguished Personages—William Pitt, Earl of Chatham—His Appearance—Character of his Eloquence—His high sense of Honor—His Enlarged and Enlightened Views—Lord North—His Character and Talents—The Difficulties of his Position—Splendid array of Parliamentary Orators of this Era—Varied Talents of Edmund Burke—His Imagination—His Erudition—His Conservative Opinions—Charles James Fox—His Contrast in every Respect to Burke—His prodigious Power as a Parliamentary Debater—His Efforts as an Author—The Younger Pitt the sole Rival of Fox as a Debater—Sheridan—His Merits and Defects—William Windham—Junius—Distinguished Jurists—Horace Walpole—Eminent Historians, Poets, and Prelates of the Reign of George III. 296

PART IV
LIFE AND REIGN OF GEORGE THE FOURTH

CHAPTER I.

Birth of George IV.—Congratulations on the Event—His Early Education—His Talents—His Disposition—His Connection with Miss Darby—Her History—Frantic Admiration of the Prince—Incidents of their Attachment—The Prince removes to Carlton House—His Peculiar Manner of Making Love—His Connection with Mrs. Crouch—He becomes the Admirer of Mrs. Fitzherbert—Her Origin and History—Her Extraordinary Beauty—She is privately Married to the Prince—Their Residence together—Unprincipled denial of their Marriage in Parliament by orders of the Prince—Mrs. Fitzherbert's Indignation at his Perfidy—Immense Debts of the Prince—They are paid by an Appropriation of Parliament 323

CHAPTER II.

Removal of the Prince of Wales to Brighton—His Attachment to Mrs. Fitzherbert—His Extravagance—His Marriage proposed to a German Princess—Alleged Invalidity of his Marriage with Mrs. Fitzherbert—His Match with Caroline of

Brunswick Consummated—Her Character and Appearance—Arrival of the
Princess in England—Her first Interview with her future Husband—Its Unhappy Result—The Marriage Ceremony—Disgraceful Conduct of the Bridegroom—His Removal to Carlton House—Liquidation of the enormous Debts of
the Prince—Domestic Quarrels between the Prince and Princess of Wales—
Birth of the Princess Charlotte—Final Separation of her Parents . . . 332

CHAPTER III.

Defects of the Prince of Wales—The Inconsistency of his Political Conduct—The
Situation of the Princess of Wales—Lord and Lady Douglas—Malicious Charges
of the latter against the Princess—Trial of the Princess for Adultery—Evidence in her favor—Her Acquittal—The Sympathy of the Nation in her behalf—
The Prince of Wales takes a new Mistress—Lady Hertford—Financial Embarrassments of the Princess of Wales—Death of Mr. Percival—Duke of
Wellington—The Prince of Wales obtains an unrestricted Regency . . . 349

CHAPTER IV.

Unpleasant Position of the Princess Charlotte—Published Letter of the Princess
of Wales—Flight of the Princess Charlotte from her Father's Residence—She is
compelled to return—Rage of the Prince Regent at her Flight—Persecutions
of her Mother—The Princess of Wales resolves to travel on the Continent—Marriage of the Princess Charlotte—Her Subsequent Death—General Grief of the
Nation—Conduct of the Princess of Wales during her Travels—The Milan Commission—Resolution of the Princess to return to England—Her Second Trial
for Adultery is resolved upon 353

CHAPTER V.

Commencement of the Scrutiny—The Famous Bill of Pains and Penalties—The
Queen's Accusers and Defenders—Imposing Scene in the House of Lords—
Distinguished Rank of the Judges, Accuser, Defendant, and Counsel—Exami-
nation of the Witnesses—Learning and Acuteness of Messrs. Denman and
Brougham—Overwhelming Power of their Eloquence—The Virtual Triumph
of the Queen—The Withdrawal of the Bill—Exultation of her Friends—Popular
Rejoicings and Processions—Mortification and Malignity of the King . . . 367

CHAPTER VI.

Preparations for the Coronation of George IV.—Intense interest felt by him in the
Ceremony—Determination of Queen Caroline to be present—Efforts made to
dissuade her from so doing—Her Unconquerable Obstinacy—Splendor and Mag-
nificence of the Ceremony—Effort of the Queen to gain admission to the
Abbey—Her Ignominious Failure—Her Dreadful Mortification—The effect pro-
duced by it upon her Health—Her immediate and rapid Decline—Her Death—
Her Character—Malignant Hatred of her Husband—His Joy at her Death—
Removal of her Remains to Brunswick—Her Burial 376

CHAPTER VII.

Death of the Duke of Kent—Historic Portrait of his Life—His early Education—
His Residence at Geneva—His Sudden Flight to England—Tyranny of George
III.—The Duke is ordered to Gibraltar—His Poverty—His Campaign in the
West Indies—His Residence in Canada—He is appointed Governor of Gibraltar

CONTENTS.

PAGE

—Character of his Administration—He returns to England—His Debts—His Marriage with the Princess of Leinengen—His Residence at Amoorback—Birth of the Princess Victoria—The Duke of Clarence—George IV. visits Ireland, Scotland, and Hanover—Abilities of Mr. Huskisson—Financial state of the Empire—Valuable services of Mr. Canning 359

CHAPTER VIII.

Disturbed state of Ireland—Miseries endured by the Laboring Classes—Establishment of Secret Societies—The Catholic Association—The Talents and Influence of Daniel O'Connell—Agitation in favor of Irish Emancipation—Repeal of the Corn Laws Proposed—Death of Lord Liverpool—Dilemma of George IV.—Mr. Canning becomes Premier—His Death—Lord Goderich succeeds him and resigns—Duke of Wellington becomes Prime Minister—Opposition of George IV. to Catholic Emancipation—Passage of the Catholic Relief Bill—English antipathy to Papists and Jesuits—Parliamentary Reform Bill introduced—Illness of George IV.—His Death—His Character 401

CHAPTER IX.

Survey of Distinguished Personages During the Reign of George IV.—Mr. Canning—Mr. Brougham—Details of their Lives and Labors—Estimate of their Talents—William Wilberforce—Charles Earl Grey—Eminent Men of Letters—Sir Walter Scott—Lord Byron—Thomas Campbell—Thomas Moore—Metaphysicians—The School of Modern British Essayists—Historians—Artists—Tragedians and Preachers of the Era of George IV.—Conclusion 413

HISTORY OF THE FOUR GEORGES.

INTRODUCTION.

EVENTS WHICH PRECEDED THE ACCESSION OF THE HOUSE OF HANOVER.

Colossal Power of Louis XIV. at the commencement of the Eighteenth Century—William of Orange—Accession of Queen Anne—The War of the Spanish Succession—Marlborough—Capture of Liege and Bonn—Events of 1704—Memorable Conflict of Blenheim—Its Results—Rejoicing throughout the Continent—Exultations in England—Events of 1705—Third Campaign of the War—Battle of Ramillies—Defeat of the French—Results of the Victory—Supremacy of the Duchess of Marlborough—Decline of her Influence—Battle of Oudenarde—Humiliation of Louis XIV.—His Appeal to the French Nation—Great Battle of Malplaquet—Defeat of the French—Influence of Mrs. Masham—Disgrace of Marlborough—Extraordinary Treaty with Louis XIV.—Death of Queen Anne.

AT the commencement of the eighteenth century, the colossal power and the restless ambition of Louis XIV. of France, were sources of apprehension to England, and to every community in Europe. He was a monarch of more than ordinary ability, and his controlling characteristic was an insatiable desire for the increase of his power, and the aggrandizement of his dominions. He was indeed intensely despotic in his views; and his whole life was devoted to the concentration of all the authority of the state in his own august person.* Every portion of Europe, in

---

* The most reliable sources from which information may be derived in reference to the events which occurred during the reign of Queen Anne, and prepared the way for the accession of the House of Hanover, are: *Life of the Duke of Marlborough, by Archdeacon Coxe; History of the Last Four Years of Queen Anne, by Jonathan Swift, London, 1758; History of Great Britain during the Reign of Queen Anne, by Thomas Sumerville, London, 1798; Bishop Burnet's History of his Own Time, London, 1734.*

addition to his own kingdom, felt the operation of this absolute and all-absorbing principle. He was the acknowledged political head of the Roman Catholic interest. He was also the invincible foe of the integrity and prosperity of the Low Countries, as was evinced by his rapid conquest of Flanders, and his declared determination to annex the Dutch provinces in the vicinity of the Eastern frontiers of France to his already compact and overgrown empire.

The most formidable opponent whom Louis XIV. had yet encountered in the execution of his gigantic plans of conquest, was the able and indomitable Prince of Orange. That remarkable and mysterious man, whose peculiar qualities have been depicted with such masterly skill by the most gifted historian whom the nineteenth century has produced,[*] devoted his whole life to the task of curbing that aspiring spirit, and humbling that haughty head. In spite of all his efforts Louis obtained, partly by treaty and partly by conquest, not only Flanders, but Bavaria, Sardinia, Naples, Sicily, while he ruled the Spanish empire through Philip V. its sovereign; but William of Orange succeeded in establishing a memorable coalition against his foe, of which England, Hanover, Prussia, Denmark, and Holland were members. Before these hostile nations could effectively array their armaments against each other, the soul of the conspiracy expired in the person of its founder; and several years of undiminished supremacy were thus insured to the French autocrat, by the death of William III.

In 1702 Queen Anne ascended the British throne. Her accession did not change the intentions of the confederated powers in reference to the common enemy; but it brought upon the stage of action great heroes who were destined to take a prominent part in some of the most momentous events of modern times. The War of the Succession still remained the all-absorbing topic of interest in England. The preservation of the balance of power on the continent, the subjugation of Louis, and the firm establishment of the Protestant religion in England, al¹

[*] Macaulay, History of England, Vol. II. page 48, Amer. Ed.

seemed to be dependent upon the events of the war which were about to ensue. Hostilities commenced in 1703. The allied army amounted to fifty-six thousand men, that of the French numbered sixty thousand. The former was commanded by two generals whose abilities and fame have never been surpassed in modern times, and whose sagacity and self-control were so remarkable, that they never permitted any jealous feeling to interfere for a moment in their perfect harmony of action. These were Marlborough and Prince Eugene. They judiciously divided the supreme command between them, each exercising it on alternate days, and this arrangement was uniformly observed during eight successive campaigns. The French army was placed under the orders of Marshal Tallard, the most able and experienced general in the French service. The first events of the war were the capture of Liege, Bonn, and Lienburg; but soon incidents of far more absorbing and thrilling interest were destined to occur.

On the 2d of August, 1704, the French and allied armies took their positions near the then obscure but now immortal village of Blenheim, in Bavaria. The former were posted between Blenheim on the right, and Lutzingen on the left. The right wing was commanded by Marshal Tallard, the left by Marshal Marsin, and the extreme left by Duke Maximilian of Bavaria. The lines extended two miles in length. Between the combatants several rivulets flowed, which it was necessary for the allies to cross, near to their confluence with the Danube, before they could reach the elevated plateau on which the French were admirably posted, protected by the whole of their artillery. Ere the battle began, Marlborough visited in person every battery and every division of his army. His lines were drawn up four deep. Before the order to advance was given, divine service was celebrated, both according to the Protestant and the Catholic ritual, at the head of each division; and the God of Battles was solemnly invoked to aid in crushing the vaunting pride and power of the most inflated and presumptuous of mortals. Marlborough and Eugene, having each received the sacrament in the centre of their lines, at the conclusion of the service the order to march was given. Instantly fifty-six thousand men stood to their arms. The rivulets and marshes in front of Blenheim and Unterglau were quickly passed, notwithstanding the heavy fire of artillery which was poured upon them by the French. The latter calmly awaited the attack. At length the combatants closed; and both sides fought with the utmost desperation. The English, under Lord Cutts, attacked the village of Blenheim, where the strongest portion of the French infantry were posted. Twenty thousand men became furiously engaged around and within the village. The charges of the allies were made with prodigious energy, and were repulsed with equal resolution. At length the French prevailed, and drove back their assailants with immense slaughter. Victory seemed about to settle upon their standards. The centre of the allied lines also failed at this crisis, in their attack upon the infantry posted under Marshal Marsin in the village of Oberglau; and the communication of the allies with their right wing under Prince Eugene, was thus very nearly cut off. The consummate ability of Marlborough, at this critical moment, alone saved the fortunes of the day, and turned the wavering tide of battle. He instantly ordered the powerful reinforcements of infantry, cavalry and artillery which had been placed in reserve, to advance to support the troops engaged both in Blenheim and in Oberglau, and against the long line of cavalry which Tallard had stationed between these two points as their connecting link. After a tremendous conflict, those formidable squadrons were broken; they fled, and were pursued toward the Danube. By this means the French infantry posted in Blenheim, became isolated, and more assailable both in front and in flank.

On the extreme right, Prince Eugene met with somewhat similar vicissitudes. At first, his attack upon the French and Bavarians posted in front of the village of Lutzingen, was repulsed with great slaughter. The Danish contingent were thrown into total confusion. Thrice were they rallied, and thrice were they broken by the French. The steadiness of the Prussians whom Eugene now led forward as a last resort, alone saved his division of the army from total defeat. They stood immovably in their ranks; then gradually advanced with a steady tread, driving before them the vast hordes of the French cavalry; and by a ceaseless rolling fire, they rejoined the position which had been first occupied by the allies. Thus, throughout the whole line, the battle which had well nigh been lost was retrieved, and victory still rendered attainable.

The allies now prepared to make a decisive movement. Blenheim had been taken, and the French on the extreme right had been routed. To break the immense squadrons of French horse posted between Blenheim and Oberglau, Marlborough ordered a body of cavalry ten thousand strong to advance. These two hosts contained the flower and chivalry of both armies, and on their conduct now depended the issue of the day. In magnificent array, and in compact order, the allied cavalry, presenting an imposing front of three quarters of a mile, advanced to the charge. They were met by a fortitude and heroism worthy of their own. In both hosts all the noblest families of England, Holland, Hanover, and France, were represented by their chivalrous sons. When the advancing lines had nearly met, they rushed forward to the attack with prodigious fury. The conflict was long and bloody. At length the cavalry of the allies prevailed, the immense squadrons of the French were overthrown, and they fled tumultuously from the field. Nine battalions were surrounded, cut to pieces, or taken prisoners. This completed the victory of the left under Marlborough.

On the right Prince Eugene still manfully upheld the fight with his Prussians. The French lines were broken, and began to waver and retreat. They took post at Lutzingen in their rear, and there a long and bloody conflict ensued. But the victory of Marlborough on the left enabled him to despatch reinforcements to the right, and the Prussians were strengthened by accessions from the Danes, Austrians, and Würtembergers. The French and Bavarians were again routed with great slaughter. Marshal Tallard, in attempting to rally his troops, was taken prisoner. So admirably did Marlborough follow up his triumph that the total loss of the French, including the killed, the wounded, the captured, and those who were drowned beneath the turbulent waves of the Danube, amounted to the prodigious number of forty thousand men. The French lost also forty-four pieces of artillery, twenty-five standards, and ninety colors. Their spirit was effectually broken. Many battalions, overwhelmed with despair and rage, burned their standards, buried their arms, and fled in the utmost disorder to remote and obscure portions of the country.

The joyful news of this great victory, the first pitched battle which had been gained over Louis XIV. by his enemies, spread rapidly throughout Europe. It created a degree of enthusiasm almost unequalled in modern times. Not even the tremendous rout of the Turks at Vienna by the heroic John Sobieski, in 1683, by which Christendom was saved from the bloody and terrible supremacy of the Ottoman power,—thrilled the inhabitants of the continent with an intenser rapture than did this sudden check upon the pernicious pride and ambition of the French potentate. Vast communities living in far distant climes—from Scotland to Wallachia—kindled with sympathetic joy at the achievement of this glorious triumph over that haughty and aspiring monarch. Long had Louis XIV. been feared, hated, and envied; and these sentiments had been combined with another which rendered them still more ignominious and undendurable, —the sentiment of despair, resulting from the assured conviction that no power on earth could resist or control so formidable and aggressive a despot. But by reason of this triumph, men rejoiced to know that, within the brilliant and gilded walls of Versailles, the vaunting spirit so long unused to any emotion except that of conscious and invincible superiority, would be compelled to chafe with mortification over a defeat at once so unexpected, so unusual, and so disastrous.

In England the exultation produced by the martial glories of Blenheim was unparalleled. It was no insignificant honor that English arms, English diplomacy, and an English general, had been the main cause of such propitious results. Envy for a time hid her malignant head, and all classes, from the grateful queen upon her throne down to the lowest and humblest citizen, united in extolling the heroism and genius of Marlborough to the skies. Parliament conferred upon him, what he valued still more than titles and honors, substantial wealth,—the extensive and valuable manor of Woodstock. This noble palace and estate had in former ages been the scene of the gentle wooings and rapturous loves of Henry II. and the fair Rosamond. Queen Anne ordered that another and more splendid palace should be constructed on the spot, more commensurate with the gratitude of the nation, and the greatness of the recipient's merits; and that the stately seat should be known to future times by the then historical name of Blenheim. In Germany, Marlborough was created a prince of the Holy Roman Empire, and other honors and dignities were conferred upon him by the grateful nations whose troops he had led to victory.

A glorious beginning had thus been made in humbling the formidable power of France; but it was necessary to follow up that beginning with the utmost energy. Accordingly Marlborough endeavored, during the campaign of 1705, to carry on operations in an extensive and effective manner; but he was constantly hampered by the backwardness of the English parliament in voting the necessary supplies, and by the parsimony and treachery of his continental allies. Had the triumph of Blenheim been properly improved during the ensuing year, it is probable that the war might soon have been ended by the complete humiliation of Louis. But during this year the conduct of the allies was extremely remiss; and at one time it even seemed not improbable that the coalition which the long toils and the deathless zeal of William III. had cemented, would be completely dissolved. The unrivalled abilities of Marlborough for negotiation and conciliation, and his prodigious self-command, alone averted so disastrous a result. His utmost efforts were able only to convert the campaign of 1705 from one of battles into one of sieges. The fortress of Huys was attacked and taken. Villeroi, the French general, entered the field with a well-appointed army of seventy-five thousand men; while the forces of the allies under Marlborough numbered but fifty thousand. Villeroi took a strongly fortified position on the Meuse, stretching through Leau to Antwerp. Marlborough, though greatly inferior in numbers to his enemy, determined to attack him. He disguised his movements with such skill, that, at four o'clock in the morning, he appeared before the French lines, when he was supposed to have been at least twenty miles distant. After a desperate, but desultory contest, the French retreated, and took up a new position eighteen miles in the rear. They had lost all their redoubts and artillery, and twelve hundred prisoners. Their new position was protected from an attack by the overhanging batteries and immense fortifications of the city of Louvain.

During the winter which ensued after the second campaign in the Low Countries, the British sovereign, court, and people were chiefly interested in preparations for recommencing the conflict in the ensuing year with greater energy and effectiveness. It was also a duty of great importance and difficulty to arouse the enthusiasm and retain the assistance of those several continental governments who were parties to the coalition against France. In this work the abilities of Marlborough were of essential service, and they assume an historical prominence which no other statesman or soldier of the time could boast. He visited the allies in person during the winter, and succeeded in reanimating their enthusiasm, their hatred to France, and their determination to persist in endeavoring to humble the power and pride of the common foe.

The third campaign of the War of the Succession now opened. Both parties had determined again to try the issue of a great battle. The French selected a strong position on an elevated and extensive plateau at Ramillies, in the province of Brabant. The descent from this plateau was abrupt, and it was surrounded by several streams and deep marshes. The heights were skilfully defended by a numerous array of artillery. On the right of the French position a high mound of singular appearance and mysterious character, reared its time-worn summit; it bore the marks of great antiquity, and carried the mind of the observer back to generations of rude Teutonic races long since crumbled into dust. It was the tomb of the ancient German hero Ottomond; and around that mouldering relic of a past and forgotten age, one of the fiercest and bloodiest struggles of modern times was destined to take place.

The allied generals formed their plan of attack with consummate skill. To deceive Marshal Villeroi as to their real intention, they pretended to assail the extreme left of the French at Anderkirch. To meet this unexpected movement Villeroi detached a large body of troops from his right and centre. This was what Marlborough had desired. He instantly began a furious assault upon the portion of the French lines thus weakened. The artillery of the latter produced tremendous havoc among their foes; yet the resistless ardor and steadiness of the allies soon drove the French from their position. The skill of the veteran Villeroi was exerted to the utmost to retrieve the consequences of the error into which he had been trapped; but in vain. Fresh troops were constantly ordered up by the commanders on both sides, and the earth shook beneath the repeated charges, as wave after wave of that living and furious flood met, recoiled, and rebounded again over the ensanguined scene. Around the tumulus of old heroic Ottomond, the deadliest combats took place. The blood flowed in torrents through the streets of the village of Ramillies. Marlborough was himself very nearly taken prisoner. But at length his superior skill and courage prevailed. In vain did Villeroi endeavor again and again to rally his broken squadrons. His troops gradually gave way along the whole line of battle. After a contest of three hours the rout became general, and the French army fled in disorder toward Louvain.

This celebrated battle took place on the 20th of May, 1706, and the trophies of the victory were immense. The French lost in killed and wounded, seven thousand men. Six thousand prisoners were taken. They lost the whole of their artillery and baggage, and eighty standards. The Princes de Rohan and De Soubise, and a son of Marshal Tallard, were among the captives.

1*

The allies lost three thousand six hundred men in killed and wounded. The results of the triumph were in the highest degree important; for Marlborough knew better than any general how to profit by success, and how to consummate the evils of a foe's defeat. The whole of Austrian Flanders immediately passed into the possession of the allies. Brussels, Louvain, Mechlin, Ghent, and Bruges, at once opened their gates to the conquerors. The joy which this victory excited in England was equal to that occasioned by the triumph of Blenheim. This feeling was heightened by the subsequent capture of Ostend, Antwerp, Menin, Dendermonde, and Ath. Both houses of Parliament voted Marlborough the nation's thanks; and gratitude more substantial, and therefore more acceptable to the hero, was bestowed on him in the shape of an annuity of five thousand pounds, and the perpetuation of his peerage to his descendants forever. The generous queen, in her doting affection for her beloved "Mrs. Freeman," the wife of the conqueror, declared that the liberality of parliament was unequal to the deserts of so great a hero, and she wrote with her royal hand as follows: "I desire my dear Mrs. Freeman and Mr. Freeman, to be so kind as to accept of two thousand pounds per year out of the privy purse beside the grant of the five thousand (by parliament); and I beg that Mrs. Freeman would never in any way give me an answer to this, only comply with the desires of your poor, unfortunate, faithful Mrs. Morley (the queen), that loves you most tenderly, and is with the sincerest passion imaginable yours."

The campaign of 1707 passed away without the occurrence of any great battle such as had illustrated the preceding years. Meanwhile strange revolutions were taking place in the court of Queen Anne. The nation had been governed by means of the intimate and sisterly friendship which had during so many years united the yielding nature of the queen to the domineering and arrogant "Viceroy Sarah," the Duchess of Marlborough. That friendship now began to cool. The duchess rendered her dominion over her royal friend too absolute to be borne, even by a disposition so pliable and tender as that of Anne. Yet it is doubtful whether the queen would ever have had the courage to break her chains, had she not been encouraged so to do by the influence of another more congenial favorite and mistress, Mrs. Masham, who, at this period, began to acquire an absolute influence over her mind. Mrs. Masham was a distant and impoverished relative of the Duchess of Marlborough. She had been introduced into the court, while yet unmarried, and bearing the name of Abigail Hill. Her position at first was a very subordinate one; but she possessed great artifice and talent for intrigue. She very soon began to gain the confidence of her royal mistress, and finally succeeded entirely in ejecting the arrogant duchess from her place in the confidence and affection of the queen, and occupying it herself. The sagacious Sarah soon perceived her waning consequence in the palace, and in the mind of the queen; nor was she very slow in discovering that she owed the ruin of her political and personal influence to the artful and ambitious intrigues of the very woman whom she had herself befriended, and introduced to the charitable patronage of the sovereign. Many successive altercations took place between the former "Mrs. Freeman" and the former "Mrs. Morley," which always terminated in a greater alienation between the parties. At length, the breach between the former friends and lovers became irreparable, and their personal intercourse terminated. A new power had arisen behind the throne, greater than the throne itself; and upon the head of the successful aspirant, the wrathful Duchess of Marlborough poured the bitter floods of her execration and enmity, until the intensity and the publicity of their mutual spite, obtained for the duchess the dignity and eminence of being the greatest and fiercest hater who ever lived.

Though the duchess now no longer ruled England, the supreme command of the allied armies in the campaign of 1708 was still, as a matter of necessity, intrusted to her illustrious husband. Marshal Vendôme, the ablest of the French generals who commanded during the War of the Succession, was now arrayed against him; and operations were commenced by the French with unusual vigor. Vendôme took Ghent and Bruges. He was preparing to besiege Oudenarde, another extensive and important fortress, when Marlborough determined to concentrate his forces at that point, and risk the issue of another general engagement. But to attain this result, he was compelled to endure pernicious delays and obstacles from the everlasting stupidity and obstinacy of the Dutch, which led to vexations which almost exceeded the bounds of human endurance.

On the 12th of July, 1708, the hostile armies came in sight of each other. The forces of the allies numbered eighty thousand men, those of the French eighty-five thousand. The battle took place in the extensive plain which surrounds the walls of Oudenarde. In the early portions of the conflict French impetuosity and gallantry achieved, as usual, some signal advantages. But soon these were retrieved by the superior skill and energy of Marlborough. Vendôme exerted his utmost efforts to break the hostile lines; he descended from his horse, and led his columns to the attack on foot. But all was in vain. Night fell upon the contending hosts, at the moment when victory decisively declared for the allies; and the thickening darkness added immensely to the confusion and massacre of the yielding French. Their whole army was completely broken up; and had an hour of daylight remained, the greater portion of it would probably have been slain or taken captive. The victory was a brilliant and effective one. The French lost six thousand killed and wounded, nine thousand prisoners, and a hundred standards. The allies lost five thousand men, and their triumph was almost equal in splendor and importance to that of Blenheim itself. In consequence of this result, Oudenarde remained in possession of the allies, and the fortress and city of Lille, the most valuable and impregnable in French Flanders, capitulated after a short siege. Ghent and Bruges were retaken from the French. At the termination of the campaign, the French had lost all their foothold in Flanders; their best armies and most experienced generals had been beaten; all their fortresses in the theatre of the war had been captured; and a series of unbroken disasters had followed all their movements.

INTRODUCTION.

The haughty spirit of the once invincible despot of France was now humbled, and all Europe exulted in his profound abasement. Never had the fall of any great tyrant from the pinnacle of power—not even the wreck of Napoleon at Waterloo—filled the world with such sincere exultation. If the allies thus continued to wrest province after province and fortress after fortress from the grasp of Louis, he would soon have need to fight, not for glory and supremacy, but for his throne, his honor, and his life. Early in 1709, he condescended to propose negotiations. The scene within the gorgeous saloons of Versailles had been strangely altered by the vicissitudes of the eight preceding campaigns. The *Grand Monarque* became gloomy and morose, and his appearance clearly proved that some great grief secretly depressed his once elastic and soaring spirit. In answer to his proposal to treat, the allies made the most ruinous and extravagant demands. They insisted on the restoration of the whole Spanish monarchy, including Naples and Sicily, to the house of Hapsburg; the acknowledgment of the title of Queen Anne to the throne of England to the exclusion of the son of James II., afterward the Pretender; the immediate banishment of that prince from France; the destruction of the harbor of Dunkirk; and the granting of an adequate barrier to Holland against the future aggressions of France, by transferring to the Dutch the cities of Ypres, Lille, Menin, Tournay, Condé, Valenciennes, Dendermonde, Ghent, Namur, and Luxemburg.

When Louis XIV. heard these exorbitant conditions of peace demanded, he burst forth in a mingled torrent of rage, grief, and despair. Greatly as he had been reduced, he could not endure so low and so humiliating a degradation. Knowing Marlborough's insatiable avarice, he sent a secret messenger to him, offering a bribe of eighty thousand pounds if he would use his influence to secure Naples and Sicily, or even Naples without Sicily, to the French monarch. He also tendered Marlborough a hundred and sixty thousand pounds if he would save Strasburg, Dunkirk, and Landau to France. But in this instance the prudent fears of Marlborough strangely prevailed over his avarice, and he refused. Louis XIV. was driven to despair, and rather than accede to the first demands of the allies, he resolved to try once more the uncertain issue of battle. During the ensuing winter he summoned all the chivalry of his realm to rally around his throne. He tasked the utmost energies and resources of the kingdom. He published a manifesto, in which he made a touching appeal to the patriotism of his subjects. The proudest monarch on earth, in this great crisis of his fate, presented the edifying spectacle of a humble and importunate petitioner, who protested to his subjects that he had abandoned all the dreams of ambition, and only wished to save his country from ruin, his throne from dishonor, and himself from impending ignominy.

Nor were these earnest appeals made in vain. The French nation responded generously and effectively to the call of their sovereign; and when the next campaign opened, Marshal Villars entered the field with a well-appointed armament of a hundred and twelve thousand men. It was with the utmost difficulty that Marlborough could persuade the allies to make preparations in some degree adequate to confront so numerous an army. After putting forth prodigious exertions, he succeeded in collecting a hundred and ten thousand troops of all arms, and many of these were raw and inexperienced recruits. The first operation of the allies was the siege of Tournay. The citadel of this fortress had been pronounced by the great Condé the most perfect specimen of the art of fortification in Europe. Its immense magazines were abundantly stored, and the works were defended by a numerous garrison. But the usual skill and good fortune of Marlborough prevailed; and after a siege of eight weeks, the fortress capitulated.

These were minor successes, and soon the combatants were ready to try the hazard of another general engagement. The French army, commanded by Villars, had taken a strong position at Malplaquet,—a spot destined afterward to rival the glories of Blenheim and Ramillies. Ninety-five thousand men stood actually under arms, around the French standards. The allies mustered ninety-three thousand, composed of a heterogeneous mass of contingents from the different countries forming the coalition. Both parties were eager for the conflict; both hoped for victory; and both were determined to contest the field with the utmost fury and resolution. The consequence was that the memorable heights of Malplaquet witnessed the most sanguinary conflict which occurred during the war.

The battle began at half past seven in the morning, with a furious cannonade on both sides. The allies then advanced and expelled the French from a portion of their position before the wood of Soisniere; but the Prince of Orange, who commanded the left wing of the allies, was repulsed with great slaughter by Marshal Bufflers. So great was the disaster that Marlborough hastened in person to the scene of it, and restored the battle by calling up his reserves. To resist the increasing strength of the allies on the left, Marshal Villars detached a large portion of his troops from his centre. The quick eye of Marlborough instantly discerned the advantage which this error gave him, and he ordered Lord Orkney to concentrate a powerful force upon the centre. This skilful movement, effected at the critical moment, decided the fortunes of the day. The centre of the French was broken. Marshal Villars resolutely led forward his troops again and again to the attack, and continued his heroic exertions until he was dangerously wounded, and was carried insensible from the field. The scene had become one of awful and terrific grandeur. Along the whole line of battle, two miles in extent, the fiery flood of musketry and artillery poured over the tumultuous hosts, while immense heaps of the dying and the dead encumbered the ground already deluged with torrents of blood. At last Marlborough ordered up a grand battery of forty cannon, placed in the centre of his army, whose murderous fires were soon decisive of the day. The French were mowed down by whole battalions in the centre, while their flanks were turned by well-directed attacks under the Princes of Orange and Eugene. The French commenced a tumultuous retreat, and so great was the confusion that they could not be re-formed until they reached Valenciennes, twelve miles from the field of battle.

The results of the conflict of Malplaquet were of the utmost importance. It not only decided the fate of the fortress of Mons, but the number of the dead and wounded was unequalled during the progress of the war. The allies lost six thousand killed, ten thousand wounded. Their entire loss did not fall below twenty thousand, being one-fifth of their whole number. The French lost in killed and wounded, fourteen thousand men; but this proportion is accounted for by the fact that their troops were protected in a great measure by the intrenchments in which they were posted at the commencement of the conflict. But the moral effect of their defeat was overwhelming. All the hopes which Louis XIV. had entertained, that this last heroic and desperate effort of his army and people would assure a tardy, but still an overwhelming triumph, were disappointed. During the winter which ensued, negotiations for peace were again resumed; but the demands of the Dutch were still so exorbitant that even Louis, humbled, enfeebled, and even terrified as he had become, could not so deeply abase himself as to accede to them. Accordingly, with the spring of 1710, hostilities were again commenced; the fortress of Douay was besieged by the allies and taken, though defended by a strong garrison, and though Villars made a diversion in their favor. Fortress after fortress fell beneath the attacks of the allies with the most extraordinary rapidity; and when the campaign closed, the fortunes of Louis were lower, the pride of the Dutch was higher, and the real power of Britain was greater, than they had ever been at any previous period.

It would naturally be supposed that the treaty which followed this memorable war, in which the most constant and invariable success attended the arms of the allies and the English, would contain the most humiliating terms for France. The fact was widely different; and the cause of this singular anomaly is to be found within the precincts of the palace of the pliant Queen Anne. That princess was then ruled by Mrs. Masham as absolutely, though more amiably, than she had ever been by the Duchess of Marlborough. This lady had already been dismissed from all her employments in the court. She was no longer the keeper of the privy purse, and no longer head of the queen's household. Mrs. Masham had succeeded to all her offices. The able ministers who composed the cabinet of the queen—Bolingbroke, Harley, and Godolphin—even brought forward against the Duke of Marlborough an accusation of fraud and peculation in the appropriation of the funds intended for the support of the war. On the 31st of December, 1712, he was dismissed from all his civil and military appointments; and the man who had achieved the most to exalt England to the rank of the first nation of Europe, was by England consigned to obscurity and disgrace.

The fall of Marlborough was the salvation of Louis. The deliberations on the terms of the treaty were progressing, when the victor in so many battles was hurled from the pinnacle of power and glory. Louis now directed his efforts to bribe Mrs. Masham the ruling favorite. He succeeded admirably; he gained Mrs. Masham, and Mrs. Masham gained the queen. On the 6th of June, 1712, the celebrated treaty of Utrecht was signed by the plenipotentiaries of the belligerent powers. England virtually gave up all the objects for which the War of the Succession had been waged. Louis XIV. was in ecstasies; he sent Queen Anne, as a token of his affectionate regard, a present of six splendid dresses, and five hundred bottles of wine! The presents made to Mrs. Masham, if more valuable, were less notorious. Louis through her means escaped from impending ruin. The great point respecting which the war had been waged—whether the vast dominions which belonged to the Spanish crown should or should not be the inheritance of the princes of the Bourbon race, was completely abandoned to Louis; for the allied powers expressly contracted that the Duke of Anjou, a Bourbon prince, should immediately ascend the Spanish throne. Never had an English sovereign and English diplomatists enacted so disgraceful, so imbecile, and so ruinous a compact.*

During the remainder of the reign of Queen Anne, the Tories

* *Du Mont, Corps Diplom., tom. VII.*

ruled the nation. Their majority in both houses of Parliament was overwhelming. But the possession of absolute power gradually engendered bitter feuds and jealousies between the members of the cabinet, which would have led to new combinations and new intrigues, had not the unexpected death of the queen, on the 1st of August, 1714, suddenly put an end, and that for a long succession of years, to the pernicious power and supremacy of the Tory party. By an act passed in the preceding reign of William III., the succession of the British crown was now to be diverted from the heads of the illustrious and unfortunate race of the Stuarts, to that of the less noble but more pliable, and therefore more acceptable, house of Hanover.

PART I.

LIFE AND REIGN OF GEORGE THE FIRST.

CHAPTER I.

Origin of the House of Hanover—History of the Family of Zell—Birth of George I.—His Visit to England—His Accession to the Electorate of Hanover—His Marriage—Sophia Dorothea of Zell—Her Attachment to Koenigsmark—The Countess Von Platen—Her crafty and malicious intrigues—Peculiar Qualities of her Family—The Imprudence of Koenigsmark and the Princess Sophia—They determine to elope—Discovery of the Plot—Violent and mysterious Death of Koenigsmark—Popular Rumors in reference to his Fate.

THE foundations of the modern house of Hanover, more properly termed that of Brunswick-Lunenberg, were laid amid the chaotic darkness and turbulent gloom of the eleventh century. In the year 1028 Azon d'Este, Marquis of Tuscany, an impoverished and adventurous nobleman, entered the service of Conrad, Emperor of Germany. He soon distinguished himself in the wars which then raged in the empire; and he subsequently had the good fortune successfully to woo the fair Cunegunda of Guelph, who, together with her immense wealth, brought him the power and influence which, at that period, were wielded by her illustrious family.

The fruit of this happy alliance was Robert Guelph, surnamed the Robust. This chivalrous prince having arrived at man's estate, obtained as his bride the widowed sister-in-law of the great Harold. She was the daughter of Baldwin de Lisle, Count of Flanders; and her first husband was the deceased Duke of Kent. This union obtained the approbation of Henry IV., Emperor of Germany; and to prove his partiality for his favorites he deprived Otho, Duke of Saxony, of the possession of Bavaria, and conferred it upon Robert Guelph. This munificent gift remained in the hands of his descendants, until his great-grandson forfeited it by his rebellion against the Emperor Frederic Barbarossa. Subsequently by means of the efficient intercession of the brother-in-law of the rebel, Henry II. of England, the unfortunate Guelph was invested with the Countships of Brunswick and Lunenberg by the Emperor Otho IV. That generous monarch in the year 1200 elevated these domains to the higher dignity, prerogatives, and title of a duchy.

The Brunswick princes having thus resumed their place among the petty potentates and nobility of the Teutonic empire, their provinces descended from one generation to another in quiet and orderly succession; and nothing either of superior distinction or of singular misfortune occurred during several centuries to signalize their career, or to render their vicissitudes worthy of special notice. The family were united, separated, and transferred by various marriages to the surrounding princes, at different times; and thus the several branches of Brunswick-Wolfenbüttel, Brunswick-Zell, Brunswick-Dannenberg were brought into existence. In the fifteenth century Duke Bernard exchanged his Duchy of Brunswick for that of Lunenberg; and thus established that particular branch from which have descended the present reigning family of the British Empire.*

The great-grandfather of George I.—William, Duke of Brunswick-Lunenberg—had seven sons. These astute German princes readily perceived that, if they all contracted the responsibilities of marriage, the revenues of their province would be utterly insufficient to meet the expenses which the proper maintenance of their ducal dignity would entail; and they adopted the prudent deter-

* The most reliable and minute details respecting the early history of the House of Hanover, both of the portion of it which was located in Germany, and of that which remained in Italy, are to be found in *Eccard's Origines Guelficæ, Muratori's Antichita Estense, Halliday's Annals of the House of Hanover*, and *Gibbon's Posthumous Works*.

mination not to form any matrimonial connections, but to draw lots to determine which one of their number should inherit the electoral dignity, should subsequently marry, and should thus continue the succession. The choice fell upon the sixth son, George, who thus became the head of the family, and subsequently the husband of Anne Eleanor, daughter of the Landgrave of Hesse-Darmstadt. The fruit of this union was Frederic Augustus. In 1658 this prince married Sophia, the daughter of the King of Bohemia. Their eldest child, George Lewis, was he whose fortunate destiny it was to elevate this petty race of German princes in his own person to the sovereignty of the British realms.

The ancestors of the Princess of Zell whom the Crown Prince of Hanover subsequently married, were fugitives from France at the ignominious epoch of the revocation of the edict of Nantes by Louis XIV. Among the many noble Protestant families who then sought safety by flight in a foreign land was that of Alexander d'Esmiers, Marquis d'Olbreuse, a native and inhabitant of Poictiers. The chief consolation of this person's exile, and the most valuable wealth which he possessed, was his only daughter Eleanora, who accompanied him. He took refuge in Brussels; and in the gay circles of that capital the young and fair Huguenot soon became celebrated for her unrivalled beauty, her intelligence, and her accomplishments. She was received into the suite of the fascinating Duchess of Tarento; but she excelled all her associates, her rivals, and even her mistress in the potency and attractiveness of her charms. Eleanora subsequently married the Duke of Zell, by a morganatic arrangement which made her his wife in the eyes of the church, but not in the estimation of the law, and which neither secured her the privileges of his rank nor the inheritance of his possessions. The first offspring of this union was Sophia Dorothea of Zell, who was born in December 1666, and was destined to a singular and melancholy fate.

GEORGE LEWIS, the comparatively insignificant prince whose enviable fortune it became, to ascend from the government of an obscure province in Germany to the throne of one of the greatest empires in the world, under the title of George I.—was born at the city of Hanover, on the 28th of May, 1660. He was the eldest son of Ernest Augustus, Elector of Hanover, and Sophia Stuart, daughter of Frederic, the Elector Palatine, and granddaughter of James I. of England. The boyhood and youth of the prince were spent, without any peculiarity of incident, at his father's court. He there received the routine of instruction usually prevalent among princes of that era; though the predominating quality of his training was military. For this department of science he exhibited not only a strong predilection, but also some capacity. When he arrived at man's estate, he enlisted in the service of the Emperor of Germany against the Turks; and somewhat distinguished himself during the three campaigns which he made in Hungary. He also acquired celebrity in the war which subsequently raged between the Emperor and the King of France.

In 1681 the Crown Prince visited England as a suitor for the hand of the Princess Anne. On his way thither he had an interview with the Prince of Orange at the Hague; confided to him the secret purpose of his journey; and requested his good offices in the advancement of his suit. But no sooner had he taken his departure than William, who was intensely opposed to the accomplishment of such a union, as it would seriously interfere with his own ambitious designs, instantly set to work and started three separate yet coöperative intrigues against the Crown Prince. One of these was centred in London, another in Hanover, and the third at Zell. It is not singular that so profound a statesman, and so crafty a tactician as William of Orange, should easily defeat the purposes of so simple and incapable a diplomatist as the Crown Prince of Hanover.

On the arrival of George in England, information was conveyed to King Charles II. that the German Prince, who still remained on board his vessel, was lying patiently in the road off Greenwich, waiting to be invited to court. Apartments were immediately prepared for him at Whitehall, and a public audience was granted him the next day. When he was in troduced to the Princess Anne he saluted her with a kiss; to perform which bold and chivalrous act he had received the king's permission. He spent four months in England, and endeavored to little or no purpose to produce some tender impression on the heart of the princess. He was welcomed to the University of Cambridge, and honorary degrees were there lavished upon him and the chief members of his suite. The father of the Princess seemed to take but little interest in the matter; he neither encouraged nor opposed the matrimonial offer of the Crown Prince. But the intrigues and influence of William of Orange seem to have been more efficacious than the indifference of Anne, or the ardent wooings of her suitor. George soon perceived that his efforts were hopeless, and was preparing to abandon all further solicitations, when he was suddenly summoned to return to Hanover. Two years after his departure Anne was married to the Prince of Denmark.

On the death of his father in 1700 the Crown Prince succeeded to the Electorate of Hanover. In 1701 he marched to the assistance of the Duke of Holstein against the King of Denmark, and eventually compelled the Danish troops to raise the siege of Tonningen. He then joined the alliance which was subsequently formed against the French monarch, and he induced his relatives, the princes of the house of Wolfenbüttel, to abandon their connection with France. In 1707 after the glorious victory of the allies at Blenheim, the Elector of Hanover was intrusted with the supreme command of the armies of the Emperor of Germany; and he performed the duties of this responsible and difficult post during three successive campaigns, with no inconsiderable degree of success and distinction. He then resigned, in consequence of the jealousies and discords of the generals who were appointed to serve under him. At the peace of Rastadt Louis XIV. was compelled to recognize the electoral dignity in the house of Brunswick-Lunenberg, as well as the right of the elector of Hanover to the succession to the British throne. That indisputable claim was based upon an act of the British parliament passed in 1700, during the latter part of the reign of William III. limiting the succession of the crown, after the death of Queen Anne without issue, to the electress Sophia of Hanover, and to the heirs of her body who were attached to the Protestant religion.*

A considerable degree of romantic interest is associated with the early matrimonial experiences of the Crown Prince of Hanover. In 1682 he married his cousin Sophia Dorothea, as already narrated. The princess was only sixteen years of age when this unfortunate union took place. The lady was remarkable for her vivacious and excitable disposition, which she had inherited from her mother; as well as for the elegance of her manners, and the beauty of her person. At the diminutive yet very gay court of Zell, she had been brought up to habits of coquetry, and even perhaps of gallantry. In no respects was this imaginative and fascinating creature adapted to the sober, dull, and heavy prince who had become her husband; and it very soon became evident that their marriage would prove a very unhappy, or at least a very uncongenial one. While the Crown Prince amused himself in his palace, and more especially when he was absent in the wars, his wife indulged in every species of frivolity and elegant dissipation. In a short time she allowed herself a still more inexcusable degree of liberty; for her rank, her beauty, her accomplishments, and her wit naturally rendered her the object of the amorous regard of several of the most accomplished and noble gallants of the day, who happened then to reside at the court of Hanover.

These suitors were not long permitted to sigh in vain; but soon the preference of the princess was fixed entirely on the accomplished and agreeable Count Philip von Koenigsmark, whose

---

* Sophia was a woman of superior talent, and of great energy of character. She had the head of a statesman and philosopher on the shoulders of a beautiful woman; and the passage of the Act of Succession by the British Parliament was in a great measure the result of the long-continued, skilful, and masterly intrigues which, during the progress of many years, she carried on with the leading minds in the British Government. See *Hannoverische Hof unter dem Kurf. Ernst August, und der Kurfürstin Sophie; von Dr. C. E. von Malortie. Hanover*, 1847.

remarkable graces of person were celebrated not only in his own day, but have been commemorated for the wonder and praise of succeeding generations. This young nobleman was descended from an illustrious and chivalrous race. The Koenigsmarks were originally an ancient Brandenberg family. The name was first rendered celebrated by Field-Marshal John Christopher Koenigsmark, who commanded with great distinction under Gustavus Adolphus in the Thirty Years' War. After the termination of that tremendous and sanguinary contest by the peace of Westphalia, the old field-marshal was made governor of Bremen and Verden; and he died at an advanced age, possessed of a great name and a princely estate. All his descendants were remarkable for their extreme personal beauty. His granddaughter Maria Aurora von Koenigsmark was one of the most accomplished and fascinating women of her time; was the mistress of the chivalrous Augustus King of Poland and Elector of Saxony; and became by him the mother of the celebrated Marshal Saxe.* But remarkable as this lady was for her personal charms she was surpassed in this respect by her younger brother Count Philip, upon whom the wife of the future King of England bestowed her ardent and impassioned affections.

Philip von Koenigsmark was born in 1662. His mother was the daughter of Count Wrangel, the favorite general and noblest courtier of the Swedish hero. His father was an officer in the Dutch service, who, after becoming distinguished for his military talents, was killed at the siege of Bonn in 1673. Philip had been

* After the connection which existed between Aurora Koenigsmark and Augustus ceased, she retired to the Protestant Abbey of Quedlinburg, in Lower Saxony, and there spent the latter portion of her life in religious exercises, and in literary pursuits. She wrote many "Meditations" which are remarkable for their intellectual and spiritual excellence. She became eventually the abbess of the institution, and under her auspices it acquired a widely-spread celebrity. It existed till 1802, when it was suppressed. It is asserted on good authority that when this royal brute, the Elector of Saxony, died, he left behind him a congregation of three hundred and fifty-two illegitimate children, whose mothers belonged to every rank and situation in life; for none of whom or their offspring had he made the least provision. Madame George Sand (Dudevant), the distinguished French writer, claims to be a direct descendant of Marshal Saxe.

brought up at the court of Zell; and already in his boyhood had been an admirer of the young Princess Sophia. Nor was his passion even then unreturned; but young Koenigsmark, in company with his brother Charles John, was suddenly sent off to England where they resided for some time at the dissolute court of Charles II. While in England both of these young men were connected with several scenes of violence and turbulence, by which they became very nearly involved in severe judicial punishments. In 1685 the brothers returned to the continent. Charles Koenigsmark was shortly afterward killed, fighting against the Turks in the Morea. His brother Philip, led by an unpropitious fate, returned to Hanover, took service under the Elector Ernest Augustus, and again resumed his habits of intimacy with the Princess Sophia, then the wife of the Crown Prince George.*

Their guilty intercourse was destined, after a considerable period of secret indulgence, to meet with a horrible and disastrous termination. The lovers frequently met; nor was their conduct controlled by much prudence.† The princess sometimes even visited Koenigsmark at his hotel. She frankly assured him in one of her letters, that if he thought that the fear of exposure, or of losing her reputation, would prevent her from seeing him, he did her heart great injustice; that his society and his love were to her more precious than her life! The deportment of the lovers was in accordance with such extravagant expressions of feeling. Obtuse and indifferent as was the nature of the Crown Prince, this connection did not escape his own notice, and that of the vigilant and jealous courtiers. Among the most malignant and artful of the latter was the Countess von Platen; a woman of strong passions and profound craft, who had herself made tender advances to Koenigsmark, which had been by him repelled. He had also added an unnecessary intensity to her hatred, by boasting in public both of his intimacy with the princess, and of his supreme contempt for Von Platen. The latter having heard of

* *Vide Archdeacon Coxe's Life of Sir Robert Walpole, Vol. I., p. 267.*
† In one of his impassioned letters which may be quoted as a sample of the rest, Koenigsmark writes: "*Demain à dix heures je serai au rendezvous;*" and adds more ardently, "*Mon ange, c'est pour toi seule que je vive et que je respire.*"

this vaunting impudence, vowed to be avenged upon the handsome count, as well as upon her more favored rival; and she set about the task of realizing her purpose.

The intense enmity which the fiendish and perfidious Countess Von Platen entertained toward the Crown Princess had additional and less honorable causes. The latter, by her amiability and affectionate deportment toward her father-in-law, the old elector, had secured his good-will, and her praises were constantly upon his tongue. Von Platen was the superannuated mistress of the venerable elector; and she became fearful that she might lose her supreme influence over her ancient lover, if his daughter-in-law secured so large a share of his affection. Accordingly she infused into his mind doubts respecting the faithfulness of the princess to her husband; and retailed with exaggerated statements all she knew about the intimacy which existed between the princess and Koenigsmark. Nor did this malignant wretch stop here. She threw her artful toils around the Crown Prince himself; and supplied him, her own aged charms being faded and impotent, with a new mistress who was not only her relative, but her most obsequious tool. It was on this occasion that she introduced to his acquaintance the celebrated "Maypole," the prodigiously tall and towering Melusina von Schulemberg. The most potent art by which she managed the prince was flattery; while to this accomplishment she added some ability in amusing his narrow and common-place mind. The consequences of these and other influences which Von Platen skilfully directed was, that soon the unfortunate princess lost the affection and even the esteem of her husband, who at length treated her with positive rudeness and insult. The birth of a son in 1683, and of a daughter in 1684, produced no permanent improvement in their relations; and even in the palace itself the unhappy princess was compelled to encounter the bold, crafty, and unblushing mistresses of the Crown Prince.*

But the grand climax of Von Platen's revenge both upon the

* It is a remarkable circumstance that this family of the Von Platens furnished mistresses to the princes of the Electoral House of Hanover, uninter-

princess and upon the Count Von Koenigsmark, yet remained to be achieved; and she patiently waited for a favorable and propitious moment.

The imprudent lovers themselves unfortunately furnished their enemy with what she most ardently desired. They had adopted the desperate resolution to escape together, first to Hamburg and thence into France. On the first of July, 1694, at eleven o'clock at night, Koenigsmark paid a secret visit to the princess in her apartment in the palace, for the purpose of making the last arrangements previous to their flight. He was disguised on this occasion in the simple attire of a tradesman. His servants and carriages were then waiting for them at the rear of the palace garden, ready to start instantly for Dresden. All these secret plans had been detected by the malignant shrewdness and vigilance of the Countess Von Platen; and she eagerly seized the opportunity both to gratify her own vengeance, and to vindicate the outraged honor of the electoral family.*

This last interview between the lovers was protracted much longer than propriety and prudence dictated. Already had the faithful female attendant of the princess, the Fraulein von Knesebeck, knocked twice at her door and urged them to separate. At length their preparations or their dalliance being terminated, Koenigsmark left the apartment of the princess, and traversed a long corridor which led through the palace, till he came to a small door in the rear, which opened into the garden. This door he expected to find as usual unlocked; but it was at that time bolted. He then returned, and passed along another corridor

ruptedly, during the progress of three-quarters of a century. The first countess spoken of in the text was the mistress of Ernst Augustus. Her daughter, Madame Kielmansegge, was the mistress of his son the Crown Prince; while the same disgraceful relation was borne toward him by Kielmansegge's sister, Madame von Busche, and by her niece the Countess Walmoden, afterward created the Countess of Yarmouth.

* See *Denkwürdigkeiten der Gräfin Maria Aurora von Koenigsmark und der Koenigsmarkschen Familie. nach ubisher unbekannten Quellen. Von Dr. Friederich Cramer.* 2 *Bände*, 8vo, *Leipzig*, 1836. This interesting and valuable work contains the most complete information which is accessible in reference to the celebrated and really remarkable family of the Koenigsmarks.

till he came to an ante-room which was built over the court-chapel, in which there was an immense chimney constructed for the purpose of receiving the smoke from the apparatus which heated the chapel. In this dark recess four armed halberdiers had been stationed by the command of the prince, at the suggestion of Von Platen; and when the unsuspecting Koenigsmark approached them, thoughtlessly humming a tune, he was suddenly and furiously attacked. He drew his sword and defended himself bravely for some time; but being overpowered by superior numbers he was mortally wounded. He was immediately dragged into an adjoining apartment, where his deadly enemy the countess awaited him. As soon as Koenigsmark beheld her, he collected his remaining strength, and overwhelmed her with curses. To these the indignant woman responded by stamping fiercely with her feet upon that bleeding face whose handsome features she had once so ardently admired. Before life was entirely extinct, the body was hurried into a small cellar, which could be filled with water by means of a pipe. There the unhappy count was drowned; and the next morning his remains were buried in an oven in the vaults of the palace, which was afterward securely walled up. Such was the sad termination of the brilliant career of one of the most gallant and accomplished courtiers of his time.*

* The authority from which these horrible details respecting the fate of Philip von Koenigsmark are derived, is a recent erudite and reliable work entitled, *Geschichte der Höfe des Hauses Braunschweig in Deutschland und England, von Dr. Edward Vehse.* 4 Bände, Hamburg, 1853. It is true that several different versions have been given of the mode of Koenigsmark's death, which vary very considerably. Thus Horace Walpole asserts, in one of his letters, that the count was strangled in the princess's dressing-room; that his body was buried under the floor of that apartment; and that when George II. subsequently visited Hanover, his remains were found in consequence of some alterations which were made in the electoral palace. Either version is sufficiently horrible; and all accounts agree harmoniously on one point, that the fiendish malice of the Countess von Platen was the cause both of the murder of Koenigsmark and the disgrace and misery of the young princess. But the narrative given by Walpole is the more improbable from the fact that, had it been true, the princess would have been able to ascertain the mode of her lover's death, as well as the place where his remains had been deposited; and she would have communicated her information to Aurora at Dresden, through whom it would have become immediately and universally known.

CHAPTER II.

Imprisonment of the Crown Princess—Her formal separation from her Husband—Evidences of her Guilt—Her mode of life at Ahlden—Her Memoirs—Accession of her Husband to the British Throne—His indifference on the subject—His arrival in England—State of Parties at that time—Doctrines of the Whigs and Tories—The Government in the hands of the Whigs—Coronation of George I.—Proceedings in Parliament—Violence of Parties—The Royal Mistresses—First Visit of George I. to Hanover—Hostility between the King and Heir Apparent.

THE sudden and mysterious disappearance of Koenigsmark excited much astonishment in Hanover. The most extraordinary reports became prevalent respecting it. His sister, the Countess Aurora, induced her royal lover Augustus of Saxony to institute the most rigorous researches into his fate. To a direct question from her emissary on the subject, the Elector of Hanover rudely replied that he was not her brother's keeper. At length the Court of Dresden succeeded by dint of heavy bribes in discovering the fate of the count, as narrated in the preceding chapter. The Crown Princess Sophia, as soon as she learned the terrible details abandoned herself to the most intense paroxysms of indignation and grief. She declared her determination to live no longer among such bloodthirsty murderers and assassins. She even attempted to destroy herself. Her violent conduct, and the fierce reproaches which she hurled at her husband and her father-in-law, widened the unfriendly breach which already existed between them; and the scandal of this family quarrel became notorious. Proceedings were then instituted for a separation, and the princess was ultimately condemned to imprisonment for life. She solemnly denied her guilt under oath, as did also her lady-in-waiting; but the recent publication of the confidential letters of the lovers clearly proves the falsehood of their asseverations of innocence.* The formal separation between the Crown Prince and his wife took place in Hanover on the 28th of October, 1694. The latter was at that time twenty-eight years of age. She was immediately conveyed to the fortress of Ahlden, situated a few miles from Zell, in the territory of her father. There she was at first closely confined, though she was allowed every comfort and luxury which she desired.†

The faithful friend and confidant of the princess, the Fraulein von Knesebeck, was imprisoned in the castle of Schwartzfels, in the Hartz mountains. After a captivity of some years this lady succeeded in making her escape. She was let down from the window of her apartment by means of a rope, by an ancient and devoted servant who had obtained access to her. She fled first to Wolfenbüttel, and thence to Berlin, where she was received into the service of the Queen of Prussia, the daughter of her mistress. The imprisonment of the Princess Sophia continued during the long period of thirty-two years. Her revenues were considerable; and she spent them in the maintenance of a select and agreeable circle of friends around her, consisting of several gentlemen and ladies. The commandant of the fortress dined with her regularly every day. She employed and amused herself chiefly with the management of her estates, with needlework, with reading, and with the society of her chosen associates.

---

* These letters, after the lapse of a century and a half, were published by Professor Palmblad in Upsala, Sweden, in 1847. Their genuineness is established by the learned editor beyond a doubt; and with the genuineness of the letters the guilt of their authors becomes clearly evident.

† She was not allowed to enjoy the society of her two children. Her son George Augustus, afterward George II. of England, was then ten years old, and her daughter, Sophia Dorothea, who afterward married the Prince of Prussia, was two years younger. During the infancy of these children their mother had always exhibited the utmost affection and solicitude for them which the progress of time and the influence of absence never diminished. In 1710 her daughter was married to Frederic William, Crown Prince of Prussia. In January, 1712, this lady gave birth to a son, afterward celebrated as Frederic the Great. Her husband proved to be a greater brute and ruffian than her father, and rendered her whole life a succession of anxieties and miseries.

She was allowed to drive out occasionally from the fortress, attended by an escort. When the elector ascended the throne of England as George I. a proposition was made to her by a commission of learned jurists, to accept her liberty and accompany him. To this offer she replied with great spirit and with some truth, that if she were guilty of the crimes with which she had been charged, she was unworthy to share her husband's throne, and if she were innocent he was undeserving of her society, and even of her friendship; therefore in either case she would remain at Ahlden. Some years later however, the princess changed her mind, and endeavored to make her escape from the fortress. She gave a certain Count de Bar a hundred and thirty thousand florins to aid her in her flight. This vile wretch having obtained possession of the bribe betrayed her; and the baseness of this treason, together with the consequent exposure and mortification, disturbed her repose for the remainder of her life.

During her imprisonment the Princess Sophia Dorothea wrote her personal memoirs.* This work commenced with the return of Philip von Koenigsmark to Hanover in 1685, and continued until the last illness of the authoress in the castle of Ahlden. The purpose of this production was to vindicate the innocence of the princess; but no effort of specious ingenuity nor of plausible reasoning has ever been able to purify her tarnished fame, or convince mankind that she was an injured and a blameless woman. Yet it must be admitted in justice to the princess, that her conduct was in no respect worse than that of her husband; that he gave her the first example of infidelity and licentiousness; that he had not only one acknowledged paramour but many; and that, whatever might be the abstract demands of morality and religion in the premises, he at least had no right to

---

* This production was entitled: *Précis de mon Destin et de ma Prison.* A German edition of the work appeared at Hamburg in 1840, and an English version in 1845, under the title—*A short Account of My Fate and My Prison.* The latter contains also a narrative written by Fraulein von Kneseback addressed to the Crown Princess of Prussia, one of the daughters of her unfortunate mistress. The second volume contains the "*Diary of Conversations*" of the talented and accomplished prisoner of Ahlden.

demand a higher degree of virtue from his wife than that which he himself displayed.

Had the mother of the Elector George, the Electress Sophia Stuart, survived but two months longer she would have inherited the English crown; for Queen Anne died on the 12th of August, 1714, and the Electress on the 8th of June previous. The latter had reached the great age of eighty-six. On the evening of the day of her death she walked as was her custom with her son in the garden of her palace at Herrenhausen; a shower of rain came on suddenly, and to escape it she ran into the palace. The moment she entered she fell to the floor in an apoplectic fit, and soon expired. She had earnestly yet vainly desired to obtain the honor of having inscribed upon her tomb the sounding title: "Sophia Queen of England," for premature death anticipated her ambitious wish.

Immediately after the demise of Queen Anne the British privy-council met, and three instruments were produced which had been executed by the Elector. By these he appointed several of his most devoted adherents to be added as lord-justices to the seven great officers of the kingdom. Orders were then issued for proclaiming the Elector of Hanover King of England, Scotland and Ireland. Lord Clarendon, the British minister at the court of Hanover, was the first to carry to the Elector the news of his accession. The British Regency appointed the Earl of Dorset to convey the official announcement of this event to the monarch, and to attend him on his journey to his new dominions. They despatched the general officers in whom they could confide to their respective posts, and appointed the accomplished Addison Secretary of State. To insult and mortify the late ministry which had been supreme during the reign of Anne, Lord Bolingbroke was compelled to wait morning after morning in the anteroom among the servants, with his portfolio under his arm, while persons selected for the purpose heaped indignities of all sorts upon him.

It is evident that, when the great and onerous dignity to which he had fallen heir stared George I. closely in the face, he

2*

viewed it with no very enthusiastic sentiments. He was perfectly sensible of the vexations and troubles which it would entail upon him. He had arrived at the mature age of fifty-four years; and was much attached to his native Hanover, where the business of government was a tranquil and easy task when compared with the same functions in the powerful, turbulent, and ambitious realm to which he was invited. He viewed his departure thither with reluctance. One evidence of this fact is furnished by a letter written by Marshal Schulenberg to Baron Steinghaus,* the ambassador at that period of the Palatinate to the Court of London, in which he thus expresses himself: "It is quite evident that George is profoundly indifferent to the result of this question of the succession. Nay, I would even bet that when it really comes to the point, he will be in despair at having to give up his place of residence, where he amuses himself with trifles, in order to assume a post of honor and dignity. He is endowed with all the qualities adapted to make him a finished nobleman, but he wants all those which are necessary to constitute a king." There is no doubt that George was conscious that he would meet with much trouble and annoyance, in his new position. He went from a small province where the sovereign ruled with almost absolute authority, to a great empire where there were many princes who had been his equals in point of wealth, who might have surpassed his former condition in every element of opulence and grandeur; where there were many talented, resolute and unscrupulous statesmen; where there were several powerful and hostile parties; where the prerogatives of the crown were shorn, by the jealousy of the nation, of nearly all their independence and authority; and where unfriendly wits, politicians, and writers of every grade of talent and influence, were ready to overwhelm the heavy and awkward German intruder into the seat of their ancient Tudors and Plantagenets, with continual floods of satire and abuse.

Accordingly, George postponed his departure to England for

* Dated 10th of August, 1714, only two days before the death of Queen Anne, which was then confidently expected.

a whole month. At length the eager expectation of his new subjects permitted no further delay. He left his favorite retreat at Herrenhausen on the 11th of September, accompanied by his son, and his daughter-in-law, Caroline of Anspach. The rest of his family followed in the succeeding October. It was a singular circumstance that the Elector of Hanover should have been chosen to ascend the vacant throne of England, while there were actually at that moment fifty-four members of reigning houses in Europe, all of whom possessed a better title to that throne than he. But of all those who possessed claims upon the British crown by the ordinary and established laws of regular or collateral succession, Sophia Stuart, the mother of George I., the daughter of Elizabeth of Bohemia, and sister of Charles I., was the only one who was attached to the Protestant religion. It was in her favor, therefore, that the act of Parliament was passed during the reign of William III. already referred to ; and George I. was wise or selfish enough not to invalidate his claim, or the title of his children, by adopting the detested superstition of Rome.* The religion, indeed, of the new sovereign of Britain, was to him a matter of small concern as far as regarded his conscience; for he was accompanied to England with an array of the most singular mistresses who ever disgraced a monarch. Their peculiarities and their repulsiveness to all other people, very soon attracted the notice and the ridicule of his new subjects. The immensely fat Countess of Keilmansegge was nicknamed the " Elephant." The tall and slender Madame Schulenberg was known as the " May-pole." Other titles were invented for the other royal favorites equally significant; and when the king shut himself up every evening in their society, as he was known to do, a fresh deluge of caricatures and satires was issued, which flooded the streets of the metropolis, and furnished sources of merriment to millions.†

---

* Another virtue which George possessed of no inconsiderable importance in the eyes of the British nation, was his bitter hostility to France, and his jealousy of the vaunting power and grandeur of Louis the Fourteenth. This peculiarity had also been one of the chief recommendations of the Prince of Orange.

† It is now clearly ascertained that George I. was secretly married to this

When George I. arrived in England, he found himself the elected sovereign not of a whole people, but only of a triumphant faction. The English nation were at that period divided into two parties possessing about equal numbers and resources, whose political ardor and rancor were equally intense, and whose mutual hostility or antagonism was irreconcilable. These parties were known as Whigs and Tories. The latter had been in power during the reign of Queen Anne, which had just terminated. The former being the main supporters of the Hanoverian succession, obtained the chief control of affairs immediately upon the accession of the Elector. The differences which divided, and the opinions which characterized these two great parties at this crisis, may be thus briefly stated:

The Whigs asserted, as their fundamental principle, that civil government was an institution of human origin and authority, which accorded with the teachings of the scriptures on the subject, and which was essentially necessary to the happiness and security of mankind. The prerogatives, therefore, which the ruler possessed, were only a trust obtained from the people; and hence it followed that the former was directly responsible to the latter, for the proper exercise of the authority with which he was invested, and liable, like every one else in a similar position, to be punished for the neglect or abuse of his functions. The Whigs further contended, that there were certain inalienable rights which all men possessed, for the preservation of which government was alone established; and that the chief of these was the privilege of worshipping God, not according to prescribed laws and usages, but according to the unbiased dictates of one's own conscience. They thus maintained the great princi-

lady "by the left hand;" an arrangement which was frequent among the petty princes of Germany, for the purpose of gratifying passion without incurring the disgrace of prostitution. This fact is proved by a letter from Etough to Dr. Birch, preserved in the British Museum, which states that the ceremony was performed by the Archbishop of York. *See Add. MSS. Brit. Mus.*, 4326, *B.* Lady Mary Wortley Montagu says respecting this lady: "She was duller than the King, and consequently did not find out that he was so." *See Works of Lady M. W. Montagu, Lord Warncliffe's Ed., Vol. I., p.* 210.

ple of *toleration* as a matter of justice, and not of charity or favor; and they insisted that it was wrong to inflict civil disabilities or personal penalties upon men in consequence of a diversity of religious opinions and observances.

All these doctrines the Tories rejected and condemned with the utmost vehemence, not only as false in themselves, but as being subversive of the welfare and even the existence of all government. Their principle was, that government was expressly ordained of God, and that from him alone princes and sovereigns derived all their authority. To him alone, therefore, they were responsible for the exercise of their prerogatives. They condemned all resistance to the will of the sovereign as being *ipso facto* resistance to the will of God; that though when the commands of the ruler were directly in contradiction to the commands of God, the subject need not implicitly obey the former; yet it is his duty to suffer passively all the consequences which may result from his disobedience, and full submission to the will of the sovereign was at all times and under all circumstances commendable and obligatory. The Tories did not deny, indeed, that it was the duty of the sovereign to do his utmost to promote the happiness and welfare of his subjects, as being the chief end and purpose of government; but if he neglected this duty, if he sought only to promote his own aggrandizement and security, if he trampled the most precious rights of his people in the dust, if he made the machinery of government an instrument only of outrage, injustice, and tyranny, and defied all laws and obligations, human and divine; there was, as they contended, no possible or allowable remedy for the evil, except passive obedience, humble remonstrance, and earnest supplication. They further contended that it was the duty of the subject to believe in that system of doctrines, to adopt those *credenda*, and to conform to that mode of worship, which the government authorized and enjoined. They held that the exercise of private opinion in matters of religion, in opposition to the combined authority of the established church and state, was both presumptuous, dangerous and culpable.* The Tories were the secret adherents of the House of Stuart; they only obeyed the intruder, the Prince of Orange, as a king *de facto*, and not as a king *de jure*. And on the same principle they submitted to the accession of the House of Hanover, as being an unavoidable necessity which they did not possess the power if they had the inclination, to resist.

The Whig party, on the contrary, had been the firm supporters of the House of Orange, and were now the equally ardent partisans of the House of Hanover. They regarded the title of George I. as clearly and legitimately established by the expressed will of the nation. That great and now triumphant party numbered among its adherents all the Dissenters in the kingdom, of every denomination; nor was this element of influence and strength by any means an insignificant one, for the Dissenters possessed an immense amount of learning, wealth, and influence throughout the nation.

George I. landed at Greenwich on the 18th of September, 1714. His public entry into the city of London took place on the 20th, and was characterized by great magnificence. As far as appearances went, he seemed to meet with a joyful welcome from the vast majority of his new subjects. Various circumstances appeared to indicate that his accession was regarded by the nation as a propitious event. Thus the day before Queen Anne expired, a false report became current that she was already dead. The public funds immediately rose four per cent., but in the afternoon, when the falsehood of the report was known, they fell again to their former value. On his entry into London, the new monarch delivered a speech to the municipal authorities, in which he expressed his regard for the happiness of his subjects, and his honest purpose to promote their interests to the extent of his ability. The poets of the day, especially those who

---

* *Vide* " *Decree of the University of Oxford, passed in full convocation July 21st, 1683, and presented to the King Charles II. on July 24th, by the Vice-Chancellor, Doctors, Proctors, and Masters Regent and Not-Regent, &c. Oxford,* 1683." This decree condemns all the leading doctrines asserted by the Whigs, and ascribed to them in the text.

were attached to the Whig party, deluged the metropolis with floods of jingling praise and congratulation.* All the great corporations of the three kingdoms also sent their addresses of congratulation to the king, whom they termed the benefactor, the father, the saviour of his people.

But notwithstanding these outward and simulated displays of joy, the nation was ill at ease. The mutual enmities of the two great parties were intense and implacable. Personal abuse and calumny reached an unprecedented virulence. The Tories charged their opponents with being a set of hypocritical schismatics and republicans, worthy only of the pillory and the gallows. The Whigs retorted by throwing similar dirt into the faces of the Tories, and characterized them as traitors, concealed papists, and rebels. What is most extraordinary of all is, that the intensest party rage and hate existed between the several factions of the established clergy; and among the thousands who were the professed teachers of a religion whose cardinal virtue is charity, there were probably not a score who possessed the slightest spark of that quality themselves. A very large proportion of these had never acknowledged William III., yet they only expressed their Tory sentiments in so far as they could safely do it without endangering their livings. The lower ranks of the clergy were generally Whigs, and maintained the more liberal and tolerant sentiments of that party; yet they hated the Tories more intensely than they hated the Dissenters. So far indeed was this detestable spirit carried, that the partisan newspapers could not even allude to an accident which had occurred to an opponent, without giving utterance to a sneer or

* Thus the Flying Post of the 7th of August, 1714, had the following:
"Keep out, keep out Hanover's line,
'Tis only James has right divine,
As Romish parsons cant and whine;
And sure we must believe them;
But if their Prince can't come in peace,
Their stock will every day decrease,
And they will ne'er see Perkin's face;
So their false hopes deceive them."

a jest. Thus one of these journals records that, "On Monday last the Presbyterian minister at Epsom broke his leg, which was so miserably shattered that it was cut off the next day. This is a great token that these pretenders to sanctity do not walk so circumspectly as they give out."* This intense hostility was partly to be ascribed to the influence which the memorable case of Dr. Sacheverell had exerted, and the conflicts which arose in reference to his sermon preached in St. Paul's in November, 1709, in which he stigmatized the Whig Lord Treasurer Godolphin, under the epithet Volpone, as a traitor and rebel; condemned the revolution of 1688, attacked the Dissenters and the Whigs, while his subsequent trial increased the existing partisan fury; until at length in December, the king was compelled to issue a proclamation forbidding the clergy to treat of political topics in their sermons.

The coronation of George I. took place on the 20th of October, 1714. The popular enthusiasm which was exhibited on the occasion of this imposing ceremony was as great as that which marked the first landing of the king. His cabinet consisted, with one exception, entirely of Whigs. The Earl of Halifax was appointed first Commissioner of the Treasury; Lord Townsend and General Stanhope were nominated Secretaries of State, with the control and direction of foreign affairs; the Earl of Nottingham, a Tory, was declared President of the Council; Lord Cowper was appointed Lord Chancellor; the chief command of the armies was intrusted to the Duke of Marlborough; the Earl of Wharton received the privy seal; and Sutherland was selected for the viceroyalty of Ireland.

The first parliament which assembled under the new *régime* convened in March 1715, and was almost entirely composed of

* See the Weekly Packet, London, of November 12th, 1715. To this sarcasm retorts like the following were administered to the Tories, speaking of the venality, licentiousness and greediness of many of the High Church faction ·

"They swallow all up,
Without e'en a gulp,
There's naught chokes a priest but a halter."

Whigs. One of the first acts of the new legislature was to impeach the leading members of the ministry of the late Queen Anne, on the charge of high treason. Sir Robert Walpole informed the house that the papers found in the office of Lord Bolingbroke afforded ample grounds for such an impeachment, inasmuch as they proved his administration to have been the most wicked and corrupt that ever existed in England. The papers which referred to the recent treaty made at Utrecht with France were specially designated as being of this character and tendency; and a committee of twenty-one persons was appointed to report upon them, of which committee Walpole was chairman. That committee soon reported; the effect of which was that a motion was instantly made in the house to impeach Lord Bolingbroke of high treason. Lord Coningsby exclaimed, before the motion was put: "The chairman has impeached the hand; I impeach the head.—I impeach Robert Earl of Oxford and Mortimer of high treason." Subsequently the Earl of Ormond was included in the act of impeachment, and both houses of parliament, after a short and feeble resistance on the part of the Tory members, passed these impeachments without any difficulty, and almost without a division.

Immediately after the passage of the act of impeachment, Bolingbroke and Ormond fled to France. Oxford remained to stand his trial, was thrown into the tower, and after a long imprisonment, escaped without any further injury. Though none of the accused ever suffered the extreme penalties of the law, yet this impeachment of the late ministry exerted a most salutary influence in one direction; it taught and asserted the great principle that the ministers of the crown could be and sometimes would be held personally responsible for the acts of their administration; which principle it was well to hold ever afterward *in terrorem* over the heads of those who occupied places of such high trust and importance. In default of the personal appearance of Bolingbroke and Ormond bills of attainder were passed against them; and their names and armorial bearings were erased from the rolls of the peerage by the orders of the house.

Although the Whig party reigned with absolute authority during the first year after the accession of George I., they were not undisturbed in the exercise of their supremacy. On the 23d of April, 1715, the anniversary of the birthday of Queen Anne occurred, and riots and tumultuous gatherings disgraced the metropolis. The mob patrolled the streets shouting : "God bless the Queen, High Church, Bolingbroke and Sacheverell." Many of the meeting-houses of the Dissenters were in danger of being burned down. Other and greater riots occurred subsequently on the occurrence of the birthday of the Duke of Ormond. At Oxford the Quaker chapel was torn down by the rabble. At Manchester all the Dissenting meeting-houses were destroyed. Gradually the spirit of disorder spread through Staffordshire, Cheshire, and various portions of the kingdom, till at length it became so formidable that the well-known Riot Act was passed, for the purpose of aiding in the suppression of the existing tumults. The royal troops were busily employed in arresting and punishing the malcontents. Nevertheless secret plots were gradually forming by the zealous Jacobites throughout England for the purpose of coöperating with the same faction in Scotland, to effect the restoration of the Pretender ; though the open and final consummation of this movement did not take place until a subsequent period.

During this interval of growing discord and confusion, the British press exhibited the utmost virulence and licentiousness. The two parties levelled against each other every species of offensive missiles, arguments, satire, caricatures and ribaldry. Songs and ballads were more numerous and popular than at any previous period.* One of the pamphlets of this period which attained a

---

* The following may be quoted as a specimen of this species of choice literature. It is entitled the " High Church Rebels," and contains several additional stanzas :

"See how they pull down meetings,
   To plunder, rob, and steal;
To raise the mob in riots,
   And teach them to rebel :
      Oh! to Tyburn let them go!"

wide celebrity was entitled: "An argument proving all the Tories in Great Britain to be fools. Price fourpence."

Nor could it reasonably be expected that, in the midst of such partisan heats, the offensive personal peculiarities of George I. would be overlooked. They became in fact the subject of an immense amount of bitter and not undeserved ridicule. His treatment of his wife, still a prisoner in the fortress of Ahlden, was severely animadverted upon; for it was well known to all men that he punished her, if she were guilty at all, for the commission of the very same crime of which he himself had been, and was even then still guilty. The evident injustice and inconsistency of this conduct did not escape censure and scrutiny. The hostile mob of Tories satirized his personal qualities, his ignorance of the language of his subjects, his heavy stupidity, his fondness for saur-kraut and punch, and above all his singular partiality for the detestably ugly, ungraceful, greedy, corpulent, and repulsive German women whom he still retained around him as his mistresses. Madame Keilmansegge was described as being a mountain of fat, having two acres of cheeks, which were thickly covered with rouge. The appalling height of Madame Schulemberg was described as being the chief charm which won for her the king's favor, and her promotion to the dignity of the Duchess of Kendall. The rapacity of this lady was publicly dwelt upon; and it was asserted that Bolingbroke had bribed her with the gift of eleven thousand pounds, to secure from the king, at the suitable period, the royal permission to return to England. Robert Walpole's interviews with the monarch were caricatured in various ways; for it was known that the king did not understand English; that the minister knew neither German nor French; and that their conversation was carried on in such Latin as would have provoked Tully and Quintillian in their graves, had it been uttered near them. Madame Schulemberg still continued to grow in the favor of the monarch, notwithstanding the ridicule and censure heaped upon their connection; for she was successively created Baroness of Dundalk, Countess of Dungannon, and Duchess of Munster. She seems to have acquired an absolute dominion over the feeble mind of her besotted lover; and her new accessions of rank and dignity called forth new ebullitions of popular contempt and indignation.

In June, 1716, George I., no doubt wearied by the everlasting strifes and jealousies of his new dominions, solaced himself with his first journey to his beloved Hanover. He appointed his son, the Prince of Wales, regent during his absence. This prince was a person of the most meagre and insignificant capacity, as his whole career abundantly testified. He was ignorant, obstinate and narrow-minded; and every quality of his nature was calculated only to excite contempt. Nevertheless during his father's first visit to Hanover, he succeeded in winning no small degree of popularity with the nation, by adopting and executing the prudent measures which the astute ministers suggested to him. During the sojourn of George I. on the continent, he refused to see his unfortunate wife; and as if for the purpose of adding irritation to her ignominy, he enjoyed the amusement of the chase in the vicinity of Ahlden, but took no further notice of her existence, or of her sufferings, than to give orders that a more rigid *surveillance* should be thenceforth exercised over her in her captivity.

After the return of George I. from Hanover the open quarrel occurred between him and the Prince of Wales, which continued during the remainder of the life of the monarch, and became disgracefully notorious. The origin of this dispute is said by some writers to have been jealousy of the popularity gained by the prince during the exercise of his regency. Whatever may have been its cause, the king banished his son and heir from his presence; and went so far as to let it be understood by the court, that whoever visited the Prince or the Princess of Wales, would fall under the royal disfavor. Yet in spite of this declaration, there were not a few among the most noble and distinguished of the courtiers who preferred to pay their devotions rather to the sun which was destined soon to rise in the political heavens, than to that which would inevitably descend beneath the horizon in the lapse of a few short years.

CHAPTER III.

The Jacobite Rebellion—The Pretender proclaimed in Scotland—The Victory at Preston—The Septennial Bill—Furious Debates in Parliament—History of the South Sea Bubble—Its Unparalleled Effects—National frenzy—Universal Bankruptcy—Judicious measures adopted by Sir Robert Walpole—Peculiar qualities of this Minister—His Personal and Political History—His Eminent Services to the House of Hanover.

THE rankling hostility which existed between the Whig and Tory parties, and which was nothing else in reality than an antagonism between the Houses of Hanover and Stuart, eventually culminated in open rebellion against the government. The first outbreak occurred in Scotland. The Earl of Mar proclaimed the Pretender, and set up his standard under the title of King James III. at Castletown; and soon ten thousand men rallied to his camp. His confederates south of the Tweed were unable to render him any effectual assistance, in consequence of the vigilance and activity of the government; which, adopting the extreme measure of suspending the Habeas Corpus Act, committed Lord Lansdown, the Earl of Jersey, Sir William Windham, and other distinguished Jacobites to close custody. These prompt measures, however, did not prevent the Earl of Derwentwater and Mr. Foster from raising an armed force, and proclaiming the Pretender in Northumberland and Lancastershire. But this movement was completely crushed by the victory of the royal troops commanded by General Carpenter, at Preston; where the insurgents were surrounded, attacked, vanquished, and compelled to surrender at discretion. At the same time the partisans of the house of Stuart, under the Earl of Mar, met their opponents, commanded by the Duke of Argyle, at Dumblane.

A furious battle ensued. The right wing of the king's army, led on by General Whitham, was completely broken by the prodigious onslaught of the Scotch; but a different result was achieved by the Duke of Argyle, who commanded the left wing of the royal troops. He drove the enemy about two miles before him; and on his return he met the victorious party which had vanquished General Whitham, when another conflict ensued in which the advantage remained with the duke. The rebels subsequently lost the city and castle of Inverness; their forces were rapidly diminished and dissipated; great incapacity was displayed by the rebel leaders; and the rebellion in both kingdoms was happily and speedily suppressed. Lord Derwentwater and other leaders of the malcontents, in spite of great efforts made to save them, were tried for treason, condemned and executed. .

The suppression of external disturbances was followed by intense discord in the Houses of Parliament. The famous Septennial Bill was introduced, the object of which was to grant the Legislature which was then in existence, and which had been elected only for the period of three years, power to extend their duration to *seven* years. The proposition, therefore, was in substance that the members should elect themselves for four years. The chief argument which was used in support of this singular proposition was, that the disaffection of the people to the government was, then so great, and the enemies of the monarch were then so numerous and so powerful both at home and abroad, that a new election precisely at that period might be destructive to the peace and even the stability of the government. It was also added, and with some show of reason, that great and deplorable evils constantly attended the frequent recurrence of parliamentary elections, in consequence of the corrupt and established modes in which those elections were carried on.

In the House of Lords the bill was opposed with great earnestness and ability by many of the peers. The Earl of Nottingham especially distinguished himself on this occasion. He contended that frequent Parliaments were of the very essence, and one of the greatest glories of the British constitution; that the members of the Legislature possessed no power thus to enlarge their functions, either as to substance or as to time; and that if they possessed the right thus to extend their functions for four years, they possessed equal right to do so for a hundred or for five hundred years. In the House of Commons the opposition to the bill was equally determined. Protracted debates ensued. Lord Raymond, afterward Chief Justice of England, delivered a speech of unrivalled power and effect against it, and conclusively answered every argument which had been advanced in its support. These he classified as follows: 1. The expenses attending frequent elections; 2. The divisions and animosities excited by them; 3. The advantages derived by the enemies of the country from these domestic feuds; 4. The encouragement which the bill, if passed, would hold out to the allies of Britain to form new and more permanent connections with her.

Notwithstanding the opposition which the Septennial Bill met with in the nation and in both Houses of Parliament, it passed by a very large majority, and immediately received the approbation of the monarch; who, in his speech on the occasion, congratulated the country upon the pleasing prospect in the future of having and enjoying *a more settled* government.

The bitter animosities which had prevailed during so many years between the two great parties which divided the nation, as well as all other excitements and conflicts, were destined, in the year 1720, to give way to one of the most singular and fantastical delusions which ever disgraced and impoverished a people. This was the celebrated South Sea Bubble.

In 1717 a Scotch adventurer named Law fled to France, to evade the consequences of a duel; and there he employed his remarkable financial abilities in projecting a company for the purpose of carrying on trade with the territories adjacent to the Mississippi River. In 1719 the French monarch incorporated the French India and China companies, of one of which Law was the president; giving them peculiar privileges and monopolies on condition that they would undertake the payment of the State bills. There was suddenly an immense advance in the shares of the company; and the success of the scheme was most extraordinary. The French Government was relieved of all its pecuniary difficulties. Many of the nobility and courtiers became immensely rich. Law rose so high in the estimation both of the court and the people, that he was admitted to the Privy Council, and appointed comptroller-general of the Finances of France. The extraordinary success of this experiment suggested to the English ministry the expediency of attempting to achieve the same magnificent results, by means of an obscure and languishing association which had been established in 1711, termed the South Sea Company. They conceived the idea of investing this company with certain important privileges, and then making it agree to liquidate the national debt, which was then regarded by the British people as an intolerable burden. Aislabie, the chancellor of the exchequer, Lords Stanhope and Sunderland, and many other leading statesmen viewed the project with special favor. Its chief opponent was the sagacious and penetrating Sir Robert Walpole, who in May, 1715, had succeeded the Earl of Halifax as first lord commissioner of the treasury. At the period of which we now speak, he was not a member of the ministry; but he deservedly wielded a great influence in the House in consequence of his superior ability and experience. The safer and wiser heads in the Legislature perceived the danger which would eventually ensue from the execution of the project. But in spite of all opposition the bill became a law; it received the royal sanction; and the enterprise was heralded forth to the world by men in high places as one deserving of the utmost confidence and esteem.

Then ensued one of the most remarkable spectacles recorded in history. Wearied with political strife and party feuds, a prodigious reaction took place in the public mind in favor of financial excitement and speculation. The rage for dealing in South Sea shares became intense and universal. In a few weeks the stock rose to above a thousand per cent. It is true, indeed, that the dealers and buyers knew very little in reference to the

real resources, capital, and securities of the company; but they
engaged in the purchase and the sale of stock because every
one declared that such a course would soon lead to the possession of immense wealth, and that millions were to be won by
those who boldly embraced the golden opportunity. Every thing
else therefore was for the time forgotten. Throughout the three
kingdoms, but especially in London, stockjobbing became the sole
pursuit of all classes and parties; of Whigs and Tories, of high-
church and low-church, of dissenters and freethinkers, of the
noble and the vulgar, of the learned and the ignorant. All these
served to constitute a tumultuous, excited, and sanguine multitude, whose whole existence seemed to be absorbed in the singular delirium which had thrown its potent spell over the public
mind. Exchange Alley and Threadneedle Street, the great
head-quarters of the company, were crowded from morning till
night by eager gamblers of every description and condition.
Elegant women, superbly dressed, elbowed their way bravely
through the throng to attain the object of their wishes, and possess
themselves of the inestimable and talismanic scrip. The highway in the vicinity was obstructed by the brilliant equipages of
princes, dukes, and prelates, adorned with illustrious arms and
coronets; whose owners eagerly joined the crowd and were lost
in its tumultuous current. Hundreds invested all they possessed in the purchase of shares. Others sold every thing and
bought stock with the proceeds. Some pledged rights in exchange for stock, of which they held only the expectancy of a
future and contingent interest. Every conceivable expedient was
adopted to raise money for the purpose of investment. At the
same time, the most artful and insidious methods were contrived
by the directors of the company to keep up the popular enthusiasm. Vast and gorgeous visions of the opulence to be derived
from the mines of Mexico and Peru through the connection which
was alleged to exist between them and the operations of the
company, were depicted before the greedy and deluded eyes of
the nation. It was asserted that the company possessed a capital of a hundred and ten million pounds, together with the

interest of the national debt, which had been transferred by government to the control and credit of the company; and they opened four new subscriptions, which increased the amount of capital, as was asserted, to the prodigious sum of two hundred and ninety-five million pounds.

Nor did the evil terminate there. The nation having once become insane with the mania for speculation, were not satisfied with gambling in one way, but a host of other companies were quickly established for the purpose of speculation in every possible shape. In three months the number of these financial bubbles exceeded a hundred, and their aggregate stock was said to amount to five hundred million pounds. They referred to every possible subject, some of them being the most impracticable and absurd which could be conceived. Among the list were companies for insuring the fortunes of minors, for securing against thieves and robbers, for insuring marriages against divorce, for obtaining pensions for widows, for trading to the Oronoko, for improving the breed of horses, for founding Arcadian colonies, for making engines to fly in the air, for purchasing lands in Pennsylvania, for curing gout and stone, for insurance against small-pox, for fabricating air-pumps for the brain, for making boards of sawdust, and for casting nativities. Some even went so far as to form a company the very purposes of which were yet unknown; "for an undertaking which shall in due time be revealed." Instances were frequently known in which several persons hired an office for a single day, opened a subscription book in the morning, took a small deposit on the shares, and after night-fall closed their shop, and dived utterly beyond soundings, carrying away with them a large sum of money. The whole nation were dancing in a jubilee of insane hilarity and enthusiasm. Some persons, indeed, who shrewdly sold out when the stock was at its maximum, realized immense fortunes. A few others connected with the court, received large bribes for their influence in procuring the patronage of the government in favor of the South Sea Company. Thus the Countess of Keilmansegge and her daughter, each accepted a bribe of ten thousand pounds for this infamous purpose. But very soon the fatal crisis arrived; these extraordinary bubbles burst; and myriads were at once and totally ruined. It would be impossible to describe the amount of misery, poverty, and despair which ensued. In October, 1720, scarcely six months after the endorsement of the South Sea Company by the royal approval, the stock fell from eleven hundred to eighty. Many of those who were thus suddenly reduced to beggary from affluence, died of broken hearts. Many others committed suicide, and a vast multitude of those who had, during all their lives, been accustomed to the enjoyment of affluence and consideration, unable to endure the disgrace of their altered state, deserted their native land to hide their shame during the rest of their existence in the obscurity of foreign countries.

As soon as the popular mind began to recover from the terrible shock which it had received, indignation against the founders of this gigantic swindle, naturally took the place of every other feeling. The South Sea Directors became objects of universal detestation and hatred. They were arrested and their property confiscated. Robert Knight, the treasurer of the Company, fled to the continent with the books of the company, which were supposed to contain important secrets which would have condemned many in high influence at court. A parliamentary investigation of the subject was ordered and made, which revealed, in the language of the report of the committee, "a train of the deepest villany and fraud hell ever contrived for the ruin of any nation." The ministry was immediately broken up, and in April, 1721, a new one was formed under the guidance of Sir Robert Walpole. Lord Stanhope, one of the previous ministry, overcome by his transports of rage at the accusations made against him, expired from the intensity of his emotions. George I. received the intelligence of his sudden death at supper. He was unable to suppress his grief, and immediately rose from the table with his eyes suffused with tears.* Through the judicious

---

* Some of the great villains concerned in these wrongs met with a punishment in some degree commensurate with their crimes. Aislabie was expelled

measures adopted by Robert Walpole, public credit was soon restored to some degree, and the evils entailed on the nation by this great calamity were ameliorated. This is the period in English history at which *political* caricatures first began to be common in England; for previous to this interval of frantic exultation and as frantic despair, they were usually mere emblems, which were so obscure and cautious, as to be rarely intelligible. The general feelings which pervaded society, after it began to recover from the blow, may be inferred from the fact, that it became a general practice when a knave turned up in playing at cards, for the dealer to exclaim : " There's a director for you."

But Sir Robert Walpole was again at the helm of state ; and soon the energy and ability of his administration made themselves widely and pemanently felt. He now adopted means for carrying on the government, which, if they were censurable, were at the same time the most efficacious. Seeing the universal perfidy and unmixed selfishness which characterized the patriots and politicians of everyparty and profession, he adopted the plan of buying over everybody to the support of the government, by using for that purpose the secret service money. It is easy for the rigid moralist to condemn this expedient on the part of the minister ; but a little reflection will perhaps convince every impartial thinker that, if men are hopelessly selfish and mercenary, and if gold alone will induce them to support good measures which are promotive of the welfare of the nation, it is better to use the nation's money for that purpose, than permit her legislators, for the want of its distribution, to adopt injurious and unjust measures. The election for a new Parliament was approaching, and an extensive system of bribery was employed to influence the result. Then was seen an exemplification of the real

from his seat in Parliament. Craggs opportunely died, and thus escaped a similar fate. Sunderland retired from office in total disgrace. Knight escaped to Brussels, where he was arrested by the British resident; but he subsequently escaped again. The immense fortunes of the Directors of the South Sea Company were appropriated by an act of Parliament to relieve the prevalent distress, and the charter of the pernicious and delusive monster was totally abolished.

baseness of humanity; not only were the common herd of politicians accessible and subservient to bribes, but many men of high standing, of loud professions of patriotism, and of great social influence, were known to be closeted with the Premier, and to have carried away with them from his cabinet, the abundant and potent wages of their infamy.

The chief defect of Sir Robert Walpole, if defect it be, was an insatiable avarice of power. He could bear no man of commanding intellect, who might dare to influence his own, to be near him in the administration. Accordingly, in forming his cabinet he omitted to confer a place upon his old and tried ally Pulteney, one of the ablest, most respectable, and most eloquent statesmen whom England had ever produced. Pulteney thenceforth became Walpole's mortal foe, and transferred the weight of his talents to the opposition. In a short time Carteret, another man of great ability, and whose knowledge of foreign affairs was most extensive and accurate, was compelled to retire from the cabinet in consequence of the all-absorbing ambition of the Premier. He also joined the ranks of the opposition. Lord Townshend was a man of a different stamp. He was less eloquent and less gifted than the two preceding statesmen; but he was more stable, more reliable, more profound. In addition to this, he was Walpole's cousin, his brother-in-law, his old friend, his former colleague in the cabinet, his neighbor both in town and in country. Yet a personal dispute respecting the exercise of their respective functions took place between them, which nearly terminated with a personal conflict or a duel; but which ended in nothing more serious or disastrous than Lord Townshend's withdrawal from the cabinet, and the loss of a faithful and attached friend. In a short time Lord Chesterfield, Lord Cobham, Lord Stair, and others, were compelled for the same reason, to adopt the same course.

Yet in justice to Walpole it must be admitted, that to him the house of Hanover were indebted, in a very great measure, for their establishment upon the throne of England. Few great ministers among the many whom the English nation, so prolific of illustrious men has produced, possessed greater talents, or wielded more absolute power, or left a brighter fame. He was descended from an ancient and affluent family in the county of Norfolk. He was originally destined for the church; but by the early death of an elder brother the direction of his life was changed, and he passed some years in the quiet obscurity of a country gentleman. His attention was first attracted to politics, at the close of the reign of William III., by the great perils which then so fiercely menaced the Protestant succession. The act of settlement which determined propitiously the future destination of the crown, was passed by Parliament only by a majority of *one;* and the death of the Duke of Gloucester, Queen Anne's son, increased the danger to a higher degree. Walpole then entered Parliament, and soon his superior capacity for the conduct of affairs became clearly evident. He took rank as one of the leaders of the Whig opposition. He gained the confidence of Godolphin, and was by him appointed Secretary at war, the first position which he occupied in the administration. When the disgraceful treaty was concluded with Louis XIV., by which that pompous and perfidious tyrant was saved from ruin, and all the glory with which the victories of Blenheim, Ramillies, Oudenarde, and Malplaquet had covered the British nation and the British arms was wiped away by the filthy skirt of the robe of a mistress of the royal bed-chamber; Walpole in honorable and reasonable disgust resigned his office, leaving Harley and Bolingbroke to govern the disgraced cabinet, queen, and nation. He boldly defended Marlborough against the attacks of the adverse faction; in revenge for which a charge of corruption when in office was made against him. He was sent to the Tower, upon an accusation of having received nine hundred pounds from a contractor; he was expelled from the House of Commons, and having been re-elected, was pronounced ineligible to a seat, by a majority of the House. The receipt of the money was never denied; the only defence was that the long-established usage of the war office justified the act. That Walpole was avaricious is evident from the vast amount of his accumulations. With a fortune originally of only two thousand pounds a year, his wealth toward the termination of his public career, amounted to two hundred and fifty thousand pounds. He entertained the conviction that all politicians were corrupt; and he is well known to have asserted boldly, that all such men had their price.* During the early part of the reign of George I. he resisted the desire of that monarch for hostilities against Prussia, in consequence of a Mechlenburg quarrel. Five years afterwards, when the stupid monarch wished to oppose the Czar of Russia, and support the Duke of Holstein in his claims on the Swedish throne, Walpole again and successfully resisted the policy of involving England with the quarrels of the continent, in which she did not possess the slightest degree of real interest. When, therefore, he entered the service of the House of Hanover for the last time in 1715, he carried with him into the cabinet the reputation of being not only an able, but also a disinterested and patriotic statesman. As an orator, and master of the great art of debate, Walpole was chiefly remarkable for his strong and manly sense, his clear statements, his contempt for all artificial ornaments, his boldness, firmness, and directness, his readiness of retort and reply, his great self-possession and command of temper, his invariable coolness and presence of mind, and his prevalent good humor. Of him it might be said, with truth, that no man has ever been a greater favorite with the House of Commons, whose turbulent and often half-drunken members it was his constant duty to lead, during many memorable years of anxiety, danger and conflict. Lord Dover, in speaking of him, justly denominates him "the glory of the Whigs." And it is the more singular that his personal influence became so despotic over his party, and over his monarch, because he had to resist the counterbalancing tendency of some great defects. His general knowledge was very deficient, and must have often excited the contempt of the polished and cultivated nobles whom he made his subservient tools. His manners were

---

* *Vide Coxe's Life of Robert Walpole, Vol. I., p. 757.*

exceedingly coarse; and his hours of relaxation were spent in noisy, licentious, and profane revelry. Notwithstanding all these and other blemishes, England, during a thousand years of national existence, may be said to have produced but one Robert Walpole.

CHAPTER IV.

Movements of the Pretender—Apprehensions felt in England—Bishop Atterbury—His Trial for Treason, and Banishment—Theological Controversies—Doctrine of the Trinity—Spirit of Religious Toleration—The Earl of Nottingham's Bill of Pains and Penalties—Bigotry and Intolerance of the Bishops—Persecution of the Roman Catholics—Relations of England with the Continental Powers.

THE Pretender to the British throne, who at this period resided at Rome, had not abandoned his ambitious schemes; and during the prevalence of the speculative mania in England, had been busy with his agents in preparing the future movements of his party. The exultation of his friends had been greatly increased by the fact that, in 1720, the Polish wife of the representative of the House of Stuart had given birth to a son. This son was destined afterwards to experience the most singular and romantic vicissitudes of fortune. The disasters resulting from the South Sea Bubble had thrown great disgrace upon the government of George I. His cabinet were compelled to resign, and on their ruins Robert Walpole rose triumphantly to power. To escape the unpopularity which surrounded him, the king spent a large portion of the year 1720 in his hereditary dominions on the continent. So badly had his affairs been administered in England, that the *debts* on his civil list for this year amounted to half a million pounds; and he was compelled to apply to Parliament for a special grant to liquidate them. This state of affairs added ardor to the hopes of the Jacobite faction. About this period the mother of the sovereign's wife, Eleanor, Duchess of Zell, expired, and the court in consequence went into mourning. It is worthy of remark that this was the only domestic incident and usage during the reign of George I., in which his unfortunate wife was permitted to participate with her family.

Early in 1722 the movements of the Pretender again assumed a formidable importance. With the assistance of Cardinal Alberoni, the prime minister of Spain, a Spanish armament consisting of six thousand troops sailed from the port of Cadiz, under the command of the Duke of Ormond.* But this fleet was dispersed and destroyed by a terrific tempest off Cape Finisterre. Two frigates only, with the Earls of Mareschal and Seaforth, and the Marquis of Tullibardine, were able to continue the voyage. These vessels contained three hundred Spanish soldiers, and arrived safely on the coast of Scotland. Here they were joined by a few Highland clans; but on the first conflict with the royal troops, they were vanquished, and the whole body of Spanish soldiers surrendered as prisoners of war. In a short time no vestige remained in Scotland of this futile and ill-conducted conspiracy.

Much greater apprehension was felt in England in reference to the movements of the Pretender, than the course of events justified. As soon as the sailing of the Duke of Ormond from Cadiz was known at London, an intense panic pervaded the capital. A camp was immediately formed in Hyde Park to protect the king and the city from the attacks of the Jacobites. It is a singular circumstance that the most prominent personage in this conspiracy in England was Bishop Atterbury, a prelate of the established church. He held the see of Rochester, and had been a minister of the crown during the brief period of the premiership of Bolingbroke under Queen Anne. On her death, the bishop had been bold enough to propose to his associates in the cabinet, that they should proclaim the reputed son of James II. as her successor. Ever since the accession of the House of Han-

* It is well known that the assistance rendered by Alberoni to the Pretender was in revenge for the part which George I. took in the Quadruple Alliance. The object of this alliance was to reconcile and adjust the rival claims and pretensions of the courts of Vienna and Madrid; in which dispute the English monarch had warmly espoused the interests of the former in opposition to those of the King of Spain.

over, Atterbury had continued secretly to plot for the restoration of the exiled family. Nor was he idle on the present occasion; for when the most active conspirators in London were imprisoned and examined, they all implicated Bishop Atterbury. These persons were a clergyman named Kelly, an Irish priest named Neynoe, the Jesuit Plunket, and Sayer, a barrister of the Temple. The prelate was therefore arrested and committed to the Tower, on the 24th of August, 1722. In May, 1723, he was brought to trial before the House of Lords, and a bill of pains and penalties was passed which deprived him of his bishopric, and banished him from the kingdom. He was placed on board a king's vessel and conveyed to France. He was followed by a torrent of execration and curses, not only from the members of his own profession, but from the large majority of the nation, such as has never before or since been heaped upon the head of any Christian minister.* The declaration which had been published by the Pretender at the commencement of the recent conspiracy, and dated from Lucca, was decreed by both Houses to be a false, insolent, and traitorous libel, and was ordered to be burned by the common hangman. In this declaration, its author had promised with singular generosity, that if George I. would relinquish the throne, he would consent to his retaining the title of king in Hanover, would unite all other European states to confirm it, and would also give him the succession to the British throne whenever his own legitimate heirs might become extinct. The Houses presented an address to the king, expressing their astonishment at such extraordinary presumption; and repeated to him their assurances of support against the impotent efforts of the attainted fugitive from whom such sentiments had proceeded.

The public mind, being thus relieved for the present from the fear of outward invasion and disturbance, reverted, with its habitual restlessness, to subjects of conflict and litigation at home.

* Vide "*England under the House of Hanover; its History and Condition during the Reigns of the Three Georges, &c. By Thomas Wright, Esq.* 2 vols. London, 1848. *Vol. I., p.* 87.

A vehement controversy arose in reference to *the Trinity*. The doctrine of the established church on this subject was assailed with great learning and ability by Dr. Whiston, in several elaborate publications. The University of Oxford then took hold of the subject, and in full convocation resolved, that the solemn thanks of that body should be tendered to the Earl of Nottingham for his noble defence of the Catholic faith, contained in his answer to Professor Whiston. Being thus encouraged, this theological and exegetical statesman introduced a bill into the House of Peers, for the suppression of blasphemy and profanity; which enacted that whoever spoke or wrote against the being of a God, the divinity of Christ, and of the Holy Ghost, the doctrine of the Trinity, the truth of the Christian religion, or the inspiration of the Scriptures, should suffer imprisonment for an indefinite term, unless he renounced and abjured his errors. The bill further proceeded to give authority to all bishops and archbishops within their respective jurisdiction to summon any dissenting teacher, and require his subscription to a declaration of faith containing the preceding articles; and upon his refusing so to do, authorizing the prelate to deprive him of the benefit of the act of toleration.

The discussion of this infamous bill furnished an opportunity to the various members of Parliament, and especially to the ecclesiastical members, to exhibit the detestable spirit which actuated them. It was evident that those who supported the most flagrant violation of every principle of religious liberty; who were tyrants and bigots equal in intensity to the worst of Romish inquisitors; who were themselves unworthy to possess the rights which they enjoyed, and were in reality a disgrace to the Christian name,— that all these would sustain the bill. Accordingly, it is melancholy to note that the prelates in the House were its most ardent and determined advocates. Dr. Wake, Archbishop of Canterbury, as he was more eminent in rank and position, became more prominent and pertinacious in its favor. He was followed by the Bishops of London, Winchester, Litchfield, Coventry, and many others. Only two secular peers sustained the bill. Many of them warmly opposed its passage with arguments of great earnestness and ability. Lord Onslow declared, that although he was warmly attached to the established church and its doctrines, he would never aid the propagation of truth by persecution. The Duke of Wharton followed; and during the delivery of his speech drew from his pocket a copy of the Scriptures, and quoted, in support of his position, passages enjoining universal charity, meekness, and forbearance. The Earl of Peterborough declared, with great eloquence and fervor, that though he was in favor of a parliamentary king, he was opposed to a parliamentary God, and a parliamentary religion; and that if the bill passed, he should much prefer to occupy a seat among the Popish Cardinals than a place in the British House of Lords. He condemned above all other outrages, those of a Protestant Inquisition. Lord Cowper stigmatized the bill as an avowal of the most execrable practices of the Romish church, which, if adopted, would eventually lead to the introduction of the rack, the wheel, and the stake. Other members of the House spoke to the same effect; and boldly asserted, what must be evident indeed to every discerning mind, that the introduction and support of this bill was another of the innumerable instances which constantly occurred, in which a pretended regard for the honor of religion was made a pretext for the gratification of the most malignant and infamous passions. The bill was lost by a vote of sixty against thirty-one.

The prevalent tone of feeling in the British nation, during the reign of George I., in consequence of, or perhaps in concurrence with, the supremacy of the Whigs, was one of religious toleration and enlightened liberty. The fate which awaited the bill of the Earl of Nottingham, just referred to, furnished an evidence as well as a result of this fact. But the advocates of ecclesiastical tyranny were not easily disheartened; and in the course of the same session another debate ensued which elicited a still more execrable display of bigotry and intolerance. A respectful petition was presented to Parliament by the Society of Quakers, who believed that the administration of oaths is always unlawful, requesting that the words "in the presence of Almighty God" might be omitted in their cases, in the legal and authorized form of adjuration, as being repugnant to their honest convictions of duty. A great storm arose in the House of Lords when this bill was proposed. A majority of the prelates vociferated their malignant spite against it, and against those to whom it referred. The Bishop of Rochester declared that he knew not why such a mark of indulgence should be extended to a set of fanatics, who had no claim whatever to the name of Christian. A counter petition was presented by the Archbishop of York from the clergy of London, expressing the most serious concern lest good men should be grieved, and the enemies of religion elated, by the spectacle of the Legislature of the nation condescending to favor the demands of a sect who renounced the divine institutions of Christianity, and particularly that one of them, by which the faithful are initiated into the church, and become Christians; meaning thereby confirmation, for which rite, however useful and commendable it may be, or may not be, in itself, not a particle of authority can be found in Scripture. But the British Parliament and nation were not to be disgraced by an approval of such a petition. It was rejected, and the request of the Quakers was finally and justly allowed; very much to the disgust of the mitred and gowned bigots and hypocrites, who, on this occasion, were the determined advocates of religious tyranny and intolerance.

It cannot be asserted, however, that the same enlightened and impartial policy characterized all the acts of legislation which were passed, in reference to the several classes of religionists in the nation at this period. In the same session of Parliament, a bill was introduced proposing that a hundred thousand pounds should be assessed upon the estates of Roman Catholics, on the ground that they had been making frequent efforts to subvert the government, to compass the expulsion of the House of Hanover, and the return of the exiled family; and because it was held to be highly reasonable that the fomentors of disturbances which it had cost the state large sums of money to suppress, should themselves be compelled to endure a portion of the burden. The Tory and Jacobite factions in Parliament, as well as in the nation, earnestly condemned this bill, as a matter of course; but it was opposed also by many others of the most intelligent and patriotic members of the House. It was contended by them, with great force of argument, that because *some* of the Roman Catholics were suspected, and even proved, to have been concerned in treasonable measures, it was unjust that the whole body of them should not only be charged with the guilt of others, but be compelled even to suffer the penalty of it; that while the law supposes every man to be responsible for his own acts, and for those only, this bill rendered one party answerable for the conduct of another, over whom it did not appear that they were disposed or were able to exercise any control; that the proposed bill specified no individual Roman Catholic upon whom either suspicion or evidence was able to affix the charge; that there was no justice in the argument, that thus to punish the Jacobites at home indiscriminately, would deter their confederates abroad from entering upon rash and treasonable enterprises, because no connection or collision had been proved between them, and because the very liability of those at home to such unwarrantable tyranny might in fact render both those at home and those abroad more reckless, more disaffected, and more rebellious; and that it was both impolitic and infamous for the government to treat a body of men as criminal, simply because they were suspected to be guilty, while as yet the vigilance and the malignity of their enemies had been unable to produce the slightest amount of evidence against them.

These considerations were not answered by the opposing faction; but prejudice assumed the place of argument, and the bill finally passed by a majority of two hundred and seventeen votes, against a hundred and sixty-eight. It then received the sanction of the sovereign. On the 27th of May, 1723, the king closed the session of Parliament by a speech from the throne, in which he expressed his satisfaction at the measures which had been adopted, especially those which appertained to the punishment of political offenders, whose guilt, though it was concealed under the veil of secrecy, was nevertheless well known to the agents of the government. He concluded by remarking that some extraordinary affairs would again render it necessary for him to visit the continent; and he indulged the hope that, during his absence, the wisdom and vigilance of his good subjects would preserve the security of their country, their religion, and their government. The special object of the royal solicitude was the coalition which the king had reason to believe had been formed between Russia and Sweden for the restoration of the Duchy of Schleswic to the Duke of Holstein; in which case the security of the king's favorite acquisitions, the Duchies of Bremen and Verden, would be seriously and permanently endangered. It was ascertained with certainty, that the Emperor of Germany had become a party to the treaty of Stockholm—an article of which referred to the restoration of the Duchy of Schleswic—in return for the adhesion of the contracting powers to the execution of the celebrated edict, termed the *Pragmatic Sanction;* which was intended to secure the vast and heterogeneous possessions of the House of Hapsburg, as a perpetual and an indivisible feofment to Maria Theresa, and to her heirs forever.*

* The term *Pragmatic* is used in this case in a peculiar sense. It is derived from the Greek πραγματικὸς, *solers in rebus tractandis*, at the same time involving the complex idea of *meddling* in affairs, and those affairs being of the greatest *importance*. The word was first employed by the historians of the Byzantine Empire, and with this precise signification. In European history the term is applied to two celebrated edicts. The first is that issued by Charles VII. of France in 1438, which secured the liberties of the Gallican Church against the encroachments and the tyranny of Rome. The other was the one referred to in the text, and was established after many years of anxious negotiation with the various powers of Europe, by the Emperor Charles VI. of Germany, but which, after his death, became as paralyzed and as impotent as its defunct author.

CHAPTER V.

Treaty formed between England and the Continental Powers—Horace Walpole—Dissatisfaction with the Treaty—Trial and Punishment of the Earl of Macclesfield—Return of Bolingbroke to England—He unites with Pulteney and Windham in opposition—Character of William Pulteney—His remarkable Attainments—Character of Windham—Description of Bolingbroke—His Early History—His Physical Advantages—His Prodigious Talents—His Political Career—Death of the Wife of George I. at Ahlden.

To counteract the dangerous influence of the treaty referred to in the preceding chapter, an alliance was formed at Hanover, in September, 1725, under the auspices of George I., to which England, France, Denmark, Prussia, and Holland became parties. The existence of this treaty was communicated to the British Parliament in January, 1726, and it immediately excited very determined hostility, on the ground that by it the British nation would eventually become involved in a war for the protection of the king's Hanoverian dominions, contrary to an express provision contained in the act of settlement. The chief agent of the king in the consummation of this alliance was Horace Walpole, the able and astute brother of the prime minister. He rose in Parliament for the purpose of discussing the merits of the treaty, answering the objections which had been urged against it, and showing the importance, wisdom, and necessity of its provisions. He explained, in an elaborate and lengthy argument, the relations and interests of the chief powers of Europe since the treaty of Utrecht. He detailed the progress and bearings of the various alliances which had been formed by them subsequent to that event. He clearly pointed out how the utmost danger threatened from the treaty of Vienna, formed between the emperor and the King of Spain; how the establishment of an East India Company at Ostend was intended as the rival of the commercial power and success of Britain; how the treaty of Vienna would probably be followed by a marriage between the eldest daughter of the emperor and the Infant Don Carlos of Spain; how the issue of such a marriage would, in time, inherit not only the imperial diadem, and the vast hereditary possessions of the House of Hapsburg, but also the monarchy of Spain, and its appendages in two continents; how the occurrence of such an event would destroy the balance of power in Europe, and endanger its liberties; and how, to obviate and resist such calamitous results, the treaty of Hanover had been consummated by the British sovereign with the best intentions, with great labor, and with profound sagacity.

The arguments of Walpole readily convinced the Parliament of the truthfulness of his position, and the treaty of Hanover was approved by an overwhelming majority. An address to the king was voted by a majority of two hundred and eighty-five against a hundred and seven, declaring the fullest approbation of the House of the treaty, expressing their gratitude to the king for his exertions in disappointing the dangerous schemes entertained by the emperor and the King of Spain, and reprobating the alliance which had been formed between them. The House further declared to his majesty that the nation would support him against the attacks which any hostile power might make against him, in revenge for the wise and judicious measures which he had adopted, even though those attacks should be directed against his Hanoverian dominions. The treaty of Hanover was strengthened in March, 1727, by the accession of Sweden; which power had till then been deterred from so doing by the influence and the dread of Russia. But that dread was dissipated when, after the death of Peter the Great, Sir Charles Wager was sent by order of George I. with a powerful fleet to the Baltic, with orders not to permit the Russian ships to leave the port of Revel until the Empress Catherine I. had duly explained her intentions in reference to the vast naval equipments which she had recently prepared for some unrevealed and unknown purpose. The reply of the empress declared that nothing was farther from her thoughts than to disturb in any way the peace of the north; and expressed a desire to maintain the most amicable relations with the British monarch. She nevertheless admitted, that she desired the restoration of Schleswic to the Duke of Holstein, though she was perfectly willing that an equivalent should be allowed for it to the Danish monarch. Being thus reassured, George I. ordered the return of his fleet to England; but the impression produced by these events was highly favorable to the superiority of the naval power of Great Britain.

During the year 1725 a domestic incident occurred, which served to show the impartial administration of public justice which at that period existed in England. The Earl of Macclesfield, lord high chancellor of the realm, was impeached by the House of Commons of high crimes and misdemeanors. This person, whose original name was Thomas Parker, commenced his career as an attorney's clerk, and rapidly rose, by means of his superior talents, through all the various grades of the law, until he attained the highest. George I. raised him to the rank of Earl in 1721. He was a partisan of the monarch against his son and future successor, in the disputes which constantly took place between them. To his care were intrusted the children of the Prince of Wales, and he exercised great influence in the royal household. But the chancellor, like his illustrious and infamous predecessor Bacon, was incapable, notwithstanding his great talents, of resisting the potency of a bribe. He sold places and preferments, and trafficked with the funds of the suitors of his court. He managed to acquire immense wealth by the abuse of his high trust, as guardian of the persons and estates of orphans and lunatics. His enemies, urged on by the Prince of Wales, resolved to impeach him, and they did so effectually. After a protracted trial of twenty days before the House of Peers, he was convicted, was sentenced to pay a fine of thirty thousand pounds, and to be imprisoned in the Tower till the amount was paid. To annoy the prince, the king promised the fallen chancellor that he would himself repay him the amount of the fine; but the promise was never fulfilled. The disgrace and ruin which overwhelmed the earl soon put a termination to his life; he predicted the day of his death to Dr. Pearce, his intimate friend; and died accordingly, more sagacious as a prophet than he had been incorruptible as a judge. He was succeeded as chancellor by Sir Peter King, Baron of Ockham.*

This period was also signalized by the return of the celebrated Lord Bolingbroke to England. During his exile he had resided chiefly in France. Having gained the influence of the king's mistress, Madame Keilmansegge, by immense bribes, her agency gradually softened the hostility of her royal lover. Sir Robert Walpole was too astute to array his authority in opposition to that of the omnipotent Keilmansegge, and he did not oppose the return of the expelled Jacobite. A bill was accordingly introduced into Parliament, and passed, restoring to him his forfeited estates, but not permitting him to resume his seat in the House of Lords. The haughty nobleman returned to England more incensed in consequence of what Walpole had failed to obtain for him, than grateful for what had actually been bestowed. He immediately joined the party of the Tories, with whom he united that portion of the Whig party which was led by the eloquent Pulteney; who, after being for many years the associate and partisan of Walpole, deserted him, along with many followers, because he believed that the premier had not rewarded his services with sufficient munificence and rapidity. Pulteney and Bolingbroke were party leaders of extraordinary ability. The opposition which they made to the administration of Robert Walpole, was more desperate and effective than any other which he encountered during his whole political career. They were joined by Sir William Windham, the able and ac-

* This excellent person soon ascertained that his abilities did not adapt him to the high post to which he had been promoted, and he resigned. He was succeeded by Lord Talbot, one of the most gifted men of his time. Talbot's death occurred in a short period after his promotion. This rapid series of changes in the highest judicial office in the realm, was terminated by the appointment of Sir Philip York, Baron Hardwicke, who presided in the Court of Chancery during nineteen years.

knowledged head of the old Tory party. Against their combined intrigues, eloquence, and activity, Sir Robert battled with the energy and ability of an intellectual giant, during twenty-three years; but he was compelled at last to succumb, though he did it with honor and gracefulness, to their protracted and unremitting hostilities.*

The peculiar qualities of this celebrated triumvirate of statesmen deserve a more minute delineation. There were two Pulteneys, William and Daniel. The latter was remarkable only for his superior capacity for business, and his familiar acquaintance with foreign affairs. He bore the same relation to his more celebrated relative that Horace Walpole maintained toward his brother Robert; he was guided in his political conduct solely by the dictation of William, and never ventured to lead. William Pulteney was the heir of immense wealth, and was descended from a highly honorable and even noble family. Having entered Parliament at an early age, he soon distinguished himself by his superior and powerful eloquence. One of the most competent judges of those times, Speaker Onslow, represents him as " having the most popular parts for public speaking of any man he ever knew."† His orations were unequalled for the polish and beauty of their style, for the spirit and effect which characterized their delivery. His most unstudied speeches exhibited the same correctness and elegance which adorned the most mature and labored effusions of other men. Every sentence and every word seemed to be placed with such singular skill and with such perfect taste, that no improvement could be made upon them by elaborate and protracted scrutiny. His wit was inexhaustible, his sarcasm scathing. Robert Walpole candidly acknowledged that he feared Pulteney's tongue far more than he feared any other man's sword. To the

---

* One of the agencies which they employed against the minister was a newspaper entitled the *Country Journal or Craftsman*, which was edited by Nicholas Amhurst, under the name of Caleb Anvers, which did great execution upon the ranks of the ministerial party. *Wright's England, &c., Vol. I., p.* 132.

† *Vide Coxe's Life of Walpole, Appendix* 3.

weight of such intellectual powers was added the influence derived from an irreproachable moral character, and from high family connections. The great fault which marked his career was his deadly opposition to the ministry of Walpole, simply from motives of personal jealousy. He knew perfectly well that the measures of that great minister were judicious and wise; that they were intended, by their pacific influence, to withhold the nation from expensive and destructive wars in which it had no real interest, and from which it could derive no possible advantage; and yet the policy of Pulteney, and of the powerful party which he led, aimed at inflaming the minds of the people with insane animosities and brutal passions; at plunging Europe into calamitous and unnecessary conflicts; at the unprincipled abandonment of allies, and the unjustifiable breaking of treaties; at the degradation of the monarchy, the overthrow of a capable, prudent, and sagacious ministry, and the triumph of insensate faction. To attain these ignoble ends, all the vast intellectual powers of Pulteney were expended; and when at last he triumphed, the throne on which he proudly took his seat, crumbled instantly beneath him; his partisans were divided by the most furious rivalry and hostility; and Pulteney became one of the most unpopular of men, both with his own former friends, with the party whom he had vanquished, and with the nation at large, who ever attained the summit of political power in England.

Sir William Windham was a much less brilliant statesman than Pulteney, but a much more substantial and reliable one.* Though descended from a noble family, his early education had been somewhat neglected; but he had drawn from actual converse with able statesmen, and especially from his intimacy with Bolingbroke, that practical and available knowledge which adapted him, in connection with his superior natural gifts, to lead in the accomplishment of great results. Speaker Onslow said respecting him: "In my opinion, every thing about him seemed great, the most made for a great man of any one I have known in this age." He was an excellent debater, and an able counsellor. He possessed perfect honesty of purpose, unflinching consistency and steadiness of principle. His style of speaking was solid and argumentative. He never used a figure or uttered a witticism in his speeches; yet few orators ever produced a deeper effect upon the minds of his auditors. At an early age he declared himself an ardent Jacobite, mingled in their councils, and was imprisoned on suspicion of being concerned in the rebellion of 1715. At a later period of life, he became convinced of the impossibility of the restoration of the Stuarts, and confined himself to the support and the advocacy of Tory principles and measures. His opposition to Walpole was based on conviction, and not dictated by personal enmity. Conscious of honest intentions, he was bold and dauntless in spirit; and his dissimilarity in many respects to his two celebrated associates added an element of power to their coalition which aided essentially in their ultimate but fruitless triumph.

Bolingbroke was nevertheless the most gifted and the most remarkable member of this famous triumvirate. His intimate friend, Dean Swift, said of him with some show of truth, that at a certain period, "he had in his hands half the business of the nation, and the applause of the whole."* Fifteen years elapsed between his entrance into Parliament and his attainder and flight; yet during that brief interval, he secured the first place among the great masters of eloquence, and won a literary reputation which classed him among the ornaments of the Augustan age of English literature.† As an orator, his is the singular and perhaps the solitary fate, to have held the first rank in the estimation of his contemporaries, and yet not to have left a solitary line of his spoken effusions on record, for the scrutiny and admiration of posterity. Nor is it strange that William Pitt, when reflecting on this unusual circumstance, should exclaim, that he would regard the possession of one of Bolingbroke's great ora-

* See his "Journal to Stella," August, 1711.
† Goldsmith says that "Bolingbroke discovered a degree of genius and assiduity that, perhaps, had never been known before to be united in one person, to the same degree." *Life of Bolingbroke, Goldsmith's Miscel. Works, Vol. IV., p.* 41.

tions, as a literary treasure more to be desired and valued than the restoration of all the perished intellectual products of the ancient world—of Cicero's translations from the orations of Demosthenes, or the lost books of Livy and Tacitus. Nor will this estimate seem absurd or exaggerated when we remember the natural and acquired attributes and qualities of this great man. His intellect was one of immense power, sagacity, and compass ; and it had been from his youth, carefully and elaborately cultivated. At Eton he laid the foundation, broad and deep, of his subsequent attainments. He was perfectly familiar with the Latin writers, nor was his acquaintance with Greek literature insignificant.* Careful study had made him at home in every department of thought, which had been adorned and illustrated by the superior intellects of his own country. His knowledge of universal history was accurate ; and his mind was capable of abstruse and long-continued speculations in morals and philosophy, the monuments and products of which yet remain in his works. He well understood the nature of the human mind, and the acutenesss of his understanding enabled him to explore the utmost depths of metaphysical and ethical speculation.† Of him it may be said, that no statesman or orator of any age, except perhaps Cicero alone, brought with him into the struggles and conflicts of the Senate, so thorough an acquaintance with the principles of intellectual and moral science, or such varied and abundant mental resources.

The physical attributes of Bolingbroke were admirably adapted to promote his success as an orator and legislator. His per-

---

* Bolingbroke furnished his friend, Alexander Pope, with a prose essay containing all the original and striking thoughts which the latter afterward elaborated into his celebrated "Essay on Man." *Vide Letter from Dr. Blair in Boswell's Johnson, I., p.* 140.

† Lord Chesterfield asserts that, "though nobody spoke and wrote better on philosophy than Lord Bolingbroke, no man in the world had less share of philosophy than himself; that the least trifle, such as the over-roasting of a leg of mutton, would strangely disturb and ruffle his temper; and that his passions constantly got the better of his judgment." *Lord Chesterfield's Works, by Dr. Maty, Vol. I., p.* 253.

son was tall and well proportioned. His countenance was handsome. All his features were symmetrical and expressive. His morals, indeed, were of the worst description, and in an age abandoned to every vice, he exceeded all others in his licentiousness. But this stigma chiefly appertains to the period of his youth and early manhood. In later life, without any change having taken place in his principles, he lost the ability, and perhaps the inclination, to commit his former excesses. His spirit was manly and generous; nor was there any thing mean or sordid in his character. In conversation he was exceedingly affable and fascinating. He captivated every one by whom he was approached, as much by the suavity and sweetness of his manners, as by the commanding vigor and superiority of his understanding. He entered Parliament as a Tory. Such had been the political faith of his ancestors. He became the most able and active supporter of Queen Anne, first in the House of Commons, afterward in the House of Lords. As one of the ministers of the queen, he exercised almost absolute power until the period of her sudden death. He plotted, previous to that event, with great skill and earnestness, for the exclusion of the House of Hanover, and for the restoration of the Stuarts. On the death of his royal mistress he was impeached; when, conscious of his guilt, and of his inability to make good his defence, he fled to the continent. Having arrived in France, he immediately entered the service of the Pretender, and was made by him Secretary of State. This promotion furnished unanswerable proof, had such been wanting, of the guilt of the fugitive statesman. After the failure of the rebellion of 1715, Lord Mar, one of the most trusted supporters of the Pretender, succeeded in overturning the confidence which that prince had reposed in Bolingbroke, and he was dismissed from his office.* In revenge he instantly forsook

---

* Various reasons have been assigned for this dismissal. The most probable is that Bolingbroke had become disgusted with the want of sagacity and prudence displayed by the chief friends of the Pretender, and ceased to take an active or sanguine interest in their movements, as being, in his judgment, perfectly hopeless. See *Memoirs of the Court of England, &c., by John H. Jesse*. Vol. II., p. 103. Bolingbroke's character might be thus briefly summed up : Na-

the service of the Pretender, and became his bitter and unrelenting foe. He succeeded in obtaining permission to return to England through the influence of one of the king's mistresses, whom he had bribed with an immense sum; and he then joined the opposition against Walpole, which he continued to support till the fall of that minister. The writings of Bolingbroke still remain the most noble and enduring monument of his genius, and bear evidence of a powerful and capacious intellect. He died at the age of seventy-four, having suffered intense agonies from a cancer in the face, which terminated his life. The chief blemish in the character of this celebrated man, was the fact that he entertained the cheerless and pernicious doctrines of infidelity, and that he prided himself in the possession of the bad pre-eminence which he held as a philosophical atheist.

Such were the character and the qualities of the three men who headed the opposition against the administration of Walpole, during the reign of George I., and subsequently during the supremacy of his son and successor. They formed for many years the most prominent and imposing figures in the living history of that stormy and eventful era.

George I. returned in safety from his visit to his hereditary dominions. One of his first acts was to elevate his favorite mistress, Madame Keilmansegge, to the peerage. She was now made Countess of Leinster in Ireland, Baroness of Brentford and Countess of Darlington in England. The illegitimate daughter of the king by the Duchess of Kendal, Melusina de Schulenburg, was also created Baroness of Aldborough and Countess of Walsingham. The weakness and complacency of the monarch could scarcely be expected to go farther.

On the 2d of November, 1726, the unfortunate Sophia Dorothea, wife of the King of England, expired, after a tedious illness, in the castle of Ahlden. She had endured a cheerless captivity of more than thirty years, during twelve of which her husband had

ture had been prodigal to him of all her best gifts; and he therefore became conspicuous in the temples of science, fascinating in the haunts of pleasure, eloquent in the halls of state, grand and potent among men everywhere.

occupied the British throne. Before she expired she blessed her children, forgave her enemies and oppressors, and solemnly summoned her absent husband, the chief cause of her unjust sufferings, as she asserted, to meet her at the judgment bar of God within a year after her own death. We will meet this prophetic summons again, before we conclude the history of her husband's career. As soon as he was informed of the death of the princess, he ordered an announcement to be made in the Gazette to the effect that a Duchess of Ahlden had expired at her residence in Germany; but no allusion was made to the fact that in her death the monarch had lost a wife and his children a mother. When he heard that the court of Berlin, over which his daughter presided, went into mourning in consequence of this event, his wrath became furious beyond measure.

To console himself for this affront after his own peculiar fashion, George I. immediately took a new mistress. This person was the half sister of the starving poet Savage; and her mother was the repudiated wife of the Earl of Macclesfield, who afterward married Colonel Brent. Unlike all the other concubines of the monarch, Miss Brent was allowed to reside in the palace of St. James. Their intercourse continued until it was unexpectedly terminated by the death of the king, who had intended—notwithstanding the intense disgust which was already expressed by the British nobility and populace at the honors which he had previously conferred upon his ridiculous mistresses —to elevate this woman to the peerage, and thus inflict upon it another disgrace. The deportment of the enfeebled monarch toward this favorite of his old age, was more childish and more contemptible than that which had characterized his earlier connections; and was the cause of serious and angry disputes with the members of the royal family. Nevertheless, Miss Brent remained supreme and triumphant in her influence, until the departure of the king on his last visit to the continent.

CHAPTER VI.

Meeting of Parliament—The Royal Speech—Loyal Address of the Legislature—The Restoration of Gibraltar—Threatened Hostilities with France—Sudden Establishment of Peace—Domestic and Foreign Prosperity—Last Visit of George I. to Hanover—His Illness and Death—Character of this Monarch—His neglect of Literature—Survey of his Reign—Joseph Addison—Dean Swift—His Genius and Irreligion—Writings of Alexander Pope—John Gay—Sir Isaac Newton—John Flamsteed—State of Morals and Religion in England during the Reign of George I.

In January, 1727, both Houses of the British Parliament again convened. This was destined to be their last assemblage during the reign of George I.; but before the termination of his career, this monarch was fated to anticipate and to prepare for a conflict with several powerful European States; and thus, during the closing months of his long career, to renew the favorite employments and associations of his youth.

After the opening of Parliament the king informed the members, in a speech from the throne, that an offensive and defensive alliance had recently been concluded between the Spanish monarch and the Emperor of Germany, the object of which treaty was to wrest the fortress of Gibraltar from the English; to place the Pretender upon the throne of Great Britain; and to injure in various ways the commercial and political privileges and interests of the nation. The king terminated his address by saying, that the Spanish monarch had ordered his ambassador to quit the realm, after having delivered to the ministers an offensive memorial which contained a formal and peremptory demand for the restitution of Gibraltar.

In reply to the royal speech, the Commons voted a most patriotic and zealous address. They expressed their determination to support his majesty with their lives and fortunes against all his enemies; to raise the supplies which were necessary to provide such armaments as might be requisite to vanquish the hostile powers; and to defend to the last extremity the succession and supremacy of the House of Hanover. The utmost enthusiasm prevailed in the Commons; and in vain did Pulteney and Windham exert all their influence and eloquence to diminish the patriotic ardor which was exhibited. In vain did they declare that it was sufficient on such an occasion to return thanks to his majesty for his gracious speech, and appoint a time for taking into consideration the measures which were proper in reference to it; without pledging themselves in so precipitate a manner to support measures of the nature and wisdom of which they were still ignorant. To no purpose did they assert, what indeed was very just in itself, that, in reference to the means of offence or of defence to be adopted, the *advice* of the House might be as necessary and as useful as its *support;* that in so great an emergency it was incumbent upon them to deliberate calmly and intelligently; and that, to effect this end, it would be expedient that those papers and other evidences upon which his majesty had based his own convictions, should be submitted to the scrutiny of the House. Sarcastic inquiries were even made by the opposition in reference to the fleets which were to convey the Pretender to the shores of his ancestors; and whether he proposed to embark on the floating island of Gulliver as a means of transportation. It was boldly asserted by others, that the alarms of the sovereign were all a delusion; that not the slightest ground existed for them; and that the fortunes of the Pretender at that moment were more depressed and more desperate than they had ever been since the expulsion of the House of Stuart from the British throne. But none of these arguments availed any thing in moderating the defiant and patriotic enthusiasm which prevailed; and the address to the king was carried by an overwhelming majority of two hundred and fifty-one votes against eighty-one.

The only assertion made in the royal speech which contained

any show of truth, was that which referred to the restitution of Gibraltar to the King of Spain. The claim of that monarch was chiefly founded upon a promise which had been given by George I. himself, to that effect, in an autograph letter addressed by him in 1721 to the Spanish monarch. In that letter the following language occurred: "I have learned with great satisfaction, from the report of my ambassador at your court, that your majesty is at last resolved to remove the obstacles which have for some time delayed the entire accomplishment of our union. Since, from the confidence which your majesty expresses toward me, I may look upon the treaties which have been in question between us as re-established; and that, accordingly, the instruments necessary for carrying on the trade of my subjects will be delivered out; I do no longer hesitate to assure your majesty of my readiness to satisfy you with regard to your demand touching the restoration of Gibraltar, promising you to make use of the first favorable opportunity to regulate this article with the consent of my Parliament."* This letter had been written by George I. at the period of its date,† in order to aid in the accomplishment of the purposes which were at that time the subject of negotiation with the Court of Madrid; and its only purpose, doubtless, was to flatter and deceive the Spanish monarch, without any ulterior intention of fulfilment, or even of remembrance.

The address of the king and the subsequent response of Parliament to it, gave great offence to the Court of Vienna. The emperor ordered Count Palin, his minister at London, to present a remonstrance to the British Court, charging the king with having made calumnious misrepresentations, and assertions void of all foundation; and declaring that no such treaty whatever had been entered into between his imperial majesty and the King of Spain, either in reference to the restitution of Gibraltar, or the restoration of the Pretender. The Parliament replied to this remonstrance in terms equally strong; and stigmatized it as an insult to his majesty, and a base and vain attempt to infuse into

* *Vide the Hardwicke State Papers.* † *June the First*, 1721.

the minds of his subjects, a distrust of the royal word. Lord Townshend declared in the House of Peers, that if the safety of the state permitted ministers to lay before their lordships the advices in possession of the Government, they would no more doubt the existence of such a treaty, than they would if they had been present at the signing of it. Count Palin, before leaving the kingdom, was ordered by his master to publish his remonstrance. He did so, adding to it a letter from Count Zinzendorf, the imperial chancellor, containing a statement of the facts of the case according to his version of them. The intemperate language of these papers gave additional offence to the British Parliament; and another address was presented to the king, reiterating, in still stronger terms, the sentiments contained in the previous one, and commanding Count Palin immediately to depart the kingdom.

Preparations for the approaching conflict were now made on both sides. The English forces were augmented by sea and land. Thirty thousand Swedes, Danes, and Hessians were taken into the British service. The king was empowered, by an act of Parliament, to apply such sums of money as should be necessary for making good the expenses and engagements which had been, or should be incurred, before the 25th of the ensuing September, for the purpose of establishing the security of commerce, and restoring the tranquillity of Europe. The sum of three hundred and seventy thousand pounds was issued in exchequer bills, and was charged upon the surplus produce of certain duties appertaining to the sinking fund. In vain did the opposition, headed by Pulteney and Windham, thunder forth their eloquent harangues against such an unwarrantable delegation of authority to the sovereign, and the reckless appropriation of funds which belonged by law to other purposes, to the sudden exigencies of the state. The ministers and the party of the court triumphantly carried all their measures by great and decisive majorities; and Parliament was at length prorogued on the 15th of May, 1727.

The only actual hostility which took place, in consequence of these disputes, and this outburst of national pride, was the siege of Gibraltar. Sir John Norris, indeed, sailed with a powerful fleet to the Baltic, where he was joined by a Danish squadron. But at this crisis the French monarch, Louis XV., perceiving that the issues at stake were not really worth the important consequences which would result from continued hostilities, and being further influenced by grave personal considerations, interposed his friendly offices between the belligerents. Preliminary articles of accommodation were signed in June, 1727. These articles provided that hostilities should immediately cease; that the charter of the Ostend India Company should be suspended for seven years; and that, after the lapse of four months, a congress of plenipotentiaries should be convened at Aix-la-Chapelle, to settle the terms of a final pacification. That congress accordingly met, and succeeded in adjusting the various subjects of controversy which had so nearly disturbed the repose and injured the prosperity of the chief nations of Europe.

Fortune thus seemed to smile propitiously upon the aged and royal representative of the house of Brunswick, both at home and abroad. In his own dominions, his administration was triumphant over the power of hostile factions; on the continent he was at peace with all his rivals and enemies; his title to the throne was respected and recognized by every European power; and the head of the Pretender lay low in imbecility and disgrace. Several years had elapsed since the happy monarch visited his favorite Hanover; and he now expressed an ardent desire once more to feast his eyes upon its familiar and beloved scenes. Accordingly, he embarked at Greenwich with a suitable retinue, on the 3d of June, 1727; and after a favorable voyage, convoyed by a large fleet of ships, his majesty arrived at Vaer, in Holland, on the 7th. He travelled thence by land to Utrecht, escorted by the guards to the frontiers of Holland. He reached Dalden at twelve o'clock at night on the 9th, still in the enjoyment of good health. There he ate a hearty supper; and at three o'clock the next morning he resumed his journey. According to the report which became afterward prevalent, it was during the succeeding day that the letter of his deceased wife, containing the "solemn summons to the judgment bar of God within one year after her death," was given him while riding in his carriage; and the same popular oracle declared, that the monarch was immediately seized with fainting fits, which continued till his arrival at the episcopal palace of Osnaburg. During his progress thither he expressed the opinion to one of his attendants, that "he was a dead man;" and at midnight of the 11th of June, notwithstanding every effort of his physicians, he expired, in the sixty-eighth year of his age, and in the thirteenth of his reign. The singular appearance of his countenance after death, caused the additional rumor to become prevalent among the irreverent multitude, that the devil had choked the king to death, at the instance of his wife, by twisting his neck!

Thus ended the career of George I.—one of those commonplace and ordinary men who, by the force of propitious accident, and through the singular influence of the institution of monarchy, was elevated to one of the highest, most difficult, and most responsible positions which a human being can possibly occupy. His personal character has never been the subject of much controversy. He was an honest, good-natured, dull, and sensual German gentleman, whose chief enjoyment consisted in the society of his equally heavy and stupid German mistresses, in drinking hot punch, in eating sauer-kraut, and in smoking his huge Hanoverian pipe. He was diffident of his own capacity, and therefore never undertook to shine among his courtiers or subordinates. He hated the cares and burdens of royalty; and had it not been that, by accepting the English diadem he thereby greatly aggrandized his Hanoverian dominions, and gave them a superiority and a consequence among the petty and contemptible German principalities by which they were surrounded, it is probable that he would have declined the brilliant but difficult post to which he was invited by the suffrages of the nation.

It is doubtless true that the intentions of George I., in the exercise of his royal functions, were good; but he always entertained a strong partiality for his German dominions, and would never allow any measures to be adopted which, however beneficial they might have been to England, would prejudice the interests of his hereditary states. It was his great good fortune to enjoy the sagacious advice and able assistance of Robert Walpole,—one of the most profound and gifted statesman who ever wielded the destinies of the British Empire; and it is not improbable that, had it not been for this propitious circumstance, the ignorance, the imbecility, the sensuality, and the unpopularity of George I. would have led to the speedy overthrow of the Hanoverian dynasty in England, and the restoration of the Pretender to the throne of his ancestors. George I. was particularly unfortunate and indecorous in his domestic affairs. His wife during his reign was an absent and detested prisoner. His son and successor was hostile to him; and by that hostility he inflicted much indignity and mortification on his father and sovereign. His mistresses were all ignorant, frivolous, and mercenary women, who ruled him with absolute authority, who turned their influence into their personal profit, and their royal lover into popular contempt. His only legitimate daughter, the Queen of Prussia, was married to the most detestable ruffian of his day, and lived a live of ignominy and misery, in consequence of his savage persecutions; yet the gross and heavy nature of George I. rendered him in a great measure insensible to the depressing influence of these calamities. He possessed some military talents, and, possibly, had he been born in an humbler station, might have risen to the distinction, and been equal to the duties, of a general of division. He understood English imperfectly, and spoke it still worse. His constant effort was to shift the responsibility of the direction of public affairs from his own shoulders to those of his ministers; thus he said to them plainly on his first accession: "I will do as you advise, and thus you become entirely answerable for every thing I do." He was parsimonious in his habits; and the only persons who were able to extort money from him were his mistresses. But even with these he was not lavish; and he allowed them knowingly to turn their influence with him to the aggrandizement of their private fortunes. He was no patron of art; cared nothing for the advancement of litcrature and science; was fond of dramatic performances simply because they amused and diverted him; and had, as a general thing, a cheerful and pleasant frame of mind. He was, in fact, an admirable and convenient puppet, by whose pliable means the machinery, and sometimes the mummery, of royalty were carried on with great success by the party then triumphant in England, headed by their able and acute leaders. The only thing recorded either of the sayings or the doings of George I. during his whole life, which reflects any credit upon him, and deserves to be handed down with honor to posterity, is the remark which he made to a German nobleman, who congratulated him on being the sovereign at once of two such glorious kingdoms as England and Hanover. He replied: "Rather congratulate me on having such a subject as Newton in the one, and Leibnitz in the other!" Yet it is doubtful whether the king deserved the credit of originality in making this remark: it was probably the echo of some graceful compliment paid him by one of his courtiers.

Although George I. did not extend the slightest degree of patronage to art, science, literature, or education, in his English dominions, they all flourished in a very considerable degree without his assistance. A brief sketch of the most eminent writers who adorned this reign, may form a fit conclusion to the preceding history of its most important events.

Joseph Addison deservedly stands at the head of those men of genius who adorned the era of the first George, although his fame was at its zenith, and the larger portion of his life had been spent, when that monarch ascended the throne. Addison was the son of a distinguished clergyman, and was born in 1672. He entered Oxford University at the age of fifteen, and soon became known for his great proficiency in Latin poetry. He subsequently took the degrees of Bachelor and Master of Arts in Magdalen College. His first poetical essay which attracted attention was an effusion addressed to the veteran Dryden, who was then at the termination of his career. About this period Addison had the good fortune to secure the favor of the Lord-keeper Somers. By his means and influence King William rewarded Addison for a complimentary poem on his military achievements, with a pension of three hundred pounds per annum. This revenue enabled the poet to indulge his passion for foreign travel; and he visited, during several years, the most interesting localities of Europe. In 1701 he returned to England, published a narrative of his adventures, and dedicated it, with an epistolary poem, to Lord Halifax. In 1704 his most celebrated political poem, entitled "The Campaign," appeared. Its popularity and success were very great. He was immediately rewarded for his loyal labors, by the appointment to the lucrative post of Commissioner of Appeals. He subsequently employed his accomplished powers in contributing the chief papers which adorn the Spectator, the Tatler, and the Guardian. He also wrote a political document entitled "The Freeholder." The superior and unrivalled excellence of these various essays, their beauty and polish of diction, their clearness and force of thought, their apt and effective illustrations, their chaste and polished wit, and their excellent moral tendency, have always been conceded, and have enrolled these productions, without a dissenting voice, among the most perfect and valuable products of English genius and English literature.

The poetical effusions of Addison occupy an equally elevated rank. In this department his supremacy may, in some respects, be disputed by Pope; but it must be admitted that, in all the higher, grander, more elaborate and inventive achievements of the muse, Addison excelled his rival. Pope could never have written so admirable and so sublime a production as the tragedy of "Cato." In truth, Pope's genius was totally destitute of dramatic power; and in his own favorite domain, in the production of polished and euphonic measures of jingling verse, he never excelled his rival. There is nothing in the "Rape of the Lock" or the "Temple of Fame" superior in this respect to the "Letter from Italy" or the "Campaign." The personal character of Addison was decorous and prudent. He was unhappy in his marriage with the Countess Dowager of Warwick, which took place in 1716; and it is probable that his domestic inquietudes led him to indulgence in the only vice which was ever laid to his charge. His excesses in the use of wine hastened his death, which took place in 1719. He presented, during his whole life, a favorable contrast to all the wits and men of letters of his day, excepting Pope, in the propriety and decorum of his conduct; and his benevolence was frequently tested and exhibited by the sums of money which he loaned, but in reality gave, to his thriftless and unfortunate associate, Sir Richard Steele. In the career of the latter wit there was nothing which deserves especial praise or mention. His intellectual eminence was chiefly derived from his connection with Addison; without whose aid and guidance he would have attained a much less distinguished place in literature than he now enjoys. In the personal incidents of his life, there was little that reflected credit upon himself, upon his associates, or upon the pursuits to which his restless and anxious existence was devoted. The incident which confers most honor upon his memory, is the fact that he was able to secure the friendship of such a man as Addison, that he retained that friendship during life, and that his name and memory will ever be preserved by their connection with the literary labors of his more gifted and illustrious friend.

Jonathan Swift was the next great literary ornament of the reign of George I. This powerful and eccentric genius was born in Dublin, in 1667. In his fifteenth year he entered the university of his native city, where he spent seven years in scholastic and learned pursuits. But even at this early period, so little was his wayward mind controlled by the dictates of prudence in the direction of his studies, that after so long a probation, he only obtained his degree *speciali gratia*. His first employment was in the household of Sir William Temple, at Moor Park, where his position was one of inferiority and even of degradation. Quarrelling with this patron, as was naturally the result, he took orders in the Church of England, and accepted an invitation from the Earl of Berkeley, one of the Lord Justices of Ireland, to accompany him thither as chaplain and secretary. He now began to distinguish himself by his talent for writing satirical and humorous verses. After Lord Berkeley's return to England, Swift obtained his living at Laracor, in the diocese of Meath, where he resided during some years. He first engaged in political writing in 1701. In 1704 he published the well-known " Tale of a Tub," in which production, while he displayed his extraordinary powers of wit, disgraced himself by sneering at virtue and religion.

When the Tories came into power in 1710, under Queen Anne, the hopes of Swift for political or ecclesiastical preferment rose high, in consequence of his friendly relations with Harley and Bolingbroke. He was admitted to their most secret councils, on terms of equality; and it is not improbable, that, had not doubts generally existed as to his belief in the truth and divinity of the religion of which he was a professed preacher, he would have been promoted to a bishopric in England. This was the great object of his selfish ambition; but so questionable was his reputation, that the highest preferment which his friends were able or disposed to confer upon him, was the Deanery of St. Patrick's, in Dublin. This promotion took place in 1713; the death of the queen occurred soon after; and Swift was condemned to spend the long remainder of his life in unavailing regrets, in a subordinate rank, in a place of abode which he detested, and beneath the slowly-gathering shadows of hopeless melancholy and insanity.

The infidelity and irreligion of Dean Swift were not the only defects which deformed his character. His relations with the female sex were such as no wise or good man will justify. While yet a young man he had attached himself to a young lady whom he has immortalized under the name of Stella; who was the handsome and amiable daughter of Sir William Temple's steward. Soon after his first removal to Ireland, he invited her to join him. In 1716 he was secretly married to her; but it does not appear that, either before or after the ceremony, there ever was any cohabitation between them. Previous to this event, in 1712, the Dean had been charmed with the wit and beauty of Esther Vanhomrigh, a resident of London. Upon her he has conferred an unenviable immortality under the name of Vanessa. The great fame and talents of her admirer soon acquired for him a despotic sway over her mind; and for some years they seem to have corresponded, she being under the expectation of eventually becoming his wife. After the Dean's secret marriage with Stella, matters came to a crisis, during which the conduct of Swift was so brutal toward both of his admirers, that he broke the hearts of both. Miss Vanhomrigh died in consequence in 1723; Stella, whose marriage with the Dean he had always refused to publish, lingered in misery till 1728. The latter years of his own life were spent in idiocy. For some months before his death, he maintained a total and morose silence. His powerful mind, imbittered by many provocations and disappointments, sank into imbecility before the termination of his physical career. He died in Dublin in 1744, in his seventy-eighth year. The peculiar intellectual merit of this celebrated writer consisted in his readiness in rhyme, in his complete mastery of the English language, similar in character and degree to that which Byron afterward displayed; in the polish and elegance of his numbers and sentences, in the humorous and sarcastic power which he possessed. His "Gulliver's Travels," and his verses on his own death, furnish an extraordinary instance of the display of the latter qualities. His prose writings are remarkable for clearness and simplicity; his poems are equally distinguished for their polished measure, their sarcastic wit, and their striking originality. Swift was a gifted man, but neither a great man, a good man, nor a happy man.

Alexander Pope occupies a position in the literature of this era midway between Addison and Swift. He was not as inventive as the former, nor so satirical and humorous as the latter; but he combined some of the best qualities of both. He was born in 1688. His family were Roman Catholics; and his earliest instruction was derived from a priest of that Church, who taught him the Latin and Greek language. From his boyhood he exhibited a fondness for poetry, and soon began to weave his fluent numbers. His associations, even in his youth, were chiefly with literary persons and with books. The most remarkable acquaintance of this early period of his life, was the comic poet Wycherley, who had been one of the ornaments of the preceding reign, and who, at the period of Pope's youth, was ending a long career of vice and literary labor by an old age of imbecility, neglect, and misery.

Pope's first publication was his Pastorals, which were printed in Touson's Miscellanies, in 1709. These were much admired, and immediately brought their author into notice. In 1712 his Rape of the Lock appeared; a mock-heroic poem, in which he exhibits more invention than in any other of his productions. In 1713 he commenced his celebrated translation of Homer's Iliad. The Odyssey followed it in subsequent years. His "Dunciad" appeared in 1728; in which poem he overwhelmed with ridicule all those rival and antagonistic authors who had either given him personal offence, or whom he had been led to dislike and despise for any reason whatever. The diction and versification of this poem are very labored and polished; but its imagery is often gross and indelicate; and while he establishes his claim to the character of a satirist, by its keen and deadly intellectual stabs, his temper becomes degraded in the estimation of the reader, as a vindictive, uncharitable, and irascible hater. His best production is his "Essay on Man," and for all the noble sentiments contained in that work he was indebted to the richer, more profound, and more inventive genius of his friend, Lord Bolingbroke. Pope expired in 1744, in the fifty-sixth year of his age, having achieved the reputation of being the most polished writer of rhymes who, till then, had illustrated and adorned the English language.

In addition to these great masters in the department of *Belles-Lettres*, other writers of less distinction added the lustre of their genius to the reign of George I. Prominent among these was John Gay, the author of the "Beggar's Opera," which was first produced in 1727, and attained a success which has been rarely equalled in the annals and vicissitudes of the drama. In the same rank, though at a considerable remove, belong the names of Prior, Parnell, Rowe, and Tickell; all of whom have left productions which confer enduring honors on the English muse. The chief writers of fiction during this period were Defoe and Richardson.

The reign of George I. was adorned by the life and labors of Sir Isaac Newton, the most illustrious of modern philosophers, although his chief fame had been won prior to the accession of that monarch to the throne. Contemporary with him were others, who displayed no mean ability in the same high sphere of intellectual endeavor. The most gifted of these was John Flamsteed, who, as an astronomer and natural philosopher, was but little inferior to Sir Isaac himself.* Associated with these in the same pursuits were Halley, Arbuthnot, and Gregory, —names of enduring eminence in the history of the achievements of philosophy and astronomy in the eighteenth century.

The ecclesiastical profession, during this reign, contained many churchmen of great talents and learning. As to the state of religion and morals, it must be conceded that it was deplorable; and that the political spirit, the party hatred and worldly ambition exhibited by the vast majority of those who occupied the various ranks of the clerical and episcopal offices, indicated the prevalence of but little religious feeling. The two great universities were regarded as the nurseries of young and aspiring ecclesiastics, from which they went forth to gain the prizes and win the renown which devotion to the interests of their political and ecclesiastical party would inevitably secure for them. The most celebrated ecclesiastics of this era were Francis Atterbury, bishop of Rochester, Dr. Wake, afterward archbishop of Canterbury, and Dr. Hoadley, bishop of Winchester; all of whom

* It is one of the many unaccountable phenomena in the history of literature, that the abilities of Flamsteed, which were of the first order, have been suffered by posterity to sink into oblivion, while they have ever been eager to accumulate extravagant praise on the overburdened head of Newton. The latter obtained some of his most important discoveries from his modest, unobtrusive, and now forgotten friend. See "*An Account of the Rev. John Flamsteed, the First Astronomer Royal; Compiled from his own Manuscripts, &c. By Francis Baily, F.R.S.*" 4to, London, 1835.

were worldly, ambitious, and unscrupulous prelates. Of the same class were Dr. Lockier,—the friend of Pope and of the most dissolute wits,—Dr. Younger, dean of Salisbury, and Dr. Chevenix, bishop of Waterford. A single circumstance, based upon the most reliable historical authority, and having reference to the most celebrated churchman in the kingdom, will serve to illustrate the state of morals which then prevailed, to a great extent, among the clergy of the establishment, in all their ranks and grades. As soon as the death of Queen Anne was announced, the Duke of Ormond, Lord Mareshal, and Bishop Atterbury, all leading Tories and Jacobites, held a secret meeting, at which the bishop earnestly besought Lord Mareshal to go forth immediately, and publicly proclaim the Pretender in form. The Duke of Ormond, who was of a more prudent and cautious temper, desired first to confer on the subject with the council. In answer to this proposal the right reverend prelate exclaimed, in great excitement: "Damn it, you know very well that things have not been concerted enough for that yet; and that we have not a moment to lose."* But it should not be supposed that, because an eminent prelate exhibited such irreligion and profanity, there were no men of piety among the clergy. It must, however, be admitted that their numbers were few, their positions obscure, and their influence exceedingly limited.

* *Memoirs of the Court of England, from the Revolution of* 1688 *to the Death of George II. By John H. Jesse. Vol. II., p.* 153.

PART II.

LIFE AND REIGN OF GEORGE THE SECOND.

CHAPTER I.

Birth of George II.—His Removal to England—His Marriage—His Court in Leicester House—Commanding Talents of his Wife—Her Female Favorites—Prince Frederic—Hostility between him and his Parents—The Accession of George II.—He destroys his Father's Will—His Cabinet—He retains Robert Walpole—Duke of Newcastle—Earl of Chesterfield—Lord Carteret—His Remarkable Talents.

GEORGE AUGUSTUS, only son of George I. and Sophia Dorothea of Zell, was born at Hanover on the 30th of October, 1683. His boyhood and youth were spent under the special tuition and influence of his talented and ambitious grandmother, Sophia, Electress of Hanover. He became well versed in the usual routine of accomplishments then prevalent among princes, and was able to speak Latin, French, and English with fluency. His person was small, his manners stiff, his bearing haughty and consequential. Ordinary as were the natural abilities of George I. those of his illustrious son were still more insignificant. Had not the accident of his birth placed him in a position of eminent importance and influence, it is probable that he would have passed through life as one of the most contemptible of men.

On the accession of George I. to the throne of England, in August, 1714, Prince George accompanied him to his new dominions. But previous to this period, in 1705, the heir apparent had married Caroline Wilhelmina Dorothea, the daughter of

John Frederic, Marquis of Brandenburg Anspach, a lady of superior mind and polished manners; to whose greater intellectual strength her dapper husband always yielded an unconscious, yet almost absolute obedience. The first fruit of their marriage was Prince Frederic, whom both parents cordially hated and despised. Their second son, William, afterwards Duke of Cumberland, was always their favorite. Nor were the relations which existed between George II. while Prince of Wales, and his august father, more friendly or more decorous. They did not speak to each other during some years.* Even the Princess Caroline was regarded by the monarch with feelings of aversion, and he indicated his sentiments by familiarly calling the future queen of England a *she devil*. It was the singular eccentricity of George I., that he hated all the members of his own family—those whom he should have loved; and that he loved only his selfish and perfidious mistresses —those whom he should have despised and shunned.

Several years before the accession of George II., he removed his residence to the palace located in "Leicester Fields," in order to be removed to a greater distance from the presence of his father. Here were assembled in an embryo court, all those who were the attached friends and attendants of the Prince and Princess, and were in bad odor with the reigning monarch. The company included many persons remarkable for talents, birth, beauty, and accomplishments; among whom were Lord Chesterfield, Lord Hervey, Lord Stanhope, Miss Lepel, Lady Walpole, Mrs. Howard, who afterwards became the mistress of the sovereign, and especially Miss Bellenden, the most beautiful woman in England. It was not long before the Prince became fascinated with the extraordinary charms, both of mind and person, which this lady possessed; and he made advances to her which could not be mistaken. His method of wooing was accordant with the inherent insignificance of his character. Remembering, and probably even imitating, the Grecian myth respecting the loves of Jupiter and Danæ, he was in the habit, when in Miss Bellen-

---

* *Horace Walpole's Letters, London, VI. Vols., Vol. I., p.* 63.

den's presence, of taking his purse from his pocket, and pouring his guineas from it into his lap. This operation he accompanied with significant glances directed to the lady. But the impression which he produced upon her, both by his person and by his gold, seems to have been very different from what he expected. Instead of adoring him as a second Jupiter, she satirized him as a villanous little bashaw offering to purchase a Circassian slave. On one occasion she became so incensed at the conduct of her princely admirer that she exclaimed: "Sir, I cannot bear it; if you count your money any more, I will instantly leave the room." The prince having discovered that Miss Bellenden was proof against his seductions, turned to the conquest of another lady of the bed-chamber, less beautiful indeed, but more necessitous and more compliant. This person was Mrs. Howard.

But the Prince of Wales was not a man of strong passions or capacities of any description; and he seems to have maintained the royal luxury of a mistress chiefly for the purpose of indicating to the world that he was not ruled by his wife. Never was there a more egregious error, and one less successfully concealed. The Princess of Wales presided over her establishment in Leicester Fields with great dignity and decorum. In 1716 she began to be regarded as the arbitress of fashion. She gathered around her also, the most distinguished men of letters who adorned the period; among whom, Pope and Newton were especial favorites. The familiarity which seems to have existed between the poet and the beautiful ladies of the bed-chamber seems to have been as indecorous as the ruder licence of those times permitted. It was at this date that the influence which one of these ladies, Mrs. Clayton, whose maiden name was Dyves, exercised over the mind of Princess Caroline became so great, that her approbation was regarded as necessary to the success of any application which was made to her mistress. This lady was a woman of talent and shrewdness, who perfectly understood the independent and sagacious disposition of the princess; and who clearly discerned precisely how far she might presume to interfere in directing or influencing her opinions. She was also used by the princess to consolidate her own influence over her royal husband; and the superior talents and discretion of Mrs. Clayton deserved the degree of confidence which her mistress reposed in her.

Mrs. Howard, the mistress of the Prince of Wales, was a woman of a different stamp. With the sacrifice of her virtue, she made no sacrifice of principle or character, for she had none to lose. In early life she had married Mr. Howard, a younger member of the great family of Suffolk. Both were very poor, and the only dowry of the bride was her beauty. Before the accession of George I. Mr. and Mrs. Howard visited Hanover, for the express purpose of securing the favor of the family to whom the royal dignities of England had fallen. It was said that, in order to defray some of the expenses of this journey, Mrs. Howard was compelled to cut off and sell her magnificent suit of hair. Even then she accorded her secret favors to Prince George Augustus, and obtained a promise from him that, as soon as he removed to England, he would appoint her one of the ladies of the bed-chamber to his wife. All this was achieved in accordance with the wishes of the husband of Mrs. Howard, who seems to have been a craven and ignominious wretch. But after the accession of George II. to the throne, it was with considerable difficulty and at some expense that he was disposed of by his subservient wife and her royal lover. His ultimate and obscure destiny is unknown.

The chief source of annoyance to which the prince and princess were subjected previous to their accession, was their aversion to their eldest son Frederic. It is difficult at this late day to ascertain with any certainty the real cause of that repugnance, though many reasons have been assigned for it. His parents did not permit him even to accompany them, when they first came to England. He was born in 1707, and seems to have always exhibited two predominating qualities, both of which were repulsive and unamiable. These were his spitefulness and his cunning. His morals were always bad. He was addicted, from a very early period, to drinking, gaming, cheating, and gross licentiousness. So completely had his conduct alienated the affections even of his mother, that she would have rejoiced had she been able to deprive him of his birthright; and she would have accomplished her purpose had not the colossal barrier of the law rendered her success absolutely impossible. Nor was Frederic allowed to visit England until after the accession of his father to the throne. In 1717 for the sake of decency, he was created Duke of Gloucester; the next year the Garter was conferred upon him, and in 1726 he became Duke of Edinburgh. His life was stormy, dissolute, and short, and he was never destined to ascend the throne which fortune had so blindly bestowed upon his family.

Previous to the accession of the Prince of Wales, and especially during the several concluding years of the reign of his father, there may be said to have existed two courts and two sources of authority in England; and it required the utmost craft and shrewdness on the part of the trimming courtiers and statesmen of the time, to conduct their relations with both courts in such a manner as not to lose the favor of the powers that were, and at the same time not fall under the ban of the powers that soon were to be. At length in June, 1727, the great event occurred which exercised so decisive an influence upon the destinies of the nation, and upon the fortunes of the courtiers. The haughty, pompous, consequential, diminutive Prince of Wales became George II., King of England, and Electoral Sovereign of Hanover.

Information of the death of George I. was conveyed by express to London on the afternoon of June 14th, 1727. His successor was then at Richmond, and thither a crowd of courtiers instantly rushed in order to tender their homage to the new sovereign. Among the number was Robert Walpole, the late prime minister; who inquired of his majesty whom he would select to draw up the usual address to the Privy Council. To his great disappointment the king named, not himself, but Sir Spencer Compton. This was as much as to intimate to Sir Robert, that his services were no longer needed in the Cabinet. But the wily and ambitious minister was not so easily to be dislodged from his ancient seat of influence and power. Compton found himself utterly incompetent to perform the duty assigned him, and was compelled to have recourse to Sir Robert. The latter induced Compton to recommend an allowance only of sixty thousand pounds per annum to the queen. Sir Robert immediately sent word to her majesty, that if he were retained as prime minister he would secure to her an allowance of a hundred thousand pounds. The queen was unable to withstand this potent bribe; and exerted all her influence with the king to obtain the retention of Walpole at the head of the administration. She succeeded; and many years of additional power, anxiety, and glory were added to the political life of that extraordinary man.

The Privy Council was then summoned. Dr. Wake, Archbishop of Canterbury, produced the will of the late sovereign, laid it before his majesty, and waited with the rest of the cabinet to hear his orders in reference to it. To the astonishment of the council, and to the utter dismay of the prelate, the king stuffed the will into his pocket, and abruptly walked out of the chamber. It is generally admitted that the document was afterward burnt, inasmuch as some of its details were not agreeable to the new sovereign.* Two copies of the will had been executed. One of these was deposited with the Duke of Wolfenbüttel, and the other with a German prince whose name has not transpired. Both of these copies were subsequently bought and destroyed by George II., so that the testamentary intentions of his father were entirely defeated. The latter could not have complained very much of this conduct, had he been living; for he had himself destroyed two wills—that of his mother, Sophia Dorothea, and that of the Duke of Zell. It is said that George I. had bequeathed forty thousand pounds to his surviving mistress, the Duchess of Kendal; and had also given a large legacy to his daughter, the Queen of Prussia. With both of these legatees the monarch was afterwards compelled to compound, by the payment of a heavy sum.

* *Letters of Horace Walpole, VI. Vols. London, R. Bentley; Vol. I. p.* 83.

George II. having concluded to retain Robert Walpole as prime minister, determined not to remove any of the members of his father's cabinet.* He ordered them all to be sworn anew. He declared his intention to preserve inviolate the constitution of the realm both as to church and state, and to maintain the same relations with foreign powers which had existed during the reign of his predecessor. Lord Townshend was appointed Secretary of State for foreign affairs. This nobleman was a relative of Walpole both by birth and by marriage. They had long been associated together in the many political changes and vicissitudes which had occurred during preceding years. The disposition of Lord Townshend was open, frank, and generous. He would have been an invaluable aid to Walpole, had not Walpole been one of the most ambitious and domineering of men. Townshend was willing to render his very respectable talents subservient to the ministerial supremacy of Walpole; but he was not disposed to be treated as a slave or a menial. Accordingly he soon quarrelled with the premier and left the cabinet; disgusted, as he well might be, with politics, and determined to be forever quit of the vexations and pollutions inevitably connected with them.

The Duke of Newcastle was also retained in the new administration. His birth was illustrious, his manners were popular and pleasing, his habits were lavish and ostentatious; but his capacities were of the most ordinary description. His chief merit was his inordinate attachment to the House of Hanover. But his character was in many respects most insignificant and ludicrous; so weak, indeed, that he would rush forth from the hands of his valet, with his face covered with soap, to embrace the envoy of the Sultan, in his joy at the establishment of friend-

* It is an incident worthy of notice, that immediately after his accession George II. placed the portrait of a lady habited in the electoral robes of Hanover, in a conspicuous position in his bed-chamber. Her features were unknown to all the courtiers. It was the portrait of the king's mother, which he had concealed for many years from the knowledge and the grasp of his father, and embraced the first opportunity to produce and honor. *See Jesse, Memoirs of the Court of England, Vol. II., p.* 197.

5

ly relations between his sovereign and the Ottoman monarch. Henry Pelham, the brother of the Duke of Newcastle, was retained as Secretary of War. His talents were respectable, and resembled those of Walpole very much as the appearance and qualities of a cat may be supposed to resemble those of a tiger. Pelham was a safe and prudent debater in parliament; he possessed considerable talent for business; his temper was yielding and accommodating; but at the same time it was timid and peevish. He possessed no large and capacious grasp of views. The circle of his vision was limited; nevertheless within the area of that circle, he saw with the clearness and accuracy of the lynx. He endured a vast amount of tyranny from Walpole, because he dreaded, above all other things, to be driven from the dignities and the ignominies of office.

The Earl of Chesterfield was appointed Lord Steward. This nobleman was celebrated as the most polite and polished gallant of his times; as possessing great conversational wit; as one who united in his own person the characters of an accomplished courtier, a man of extreme fashion, and a writer of no mean literary ability. Though he abhorred gross and vulgar licentiousness, he was tarnished by all the elegant and refined vices of the times. After quitting the University he made the tour of Europe. Having returned to England he entered parliament for St. Germains in Cornwall. He became a favorite of George II. while Prince of Wales, and on the accession of that monarch, was appointed a member of the Privy Council, and sent as ambassador to Holland. His chief defect was his fondness for gaming. In 1733 he married Melesina von Schulemberg, the daughter of George I. by the Duchess of Kendal. In the preceding year he had been dismissed from the cabinet in consequence of his opposition in parliament to the passage of the Excise Bill, which was a favorite measure with George II. and his able prime minister.

But the most remarkable man in every respect who held a place in the new cabinet, was Lord Carteret, afterward Earl of Granville. He was the most brilliant and powerful orator who had, previous to that period, displayed his abilities in the British parliament. His eloquence was rapid, stately, imposing and impressive. His commanding person and graceful manner set off his extraordinary talents to the greatest advantage. His learning was remarkable for its richness, accuracy and variety. He was familiar with all the most important languages of modern Europe. His knowledge of the literature of ancient Greece and Rome was such as a Grotius or a Parr would not have disdained. His acquaintance with the great ecclesiastical writers of the Middle Ages would have conferred credit upon a Roman Catholic Doctor of Theology; and the sophisms of Aquinas, Duns Scotus and Occam were neither secrets nor enigmas to his well stored mind. His opinions in International Law possessed great depth and soundness. He alone of all the members of the cabinet could address the king in his native German; and the facility with which he frequently poured forth his Teutonic gutturals in conversation with the monarch, excited the jealousy and apprehension of his less accomplished associates. Beside all this, Carteret was not merely a man of words. He was practical, utilitarian and effective; and his measures were always prompt, decisive and adroit. In parliament no man dared to stand before him as a debater, and when at last his forensic glory was eclipsed, it was eclipsed by that of William Pitt alone. His temper was constantly cheerful and hopeful. The most disastrous events never threw a cloud of sadness over his exultant spirits. He had but one vice, and that was a fondness for wine. When at last, after years of coöperation with Walpole, he retired with him from office, he alone descended from his eminence with an easy and willing grace, and retired laughing to the obscurity of private life; and soon convinced the world that neither ambition, resentment, nor jealousy was the ruling passion of his soul, but that he felt within him the raging of no other yearning except an insatiable *thirst*. No man ever enjoyed the possession of power with less arrogance; none ever resigned it with greater indifference, than Lord Carteret, Earl of Granville.

CHAPTER II.

Revenues and Expenses of the Government—Spanish Aggressions on British Commerce—The Treaty of Vienna—Walpole's Law of Excise—Marriage of the Princess Anne to the Prince of Orange—Incidents connected with the Marriage—Mortifying conduct of Frederic, Prince of Wales—He leads the Opposition against Walpole—Motion to repeal the Septennial Parliament Act—Increase of the National Forces by Land and Sea.

Such were the men who formed the cabinet of the second sovereign of the house of Hanover in England. The first measure which demanded the attention of parliament was the settlement of the civil list. The usual revenues of the government amounted to eight hundred thousand pounds a year. Sir Robert Walpole proposed to allow the whole of this enormous sum for the regular use of the king. The measure met with some opposition. It was alleged that so great a revenue had never before been granted to any British monarch; that during the reign of George I. five hundred thousand pounds had twice been voted to discharge the debts which had accumulated on the civil list; that a hundred and twenty-five thousand pounds had been voted for a similar purpose but a short time before; and that a debt of half a million of pounds contracted by the late sovereign yet remained to be accounted for. But parliament was in a compliant mood, and granted every demand which was made of them, including a settled revenue of a hundred thousand pounds per annum for the queen, according to the lavish promise of the minister.

In 1729 the attention of the British people was attracted to the outrages which had been committed upon their commerce in the West Indies by the Spanish cruisers. Parliament passed a resolution, authorizing Admiral Hosier to seize the vessels of that nation which might fall in his way; and an address was voted to his majesty desiring him to use his utmost exertions to procure satisfaction for the injuries which had been already perpetrated; and especially that means should be taken to secure Gibraltar and Minorca. In accordance with these suggestions, a congress was soon convened at Seville, composed of diplomatic representatives of England, France, and Spain, which settled upon favorable terms of pacification. When Parliament opened in January, 1730, the king informed them from the throne, that the peace of Europe was firmly established by the enactments of the treaty of Seville; that Spain by that compact, had agreed to make ample reparation for all her depredations in the West Indies; and that the rights and possessions of his subjects every where were guaranteed. Notwithstanding these assurances, complaints were soon renewed that the former cruelties and injuries of the Spaniards in the Indies had only been suspended, and had again been resumed. The Legislature presented another petition to the king, requesting the protection of the crown in behalf of those subjects who were engaged in commerce among those Islands. The sovereign devoted his immediate attention to a delicate matter which so nearly concerned both the honor and the interests of the nation; and before parliament was prorogued in May, 1731, he was able to inform them from the throne that another treaty had been signed at Vienna in the preceding March, which would effectually attain the results which had been fruitlessly attempted by the treaty of Seville; that the Ostend East India Company should be totally abolished, and thus an end would be put to the pernicious rivalry which that corporation had so long maintained with the English Company; and that the previous dispute in reference to the sovereignty of Parma and Placentia was amicably adjusted; in exchange for all which important advantages, the King of England only bound himself to adhere to the demands of the Pragmatic Sanction. The consummation of this treaty was due, in a great measure, to the able and skilful exertions of Robert Walpole; whose whole administration was based upon the principle of preserving the general tranquillity of Europe, and the friendly relations which existed between England and the continental powers; and not permit the former to become involved either in any compacts or any wars which concerned simply the interests of the Hanoverian dominions of the king.

It was in February, 1732, that the premier devised and proposed his celebrated project in reference to the duties of Excise. His intention was to effect a radical change in the national system of taxation. He contended that the taxes on real estate, and all immovable property, such as houses, lands, hearths, and windows, were oppressive, partial, and unjust; while at the same time he thought that it was more equitable to lay taxes on consumable articles, to which every citizen contributed in an exact proportion to his consumption. He desired to convert the greater part of the customs into excise taxes, or taxes laid upon commodities both manufactured and consumed within the realm. In accordance with this plan, Walpole proposed a bill in parliament to revise the duties on salt, which had been repealed, in exchange for a land tax of a shilling in the pound. The most violent debates ensued in the House of Commons, in consequence of the introduction of this celebrated bill. The minister was charged by the opposition—among whom Pulteney shone forth preëminently for the unrivalled brilliancy and fervor of his eloquence—with the most malignant and perfidious designs against the liberties and the welfare of his country. These charges were repelled with equal fierceness and determination by the orators of the administration, led on by the dauntless Carteret; and after a desperate conflict, the bill was passed by a majority of two hundred and seven votes over a hundred and thirty-five. In June, 1732, the king prorogued parliament, and announced his intention immediately to visit Germany, and receive the investiture of the Duchies of Bremen and Verden. He appointed Queen Caroline Regent during his absence, who administered the government with much more energy, intelligence, and ability than her husband.

At this period an event of importance occurred in the domestic affairs of the monarch. This was the marriage of his eldest, proudest, and vainest daughter, Anne, to the deformed and sickly Prince of Orange. The lady had already attained the mature age of twenty-five. The birth of brothers had defeated her inheritance of that crown, respecting which she declared that, to be allowed to wear it for a single day she would willingly expire on the next. When she was sixteen years old, a match had been contemplated between her and Louis XV. To this high alliance the aspiring princess had no objection; but it was eventually prevented by the fact that she was a Protestant, and that to have changed her religion would have destroyed the confidence of the British nation in the Protestantism of her whole family, thereby threatening the security of their throne. Years quickly rolled by, and the fair princess still remained unmarried. Equal suitors had not proposed; unequal ones had not ventured to offer. At length the Prince of Orange, whose only merit was that he belonged to the high and mighty class of *reigning* princes, resolved to interpose his own deformed figure between the princess and her unwelcome solitude. At first the British sovereigns laughed outright at the proposition. Queen Caroline called the prince "an ugly animal." George II., who had seen his proposed son-in-law, abhorred him. Anne, who had formed her opinion of his person only from the exaggerated miniatures which his flatterers had executed of him, thought him at least endurable. Her father, aware of the sources from which her ideas had been derived, informed her that the prince was the ugliest man in Holland. She replied, in her determination no longer to be deprived of something in the shape of a husband, that she would marry the prince "though he were a Dutch baboon." Her father sarcastically replied: "Then have your own way; I promise you that you will have baboon enough."

This fascinating bridegroom arrived at Greenwich in November, 1732, and took up his residence at Somerset House. Before the marriage could take place he fell sick. The ceremony was consequently postponed. It was not till the succeeding January that he was so far restored, as to be able to travel to

Bath to imbibe renewed vigor and strength at that fashionable resort. In March his serene Highness had become to some extent restored to health; and announced himself as prepared to undertake the responsibilities of matrimony. On the 24h of March the ceremony was performed by the Bishop of London in the chapel of St. James. The groom was dressed for the occasion in a suit of cloth-of-gold. The princess was arrayed in robes of silver tissue, having a train six yards long, which was supported by the fair daughters of ten dukes and earls. The bride and groom were an odd-looking couple; and their appearance was extremely ludicrous when, after the ceremony and the supper, they were put to bed and sat bolt-upright together in their night-dresses, while the court and nobility defiled before them, according to the established etiquette of the court. The princess was marked with small-pox, while her figure was short, fat, and shapeless. The bridegroom was absolutely deformed, and his person was remarkable for an odor which was neither agreeable in a prince nor a peasant. His figure was so peculiar that, while sitting in bed, when seen from behind he seemed to have no head; when seen from before he appeared to have no legs. When Queen Caroline saw the ridiculous and melancholy spectacle presented by this hymeneal pair, she could scarcely retain her tears of mortification; yet the absurdity of the scene in the next moment compelled her to laugh in despite of herself. Never had a more intensely serio-comic exhibition been made in the annals of royal marriages in England. When the matter of the dowry of the princess was proposed in parliament, the House resolved to sell lands in the island of St. Christopher to the amount of eighty thousand pounds, and appropriate that sum for the purpose. In justice to the Prince of Orange, it must be admitted that, though deformed in person, he was a man of intelligence and good sense. His conduct was always marked by a proper regard for propriety and decency; which redeemed him in a great measure from the derision occasioned by his physical defects, and secured him the respect and esteem of his subjects.

After the marriage, the Prince of Orange was conducted by his brother-in-law Frederic, the heir-apparent, to examine the wonders and novelties of the metropolis. A bill was also passed by parliament, conferring upon him the rights of a British subject. The king further preferred a request to parliament that they would settle five thousand pounds per annum upon the Princess of Orange; to which proposition they generously acceded. In April, 1734, the bride and groom started for Holland. The match seemed to be a happy one. The princess at least appeared to be pleased with her husband, and treated him with great tenderness and affection; which was reciprocated by him, not with ardor indeed, but with the solemn and honest phlegm which characterized his nation. The queen was satisfied, notwithstanding her previous apprehensions, that the happiness of her daughter had not been sacrificed by the alliance.

It was well that no domestic anxiety tormented the king and queen from this source, inasmuch as they found a constant cause of vexation and mortification in the conduct of their eldest son, Frederic. Parliament allowed this prince a hundred thousand pounds a year; of which sum his father only paid over fifty thousand. In his rage he joined the opposition, and became its most violent and vindictive leader. His parents cordially detested him for his debauched morals, for his disrespect to them, for his opposition to the government, and for the general worthlessness of his character. It was fortunate for the British Empire that he never ascended the throne. He feared his mother, with great justice, more than he did his father. He readily perceived her intellectual and moral superiority. It was she who vanquished Lord Stair in a set argument, and humbled him as he never before had been humbled.* It was she who overawed the satirical and irreverent spirit of Lord Chesterfield; who removed the in-

* This nobleman had been selected by a large number of peers to wait upon the Queen, and represent to her the unconstitutional nature and the destructive tendency of Walpole's great measure in reference to the excise. This was a favorite scheme with Caroline as well as with her minister; and Lord Stair, though a man of talent and experience, found that he was no match for the shrewdness and resolution of the Queen.

5*

tense hatred which her husband had felt, on his accession to the throne, against Robert Walpole; and who continued him firmly seated in his high place for many years, so that he was generally called, with perfect truth, the Queen's minister.* Yet notwithstanding all her sense, prudence, and decorum, the hatred of the queen against her eldest son was so intense, that on more than one occasion she declared that she would rejoice at his death; and upon him alone of all her family or subjects was she unable to impress any sentiment of esteem or affection. The union of the prince with the Opposition gave that party great courage and energy. They took countenance from the fact that their measures were supported by the heir apparent, who might at any moment, by the sudden demise of the king, ascend to the supreme conduct of affairs; and they thus rendered the position of the minister one of increased difficulty, and that of the nation one of more imminent danger.

An important illustration of this fact, may be found in the effort which was made by the opposition in the session of 1734, to repeal the Act authorizing septennial parliaments. These were represented as a flagrant encroachment upon the rights of the people; as giving a pernicious degree of power to the crown; and as being the cause of many great evils and misfortunes to the state. The motion to repeal the Act was supported with great ability; especially by Sir William Windham, who on this occasion gave utterance to a burst of eloquence which has since become classical. Sir Robert Walpole answered him with equal effect, and defied the enemies of the government to point out a single instance in which the nation had been injured by the operation of the existing law. His resolute efforts prevailed, after a desperate conflict, in which the whole strength of both parties was fully exerted and displayed; and the motion to repeal was

---

* We may call this a very great triumph on the part of the Queen, for her husband was one of the most obstinate of men. George II. under her influence, finally became enthusiastic in praise of Walpole; called him a "noble fellow" and frequently shed tears when speaking of his heroic battles in Parliament with the opponents of the Government. *Doran's Queens*, Vol. I., *p.* 253.

lost by two hundred and forty-seven votes against a hundred and eighty-four.

A further effort was made during the same session to limit the authority of the monarch by the passage of a law, which took away his power to divest officers of their military commissions, otherwise than by the judgment of a court martial, or by an address of either house of parliament. This motion gave great alarm to the court; as it was supposed that the passage of such a law would render the military arm of the government independent in a great degree of the sovereign; and as giving licence to the commission of every species of military cruelty and oppression. An animated debate again ensued, after which the motion was lost by an overwhelming majority. The ability, tact, and *secret bribes* of the prime minister continued to carry the government successfully through all its proposed measures, during several successive sessions of parliament. He triumphed on the motion to grant the king a supply of sixty thousand pounds to increase his forces by sea and land; on the motion to allow a subsidy to the King of Denmark, in accordance with the requisitions of an existing treaty; on the motion to repeal the ancient statutes which still disgraced the nation in reference to witchcraft and conjuration; and in its opposition to the motion which was introduced in March, 1736, to repeal all those clauses of the test act which obstructed the admission of Protestant Dissenters to civil employments under the government, which measure was represented by the administration to be at that time premature and impolitic.

CHAPTER III.

Domestic Life of George II.—Quarrels with Prince Frederic—The King's Visit to Hanover—Singular Correspondence between the King and Queen—The Monarch's Contempt for the Bishops—Marriage of Prince Frederic proposed—First Speech of William Pitt in Parliament—The Princess Augusta of Saxe-Coburg—Her Marriage to the Heir Apparent—Her Arrival in England—Visit of George II. to Hanover—His Intrigue with Madame Walmoden—Popular Satires and Caricatures of the Monarch at Home.

THE domestic life of George II. at this period was not one of much comfort, dignity, or decency. In 1734 Mrs. Howard, who for some years had been his mistress, married, and was dismissed from her disgraceful relation to the monarch. It is probable that the immediate cause of her dismissal was an adroit effort on the part of the talented queen to crush her rival, in which the polished Lord Chesterfield was made an unconscious tool.* The treatment which the king bestowed upon Frederic, the Prince of Wales, was probably such as he deserved. The prince frequently attended the levées of his royal father, on which occasions it was curious to observe how completely the latter ignored his presence. He would pass by him, stand near him, and converse with courtiers next to him, and never seem to be conscious of his presence. Lord Harvey, in his memoirs, describes with great effect the skill which the king exhibited in

* It would appear that different sentiments were entertained by the members of the royal family in reference to this event. The Princess Anne, who had married the *handsome* Prince of Orange, being in England at the time, remarked: "I wish with all my heart that the king would take somebody else, that mamma might be a little relieved from seeing him eternally in her room." *Doran's Queens of the House of Hanover*, Vol. I., p. 262.

thus pointedly and repeatedly giving the cut direct to his detested son. "It put one in mind," says the supple courtier, "of stories that one has heard of ghosts that appear to part of the company and were invisible to the rest; and in this manner, wherever the prince stood, though the king passed him ever so often, or ever so near, it always seemed as if the king thought the prince filled a void space."

In 1735 the king made another visit to Hanover. He appointed the queen regent during his absence, which he expected would continue during half a year. The conduct of the monarch on this occasion was singular and disgraceful in the extreme. He wrote almost daily to the queen enormous letters containing thirty or forty pages, in every line of which he loaded her with praises.* At the same time he seduced a young married lady named Walmoden, residing in the City of Hanover; had the turpitude to induce her to desert her husband; and disgraced her and him in the eyes of the whole world by making her his acknowledged mistress. To render his conduct still more singular, in his interminable letters to his queen he gave her all the details of this amour, and even asked her advice in reference to the woman's removal to England, and bespoke for her the affection of his wife! He also urged her to invite the daughter of the Duke of Orleans to visit her court, in order that he might have an opportunity to commence an intrigue with her. In regard to some of these interesting points, he suggested to her that she should consult with Sir Robert Walpole as an oracle of sagacity and wisdom. We question whether a parallel to such incidents could be found in the whole range of royal or princely correspondence.

On the 26th of October the king returned to England, leaving behind him his new mistress, Madam Walmoden, and with

---

* The language of the king was, in part, as follows: "Un plaisir, que je suis sûr, ma chère Caroline, vous serez bien aise de me procurer, quand je vous dis combien je le souhaite." *See Lord Hervey's Memoirs of the Court of Queen Caroline.* This young nobleman was chamberlain to the Queen, her constant attendant, her chief confidant and her favorite.

her his good temper. On his arrival at the palace of Kensington, he treated his queen and family with unusual petulance and rudeness. He missed the wanton and fascinating charms of Walmoden; he preferred the small Electorate of Hanover, where his power was absolute; and he felt vexed at his return to a family who either despised or abused him—and to a kingdom where his tyranny was restrained by the operation of law, and by the boldness and resolution of a great people. At breakfast he snubbed the queen, and told her that she was always stuffing. He accused the Princess Caroline of growing abominably fat; and he charged the Duke of Cumberland with standing as awkwardly as a monkey. The irate monarch seemed on this occasion to be pleased with nobody. Lord Hervey having remarked to him that a work of Bishop Hoadly on the sacraments had just appeared, he replied, that "he was always talking of such nonsense, and that were it not that there were fools to speak of such things, the fools who wrote such books would never think of publishing their nonsense, thereby disturbing the government by their disputes." The monarch then fell upon the character of the learned and pious prelate in question, and called him "a great puppy, a very dull fellow, and a very great rascal." He continued by saying: "It is very modest for a canting hypocritical knave to be crying that the kingdom of Christ is not of this world, at the same time that he, as Christ's ambassador, receives seven thousand pounds a year; and is ready to receive the best pay for preaching the Bible, though he does not believe a word of it." During this outburst the skilful queen did her best, by smiling and nodding assent at the proper places to win the favor of her husband; but all to no purpose, as he concluded by snubbing her again, in reference to her *grotto* in Richmond Gardens. The indignant and petulant little monarch only regained his usual temper after he had written several immense letters to the absent Walmoden; to whom he promised to return, to receive the renewal of her hypocritical and purchased embraces on the 29th of the ensuing May.

In 1735 Prince Frederic, the heir apparent threatened to

bring the matter of his limited pecuniary allowance before parliament. To avoid the disgrace and vexation of this step, Queen Caroline adroitly proposed to marry the prince to somebody, and at the same time provide for him a more suitable establishment. She readily obtained the consent of the king to this measure; and the royal matchmakers looked around for a suitable bride. At this time the prince had two mistresses, Miss Vane, and Mrs. Archibald Hamilton, already the mother of ten children. These, however, were no impediments to the accomplishment of the proposed marriage. At first the king wished to unite the prince to the eldest daughter of the King of Prussia; and suggested at the same time, that his second daughter should marry the king's eldest son. Proposals to this effect were made in due form; but the Prussian monarch replied that if he gave his eldest daughter to the Prince of Wales, he would require the *eldest* daughter of the British monarch for his son. Queen Caroline would have consented to this arrangement; but her husband was inflexible. His refusal excited the most ungovernable fury in the royal madman who ruled in Prussia; and the two monarchs reviled each other, in consequence, in the grossest language. The quarrel became more and more violent; until at last it ended in one of the most singular incidents which ever occurred in the history of royal animosities. They determined to settle the dispute by a *duel*. These two fathers, sovereigns, allies, and brothers-in-law, determined to meet on the field of blood, and settle their controversy by an attempt at each other's lives. The territory of Hildesheim was the spot chosen for this extraordinary scene. The British monarch selected General Sutten for his second. The King of Prussia conferred a similar distinction on Colonel Derschein. George was to reach the battle-ground by travelling from Hanover. Frederic was to confront him by passing through Saltzdahl. All the fearful preliminaries were definitely arranged, except the single item of the *time* of the conflict. On this point the combatants could not agree. Their respective advisers and courtiers, perceiving the unutterable folly and foolishness of the dispute, and its proposed conclusion, continued to raise difficulties on both sides in reference to this point, to procrastinate, and eventually to defeat the belligerent purposes of the two monarchs entirely. The royal duel never occurred; and posterity, instead of sighing at the miserable weakness, may more comfortably laugh at the ridiculous absurdity, of the whole transaction; although great coldness continued to exist between the courts of London and Berlin for many years in consequence of this quarrel.

Queen Caroline at length proposed a suitable bride for the heir apparent, the handsome and accomplished Princess Augusta of Saxe Coburg. Lord Delaware was sent to demand her hand from her brother, the Duke of Saxe Coburg. The proposition was very agreeable to that petty monarch, and the match was quickly agreed upon. The subject of the prince's marriage was proposed in parliament for the first time in the beginning of April, 1736. In the following session, Mr. Pulteney moved that a hundred thousand pounds per year should be settled on the prince, out of the civil list. It will be observed that the proposition was, not to vote this sum directly to the prince, but to deduct it from the immense revenue of a million already allowed for the regular expenses of the government. It was on this occasion that William Pitt, the most illustrious and powerful statesman who has guided the destinies of the British nation, made his first speech in that Legislature which was destined, during thirty memorable years of conflict, disaster, and glory, to be the theatre of his prodigious achievements and abilities. The House of Commons moved an address to the king. Pitt had listened to the debates for several months in silence. On this occasion he arose and addressed the house on the side of the opposition to the government. His splendid person, his graceful delivery, his sonorous and melodious voice, his boldness of manner, and the temerity of his sentiments, at once attracted to the young cornet the attention of every member. The substance of his effort was not remarkable for any thing but the magnificent and brilliant declamation which characterized it. Nevertheless the effort was a worthy introduction to that long series of oratorical displays which, improving with the progress of time in substantial merit, will remain to the end of time the most admirable which any British statesman has ever achieved. After an animated debate the motion of Pulteney was lost; but it was lost by a majority only of thirty votes. Never before had the government been so nearly defeated since the accession of George II; and the event struck terror into the hearts of his courtiers and servants.

Prince Frederic was compelled to accept such a support as his royal father was disposed to allow him. The yacht William and Mary was sent to convey the young bride, seventeen years of age, to the British shores. She arrived at Greenwich on the 25th of April, 1736, and attracted general admiration by her cheerful manner, her healthy appearance, and her elegant attire. She first set foot on the soil of her adopted country on Saint George's day; an incident which was deemed auspicious to the future fate of the princess who was destined to be the mother of the first king born and reared in England since the birth of James II. As soon as she had landed, the king, queen, and other members of the royal family sent her their compliments. The next day her intended husband reached Greenwich, where she still remained, and the first interview took place between them. The princess was conveyed in one of the royal carriages to Lambeth. Her reception at St. James Palace was cheerful and even magnificent. On her arrival at the palace, the bridegroom took her hand and conducted her into the presence chamber of the monarch, where the whole court had been assembled. As she approached her future father-in-law, she prostrated herself before him. She had been informed that the haughty and punctilious little king would be gratified by such a profound act of homage. He courteously raised her from the floor, kissed her on each cheek, and handed her over to the embraces of the queen. The princess, who was unaccompanied by a single friend, behaved on this somewhat trying occasion with extraordinary self-possession and grace. She won the admiration of all observers, except that of a few venerable females of the court, in whose breasts jealousy absorbed every other sentiment.

On the evening of the day of the arrival of the princess, the marriage was celebrated at St. James's by the Bishop of London, dean of the Royal Chapel. After the ceremony was concluded, a supper followed. When the hour arrived for the observance of that most ridiculous of royal ceremonies, the "bedding" of the youthful pair, the bride was conducted to her sleeping apartment by her attendant ladies, where she was disrobed and arrayed in her night dress. While this was going forward, Prince Frederic was undergoing the same process in another apartment, where the king did him the honor to hand him his shirt, and even aid in putting it on. The princess having been placed in her bed, her husband was conducted thither by several noblemen. He was arrayed in a night-gown of silver stuff, and a cap of the finest lace. The attire of the princess consisted of a night-dress of equal elegance. The prince took his place in bed beside his wife; and both sat upright to give the courtiers an opportunity to behold this rare and edifying spectacle. After the royal family and all the court had sufficiently satisfied their curiosity, they gradually withdrew, the lights were put out, the doors were locked, and the young couple were left to themselves.

When the end of May arrived the king repeated his visit to Hanover, as he had promised his fascinating Walmoden that he would do. He again appointed the queen regent during his absence. As Walpole was the favorite minister of the queen, the kingdom was governed during the absence of the monarch on the same principles as during his presence. On this occasion the peace of the kingdom was disturbed by riots in the western counties, which were caused by attempts to prevent the exportation of corn; by riots in London occasioned by the presence of Irish laborers who offered to work for less wages than the English; by riots in Edinburgh in consequence of the execution of a noted and desperate smuggler. While the queen regent and her able minister were suppressing these commotions, and preserving the peace of the kingdom as best they could, the amorous king was still luxuriating in the society of the fair Walmoden in Hanover; and so potent had her charms become over her royal dupe, who was old enough to be her father, that he overstayed his birthday. This was an event which had never before occurred; and the consciousness of its disgraceful cause inflicted intense suffering upon the heart of the queen. Once only was she seen by her confidants to weep. She instantly mastered her feelings, probably being consoled by the just reflection that the worthless and conceited libertine whom she had the misfortune to call husband was unworthy of her sensibility.

But while the conduct of the king afflicted his wife, he became annoyed, as he deserved to be, by the discovered unfaithfulness of his mistress. He ascertained that she gave secret interviews to Captain von Schulemberg, a relative of the Duchess of Kendal. In the midst of his mortification, and in accordance with the folly and meanness of his character, he wrote to the queen on the subject of his cuckoldry, and asked her advice under such painful circumstances! At the same time he desired her to consult with Walpole, as a man "who has more experience in these matters, my dear Caroline, and who, in the present affair, must necessarily be more unprejudiced than I am." The king himself thought that the best expedient would be to convey the fair but perfidious Walmoden to England. Meanwhile his despicable conduct began to excite the public derision and contempt. Caricatures and pasquinades against him flooded the streets of the metropolis. A famished old blind horse, with a saddle and a pillion behind it, was sent hobbling through the streets, with an inscription attached to its forehead requesting that nobody would stop him as he was the " King's Hanoverian Equipage going to fetch his majesty and his mistress over to England." A written notice was boldly affixed to the front of St. James's Palace as follows: " Lost or strayed out of this house, a man who has left a wife and six children on the parish. Whoever will give any tidings of him to the churchwardens of St. James's parish, will receive four shillings and sixpence. Nobody supposes that he is worth a *crown*.* From incidents such as these it will not be difficult to estimate the real opinion which the majority of the subjects of the second George entertained of his public character, and his private worth.

* *Lord Hervey's Memoirs of the Court of Queen Caroline.*

CHAPTER IV.

George II. embarks for England—A Storm arises—Apprehensions for his Fate—He narrowly escapes Shipwreck—Congratulations of the Royal Family and of Parliament—Revenues of Prince Frederic—Coarseness and Vulgarity of the King and Queen—Confinement of the Princess of Wales—Disgraceful feuds in the Royal Family—Declining health of the Queen—Domestic Scenes—The Queen's last Illness—Her Death—Ridiculous Conduct of the Bereaved Monarch.

George II. took his leave of the capital of his Hanoverian dominions, to return to England, on the 7th of December. On the night previous to his departure the fair and fascinating Walmoden entertained her royal lover with a sumptuous farewell supper, at which both wine and tears were shed abundantly. The king having reluctantly torn himself away from the siren, arrived at Helvoetsluys on the eleventh; and although his daughter, the Princess of Orange, lay at that moment very dangerously ill at the Hague, he hurried on without even inquiring into her condition, or sending her any message of condolence. He immediately embarked on board the royal squadron; and then ensued a series of thrilling incidents which very nearly changed the future destinies of the British succession. While the inhabitants of London were expecting to hear of the safe arrival of the king at Harwich, the wind suddenly changed, a hurricane blew from the west with terrific violence, and such an unparalleled storm swept over the deep, that every one concluded that, if the king had embarked, he had inevitably gone to the bottom. The excitement in London and in the court, in reference to the royal fate, became intense. Bets were laid upon the issue. The adroit and provident Walpole began to discuss with the queen the probable results which would follow, should their fears in reference to the king be realized. The queen became greatly agitated; for she knew that if Frederic, Prince of Wales, then succeeded to the throne, her fate would be an unenviable one, in consequence of the hostile feeling existing between them. While this state of anxiety continued, news of disasters at sea began to reach London. Signals of distress had been heard at Harwich, booming over the face of the troubled waters. It was supposed that these came from the foundering royal fleet—the solemn funeral dirge of the drowning monarch. While the tempest still raged over land and sea, and while the apprehension was at the highest, a courier from the king arrived at St. James's, who had miraculously escaped the devouring waves; and informed the queen that her husband had never embarked at all, but that he was taking his comfort contentedly at Helvoetsluys, awaiting the arrival of fair weather and propitious winds.

The king became impatient of delay, and as soon as the storm had partially lulled, he informed Sir Charles Wager that he had determined to embark. The Admiral declared that he judged the weather to be still unsettled, and the sea dangerous. "Be the weather what it may," said the king, "I am not afraid." "I am," responded the veteran seaman. The king answered that he wanted to see a storm, and would sooner be twelve hours in one, than be shut up twenty-four in Helvoetsluys. "Twelve hours in a storm!" exclaimed the Admiral: "four hours would do the business for you." After some further delay the impatience of the monarch prevailed, and the fleet set sail. A tempest still more terrible than the first instantly arose, and the condition of the royal fleet became perilous in the extreme. Sir Charles made signal for every vessel to provide for its own safety; and immediately endeavored to regain the port of Helvoetsluys by tacking. Meanwhile at London, with the renewal of the storm, the public anxiety was increased. It was Christmas; and never before had so dull a holiday been known in the palace of St. James. Walpole informed the queen of the more assured apprehensions now entertained by her subjects as to the king's fate; and she burst into tears at the announcement of his certain danger. The day was also Sunday, and the queen determined, notwithstanding her intense anxiety, to attend divine service as usual. In the midst of the service, she received a letter from the king's own hand, in which he told her to dismiss her fears, and informed her that he indeed had embarked, that the royal fleet had been scattered by the storm, that he had been tossed about for twenty hours on the deep, in constant danger of death; but that he had at last reached Helvoetsluys, and that he was alive and safe. During the interval of suspense which prevailed in London, the query rapidly passed from mouth to mouth, "how is the wind for the king?" and the answer uniformly given was: "Like the nation; against him."

The escaped and impatient monarch had seen enough of storms. He had been terribly shaken by its violence; and nothing could induce him to venture again upon the treacherous deep, until the weather seemed most unmistakably propitious. He delayed, therefore, five weeks in port, and at length embarked, made a successful voyage, and arrived in London on the 15th of January, 1737; greatly to the joy of the queen, Robert Walpole, and the court of St. James, and as greatly to the regret of the Prince of Wales, the opposition, and the diminutive court in Leicester House.

No sooner were the congratulations tendered to the king in consequence of his escape concluded, than he was again annoyed by the introduction into parliament of the question of the revenue of his detested son Frederic. Walpole did his utmost to prevent this result; but the friends of the prince, especially Lord Carteret, were not to be deterred from their purpose either by entreaties or by threats. The prince demanded an absolute and regular income of a hundred thousand pounds per year. A compromise was proposed by Walpole in the name of the king, which was declined by the prince, because it was inadequate to his necessities. After an animated debate in the House of Commons, the bill was lost by a small majority; but this victory of the court was gained only by heavy bribes to leading members, amounting to several thousand pounds. The same proposition was lost in the House of Peers by a still greater majority; although it was there supported by all the eloquence and resolution of Lord Carteret.

It will readily be supposed that these disputes in the royal household increased the ill feeling already existing between its members. This was the fact; and they were not backward or decorous in expressing their cordial hatred and disgust of each other. Prince Frederic, according to court etiquette, led his royal mother to dinner by the hand every day; and yet she repeatedly "cursed the day in which she had given birth to that nauseous beast." His sister, the Princess Caroline, was equally malignant, and prayed publicly and repeatedly that "God would strike the brute dead with apoplexy." The king spoke of him always as "a brainless, impertinent puppy and scoundrel." Such was the singular state of feeling prevalent among the members, both male and female, of this exalted and exemplary family.*

The chief defect in the character of the queen was the coarseness and bitterness exhibited by her in reference to this subject These qualities she displayed on many occasions and in different ways. The king having remarked to her that he understood that Lords Carteret, Chesterfield, and Bolingbroke, were each writing the history of their times, she replied that the three histories would be three heaps of lies; but they would be lies of very different descriptions. Bolingbroke's would be great lies, Chesterfield's would be little lies, and Carteret's would be lies of both sorts. We may admit the wit, and even the truth of this sarcasm, but it would be difficult to excuse its coarseness and indelicacy when emanating from a woman.

The attention of the royal family and of the public was now attracted to the anticipated birth of a lineal heir to the throne. The Princess of Wales was near her confinement. When Queen Caroline was informed of the fact, she immediately expressed

---

* The *Memoirs of Lord Hervey* furnish throughout the most abundant evidence that the representations above given of the hostility which existed between the prince and his relatives are not exaggerated, nor even fully equal to the revolting truth.

her determination to be present, inasmuch as she doubted the genuineness of the pregnancy. She declared that her son, the prince, was such an "infamous liar," and so "great a knave," that he would willingly attempt to impose a false issue upon the nation. Moreover, she added: "I am resolved to be satisfied that the child is the princess's; and it can't be got through with"—she added with characteristic coarseness, "as soon as one can blow one's nose!" To aid in preventing an imposition the king gave a peremptory order to the prince that the birth should take place at Hampton Court Palace.

As the period of the *accouchement* of the princess approached, her husband resolved to defeat the interference and scrutiny of his parents, and remove his wife to his own residence at St. James's Palace. He accomplished this purpose at midnight on the 31st of July, only several hours before her delivery. She was secretly conveyed thither in a carriage, even after her sufferings had begun; and she came near dying before she reached the termination of her journey, her husband constantly urging her to take courage, and assuring her that "it was nothing, and would soon be over." The princess was safely delivered, however, in the presence of as many of the great officers of the crown as could be summoned under the circumstances. The Lord President Wilmington and Lord Privy Seal Godolphin were the chief of these. Lord Hervey and Queen Caroline soon afterward arrived; and the former describes the infant as a "little rat no bigger than a toothpick case." The queen, taking the child in her arms, closely scrutinized it, and exclaimed: "May the good God bless you, poor little creature, for you have arrived in a most disagreeable world." And the subsequent fate, during many long years, of this infant, who proved to be a daughter, amply verified the declaration of the queen; for she afterward became the wife of the Duke of Brunswick, and the mother of the unhappy spouse of George IV., in connection with both of whom she suffered infinite sorrows.

But the birth of this princess did not alleviate the existing family feuds. After an interval of nine days the queen again visited her daughter-in-law. She remained an hour, during the whole of which time the Prince of Wales did not address a single word to his mother. Etiquette required that he should conduct her both to his chamber and from it; but he performed even this duty in such a manner as to render his courtesy a vehicle of contempt. It must be admitted that the queen had some excuse for the indecorous and bitter hostility which, during many years, she exhibited toward the heir apparent to the throne. This was the last occasion on which they ever met each other; so unexpectedly near was the death of the queen, and so implacable was her hatred, that during her last hours the very name of her son elicited the most intense execration. On the part of the prince, he publicly boasted what he would do when he became king. His mother should be fleeced, flayed, and minced. The Princess Amelia should be kept in strict confinement. He would leave the Princess Caroline to starve. Of the youngest princesses, Mary and Louisa, at that time fourteen and thirteen years of age, he made no particular mention; nor of his brother, the Duke of Cumberland, who during all his life had been the special favorite of his parents. Efforts were indeed made by the Princess of Wales, by the Duke of Newcastle, and by other courtiers to heal this unseemly and disgraceful feud, but all to no purpose.* The same hostile sentiments continued to exist until the father, mother, and son, all reposed in the dreamless slumber of the tomb. In this domestic controversy the prince stood arrayed against his whole family. George II. himself was as bitter as his queen; but the undutiful conduct of his son produced far less effect upon his spirit, than upon that of his more susceptible wife. His nature was too cold, too selfish, too unsympathizing,

---

* This will readily be believed when it is remembered that the Queen, in speaking of her detested "Fritz," thus addressed herself to Lord Hervey: "My dear Lord, I will give it you under my hand, if you have any fear of my relapsing, that my dear first-born is the greatest ass, the greatest liar, the greatest canaille, and the greatest beast, in the whole world; and that I most heartily wish he was out of it." What a singular utterance of maternal feeling is this, in reference to the first offspring of conjugal affection!

to be lacerated by any misfortune which did not directly affect either his pocket, his prerogatives, his safety, or his pleasures.

In 1737 Queen Caroline began to feel the certain approach of death. For some years she had been afflicted with rupture; but she had imprudently concealed both the nature and the existence of her malady from her medical attendants, and even from her husband. She always shuddered at the thought of death, and she avoided all allusions and references to so repulsive a subject. She also feared that, if it were known that she was thus afflicted, the possibility of her death might diminish her influence over the king and over the courtiers. But the monarch long suspected, from certain indications which the queen could not conceal, that she was thus diseased; but to all his inquiries she constantly returned a positive and absolute denial. Sir Robert Walpole, in the long interviews which he held with her, had discovered that she was afflicted with some secret malady; but she endeavored to deceive him also, and often *stood* for a considerable length of time in his presence, to convince him of the fallacy of his conjectures.

But this system of deception could not continue forever; and at length in August 1737, the Queen became worse. A report soon became prevalent that she was dead; but it was premature and false. She rallied for a few days, yet on the 9th of November she was seized with the illness which terminated in her dissolution. Dr. Tessier was called in, who administered an elixir which for a time alleviated her pains. The improvement was only temporary, and her sufferings increased while her strength diminished. Cordials and various other remedies including Usquebaugh were given, but without any alleviation of her condition. The Princess Caroline seemed much affected at the sufferings of her mother; but the king exhibited his usual apathy. Even yet, until the 12th of November, the patient obstinately concealed from her physicians the true nature of her disease. Dr. Ranby was by this time also in attendance. He was permitted to examine the person of the queen; and he contrived to satisfy himself without her aid of the real cause of her sufferings. He immediately gave utterance to his suspicions in the royal bed-chamber; but the queen, ill as she was, abused him for his frankness as a "blockhead." So mortified was she at the discovery, that she actually shed tears. Shipton and Bussier, the most distinguished surgeons of the time, were instantly summoned. After an examination of the person of the queen they promptly suggested an operation. The patient submitted, and endured the agony which ensued without a murmur. Her wit and sarcasm did not forsake her even when under the knife; for she remarked to Dr. Ranby the operator at that moment, that she had no doubt he was sorry that his patient was, not herself, but his own aged and ugly wife.

While in this critical and painful condition, she was thrown into a paroxysm of rage in consequence of a message which was sent to the palace from Prince Frederic, inquiring after the health of his mother. She knew that the information was asked in the spirit of satirical exultation; and almost with her dying breath she cursed the son, whom she hated with a hatred passing that of a step-mother. She besought the king not to permit the reprobate to approach her chamber while living, nor to see her remains when dead; she said she knew "he would blubber like a calf in her presence, and laugh at her the moment he left it."

The remedies which were applied for the rupture with which the queen was afflicted proved unavailing because they came too late. On Sunday the 13th, she was much worse. The wound had begun to mortify. The queen was apprised by her medical attendants of her critical condition; and she bore the announcement with great calmness and self-possession. The feeble-minded king was much more affected at the near prospect of the dissolution of his wife than she; and began to be impressed with the solemnity of the occasion. As her last hour was supposed to be near, the royal family were all summoned to her bedside, except the Prince of Wales, who was excluded, and the Princess of Orange, who was absent. Then ensued one of the most extraordinary death-bed scenes which has ever been witnessed either among royal or plebeian moribunds. The queen took a solemn leave of her children. She spoke kindly to her daughter Amelia. She used still more tender words to the Princess Caroline. Her farewell to her favorite son, the young Duke of Cumberland, afterward the hero of Culloden, was affecting in the extreme. Her two youngest daughters, Louisa and Mary, she intrusted to the special care of the gentle Caroline. The utterances of the queen were rendered almost inaudible by the exclamations of grief which filled the chamber. Last of all the king himself approached to bid his wife farewell. She took from her hand her marriage ring, and placed it on the finger of her husband. She declared that for all the greatness and happiness which had fallen to her share in this world, she was indebted alone to him, and that all she possessed should return to him. The little monarch seemed to be overcome by his emotions, and he was heard to exclaim, amid his sobs and groans, that she had ever been to him the best of wives. The dying queen was comforted by this assurance; and proceeded to say that she hoped her husband would marry again after her death. He appeared to be quite astounded at this suggestion; and declared that, after the loss of so admirable a wife, he never could think of placing any substitute in her stead. The queen persisted in her recommendation, and the king persisted in his refusal; but at length, in the midst of his heart-breaking sobs, he added that, though he never could marry again, he might go so far as to take a mistress or two. "My God," exclaimed the queen almost with her dying breath, "why not do both? the one does not prevent the other!"

Nor was this extraordinary threat of the king an empty one; for immediately after the burial of the queen, he sent orders to Madam Walmoden to remove without delay to England, and assigned her apartments in the palace of St. James; while at the same time he promoted, or degraded, Lady Deloraine to the same bad eminence as one of the royal mistresses.

The patient sank very rapidly; and the princess Amelia suggested to the king, the father of this family of royal heathens, that it might perhaps do no harm to the queen if a priest were sent for, and the usual forms of religion were observed. The king was indifferent either way; and Dr. Potter, the Archbishop of Canterbury, whom the queen had often complimented with the assurance that he was a fool, was ordered to attend. What passed in the royal bedchamber is not known. It is certain, however, that the queen did not receive the eucharist. It is also certain that she refused to the last to be reconciled to the "cursed Fritz." The king uniformly kept out of the way, as long as the visits of the Archbishop continued. The curiosity of the courtiers to ascertain what occurred in the bedchamber was not satisfied; and all that the most adroit questioning could extort from the prudent prelate was, that "her majesty was in a heavenly state of mind."

This indeed is very doubtful; for, during her last hours, the sufferer became profanely impatient and restless. " How long can this last?" she demanded of Dr. Tessier. He replied: "It cannot be very long before your majesty will be relieved from your sufferings." "The sooner that happens the better," was her sharp response. Sunday the 20th of September dawned; and it was the last day she was destined to live. She now sank rapidly, the mortification had greatly extended, and at eleven o'clock in the morning, drawing a long sigh, uttering the word "so" with a deep aspiration, and with a queenly and farewell wave of the hand, she gently expired. The princess Caroline approached, placed a glass before the mouth of the corpse, and finding it unsullied by a breath, exclaimed, " 'Tis over." The widowed monarch repeatedly kissed the hands and face of the defunct with passionate ardor; and turning round to the courtiers and attendants delivered a long harangue upon the extraordinary virtues and merits of his wife. While thus engaged the king discovered Horace Walpole in the background, who was trying to weep for fashion's sake; but who accomplished the feat in so ludicrous a manner, that the monarch stopped his speech, gazed at Walpole for a moment, and then burst into a roar of laughter. Such were the mingled scenes of solemnity and buffoonery which were enacted around the deathbed of Caroline

Wilhelmina Dorothea of Brandenburg-Anspach, the most talented of all the queens of the royal house of Hanover. For many weeks after her death, the king continued to expatiate at great length to the circle of the court, upon the unparalleled excellences of his departed spouse, assured them that she was the only woman in the world whom he would have married; and declared that if he could not have made her his wife, she should inevitably have been his mistress. The only word or deed of the king in reference to her, which deserved to be recorded to his praise, was the order which he gave that the salaries of all her officers and servants should be continued, as well as her benefactions to benevolent institutions, so that no one might suffer by her death except himself.

CHAPTER V.

Fate of the Queen's Favorites—Lord Hervey—Intellectual and Moral Character of the defunct Queen—Spanish Aggressions—The National Forces Augmented—War Declared against Spain—Events of the War—Cabal in Parliament against Walpole—Its Failure—Hostility of the Prince of Wales to the Minister—Walpole compelled at last to Resign—His Services to the Monarch.

THE death of Queen Caroline produced but little alteration in the pursuits, employments, and pleasures of the king. He had been her unconscious slave during her lifetime; and after her decease he was governed directly by Sir Robert Walpole, who had previously used the queen as his pliant intermediate instrument. With her passed away for a time the influence and importance of her favorite, John Lord Hervey, who, for some years had occupied the post of confidant, attendant, and purveyor of amusements to her majesty. He was a singular man, and was possessed of considerable ability. His appearance and manners in conversation were effeminate in the extreme; yet his political writings, in which he particularly assailed Bolingbroke and Pulteney, were unsurpassed for the bitterness of their satire, the fierceness of their invective, and their general spirit and vigor. In 1730 he was challenged by Pulteney to the field of combat, in consequence of an acrimonious and bitter attack which he made upon that statesman. They met; both were slightly wounded; and Mr. Pulteney would have inevitably run his antagonist through the body had not his foot opportunely slipped. The former immediately embraced Lord Harvey, congratulated him on his escape, and promised never to attack him again.* The friendship of Lord Hervey, and afterward his enmity toward the poet Pope, have also been celebrated. They both wrote poetical satires against each other, in which they descended to the most bitter ridicule and abuse of each others' personal deformities, and neither gained any credit. In May, 1740, Lord Hervey attained his highest political elevation; being appointed Keeper of the Privy Seal, and one of the Lord Justices for governing the kingdom during the absence of the monarch in Hanover. The character of this singular man was marked on the one hand by extreme affectation, by great bitterness of invective, and by abject flattery of his superiors; and on the other by a disposition to pratronize men of letters, and an ability to be exceedingly agreeable and fascinating in his manners. The foundation of the decided partiality which Queen Caroline entertained for him, and which continued unabated until her death, was her admiration of his admirable conversational powers, and his unrivalled capacity to amuse her by his mingled wit, satire, gossip, and sympathy. It is well known that he inspired the amiable princess Caroline with a most romantic passion, even after he had married the beautiful Mary Lepel; which did not terminate at the premature death of its object, but which rendered the princess the victim of a morbid, a hopeless, and eventually a fatal melancholy.

But little difference of opinion has ever existed in reference to the intellectual character of the wife of George II. She possessed a strong, clear, and penetrating understanding. She was not deficient in adroitness and cunning. She generally estimated persons and things according to their real value. She was to

---

* The satirists of the time attacked this duel with their usual keenness. One of their effusions was as follows, addressed to Mr. Pulteney:

> Lord Fanny once,
> Did play the dunce,
> And challenged you to fight;
> And so he stood,
> To loose his blood,
> But had a dreadful fright.

some extent a patron of literature, but she was injudicious in the distribution of her favors. She was particularly partial to divines who belonged to the heterodox school, among whom were Whiston, Clarke, and Bishops Gibson and Berkley. It was certainly a singular whim in a worldly, ambitious, and fashionable woman, such as Caroline unquestionably was, that she became fond of reading "Butler's Anology," the most abtruse and profound production within the whole range of English literature; in reference to which work Bishop Hoadly declared that even to look at it gave him a headache. She was also particularly pleased with Warburton's "Alliance between Church and State." She derived great pleasure from the controversies of those intellectual colossi, Dr. Clarke and Leibnitz. She watched the progress of their disputes with intense interest, and applauded with discretion where applause was due. A woman who could understand and appreciate the writings of such men, must herself be the possessor of no ordinary intellect. The chief blemish of her character was her disposition to excuse and encourage the licentious partiality of her husband for mistresses. She saw that his weakness lay that way; that to oppose or condemn him would but weaken her own influence over him; that nothing would please him better than to submit to his will, and acquiesce with a good grace; that by protecting the royal favorites, she transformed them into complacent and effective tools to accomplish her purposes; and neither her principle, her pride, or her affection allowed her to hesitate for a moment in pursuing such a course of conduct. Morally speaking, therefore, she became a partner in his guilt, and she deserves a portion of the blame which justly attaches to it. Many incidents occurred after her death to illustrate the intense admiration with which she had inspired the mind of her weak, vain, and superficial husband. When speaking to Walpole respecting her merits, he frequently burst into tears. Having been informed that Baron Brinkman possessed an excellent portrait of her, which he had never seen, he sent for him, and requested him to produce it. The Baron obeyed. The king contemplated the picture for some time intently, and then exclaimed: "It *is* like her." He then ordered the owner of the treasure to leave him alone till he rang for him. During two hours the Baron waited in the ante-chamber, while the bereaved monarch continued to contemplate the counterfeit resemblance of the only woman who had ever impressed his mind with any thing like respect and esteem. Having at length summoned the Baron, he said: "Take it away! take it away! I never yet saw the woman worthy to buckle her shoe." No sooner had the Baron disappeared with his prize, than the aged king, grasping his amber-headed cane, hurried off to the apartment of Madam Walmoden, to whom he had given the title of Lady Yarmouth.

In regard to the religious opinions of Queen Caroline, it is difficult to attain any definite conclusion, as she was most probably herself unsettled on the subject. She attended the regular services of the established church, and conformed to all its ceremonies; but Lord Chesterfield declares that, in reality, after having studied all systems and all schools, she had ultimately settled down in Deism, being convinced only of the existence of a God, and of a future state. It is probable that the judgment of this celebrated *magister elegantiarum* is correct; and that the character of his royal mistress might be thus briefly and truly summed up: she was a talented, amiable, and benevolent woman; but scarcely a good, and much less a pious or devout woman.

Having thus traced the chief incidents of the domestic life of George II. until the death of his queen, it will be proper to resume the history of the public and political events of his reign. The propitious era of peace terminated with the life of Caroline; for her potent influence, combined with that of Robert Walpole, uniformly succeeded in allaying the hostile and warlike propensities of the king, and ending all disputes with foreign powers in amicable adjustments. In 1738, continued Spanish outrages upon English commerce in South American waters drove the ministry into a war. Early in that year petitions were presented to parliament from the mercantile cities of the realm, setting forth the losses which they had suffered from this source, and earnestly demanding protection and relief. The House proceeded to hear counsel for the merchants and to examine the evidence. They became greatly incensed at the cruel excesses which that evidence revealed on the part of the Spanish cruisers; and they voted an unanimous address to the king beseeching him to use his endeavors to obtain effectual relief for his injured subjects, and demand full indemnity from the King of Spain, promising to support him in the execution of any measures which he should deem necessary and expedient. To this memorial the king returned a favorable answer, and in May the parliament was prorogued.

During the ensuing recess Walpole put forth his utmost efforts to arrange the difficulties which existed between the two countries by new negotiations. A treaty was eventually signed at Madrid, by which the King of Spain once more bound himself to make reparation for the losses already inflicted on British subjects by Spanish cruisers, and to prevent similar outrages in future. Parliament again convened in February, 1739; and when the minister communicated the terms of this new compact, they were treated with the utmost ridicule and contempt. The amount of indemnity allowed by Spain for the injuries inflicted, which did not exceed ninety-five thousand pounds, was especially deprecated as utterly inadequate to the real demands of the occasion; and the opposition declared, with much bitterness and with some truth, that this sum would scarcely cover the expenses incurred by the English commissioners who were sent to effect the treaty. After those expenses were accurately ascertained, it was found that a balance of only twenty thousand pounds would have remained over their outlay.

The ministry, at the conclusion of an animated debate, carried an address of approbation to the king by a small majority of twenty-eight. In the House of Peers seventy-three members voted against it; and after its passage, thirty-nine signed a bold and decisive protest against the treaty. The Commons then allowed the sum of five hundred thousand pounds, to augment the forces of Great Britain in case of emergency. In June, 1739, parliament was informed that the Spanish monarch had not yet paid the sum stipulated in the recent treaty of Madrid. The patience of the house was at length exhausted; the neglect was justly regarded as an insult to the nation and the monarch; and a vote was passed ordering letters of marque and reprisal to be instantly issued against the Spaniards. This decisive step was in substance a declaration of war. In October, 1739, the formal declaration of hostilities against Spain was made. The nation received the announcement with universal exultation, and Admiral Vernon was immediately sent with a powerful squadron to the West Indies. That exultation was increased when the news arrived that the city of Porto-Bello, situated on the Isthmus of Darien, had been bombarded and taken by that gallant veteran. The Admiral received a vote of thanks from the House of Commons, and became at once the popular idol of the nation. Having returned to England covered with glory, he was placed in command of a formidable armament intended to attack Carthagena on the Spanish main. Lord Wentworth was appointed commander of the land forces. But not a single achievement of any importance followed; and the elated Admiral fell at once from the sudden and giddy elevation which he had attained in the popular estimation, to a place even lower than that which he actually deserved.* A squadron dispatched to the South Seas, under the command of Commodore Anson, to annoy the Spanish settlements located there, was more successful. The Commodore took a great number of valuable prizes off the coasts

---

* The Admiral was assailed after his return, according to the fashion of the times, with a flood of satires and caricatures. As a specimen of the former we may quote the following, which is but a single stanza of a lengthy ode:

"I, by twenty sail attended,
   Did this Spanish town affright:
Nothing then its wealth defended
   But my orders not to fight.
Oh! that in this rolling ocean
   I had cast them with disdain,
And obey'd my heart's warm motion
   To have quell'd the pride of Spain!"

of Chili and Peru; he plundered the town of Païta; and he even threatened to attack the capital city of Lima. On his return home he captured a Spanish galleon freighted with an immense treasure; and after having circumnavigated the globe, he safely reached England, the object of universal applause, and the possessor of the same dizzy eminence in the popular estimation, from which the unhappy Vernon had so ignominiously and suddenly fallen.

The year 1740 was distinguished by a desperate attempt made in both houses of parliament, to expel Sir Robert Walpole from the post of prime minister. The war with Spain was popular with the nation; but it operated singularly and adversely upon the minister's influence, because it was known that he was reluctantly driven into it. During the year 1739, nothing but disasters and defeats attended the British arms; and these were ascribed to his lukewarmness and treachery in conducting hostilities. The Spanish cruisers captured a vast number of British prizes. The fleets stationed off the coasts of Spain accomplished no honorable achievement. The French government, emboldened by the posture of affairs, repaired the fortifications of Dunkirk, in violation of the express stipulations of the treaty of Utrecht. A French fleet even sailed to the West Indies to aid the Spaniards in their aggressions on British commerce. Very great apprehensions were felt lest Jamaica should fall under their combined attacks. All these calamities were charged upon the minister, who was condemned by the popular voice, both for the part which he took in the war, and for the part which he did not take. Mr. Sandys, soon after the opening of parliament in November, 1740, having made a furious attack in the Commons upon the measures which had been pursued by the minister during his long tenure of office, moved that an address be presented to the king " beseeching his majesty that he would be graciously pleased to remove the Right Honorable Sir Robert Walpole from his majesty's presence and counsels for ever." A violent and protracted debate ensued, during which Mr. Pulteney especially distinguished himself by the fierceness and acrimony of his attack upon his former associate and friend. Sir Robert defended him self with more than his usual power and ability. He proved that all the successive measures of his administration had been adapted to the changing exigencies of the times; that they had received the repeated and decisive approbation of parliament; and that they had uniformly promoted the national prosperity and glory. The motion of Mr. Sandys was finally rejected by a large majority. A similar proposition, introduced into the house of Peers by Lord Carteret, met with a similar fate; though it became apparent that these violent attacks upon the measures and the authority of the premier weakened his position, and foreshadowed his approaching fall at no very distant day.

The party both in parliament and out of parliament who were the implacable opponents of Walpole, grew in strength, numbers, and resolution from day to day. When the Legislature assembled in December, 1741, the king delivered a speech from the throne, in which he recommended the support and defence of the Pragmatic Sanction. This step was equivalent to inviting the British people to expend their blood and treasure in protecting the vast dominions of Maria Theresa—in whose integrity and safety they had not the slightest interest—from the attacks of her continental enemies. When the usual address of thanks was proposed, a storm of opposition arose against the motion. It was urged with great force and reason, that the British nation had been fighting the quarrels and defending the interests of their allies long enough; that such a policy had entailed a debt upon the nation numbering many millions; and that England had been during some years constantly engaged in war, in order that others might enjoy all the advantages of peace. The address underwent some material alterations, and was then passed, in consequence of the prodigious exertions of the ministry.

But the storm had not passed away. It yet lowered over the head of the minister; increased continually in blackening fury; and at last burst upon him with such resistless violence that he was utterly swept away. A number of candidates belonging to the court party had been returned for Westminster. Their seats were contested, and ultimately declared void by a majority of four. The loss of these votes placed the minister in a minority. A great party, composed of the leading men in the nation had by this time organized an opposition to Walpole, so compact, so resolute, and so able, that even that veteran giant was overwhelmed by them. They included in their number, Carteret, Pulteney, Bolingbroke, Chesterfield, Argyle, Doddington, Pitt, Windham, Littleton, Pope, Swift, Gay, Arbuthnot, Johnson, Akenside, and Thompson; each of whom assailed Walpole with their respective weapons of intellectual gladiatorship, with unsurpassed fierceness and acrimony. All the resources of eloquence, logic, satire, invective, philosophical disquisition, poetical effusion, political strategy, diplomatical craft, aristocratical influence, popular enthusiasm, and demagogical frenzy, were brought to bear upon the fated minister. The opposition had gradually drawn within its bosom all the young and aspiring men of talent, all the mature and experienced statesmen of riper years, all the disappointed place-hunters and Whigs about the court and in parliament, all the personal enemies of Walpole, all the political and private friends of Frederic, Prince of Wales, and the whole Tory party in a body. After the death of the queen, Walpole had, beside the energy of his own extraordinary abilities, but one supporter—the unprincipled, feeble and selfish king. It is true that this heterogeneous company were not united in their views of policy. They differed, and differed widely, on many grave and fundamental points—in reference to septennial parliaments, in reference to increasing the revenue of the heir apparent, and in reference to the war with Spain. But unhappily for Walpole they all agreed, without a single dissenting voice, on the propriety and necessity of pulling him down from his high place. They either believed him to be, or they represented him as being, the great and sole cause of all the evils, both external and internal, domestic and foreign, which afflicted the country. Were he removed they contended that all would be well. They even went so far as to declare that the other members of the administration, whom they well knew to be but cyphers under the influence of the overshadowing ambition of Walpole, might, if he were crushed, still be allowed to retain their offices.

Long as Walpole had fought the battles of the king, and contended for his own honor and supremacy, he was determined manfully to continue the contest to the last. He tried various expedients to avert his doom. He skilfully attempted to compound the differences which existed between the king and Prince Frederic; but the prince declared that he would enter into no terms whatever with the great enemy of the state. He then endeavored to detach some of the leaders of the opposite party from their friends, and enlist them in his own service. Greater bribes were offered them to retain their adhesion to their old associates, and this effort also failed. At length the great, crafty, and once absolute minister, was left upon a vote of importance, in a decisive and hopeless minority in the Commons. When the adverse vote was announced Walpole arose, declared that he would never again enter that house, and retired. On the next day, February 3d, 1742, the king adjourned parliament till the 18th. In the mean time, on the 11th of the month, Walpole resigned his employments and offices, obtained from his royal master security and protection for all the measures of his past administration, was created Earl of Orford in return for his long and faithful services, and retired after twenty years of almost absolute power, to the repose and the dignities of private life at his sumptuous seat at Houghton ; there to enjoy that happiness which the turbulent and uneasy splendors of his former state had never been able to bestow.

CHAPTER VI.

The Members of the New Cabinet—The Pension Bill—Lord Carteret Prime Minister—The Seven Years' War—George II. present at the Battle of Dettingen—Events of 1745—Battle of Fontenoy—Movements of the Pretender in Scotland—His Successor—His Defeat at Culloden—Success of British Arms at Home and Abroad—Treaty of Aix-la-Chapelle.

THE DUKE of Newcastle and Mr. Pelham still remained in the cabinet. The Earl of Wilmington succeeded to the premiership. Mr. Sandys was appointed Chancellor of the Exchequer. Lord Carteret took the Seals, and Mr. Pulteney was sworn of the Privy Council. The sentiment which first prevailed throughout the country when the resignation of Robert Walpole became known, was one of general joy. The bells were rung and bonfires were lighted in most of the towns and cities of the realm. The opposition papers teemed with ungenerous insults to the fallen statesman, and he was boldly threatened with impeachment and the scaffold. His Earldom, his Garter, his Knighthood of the Bath, were all made the subjects of satire and invective.* His daughter by his second wife, who was illegitimate,

---

* The *Champion* of February 16, 1742, (a more scurrilous paper even than the *Craftsman*,) contains the following epigram, which may be taken as a sample of effusions to which the ex-minister was exposed daily :

"Sir —— [*Robert*], his merit or interest to shew,
Laid down the red ribbon to take up the blue :
By two strings already the knight hath been ty'd,
But when twisted at —— [*Tyburn*], the third will decide."

was given precedency as an Earl's daughter by a separate patent from the king; and this step aroused a furious storm of indignation around his ears from the incensed aristocracy, and the "modern quality of Miss Maria Walpole" became the subject of several pointed satires and poems. The young patriots, whose chief and confessed leader was William Pitt, being disappointed in obtaining a place in the new cabinet, absurdly vented all their spleen on the ex-minister.

This storm gradually subsided, to be followed by another of almost equal fury, resulting from the disputes which divided the new ministry. The Pension Bill, the Place Bill, and a Bill to repeal the septennial parliaments, called forth the antagonistic and irreconcilable sentiments of the heterogeneous multitude who had triumphed over the Earl of Orford. An effort was again made to authorize a formal investigation into the measures of the last ten years of his administration. It was in the discussion of this motion that William Pitt, then rapidly rising in favor and popularity by means of that stately and powerful declamation in which he eventually excelled all men—particularly distinguished himself. He dwelt with great effect upon the detestable use which the recent minister had made of the secret service money; of which one million and a half pounds had been expended, as was asserted, during the preceding ten years, in bribing the members of the legislature. He denounced the defunct administration as rotten to the core, and as tarnished with the cadaverous hue of moral corruption and disease. But all the threats of impeachment and punishment which were hurled at the head of the ex-minister eventually amounted to nothing; and he remained secure in the possession of that political innocence of which he fearlessly boasted when he first heard the threat uttered in parliament.

In 1742 the attention of the king, the parliament, and the nation, was chiefly engaged by the stirring events which were transpiring on the continent. The Austrian Empress, Maria Theresa, was contending heroically for the integrity of those vast and heterogeneous possessions which she had inherited, and which had been guaranteed to her by the Pragmatic Sanction. Under the influence of Lord Carteret, George II. became decidedly warlike in his tastes and feelings. He even conceived the desire to distinguish himself as a great hero on the field of battle. Sixteen thousand regular troops, under the command of Lord Stair, who had succeeded the Earl of Argyle in the new ministry, were sent over to Flanders in April, where they were joined by a large body of Hanoverians and Hessians in British pay. These troops were destined to operate in support of the Empress-Queen. But Lord Stair had been directed, in the first place, to try the effect of negotiation, to induce the States General to join the coalition, and concur in the projects of the King of Great Britain. These provinces determined however to adhere to their neutrality ; and thus the summer glided away without any military operations having been attempted. The troops were placed in winter quarters; but during the ensuing session of Parliament, the conduct of the new ministry, with reference to the continental war, was bitterly and furiously assailed. Nevertheless, in the following spring the warlike policy was resumed, and larger detachments of troops were sent to the Low Countries, to unite with those already collected there under the command of the Earl of Stair. The first purpose of this commander was to enter the French territory on the side of the Moselle. Baffled in this attempt, he changed his line of operations to the banks of the Maine. The Court of Versailles immediately ordered sixty thousand troops, under the command of the Marshal de Coigné, to confront the foe in this new position. In June the warlike fever had so completely taken possession of the nature of George II., that he journeyed in person to the continent, in company with his son the Duke of Cumberland, and arrived at the camp of Lord Stair at Aschaffenburg. He desired to see the operations of the great conflict going forward, and if possible to win some of the laurels which were about to be distributed among the combatants. But the little king was soon treated to more of the stern realities of war than he had anticipated. The Marshal de Noailles, who had in the meantime taken the command, carried on his operations with such consummate skill and vigor, that he soon placed the English commander in a very critical position. Lord Stair was compelled to decamp in haste from Aschaffenburg, and direct his march toward Hanau. There he expected to obtain large reinforcements. But Marshal de Noailles had anticipated this movement, and had taken effectual measures to intercept it. On approaching the village of *Dettingen*, the British commander, who was accompanied by the British king, found the French army drawn up in battle array to oppose his further progress. The position was a dangerous one. The enemy occupied the defiles of Dettingen in front; on the left flowed the deep and turbulent waters of the Maine; and on the right were impassable forests and morasses. A retreat even was impossible, for the French commander had promptly taken possession of Aschaffenburg with a powerful force, immediately after it was deserted by the English. A decisive battle was now unavoidable, in which every probability of defeat and ruin conspired against the English. Lord Stair instantly made very admirable dispositions for the conflict. The French charged with their usual impetuosity. They were received by their foes with great steadiness and intrepidity. Yet the disadvantages of their position, the superiority of numbers on the part of the French, and their better condition, would have inevitably secured them a decisive and overwhelming triumph, had not the skilful plans of the French Marshal been disarranged and ruined by the rash and inexperienced valor of the Duke de Grammont; who, contrary to express orders, advanced his troops through the defiles at an unfavorable moment, thereby compelling the whole army to sustain an unseasonable movement. During the conflict, George II. behaved with considerable fortitude. Had the French been victorious, he would most probably have been taken prisoner. But a propitious accident saved his army from defeat, his person from captivity, his reputation from disgrace, and thousands of brave men, who would have had no possible means of retreat, from certain death. The French lost six thousand killed and wounded. After the battle, George proceeded to Hanau, where he received the expected reinforcements. No further operations of importance afterward occurred during the summer; and having passed the Rhine at Maintz, Lord Stair fixed his headquarters at Worms for the ensuing winter. The king, having had enough of the realities and splendors of war, returned immediately after the termination of the campaign, to his British dominions, to congratulate himself upon the laurels which he had won, and still more heartily and justly on the destruction or captivity which he had escaped.

In the spring of 1745, hostilities were resumed on the continent between France and the Allies. The commander of the French troops was the celebrated Marshal Saxe, a hero of great military abilities. He was the son of Augustus, King of Poland and Saxony, and that accomplished and beautiful Aurora, Countess of Kœnigsmark, to whom reference has been made in a preceding page of this work. The Marshal inherited the remarkable beauty of his uncle, the unfortunate lover of Sophia Dorothea of Zell; the fascinating manners and the superior intellect of his mother; and the vast bodily size and strength of his royal and voluptuous father. His whole life had been one of adventure, luxury, and vicissitude. He was one of the last and most eminent representatives of that class termed soldiers of fortune; who, in preceding ages, hired their swords to the most lavish or opulent bidders, and became celebrated for martial deeds in the results of which they did not feel a particle of personal interest. At this period the military fame of the gallant Marshal stood very high; but the campaign which now ensued was destined to elevate it to the summit of glory. The Allies, commanded by the Duke of Cumberland, by Marshal Königseg, and by the Prince of Waldeck, marched to the relief of the city of Tourney, which the French under Saxe had invested. The combatants met near the village of Fontenoy, to which the prodigious scenes of carnage which ensued in its vicinity has given an enduring and melancholy celebrity. During the early stages of the battle the Allies, especially the English and Hanoverian infantry, drove the French repeatedly beyond their lines, and the victory seemed to be secure. Their artillery had been posted with such skill by Marshal Königseg, the commander of the Austrian contingent, that immense numbers of the French were slain. The position of Saxe was becoming critical. He was ill at the time, and was conveyed from post to post in a litter. But this hero's fortitude and presence of mind never deserted him, even in the most imminent dangers, or amid the darkest gloom. The centre of the French having been broken, the Allied column of attack should have been divided. But advancing in a solid mass into the heart of the French lines, its isolated position rendered it at once an object of assault to the whole French army. Saxe instantly took advantage of this error, and ordered up all his *corps de reserve*. A circle of fire from the redoubts which they had already passed, and from other powerful batteries ranged on their flank, was skilfully drawn around the hapless column, which then melted like frost-work before it. Total destruction now impended over it; rapid retreat became inevitable; nor was this effected until the Allies lost ten thousand men, killed and wounded on the field of carnage and conflict. The victory of the French was complete, and its consequences were important. Tournay surrendered, Ghent and Bruges were captured by a *coup-de-main*, Ostend, Dendermond, and Newport successively capitulated to the conquerors.

The British nation now fell into one of their fits of spleen and spite in consequence of these disasters; but misfortunes and perils nearer at home were soon about to ensue. The French monarch observing that all the British forces were engaged upon the continent, regarded the opportunity as favorable to the promotion of the interests of the Pretender. Prince Charles, the son of the "Chevalier de St. George," being equipped by Louis XV. and incited by him, landed in the Western Islands of Scotland, in August. The movement was propitious to his interests in many ways. George II. was then absent in Hanover. His British dominions were almost destitute of troops. The ablest military commanders were engaged in the absorbing events transpiring in the Low Countries. The Scotch were in a great measure partial to the cause of the Pretender; and the English were exceedingly disaffected toward their own government. As soon as the news of the arrival of Prince George reached London, a messenger was despatched to the continent entreating the monarch to return to his capital. Several British regiments were recalled from the Netherlands. Six thousand troops were demanded from the Dutch, who were bound to furnish them by the requirements of an existing treaty. The Lieutenants throughout the kingdom were ordered by the Lords of the Regency to muster the militia in their respective counties, and commissions were issued to raise new regiments. Divided and dissatisfied as the nation had been, the greatness of the impending danger at once united them, and all parties except the Jacobite alone engaged heartily in energetic preparations for defence.

In a short time Sir John Cope, the commander-in-chief of the forces in North Britain, advanced to Inverness at the head of such troops as could be hastily summoned. The Pretender had already reached Edinburgh, had entered it in triumph, had caused his father to be proclaimed king, and himself regent, of Great Britain; and had fixed his head-quarters in the ancient abode of his ancestors, the venerable palace of Holyrood. On the 20th of September, Sir John Cope encamped at Prestonpans, in the vicinity of the Scotch capital, in command of three thousand regular troops. He was attacked in his position on the ensuing day, by the Pretender, at the head of an equal number of Highlanders. Nothing in modern warfare equalled in ferocity and fury the onslaught made on this occasion by the rude and fierce sons of the Caledonian hills, upon the lines of the royal troops. The shock of battle was prodigious. The Scotch hewed down their foes with their broadswords and Lochaber axes as if they had been so many cattle. The field of conflict was deluged with blood, the royal army was totally routed in ten minutes, and the Pretender at once found himself master of the whole of Scotland. He now received large supplies from France, and was joined by Lords Kilmarnock, Cromarty, Balmerino, Lovat, and the Earl of Derwentwater. After his first triumph, the Pretender marched with an increasing army southward. The city of Carlisle surrendered to him in November. At Manchester he was welcomed with general demonstrations of joy. He advanced as far as Derby. By this time the panic which pervaded the nation was intense and universal. Had the Pretender then continued his progress to London, it is highly probable that his descendants would, even at this moment, be seated upon the British throne. The fall of Rome, after the overwhelming carnage of Cannae, was not more certain, had Hannibal hastened directly thither and thundered before her gates, than was the submission of the British capital to the representative of the Stuarts, had he at that crisis summoned her to surrender. But as Hannibal unaccountably failed in the decisive moment of his destiny, so also did the aspiring rebel chief on this occasion. Being informed that Lord Stair had been appointed to the supreme command of the royal troops, and that he was advancing against him, he began, on the 6th of December, to retreat northward. On the 21st of the month, Carlisle was invested by the Duke of Cumberland, who had been appointed commander of a portion of the royal troops. At Falkirk, the Pretender gained another victory over his enemies, led on by General Hawley. He then retired to Glasgow and invested the castle of Stirling. But a great and decisive battle could alone determine the controversy which seemed to be involved in such ultimate uncertainty. In April, 1746, the Duke of Cumberland, having been made generalissimo of the royal forces, met the Pretending Prince on the famous field of Culloden. The heroic Highlanders had lost none of their military ardor, but their foes had by this time become familiar with their method of fighting, and had been taught how to resist it. The engagement began at one o'clock in the afternoon. The Highlanders, who had been drawn up in thirteen divisions upon a favorable eminence, rushed down upon their approaching foes with prodigious fierceness. But they were steadily received on fixed bayonets; a continual firing by platoons was kept up upon them; the weapons of the Scotch could produce but little effect upon the solid barrier of steel which confronted them; their ranks rapidly thinned; the survivors gradually became exhausted; terror took the place of heroism; their tumultuous masses were thrown into confusion; the royal cavalry and artillery were then brought to bear upon them with destructive effect; a retreat became inevitable in less than an hour; and a dearly bought victory was at last attained by the steadiness and valor of the royal troops. The rout was complete, and more bloody than complete. No quarter was given. A savage thirst for revenge actuated the conquerors; and the most cruel barbarities were inflicted even upon the families of the discomfited rebels long after hostilities had terminated.

The cause of the Pretender was utterly ruined. He fled from the kingdom, and only reached France after passing through a series of imminent perils and romantic vicissitudes such as were paralleled by no other scenes in the history of princes, except those experienced by Charles II. after the battle of Worcester. Hundreds of the rebels were executed, including many distinguished noblemen. To all intercessions in their behalf, the incensed and inexorable monarch turned a deaf ear, and an unrelenting heart. The victory was indeed great, and the delivery from national commotion and civil war most fortunate. Parliament presented an address of congratulation to George II. with which he doubtless sympathized more heartily than he had ever done before on any similar occasion; and the triumphant hero of the day, the Duke of Cumberland, received an addition of twenty-five thousand pounds per annum to his revenue, a vote of thanks from parliament, and the hearty praise and adulation of the nation.

During the year 1746, the popularity of the court and the supremacy of the ministry in parliament again returned, in consequence of these domestic victories, and the brighter aspect of affairs on the continent on behalf of the Allies. Changes also occurred in the Cabinet; but they produced little effect on the policy pursued by the government, either domestic or foreign. Lord Carteret, now created Earl of Granville, still retained a paramount influence over the mind of George II., and was made

President of the Council. This office he retained for many years. During 1747, the ministry constantly commanded a decisive majority in both houses of parliament; and the opposition languished so greatly that it could scarcely be said to exist. At this period the military operations in the Netherlands terminated; and a treaty was eventually signed between the Plenipotentiaries of the French monarch and those of the Allies at Aix-la-Chapelle, the terms of which were decidedly favorable to the latter. Thus at length security and peace, both at home and abroad, became again the portion of the British people; who had become heartily wearied of the expenses, the anxieties, and the vicissitudes inevitably attendant upon domestic strife and foreign levy, and earnestly desired to be relieved from their pernicious effects.

CHAPTER VII.

Death of Frederic, Prince of Wales—Peculiar Conduct of the King on the Occasion—Decline of the opposition in Parliament—Increasing Eminence of William Pitt—Character of his Eloquence—Mr. Murray—Henry Fox—Acts of Parliament—Death of Henry Pelham—Duke of Newcastle Prime Minister—War between the English and French Colonies in North America—The King's Address to Parliament in November, 1755—Furious Debates which Ensued—War with France—Cowardice of Admiral Byng—The Disappointment and Rage of the Nation—The Trial, Conviction, and Execution of the Admiral.

THE commencement of the year 1751 was rendered remarkable by a domestic event of great importance to the royal family, and to the nation. On the 20th of March, Frederic, Prince of Wales, and heir apparent, died after a short illness. He had been previously attacked with pleurisy, had partially recovered, and had again been injured by a fall from his horse. Early in March he was present in Parliament. The house was crowded, and the heat intense. In returning late at night to Carlton House, he rode with the windows of his carriage open. He then changed his dress, and reposed for several hours upon a bed in a cold and damp apartment. He became seriously ill, and the next day his life was in danger. He immediately sent for his eldest son, afterward George III., and bade him farewell. His medical attendants, Doctors Wilmot and Hawkins still continued to indulge hopes of his recovery. But at the very moment when they were uttering words of encouragement, the Prince, placing his hands upon his stomach, exclaimed: *Je sens la mort*, and commenced to sink. His cough returned with increased violence. His body shivered convulsively from head to foot. By this time his wife and some of his children had reached his bedside; sympathy and medical treatment were of no avail. The prince was held up in his bed by Desnoyer, his favorite and athletic dancing-master. After a few minutes of convulsive agony, the heir of the British Empire expired in the arms of a French fiddler. The king had heard of the sudden illness of his son; but with his usual indifference and cruelty, he had taken no notice of the event. As soon as the Prince had ceased to exist, Lord North conveyed the sad intelligence to the bereaved father. The latter was, at that moment, at Kensington, and was looking over a card table at which the Princess Amelia, the Duchess of Dorset, the Duke of Grafton, and Lady Walmoden were playing. In answer to the information conveyed by Lord North the king merely replied: "Dead, is he?" Then going round to Walmoden, he observed to her in an indifferent tone: "Countess, Fred is gone!" and then the game proceeded. The funeral of the defunct Prince was simple and unostentatious in the extreme. Not a single bishop was present. The reason of the neglect was, that these sanctimonious courtiers were apprehensive of injuring their interests with the surviving monarch, who was known to have been at enmity with his son. Their presence at the obsequies of the heir apparent, though a custom and a duty enjoined by immemorial usage, would have endangered certain mitres, fat benefices, and august promotions to still more opulent and powerful sees, which loomed invitingly in the future before their unambitious and unworldly eyes. The same fear of displeasing the court and king kept all the temporal lords and peers away, with the exception of a solitary Irish nobleman. The Earl of Limerick alone honored with his presence the last mournful journey of his unfortunate friend. Neither canopy, nor funeral service, nor anthem, nor priest, nor organ, were permitted to impart a seemly dignity and solemnity to the exit of the inheritor of such proud hopes, and so exalted a destiny; who in truth scarcely deserved a better fate. The widow of the Prince, Augusta, was at that time the mother of eight children. She behaved on this mournful occasion with great propriety; and among other things displayed her usual discernment and prudence by burning all her husband's private papers. The sensation produced by the death of the Prince throughout the nation was not intense. His character had not commanded their confidence and esteem, and his demise was probably regarded by the majority of them as a public blessing.*

Immediately after the death of the Prince of Wales, his Royal Highness, his eldest son, was committed to the Earl of Harcourt as governor, and the Bishop of Norwich as preceptor. It was at this period that the Earl of Bute began to ingratiate himself with the Princess of Wales, the mother of the heir apparent. She then resided at Leicester palace, and Bute was a member of her household. His handsome person, his agreeable manners, his graceful deportment, his high birth, his prudent and crafty nature, all adapted him to the attainment of great influence over the vacant heart of the widowed but worldly, aspiring, and sensual Augusta. The ambitious plot which was contrived between these lovers amounted to nothing less than a determination to rule the nation through the young Prince of Wales, after he should have attained the throne. They commenced by placing such books in the hands of the prince, as inculcated political doctrines, little in harmony with British ideas of liberty and constitutional monarchy. The preceptors of the Prince soon detected this intrigue, and they informed the House of Peers that they no longer possessed any authority

* The following elegant epitaph was written for him by the Jacobite press:
"Here lies Prince Fred,
 Who was alive and is dead.
 Had it been his father,
 We had much rather;
 Had it been his brother,
 Still better than another.
 Had it been his sister
 No one would have missed her.
 Had it been the whole generation,
 Still better for the nation.
 But since 'tis only Fred,
 Who was alive and is dead,
 There is no more to be said."

over his education, in consequence of sinister influences which were brought to bear upon his mind; and they resigned their offices. Lord Waldegrave and the Bishop of Lincoln were appointed in their places; but the same secret bias remained, though its operation was rendered more subtle and concealed.

After the death of Prince Frederic, the opposition to the court which he had headed in Parliament, may be said to have expired. All the men distinguished for talent and eloquence in the Legislature, were enlisted in the service of the government. Three mighty and turbulent spirits had been laid to rest, for the time being, by the potent spell of official rank, influence, and emolument. These were William Pitt, afterward Earl of Chatham, Murray, afterward Lord Mansfield, and Fox, afterward Lord Holland. Pitt occupied the post of Paymaster of the Forces; Murray was appointed Solicitor-General; Fox held the office of Secretary of War. Never were three more remarkable and gifted men combined together in the support of any government.

William Pitt was still comparatively young, and in the pride and splendor of his manhood. He was already the most popular man in the nation. He had gained the hearts of his money-loving countrymen, by the disinterested honesty with which he had refused to pocket several hundred thousand pounds which he might have claimed on the ground of custom, as per centage upon the moneys which passed through his hands as Paymaster of the Forces. The British people looked upon him as a rare and unequalled specimen of an incorruptible and disinterested statesman. In addition to this great moral influence of which he was the possessor, he exhibited other commanding and attractive qualities, which were equally valuable. His eloquence was characterized by such force and splendor of diction, by such clearness and directness of argument, by such prodigious power of invective and repartee, as overwhelmed his hearers with admiration and astonishment. He was the ablest supporter, and the most destructive assailant, who figured in the house. He may be said to have annihilated whomsoever he elevated to the dignity of an opponent. His bursts of eloquence were not unfitly compared to the lightning which flashed from heaven, blasting whatever it smote, and withering the crushed form of every antagonist. During a memorable period of thirty years he continued to reign the *Jupiter Tonans* of the British Parliament; and he is deservedly regarded as the most important, imposing, and magnificent historical personage, whom the English people have ever produced, during many generations of national existence.*

Murray, afterward the Chief Justice, was a person of very different stamp. He was inferior to Pitt in all the shining qualities of a great statesman, and in all the brilliant attributes of a popular orator. His parliamentary eloquence was clear, placid, impressive, and convincing. His nature was not impulsive nor inflammable; neither were his measures nor his eloquence. He was cautious, calculating, and prudent. But his intellectual grasp was vast, comprehensive, and profound. As a whole, the greatness of his mind was not inferior to that of Pitt's. He successively filled the posts of Solicitor-General, Attorney-General, and Chief Justice of England; and in all three offices he achieved a legal fame unsurpassed in British history; for Lord Mansfield stands at the very head of the illustrious array of jurists and lawyers of the land of Coke and Eldon.

The third most remarkable person connected with the tranquil administration of Henry Pelham, who now served the king and the nation without encountering the difficulties and dangers of an organized opposition in Parliament, was Mr. Fox. His eloquence and his abilities occupy a middle position between those of his two chief associates. He was in every respect less brilliant than solid. He possessed none of the outward advantages

---

* Pitt's celebrated retort upon Horace Walpole, who had charged him with being a young man, and therefore ignorant and inexperienced, is a memorable instance of the power of reply and invective which he possessed, and frequently exhibited. See *Belsham's Memoirs of the Kings of Great Britain*, Vol. II., p. 127. *History of the Rt. Hon. William Pitt, &c.; by Rev. F. Thackeray*. London, 1827, 2 vols. 4to.

which the others exhibited. His figure was heavy and awkward; his countenance was coarse and unintellectual. His delivery was hesitating and embarrassed; and his gestures devoid of grace or appropriateness. But as a declamatory logician, he excelled every man whose voice had ever been heard in the British Parliament. No orator of modern times surpassed the ability with which he took hold of the positions and the arguments of his opponents, and sifted their weakness, absurdities, falsehoods, and errors. Even the very homeliness of his language often operated prodigiously in his favor; while the logical power with which he scoured every nook and corner of the debatable land, astonished, terrified, and crushed his opponents.

With such an array of various talent in support of the administration, it is not singular that some years of pacific government ensued under the crafty and supple guidance of Henry Pelham; a man every way adapted to preside prudently and warily over the movements of so many powerful and impetuous subordinates. During this period the foreign relations of Britain were friendly, and the acts passed by Parliament were all of a domestic, internal, and local character. A company was incorporated to promote and encourage British Fisheries; another to reform the Gregorian calendar for the computation of time; and a third, for permitting the naturalization of Jews who had been born out of the realm. The last was subsequently repealed; it being absurdly contended that the adoption of "vagrant Jews" as British citizens would endanger the constitution in church and State, and would be a disgrace to a Christian nation! The repeal of this law was the last event which occurred during the administration of Henry Pelham. He expired suddenly, unexpectedly, and prematurely in March, 1754; thereby throwing the whole machinery of government into a temporary confusion.

When George II. was informed of the death of the minister, he exclaimed: "Now I shall have no more peace;" and though the prophet, in this instance, was neither a good nor a wise man, the prophecy proved in a great measure to be a true one. Much

7

difficulty was experienced in obtaining a suitable successor, who was in every essential respect adapted to that high and difficult place. In a few days the Duke of Newcastle was selected to fill the vacant office; but with his selection, the embarrassments of the court were increased instead of diminished, in consequence of the impracticable and all-absorbing ambition of the Duke. He would allow no man of commanding ability to share the government with him; and yet unassisted, he was utterly unable to stand. A compromise was at last effected with Mr. Fox, who was appointed Secretary of State, yet without the powers which usually belonged to that office—without the control of the secret service money; and without being informed what use was to be made of that detestable fund by those who actually controlled it. Thus hampered, it was impossible for even Mr. Fox to discharge his duties so as to secure the permanency of the administration; and after a few days of imbecile and mortifying effort he resigned.

Pitt was too bold and dangerous an ally to be placed by the Duke of Newcastle in a position of great prominence in the cabinet, for in that case the latter well knew he would soon himself become a cypher. Pitt was therefore cautiously passed by. At length Mr. Legge was made Chancellor of the Exchequer, and the seals were consigned to Sir Thomas Robinson, together with the lead in the House of Commons. Sir Thomas was utterly unfit for this difficult post. He had formerly been ambassador to Vienna, and had proved himself scarcely competent even for that office. When Pitt, therefore, heard of his appointment, he exclaimed in astonishment: "Sir Thomas Robinson lead us! Newcastle might as well send his boot-jack to lead us." A short time only was necessary to prove the total incapacity of this cabinet. In addition to the management of the domestic legislation of the nation, its foreign relations, which were daily becoming more complicated and perplexed, engrossed their attention and confounded their abilities. The first difficulty arose between the French and English Colonies in North America. The limits of the territory of Nova Scotia, which had been ceded to England, became the subject of dispute. France was erecting a long chain of forts on the Mississippi, to connect together her possessions in Canada and Louisiana. The British cabinet gave orders to the governors of the American provinces, to repel force by force, and to dislodge the French from their settlements and fortresses on the Ohio. In March, 1755, the king informed Parliament that the existing state of affairs made it necessary to augment the national forces by land and sea, with special reference to the increasing difficulties and exigencies in America. A million pounds were voted by the House in accordance with the demands of the monarch, in consequence of the fact, that at that moment information reached England, that a powerful French armament was preparing in the ports of Rochefort and Brest, destined to operate in America. Admiral Boscawen was immediately dispatched with a numerous squadron to the banks of Newfoundland, to intercept the entrance of the French fleet into the gulf of St. Lawrence.

The French monarch at this crisis recalled M. Miressoix, his minister at the court of London. Letters of general reprisal were then issued by the English government. In April, 1755, General Braddock sailed from Cork with a large body of regular troops for the purpose of operating against the French on the Ohio. His rash and unfortunate career was terminated by the memorable and disastrous defeat at Fort Du Quesne; where for the first time British troops learned to appreciate the nature of conflicts with the savage aborigines, amid the primeval forests and pathless solitudes of the then uninhabited and unfrequented wilds. General Braddock was among the slain, and the command devolved upon General Shirley. The French, under Montcalm took Oswego, on Lake Ontario. The same fate subsequently befell fort William Henry; and by these successes the French acquired the entire command of the great chain of lakes which connect the St. Lawrence and the Mississippi. In November, 1755, George II. informed Parliament in a speech from the throne, that he had done his utmost to carry on hostilities against France effectually; but that the result had not yet been commensurate with his wishes. He concluded by asking for further appropriations for the continuance of the war, and for the preservation and security of his Hanoverian dominions, which were then threatened by the French monarch with invasion.

The passage of the address of Parliament in answer to the royal speech, called forth the most violent and lengthy debate which had ever occurred in the House within the memory of that generation. Very great offence was taken by many leading statesmen at the proposition which was made, to engage England and bind her to the defense of the king's Hanoverian dominions. It was on this occasion that Gerard Hamilton delivered that celebrated speech, whose extraordinary eloquence astonished and transported the House; which eclipsed every other orator who took part in the debate; and which has rendered his memory immortal by affixing upon its author, who never delivered another, the epithet of "Single Speech Hamilton." Pitt spoke an hour and a half against the subsidies, with immense energy and effect. Although he still retained the office of Paymaster of the Forces, he did not in the least degree moderate his opposition on that account. He declared, in tones of thunder, that the protection of Hanover would in a few years cost England more money than the fee simple of the electorate was worth, whose extent was so insignificant that even its name could scarcely be found upon the map; and he concluded with wishing for the day when those fetters would be broken which bound England, like Prometheus, to that barren and pernicious rock. This deadly thrust against the honor of his favorite province, George II. never forgave. He instantly dismissed Pitt, and his friend Legge, from their offices. Sir Thomas Robinson soon afterward resigned. Fox was appointed Secretary of War, and he exerted his utmost abilities to serve the imbecile king and government. The address of the Parliament was finally passed, the amendment moved by the opposition having been rejected by a large majority.

The chief event which now engaged the attention of the English government and people, was the war with France. A formidable fleet was equipped at Toulon for the purpose of making

LIFE AND REIGN OF GEORGE THE SECOND. 157

a descent on the island of Minorca. To resist this movement, a squadron, under the command of Admiral Byng, was ordered to sail from Spithead in April, 1756. On approaching Minorca, Byng discovered the British colors still floating from the fortress of St. Philip; thereby being assured that the French had not yet attempted or accomplished their purpose. Their ships were seen to the south-east, formed in line of battle. The British admiral declined a general engagement, on the ground of the inferiority of his fleet, and set sail for Gibraltar.

When the news of this ignoble cowardice reached England, a great storm of popular fury burst upon the head of the unhappy admiral. The nation was at that moment highly incensed at the French, and they could ill brook the disappointment of their anticipated vengeance. The ministry, not daring to resist the popular torrent, appointed Admirals Hawke and Sanders to take the command, and ordered Byng to be sent home under arrest. On his arrival he was committed a close prisoner to Greenwich hospital. The angry nation demanded his blood, and would hear of no defence or palliation. He was charged with cowardice, treachery, and gross ignorance. The shop windows were filled with libels and caricatures. Numerous addresses were sent up to the king, demanding the punishment of the criminal; and special instructions were sent to many representatives in Parliament, by their constituents, requiring them to vote against the unfortunate Admiral, and insist on the penalty of death.

Byng was accordingly tried, convicted, condemned, and executed.* No crime was proved, or could be proved against him, except an involuntary error of judgment, in supposing that his fleet was too small to cope successfully with the much more numerous armament of the French. Had he fought and been beaten, it had been, in the opinion of the nation, much better than not to have engaged at all. But Byng expiated his offence with his blood, and thus the vengeance of the people was slaked for the

---

* His trial commenced on December 28th, 1756; and he was executed on the 14th of March, 1757.

time. George II. seemed to partake of the fury which convulsed his subjects; and approved of the execution of the unfortunate Admiral. But his death did not bring back popularity and power to that feeble ministry. It held power precisely five months, and new changes became absolutely necessary. Pitt and his brother-in-law Temple, again came into office, and again went out, after a short collision with the impracticable and narrow-minded Newcastle; with whom no liberal-minded statesman could co-operate, as long as he remained at the head of the government.

CHAPTER VIII.

England without a Ministry—New Cabinet formed—William Pitt becomes Premier—His Extraordinary Character—The Vigor and Energy of his Government—Success of the British Arms by Land and Sea—National Exultation—The British Empire in India—Its History and Vicissitudes—The French Power in India—Conflicts between the two Nations—Brilliant Victories of Clive—Surajah Doulah—Horrors of the Black Hole—Popularity of Pitt's Administration at Home—Death of George II.—His Intellectual and Moral Character—Eminent Men of Letters during his Reign—State of Religion and of the Established Church—Cardinal Principle of the Government of George II.

DURING eleven weeks England remained in the anomalous position of possessing no ministry, although during that interval the Parliament was in session, and the war with France was raging. Pitt was evidently the only person who could grasp the helm of the ship of state in that great crisis, with a powerful and steady hand, and conduct her safely into port. But George II. hated and feared Pitt as he hated and feared no other man; and he resisted every proposition which was made for the purpose of effecting his recall to power. At length, after trying every other expedient in vain, and sending Newcastle smirking and chattering around the court, and through the Parliament, to confer with every available person, the king was compelled to yield; and the Great Commoner was called at last to fill the exalted post for which, of all other Englishmen, he was best adapted. By this new arrangement Pitt became prime minister, Newcastle took the Treasury and Foreign Affairs, Fox became Paymaster of the Forces, Lord Anson, first Lord of the Admiralty, Mr. Legge, leader in Parliament, and Sir Robert Henley, keeper of the Great Seal. By this coalition, all opposition in Parliament seemed to be annihilated; a powerful and compact ministry appeared to have been placed at the head of the country; and the entire direction of the war was thus intrusted to Pitt, the boldest, most energetic, and most patriotic of statesmen. At this fortunate consummation the nation rejoiced, and George II. was glad in spite of himself; inasmuch as it promised him a release from the cares of government, and greater leisure to divert himself with the puerilities which, together with the society of the "Countess Walmoden" filled up the empty and useless vacuum of his existence.

From the moment that Pitt seized the helm, the tide of victory and glory began to turn in favor of the British arms, both by land and sea. A large fleet was ordered to sail from Portsmouth in the beginning of September for the purpose of reducing Rochefort. As soon as Lord Anson of the Admiralty was informed that a specific time had been fixed for the departure of the fleet, he replied that it was impossible to comply with the requisition. Pitt boldly answered that it *was* possible; and that if the ships were not then ready he should impeach his lordship for neglect in the House of Commons. This sort of address to the first lord of the Admiralty was new; but it was effective; and the ships were all ready at the appointed time. The fleet sailed under the command of Admirals Hawke and Mordaunt. The island of Aix was taken. Rochefort was threatened. Some of the enemy's ships were burned in the harbor of St. Maloes. In July, 1758, Louisburgh capitulated to General Amherst; by which means the island of Cape Breton, six ships of the line, and five frigates, also became the trophies of the British commander. In the next campaign the important fortresses of Ticonderoga and Crown Point fell into his hands. But the most glorious achievement which had yet honored the arms of Britain during the war was the assault and capture of Quebec, the capital of the French possessions in Canada. Both nature and art had conspired to render this place almost impregnable. Its elevated position, the abruptness of the heights on which it was built, and the extent and strength of the fortifications, seemed to justify the prevalent opinion that it was unassailable. The heroic Wolfe commanded the British troops on this occasion. He reached the works by scaling the almost perpendicular heights of Abraham —an achievement which had been itself regarded as impossible. The commander of the French forces, General Montcalm, abandoning his intrenchments, advanced to meet his foe. A furious combat followed. General Wolfe was mortally wounded, but he refused to leave the battlefield, though rapidly sinking. When he heard some one exclaim, " They fly !" the dying hero, raising his head, inquired, " Who fly?" Being told that the French were beaten, he exclaimed, " I die content." The victory was complete; Quebec capitulated; and the whole French armament fled to Montreal.

When the news of this splendid series of triumphs reached England, the nation, so long unaccustomed to receive tidings of success, became almost delirious with joy. Those who returned from the scenes of conflict were received with the highest honors. The standards which had been captured from the foe on various fields of blood, were carried in public procession to the Cathedral of St. Paul, and there suspended as trophies. The heavens were rent with the acclamations of great multitudes. Bonfires, addresses of congratulation, and discharges of artillery, attested the national joy. Parliament voted immense subsidies to carry on the war ; and decreed a monument to be erected over the remains of General Wolfe, to whose fortitude and genius the most important of these victories was due. While these scenes of exultation were being enacted at home, Admiral Hawke attacked, defeated, and scattered, in November, 1759, a large French armament in the Bay of Biscay, and obtained a victory which completely destroyed the French marine. This event added greater intensity to the prevalent rejoicing. Thus both upon land and sea the tide of fortune had turned; and the ability and energy of Pitt had introduced an era, in which a conquest and a triumph became an everyday occurrence. Yet the most brilliant and gorgeous of all the achievements which British arms, enterprise, and diplomacy were destined to make, were still to come ; and that too in a far distant clime, in a vast and extensive country, among strange and unfamiliar people, and amid scenes of romantic oriental splendor.

The origin, establishment, and supremacy of the British Empire in India form one of the greatest marvels of modern times. That a purely mercantile company, organized for the peaceful purposes of commerce and trade, should eventually become the despotic rulers of a cluster of great nations, numbering fifty millions of people, inhabiting a territory two thousand miles in extent, and they the descendants of the soldiers of mighty and world-renowned conquerors of former times, the fame of whose achievements had long been familiar even throughout Europe; —that was an event perhaps unparalleled in history. In the seventeenth century, the British East India Company having been chartered, and established by law, its first foothold within the limits of the vast empire which it was destined afterward to possess, was obtained by purchase. The island of Bombay and the factory of Surat, on the Malabar coast, Fort St. David, and Fort St. George, usually styled Madras, on the opposite shore of Coromandel, and several villages in the vicinity, had been bought by the company from the King of Golconda; and their commercial operations were immediately commenced. Fort William, and the town of Calcutta, at the mouth of the Ganges were soon added to the possessions of the enterprising traders; and thus the foundations of the British Empire in the land of Tamerlane and Aurengzebe were laid.

At this same period the sagacity of the French had enabled them to take hold of the same glittering and inviting prize. They had established extensive commercial relations at Pondicherry, on the Coromandel coast, at Chandernagore, on the Ganges, at Rajapore, Calicut, and Surat, on the continent; and at the period of the accession of the house of Hanover to the British throne, their wealth and influence in India greatly exceeded that of their English rivals. The commanding genius of the French in India—he whose daring and sagacious intellect had foreseen the splendor and extent of the empire which European ability and energy might establish in the East, and who carried out his ambitious plans for a period with consummate talent and signal success—was Dupleix. He took advantage of the domestic disputes existing between the princes who ruled the province of Arcot, and the Viceroy of the Decan. He proposed to rear, upon the crumbling and decrepit dynasties of India, a vast and magnificent empire, which should rival or exceed those of the West; and the chief means by which this result was to be obtained, he clearly saw, was to use European soldiers, trained according to the tactics, and expert in the military science of Saxe, Vendôme, and Turenne. He also perceived that it would be a profound stroke of policy in any European adventurer, were he to use some feeble and debauched native prince, as the pretext and the veil whereby to hide the ambition, the avarice, and the tyranny, which would be the prominent characteristics of the career of the bold and successful aspirant. Such a puppet he quickly found in Muzapher-Zing, whom eventually he raised to the throne of the vice-royalty of the Decan and the government of the Carnatic. This was but the opening of the gigantic plans which Dupleix had conceived; and it is probable that this very resolute and unscrupulous adventurer would have succeeded in the full realization of his vast conceptions, had not accident placed an obstacle in his pathway, in the person of a man whose extraordinary qualities rendered him eventually one of the most illustrious men of his time. Robert Clive alone, of all living Englishmen either in England or in India, possessed the genius and the determination to crush not only the aspiring head of Dupleix, but that of every native prince or hero who dared to oppose him. This man had received neither a military nor a diplomatic education. In fact, he may be said to have had no education at all; for his boyhood and youth were spent in a turbulent resistance to all restraint, and in the uncontrolled gratification of every passion. But when surrounded by the vortex of perilous and critical affairs, which demanded the rarest combination of elevated natural gifts, this young mercantile clerk, accustomed only to the inspection of bills of lading, at once displayed his native superiority; exhibited in a wonderful degree both sagacity, fortitude, craft, prudence, self-control, and an unconquerable heroism, which eventually secured to England the possession of the greatest and richest empire in the East.

In four years Dupleix had become the most powerful personage in India, and the French were everywhere supreme. They looked with a contempt which they took no pains to disguise, upon the imbecile English traffickers of Madras and Calcutta, who seemed to have no aspiration save that for the accumulation of gold. In the progress of their conquests, the French besieged Trichinopoly, the residence of Mohammed-Ali, the rival claim' ant to the Viceroyalty of the Decan. This prince was the ally of the English; and if he should be taken or destroyed, the last obstacle to the supremacy of the French in India would be removed. Clive, seated at his desk in the counting house of his employer, perceived the greatness of the crisis, and persuaded the authorities at Madras to permit him to lead a small English force to attack Arcot, the capital of the Carnatic; hoping by this means to attract the French from the siege of Trichinopoly. Two hundred English soldiers, and three hundred sepoys, armed and trained in European tactics, was the insignificant force appointed to this difficult and dangerous enterprise. Clive marched with incredible rapidity to Arcot; and the boldness and suddenness of the movement so appalled the French garrison, that they evacuated the fort without any resistance. The English entered it in triumph, and began immediately to prepare to resist the force which they well knew would very soon be brought to bear against them. In a few days ten thousand troops, among whom were several hundred French soldiers, commanded by French officers, surrounded Arcot; and the destruction of the insignificant garrison whom Clive commanded seemed to be inevitable. Then ensued one of the fiercest and bloodiest struggles on record. During fifty days a hand-to-hand fight was kept up. The garrison became greatly reduced. At length an effort was made to storm the works by a general assault. Four officers and three hundred soldiers alone remained to confront nine thousand, aided by a powerful artillery, and many armed elephants. The heroic garrison received the assailants with undaunted resolution, and an unparalleled conflict of an hour's duration ensued. Thrice did Rajah Sahib, the native commander, seated on his milk-white elephant, lead forward his whole line to the attack. Thrice did the thinly scattered garrison hurl death and destruction into his serried ranks, and compel them to retire. The musket balls of the English, directed against the huge foreheads of the elephants prostrated some as dead masses and sent others flying over the field frantic with pain, trampling the native troops beneath their feet, and adding to their consternation and disasters. At length the Rajah, perceiving the hopelessness of further effort, commanded his disorderly host to retire from the attack. The result of this glorious defense of Arcot was, to establish the British name and authority in a large portion of India, in the place of the supremacy of France, which had proportionably fallen. Other military operations ensued, equally honorable to the English. The siege of Trichinopoly was raised soon after the attack on Arcot.

In 1756 other events of equal importance and interest transpired in India. The Viceroy of the vast province of Bengal, Surajah Dowlah, though nominally a subject of the Great Mogul at Delhi, was in reality an independent prince. From his youth he had conceived a violent dislike to the English. As long as they remained feeble and obscure, he despised them. Now that they had become formidable and dangerous, he feared and hated them. He apprehended the future growth of their power, and he formed the determination to crush them before they could become greater. He collected a vast army and marched to the siege of Fort William, which was then occupied chiefly by unwarlike traders. These fled in terror as soon as the Viceroy's army appeared in view. A few soldiers and traders only remained behind. Surajah Dowlah, who was a cruel and sanguinary monster, entered the fort, and ordered all who were to be found in the factories, or in the fortifications, to be brought before him. He wished to see specimens of that detested race upon whose destruction he was so intent. His com mand was complied with, and after he had inspected and insulted these unfortunate men, he directed them to be imprisoned. That order was equivalent, as the despot well knew, to a warrant for their execution. Within the fort, shut out entirely from the free air of heaven, there was a dark and deep dungeon, fitly termed the Black Hole; intended for the occasional use of the diminutive garrison. It was only twenty feet square, and had never been occupied by more than two or three culprits at a time. At that season of the year when the ardent sun of Bengal almost consumed the vegetation of the earth by the intensity of its heat; when even the natives could scarcely exist, with every convenience and freedom which their habits of living allowed them; and all were parched and suffocated by the closeness of the atmosphere, a hundred and forty-six Englishmen were confined in that hideous furnace. When their guards first ordered them to enter it, they believed them to be jesting. The order was peremptorily repeated; and after expostulating and beseeching in vain, they were compelled to obey at the point of the sword. The bolts were then drawn, and the unfortunate captives were left to their fate in the stifling tomb to which they had been consigned. No language can adequately depict the horrors which ensued. The prisoners made every effort at first, to move the sympathy and the avarice of their jailers. They offered immense bribes to be released. Their guards laughed at their agonies, which were but commencing; and remained uninfluenced by their gold, their supplications, their execrations, and their tears. Soon the pangs of that great agony became insupportable, and the sufferers began to be delirious. Then they fought with each other, and contended with murderous and desperate violence for places near the several small loop-holes, which perforated to little purpose the massive walls. Some prayed, some laughed, and some blasphemed. Others implored their comrades to put an end to their existence, and others still attempted by their own hands to terminate their sufferings. Death, more merciful than the jailors of Surajah Dowlah, soon relieved them. Their screams of agony and despair gradually subsided into melancholy moans; and as the heated hours of the night wore slowly on, one after another of the captives expired. When at length the morning dawned, and the door of that memorable prison was opened, it was crowded from floor to ceiling with irregular piles of corpses. Out of the whole number who had entered it on the preceding night, but twenty-three survived, and they themselves were little better than dead men.

Surajah Dowlah exhibited no sorrow for the horrible fate which had befallen his captives. But they were speedily avenged. He was subsequently attacked by an English force under the command of Clive, on the memorable plain of Plassey; where three thousand European troops confronted and vanquished with great slaughter an army of seventy thousand men, accompanied by fifty pieces of artillery. This numerous armament, composed of the best native troops of India, some of which were infantry and some cavalry, covered the plain as far as the eye could reach; yet the heroism of the British commander and troops achieved an overwhelming victory. The viceroy was compelled to flee. His army was scattered. Having returned to Moorshedabad, his capital, he was forced to escape thence at midnight, and being discovered in his flight, he was taken and executed. The shades of the unfortunate captives of the Black Hole were avenged; and the British power was established on a firm and permanent basis throughout the whole of the Carnatic, both over the native population, and over the dispirited and subjugated French residents.

At home the administration of William Pitt still continued to win the popular favor. His measures were patriotic, energetic, and successful. He secured the establishment of a national militia, which produced a comprehensive and effectual system of national defence; although the number of men was reduced by the House of Peers from sixty-four thousand to thirty-two thousand. At the opening of parliament in December, 1757, George II. officially informed the House of the successes which had recently attended the arms of his illustrious relative and ally, the King of Prussia; and requested that such assistance might be granted him by the English government, as would enable that hero to continue his heroic defence of the Protestant religion, and of the liberties of Europe. The Seven Years' war was then in progress; but neither the Protestant religion nor the liberties of Europe had the slightest connection either with its origin, its progress, or its results. Nevertheless the Commons returned a most dutiful and loyal answer, and subsidies to the immense amount of ten million pounds were unanimously voted.

Successes still continued to attend the British arms and to add unmerited lustre to the reign of the aged and decrepit monarch. When parliament met in November, 1759, the Lord Keeper dwelt exultingly upon the long and brilliant series of victories which British valor had won in North America, in the West Indies, in the East Indies, and upon the high seas. In truth, as George II. became more feeble and insignificant, the splendor of his reign became more imposing, in consequence of the energy and ability with which William Pitt directed every department of the government, infusing into each branch of the service some portion of the peculiar qualities which he himself possessed.

Just at this crisis of universal success and triumph George II. expired. A large portion of his family had preceded him. Prince Frederic, the heir apparent, first passed from the scene. In 1751 Louisa, Queen of Denmark, died. Young Prince Edward also was cut off prematurely by an imposthume in his side. The Princess Anne of Orange had also been called away. And at last the aged monarch received the summons to follow them. On Friday, the 24th of October, 1760, he retired to rest at his usual hour, and in the enjoyment of his ordinary health. He slept well during the night, and at six o'clock in the ensuing morning he rose, drank his usual cup of chocolate, walked to the window, looked out upon the Kensington gardens, and remarked that the wind was unfavorable for the arrival of the expected packet which conveyed his dispatches from Holland. He remarked to his attendant that he would take a short walk in the garden. He started through the adjoining apartment in pursuance of this purpose, when he suddenly fell to the floor. In falling, he inflicted a wound on his right temple, produced by striking it on the corner of a bureau. His attendants, hurrying to his side, found him gasping for breath. He feebly said, "Send for Amelia," and expired. He was instantly conveyed to the bed from which he had so recently risen, and every effort was made by the physicians, who were quickly sent for, to resuscitate nature; yet to no purpose. His daughter the Princess Amelia arrived; but it was only to embrace the lifeless corpse of her father. His grandson, the Prince of Wales, now monarch of the British realms, was sent for, and informed of the momentous event which had occurred. He was riding at a distance from the palace when the message reached him. Without exhibiting much surprise or emotion, he remarked to his attendant that his horse was lame, and wheeling round returned. It is singular that the longest reign in British annals should have commenced with the utterance of an unnecessary and puerile falsehood.

George II. being dead, he was buried in the ancient vault of the Kings of England, with the gorgeous and impressive ceremonies which usually attended the funeral of the defunct monarchs. This undeserving and insignificant man expired in the propitious hour of victory and universal national joy; and in this peculiarity of his fate, he furnished another illustration of the disparity which exists in the dispensations of Providence among royal as well as among plebeian personages; for while many of the former have ended their unfortunate or turbulent careers in disappointment and gloom, with the future fate of their dynasties wrapped in uncertain perils, George II. enjoyed the rare felicity of being permitted to expire on the bosom of victory, in a ripe old age, with peace, contentment, and prosperity richly possessed by his subjects at home; with the national glory honored and revered by the whole world, and with the prospect of a tranquil and secure succession being inherited by his descendant.

Although the character of George II. was in every respect an ordinary one, and though he exhibited but very few qualities which entitled him to admiration and esteem, his death was mourned by the popular poets by the effusion of an immense quantity of rhyming and jingling grief. The nation at large were indifferent at the event, and prepared themselves quietly to acknowledge the accession and the authority of his successor. Thus far indeed the House of Hanover had exhibited but few attributes which were calculated to engage the affections of their subjects; and George II. was the least attractive of the two sovereigns of that race who had occupied the throne.*

In his person George II. was diminutive and undignified. His intellect was superficial and imbecile; and he remained a German until the day of his death, in every essential feature. In his youth he had received the usual routine of the education of princes, which had been, in truth, fully equal to the extent of his faculties. He was utterly indifferent to the promotion of science and literature, and never extended to them the least patronage. He never became a master even of the prevalent dialect of his subjects; and, to use his own inelegant language, he cordially hated "boetry and bainting." Yet in spite of his total disregard of the importance and charms of literature, education, science, and art, they all flourished during his reign in an unusual degree. It seemed indeed to have been the singular and fortunate lot of George II. to behold the triumphs, both of arts and arms, of intellectual and physical power, among his subjects, while he himself, by his example of indifference to these results, exerted his influence to prevent or postpone so felicitous a result. During his reign, and especially in its concluding years, the genius of the British people shone forth brilliantly in every department of its power. This was the era in which the graceful pens of Gray, Young, and Thompson, produced their matchless

---

* George II. was possessed at the period of his death of considerable personal property. He bequeathed fifty thousand pounds to his favorite, the Duke of Cumberland, and the Princesses Amelia and Mary. To the Countess Walmoden he left a cabinet, the contents of which were estimated at eleven thousand pounds. He also willed to the Duke of Cumberland a number of mortgages amounting to the sum of a hundred and thirty thousand pounds.

numbers, so descriptive of the beauties and the attributes of nature; for the Church-yard Elegy, the Seasons, and the Night Thoughts, will ever remain contributions of the richest value to the poetical literature of the language. In the department of the drama, the pathetic effusions of Otway, and the elegant compositions of Rowe, deservedly attained great eminence; although their labors were so little appreciated by the monarch, or by the court, that the gifted author of Venice Preserved, absolutely starved to death.* In comedy, Congreve, Vanburgh, and Farquhar, produced works of sterling merit, which are to this day admired and represented. Two great historians began to flourish during the life of the second George, and culminated during the succeeding reign; for the names of Hume and Robertson will ever rank among the first in that difficult yet attractive species of composition. The History of England, and the Reign of Charles V., possess peculiar and distinctive merits which have rendered their authors immortal. In the department of philosophy or metaphysics, Hartley became greatly distinguished by introducing a system which was remarkable for its simplicity and clearness, and for its accurate accordance with the real phenomena of human nature. Bentley was celebrated as a philologist. Warburton, Samuel Clarke, and Hoadley, were eminent as theological writers, and deservedly ranked among the most profound and learned thinkers of the age. To these may be added the names and productions of Foster, Chandler, Leland, Lardner, and Lowth, as possessing equal distinction and merit.

Nor were the fine arts left without illustrious representatives.

---

* The climax of the literary misery of this period, the harrowing details of which have reached us, was found in the person of Samuel Boyce, whose name and works are now almost unknown, yet whose genius was of a high order. This unfortunate man was born in Ireland in 1698. He first migrated to Edinburgh, and thence to London. He lived and died in the most abject poverty. In 1740 it is recorded of him, that he had not a shirt, a coat, or any kind of apparel to put on, and the bed sheets on which he lay were sent to the pawnbroker. He frequently wrote sitting in bed with no covering but a blanket, in which a hole had been cut to receive his head, and others to admit his arms. He died at last in the alms-house, and was buried by the parish. *Cibber's Lives of the Poets*, p. 168.

Sir Joshua Reynolds in painting, Wilton in sculpture, Handel, Arne, and Boyce in music, contributed to add to the lustre of this period. In one single respect does George II. deserve the esteem of posterity for his personal conduct and opinions : he declared that, during his reign, there should be no persecution for conscience sake. Accordingly it was at this era that those penal statutes which had for so many ages been the disgrace of the English nation, and which exhibited and authorized a degree of tyranny which would have dishonored the sceptre of a Nero or Heliogabalus, were ameliorated, reformed, and finally in a great measure abolished. This cheering feature, together with the flourishing state of literature, and the prevalence of mental activity, render this reign one of the most attractive and pleasing in British history ; for these are not to be attributed in the least degree to the fostering and partial care of a Mæcenas or a Dorset, nor to the encouragement received from academical patronage and premiums, but to the cultivation, intelligence, and generosity of the nation. Yet religion did not flourish at this period in the same degree ; for in the established church an unexampled spirit of indifference and even of infidelity prevailed. There were hundreds of clergymen who, like Dr. Conyers Middleton, the author of the life of Cicero, subscribed to the Thirty-nine Articles for the purpose of obtaining a sumptuous or a competent living, while in their hearts they disbelieved and despised the doctrines which they professed. The king and queen were both regarded as sceptics in religion ; the leaders of the *beau monde*, Lords Chesterfield and Hervey openly entertained the same sentiments ; the *esprit fortes* of the period, such as Lady Mary Wortley Montague and Horace Walpole, were scoffers at every thing serious or devout; and a disposition to ridicule and neglect the obligations of Christianity prevailed among the higher and more cultivated ranks of society.*

Such was England at the period of the death of the second monarch of the House of Hanover. If, during his reign, no events occurred possessing the absorbing and thrilling interest

* See Short's History of the Church of England, *passim*.

which characterized the era of Cromwell, of Charles II., or of William of Orange, yet one very great advantage was enjoyed by his subjects, which was infinitely more to be desired and valued than more startling and illustrious characteristics : George II. was content to rule in harmony with the requirements of the British Constitution; without any violation of the established laws and the chartered liberties of the kingdom ; and in accordance with liberal, impartial, and equitable principles of administration. But the intelligent student of his life and reign must admit that, in his own character and measures there was little to admire ; while all that was fortunate, or glorious, or felicitous therein, was due to the superior genius of those great ministers whose steady and skilful hands so ably guided the ship of state during many perilous and troubled years.

PART III.

LIFE AND REIGN OF GEORGE THE THIRD.

CHAPTER I.

Birth of George III.—His Connection with Hannah Lightfoot—Lady Sarah Lennox—Proposals for his Marriage—Researches of Colonel Graeme—The Prince's Marriage to Charlotte of Mecklenburg Strelitz—Her Character—Accession of George III.—His Mental Qualities—His Personal Appearance—Administration of William Pitt—Lord Bute—His Relation to the Princess Dowager—A New Ministry—Meeting of Parliament—War declared against Spain—Incidents of the Conflict.

GEORGE III. was born at Leicester Palace on the fourth of June, 1738. He was the eldest son of Frederic, Prince of Wales, the heir apparent to the throne, who died, as we have already narrated, in 1751. His mother was Augusta of Saxe-Gotha. The young prince was placed, when at a suitable age, under the tuition of the learned and amiable Dr. Ayscough, Dean of Bristol. He was intelligent, diligent, and displayed considerable aptitude for the acquisition of knowledge. On one occasion his grandfather George II. sent Baron Steinberg to examine him in his studies. He exhibited more than ordinary proficiency for his years in Latin; but when Steinberg remarked that he ought also to study German, he exclaimed: "German! German! any blockhead can learn that." In every other branch of knowledge the future king was quite respectable.

The principal incident of the boyhood of George III. was his investiture with the order of the Garter by his grandfather, in 1749. The juvenile knight was carried into the royal presence by the Duke of Dorset. He immediately commenced to deliver himself of a speech which had been taught him by his tutor; but his eloquence was suddenly stopped by the king, who proceeded to the conclusion of the ceremony. At an early age the prince proved himself susceptible of the tender sentiment. The first object of his amorous regard was a young Quakeress, named Hannah Lightfoot, whose beauty and amiable disposition exerted so powerful an influence over him, that it was the prevalent report that he had been married to her privately in 1759, in Curzon Street Chapel, by the Rev. Mr. Keith. The witness of the ceremony was said to have been his brother Edward, Duke of York. The reality of this occurrence has been as positively denied as it has been strenuously asserted; and it is impossible at this late day to ascertain the truth with certainty. But it is well known that the lovers kept house together; that they were devotedly attached to each other; and it is added by some authorities that there were children born to them. In the progress of time, however, George became indifferent to the sedate and monotonous charms of the Quakeress; and she was disposed of by being married to a person named Axford, who received her and her very considerable dower without asking any impertinent or inconvenient questions. From that period Hannah and her subsequent fate disappear beneath the shadows of oblivion.

The fair and fascinating Lady Sarah Lennox was the next object of the affectionate regard of the young prince. On a certain occasion the tragedy of Jane Shore was enacted at Holland House. Charles Fox represented Hastings, and Sarah Lennox played the part of the unfortunate yet beautiful heroine of the piece. Her acting was so natural and affecting, and her personal charms were so powerful, that she completely stormed the heart of the susceptible prince, who witnessed her performance; and had she not been a British subject, her lover would have led her to the altar; but against such a proceeding a stringent statute had been made and provided, which rendered it absolutely impossible. It accordingly became necessary for the friends of the prince to look elsewhere for a suitable and lawful partner of his fortunes.

Various persons were suggested in this emergency. The mother of the prince, and Lord Bute, who already occupied the questionable relation toward her which afterward led to his elevation to the premiership, were in favor of a member of the house of Saxe-Gotha, to which she herself belonged. But George II. declared, in no very delicate manner, that he had had enough of that family already. At length Colonel Graeme, a Hanoverian favorite of the monarch, was despatched to the continent with orders to visit all the German courts without divulging his purpose; to scrutinize the merits and peculiarities of the several eligible princesses; and report the results of his observations. In the execution of this commission, the Colonel happened to pass a few days at the famous baths of Pyrmont. There were collected together a number of noble families, for the purpose of enjoying the salutary effects of the waters. Etiquette and formality were in a great measure thrown aside; and delicate and fair young ladies, who at home were models of obedience to the rigors of an iron restraint and formality, enjoyed themselves with a perfect and healthful freedom. Among the handsomest and wildest of these enfranchised young slaves were the two daughters of the Dowager Duchess of Mecklenburg Strelitz. The vigilant Colonel soon became sensible of the superior beauty and intelligence of the younger of these ladies, the Princess Charlotte Sophia, and immediately fell vicariously in love with her. He sent information directly to the court of London, of the important discovery which he had made; expatiated at length upon the merits of the princess; and thus became the means of eventually providing a queen for England. Nor does the choice of the acute Colonel appear to have been a bad one. Charlotte was the daughter of Charles Louis, the Duke of Mirow, the second son of the Duke of Mecklenburg Strelitz. She was born in May, 1744. She had in her earlier youth been instructed by Madame de Grabon, who has generally been termed the German Sappho. She had been carefully educated by Dr. Geitzner in Lutheran theology, in natural history, and other useful sciences. She was a good linguist, a good musician, and an admirable

8*

dancer. She was a young lady of sense and spirit; and to all these charms she added the less impalpable ones of a very intelligent and pleasing countenance, and a figure of medium size, perfect in its mould and proportions. After the death of George II., and the accession of his grandson, the latter communicated to his council his approaching marriage in July, 1761. At first the announcement was not received with any great enthusiasm either by the cabinet or by the people; for Mecklenburg Strelitz was one of the most insignificant of the many insignificant principalities of Germany, and unworthy of the connection. But soon every body became reconciled to an event, to which indeed there could be no valid objection; and Lord Harcourt was deputed to visit Strelitz, and demand the hand of the young princess in form. There were few or no difficulties in the way. A favorable answer was readily given. The treaty of marriage was signed at Strelitz on the 15th of August; and the Earl of Hardwicke was sent to convey the intended queen to England. He was accompanied by two ladies of extraordinary beauty, the Duchesses of Hamilton and Ancaster. The princess was astonished, as she well might be, when she first beheld the fair companions of her voyage, and inquired with some apprehension, if there were many such beautiful women in the English court. These ladies had in fact no rivals in this respect in England; yet even in their presence the graceful and talented young bride of George III. need not have been in the least degree discouraged.

The bride traversed the channel in the fleet commanded by Admiral Anson. The passage was stormy but not dangerous. Having at length disembarked at Harwich, she commenced her journey toward London, accompanied by a large retinue of noble ladies and their attendants who had been sent to meet her. She retained her buoyant spirits until she arrived in view of the Palace of St. James, where her public presentation was to take place. Here for the first time she became somewhat disconcerted and grew pale. The Duchess of Hamilton endeavored to cheer her, when she replied: "My dear Duchess, you may laugh, you have been married twice; but it's no joke to me!" She soon recovered her usual self-possession; her intended husband met her at the palace gates; and as she knelt on one knee to pay him her homage, he prevented her, and kissed her with more than an ordinary show of princely affection. During the whole scene of her presentation to the old monarch and the court, she conducted herself admirably, and proved herself worthy of the high alliance which had been tendered her. The marriage ceremony took place a few hours after her arrival, and was celebrated in the chapel of the Palace of St. James.

Few monarchs ever ascended a throne under more favorable circumstances than those which attended the accession of George III. His aged predecessor had expired in the arms of victory, and amid general national prosperity. In every quarter of the globe, the valor and power of Britain were triumphant, while at home peace and prosperity prevailed to a degree rarely exhibited in the chequered history of the nation. When George III. at length mounted the throne of the ancient yet ruined house of Stuart, the British people rejoiced in the possession of a sovereign, who, among other valuable attributes, was a native of the soil. That feeling of ill-concealed dislike with which the nation had regarded the rule of a foreign prince had passed away. Beside all this, George III. was young, and he secured that partiality with which youth when invested by no act of its own with great powers and dangerous responsibilities always secures. He had also some claim to hereditary right. His person was handsome, his manners agreeable, his intellect respectable, his character unstained by any known vice. The affections of the nation gathered around him, and became the strongest bulwark of his throne. Those qualities of his mind which were repulsive—his obstinacy, his narrow views, his exalted ideas of his prerogatives—had not yet been developed. During the reign of his predecessor he had abstained from any interference in the affairs of government, and if he had in consequence no powerful party particularly devoted to his interests, there was none which declared an intense and deadly hostility to him. The two great factions of Whigs and Tories still indeed existed. The former had retained possession of the chief offices of the state until the death of George II. Had his son Frederic Prince of Wales, succeeded, the Tories, to whom he had joined himself in his mad opposition to his father's measures and person, would have secured an ascendency as absolute and as pernicious as that of Harley and Bolingbroke during the reign of Queen Anne.

On the accession of George III. he was supposed to entertain sentiments which might be designated as those of the moderate Whigs. On the 18th of November, 1761, he delivered a speech to Parliament from the throne, in which he gave utterance to the most popular opinions. Said he: "Born and educated in this country, I glory in the name of Briton; and the peculiar happiness of my life will ever consist in promoting the happiness of a people whose loyalty and warm affection to me, I consider as the greatest and most permanent security of my throne. The civil and religious rights of my loving subjects are equally dear to me with the most valuable prerogatives of my crown." * Other sentiments of a similar character followed, in which he declared that it would be the aim of his administration to maintain as far as possible the future peace of the empire, to protect the Protestant interest at home and abroad; and he concluded with expressing the hope and the assurance that, in the accomplishment of these and other great results, he would possess the assistance of every honest man and good citizen. † The royal speech was received by the nation with acclamations of grateful pride and pleasure.

The powerful hand of William Pitt still guided the helm of the ship of state with consummate ability. Had he been permitted to retain his influence and to execute his favorite measures, the same halo of glory which had illumined the nation ever since his accession to power, would undoubtedly have continued to exist. But a dark and malignant spirit hovered behind the throne of the youthful monarch, which was destined to exert its powerful spell in effecting the removal of the nation's favor-

* *Belsham's Memoirs of the Reign of George III.*, Vol. I., p. 6.
† See *Croly's Life and Times of George IV.*, p. 13.

ite, and in entailing a long series of pernicious measures and disasters. That spirit—the evil genius of George III.—was the celebrated Lord Bute.

Bute was a Scotch nobleman who possessed large estates in one of the Hebrides Islands. At an early age he had been chosen to fill a vacancy among the Scotch representative peers in parliament. He was a man of very ordinary ability, and was never reëlected. During twenty years he remained in obscurity, either at his remote seat in the Hebrides, or subsequently as a member of the household of Prince Frederic. After the death of the prince, he succeeded in ingratiating himself into the affections of the widowed princess. He became her favored lover. His chief recommendation for this place was the possession of a pleasing countenance, and a figure of rare beauty and symmetry. He was also a person of some literary cultivation, while his manners were courtly and agreeable. He gradually obtained an absolute influence over the mind and heart of the Princess Dowager; and through her he began to govern the young king with a degree of success which daily acquired increasing strength. Bute was a Tory in sentiment, though his Toryism had been somewhat modified by the influence which had been exerted upon him, by the statesmen with whom he associated in the household of Prince Frederic, whose opinions more nearly resembled those of Lord Bolingbroke than those of any other British statesman. The very day after the accession of George III., Bute was sworn a member of the Privy Council. Shortly afterward, the Rangership of Richmond Park was taken from the Princess Amelia, and conferred upon him. It was very evident that other and much more important promotions would soon follow. Pitt became aware that a desperate cabal was already formed by Bute, for the purpose of changing the whole policy of the administration; by which means he himself would be precipitated from power, and the glory of the nation tarnished and obscured. Nor was this disagreeable apprehension long in being realized. Lord Bute soon informed his friend Doddington, that Lord Holderness, then a member of the Pitt cabinet, had agreed to quarrel with his associates and resign. The vacancy thus created was to be supplied by himself; and a favorable opportunity was only waited for to put this initiatory step of the intrigue into operation. In March, 1761, the first parliament which sat since the accession of George III. was prorogued, after a speech from the throne in which the young monarch commended and approved all that they had done. On the very same day the downfall of that great and powerful ministry which had made England the wonder and envy of the world, began by the dismissal of Mr. Legge, the Chancellor of the Exchequer.* He was personally offensive to the king in consequence of his refusal to obey the will of the monarch while Prince of Wales, in not withdrawing himself as a candidate for the knightship of the County of Southampton; in order to allow the substitution of a friend and favorite of the prince. George had not forgotten that act of independence, and punished it upon the earliest possible opportunity. The fall of Legge was followed two days afterward, by the resignation of Lord Holderness; who, by a species of bribery which covers his memory with indelible disgrace, sold his office for the reversion of the Wardenship of the Cinque Ports.

* Horace Walpole, in his Memoirs of the Reign of George III., (edited by Sir Denis de Marchant, 4 vols., London, 1845,) thus speaks of the several persons referred to on this occasion:

"*Mr. Legge—chancellor of the exchequer:*

"With all his abilities, Legge was of a *creeping, underhand* nature, and aspired to the lion's place by the *manœuvre of the mole.*" Vol. i., p. 301.

"Winchelsea said Legge had had more masters than any man in England, and had never left one with a character." *Ib.* p. 30.

"*Lord Temple—privy seal:*

"This *shameless* and *malignant* man worked in the minds of successive factions for nearly thirty years together. To relate them is writing his life." (Vol. ii. p. 359.) "Nothing could be more offensive than Lord Temple's conduct, whether considered in a public or private light. Opposition to his factious views seemed to let him loose from all ties, all restraint of *principles;* and his brother was the object of his *jealousy* and *resentment.*" Vol. i., p. 295.

"*Lord Holderness—secretary of state:*

"Orders were suddenly sent to Lord Holderness to give up the seals of secretary of state: the king adding, in discourse, that he had two secretaries, one (Mr. Pitt) who would do nothing, and the other (Lord Holderness) *who could do nothing;* he would have one, who both could and would. This was Lord Bute.

The Earl of Bute was instantly promoted to the place vacated by Lord Holderness. He appointed Lord Hawkesbury his under-secretary. Legge was succeeded by Sir Francis Dashwood, a zealous Tory, but one of the most incompetent men who ever occupied a place of high trust and responsibility. Thus an effectual beginning had been made in accomplishing the entire change of the cabinet. Pitt still remained nominally at the head of affairs; but it was easy to see that, with two determined and hostile ministers in the cabinet, the energy and boldness which had for some years wrought such wonders in the fortunes of England, would be shorn of a large portion of their strength. In addition to this adverse influence, there were other causes which aided in the eventual downfall of the great minister; and substituted in his high place a man whose only recommendation was his fitness and acceptableness as the paramour of the Princess Dowager. Yet while the vigorous and powerful genius of Pitt was achieving brilliant triumphs at one and the same time in America, in India, and in Germany; while he made his coun-

But, however *low the talents* of Lord Holderness deserved to be estimated, they did not suffer by comparison with those of his successor." Vol. i., pp. 42, 43.

And again, when he reappeared as *governor to the Prince of Wales* in 1771: "Lord Holderness owed his preferment to his *insignificance* and to his wife, a lady of the bed-chamber to the queen, as she did hers to her daughter's governess, whom the queen had seduced from her, to the great vexation of Lady Holderness. The governess, a French Protestant, ingratiated her late mistress with the queen, and her mistress soon became a favorite next to the German women." Vol. iv., p. 314.

Of Lord Bute who succeeded Lord Holderness, and soon became *first lord of the treasury*, we need not repeat any of Walpole's general opinions, but we may extract the following summary of his character while minister:

"Success and the tide of power swelled up the *weak bladder of the favorite's mind*," (vol. i., p. 177.) "His countenance of Fox was but consonant to the *folly* of his character," (p. 249.) "His *intrigues* to preserve power—the *confusion* he helped to throw into each succeeding system—his *impotent and dark* attempts to hang on the wheels of government, *which he only clogged*—all proved that neither virtue nor philosophy, but *fear*—and fear only—was the immediate and precipitate cause of his retreat. Yet let me not be thought to lament this *weak* man's *pusillanimity;* had he been firm to himself, there was an *end of the constitution.*"

try the mistress of the seas and the umpire of the continent; while the guns of the Tower were reverberating from day to day with salvos of victory; while the dwellings of the metropolis were frequently illuminated, and French banners were repeatedly carried through the streets, in honor of new achievements; while his resistless eloquence resounded in the Commons, prostrating every opponent of his measures; kindling the enthusiasm, stirring the blood, and summoning tears to the eyes, of the patriotic representatives of the realm, and causing them to vote heartily and unanimously in favor of those immense subsidies which were necessary to the execution of his vast measures of offensive and defensive war; during all this time the more thoughtful portion of the nation began to recover from the delirium into which they had been thrown, and to survey the opposite side of the brilliant but delusive picture. They discovered that some of the acquisitions and triumphs which had been achieved, though they were honorable, were also expensive and unprofitable; that England had been involved in the defense of the Hanoverian provinces of the king; that British gold had paid for the military glories which clustered so thickly around the brow of the Prussian hero; that while the whole attention of the minister was absorbed in these engrossing events, peculation and embezzlement had crept into the Home government to a shameful and alarming extent; that the National Debt had, in one short year, become so much increased, that it would require forty years of prosperous peace to liquidate the amount; and that eight million pounds had been borrowed by the nation in twelve months. It was the assured conviction of thousands of the wisest Englishmen, that triumphs and splendors won at such a sacrifice were dear indeed; and a sentiment of fear began to mingle with that prodigious admiration with which the greatest of English ministers was regarded by his prudent and calculating countrymen. To all this must be added the fact, that the peculiar doctrines of the great Tory party, of which the chief were a standing army, a national debt, a septennial parliament, and a government by aristocratic influence, no longer excited the apprehension and alarm which they formerly produced.

This was the state of affairs when a crisis unfortunately occurred in the measures of the administration. Charles III. was now King of Spain and the Indies. He hated England with an intense hatred. He greatly envied the successes which had followed all the measures of Pitt. He secretly concluded a treaty with France termed the "Family Compact," the object of which was to make war conjointly upon England. But war was not to be declared in form until the arrival in Spain of an expected squadron from the Brazils freighted with a vast and prodigious treasure. Pitt had received information both of the treaty and of the treasure; and he proposed in Council that an armament should be instantly dispatched to intercept the fleet, while at the same time war should be declared against the confederate powers. In this proposition he was supported by his brother-in-law, Earl Temple; but the influence of Bute and his allies predominated, and the inestimable argosy amounting to several hundreds of millions in bullion was safely disembarked in the port of Cadiz. Pitt immediately resigned his place in the cabinet; declaring that he would no longer remain responsible for measures which he was no longer permitted to guide.

Thus ended the most brilliant administration which England ever enjoyed. The Great Commoner was succeeded by the Earl of Egremont, a descendant of Sir William Windham, and a moderate Tory. He was a fair representative of that class of statesmen who were at that moment winning their way, under the guidance of Lord Bute, to supreme power in the state. Lord Temple and the Duke of Newcastle also resigned. To avert the unpopularity which the withdrawal of Pitt would inevitably entail on the court, large offers of pecuniary provision were made him, and he was even invited to enter the peerage. The latter proposition he prudently refused; but he was compelled by his necessities to accept a pension of three thousand pounds per annum, while his wife was created a peeress in her own right. By this means the popularity of the ex-minister was preserved, his pressing wants supplied, and the odium of the nation averted in some measure from the king and court, in consequence of the removal of their idol.* This event was still regarded as a national calamity. George III. received an unpleasant intimation of the wane of his popularity, upon the Lord Mayor's Day, which occurred shortly after these events. He dined according to custom at the Guildhall. The monarch, his young bride, and his cabinet, were scarcely noticed; while Pitt's entrance was greeted by long and loud acclamations; and on the return of the royal party to the palace, the carriage of Bute was hooted and pelted by a great multitude of the indignant and scurrilous populace.†

On the fourth of January, 1762, war was declared against Spain with the usual formalities; and letters of marque and reprisal were granted to privateers against the enemy. The king expressed in his address to the Commons "his regret at the unsuccessful termination of the late negotiations for peace, and his resolution to prosecute the war in the most effectual manner, till the enemies of Great Britain, moved by their own losses, and touched with the miseries of so many nations, shall yield to her equitable conditions of an honorable peace." In accordance with these declarations, the new ministry endeavored to emulate the energy which had characterized the measures of Pitt. Bute led the court party in parliament; and he acquitted himself with more success as an orator than had been anticipated from his limited abilities, and from his want of experience. An armament consisting of eighteen ships of the line was sent under the command of Sir G. Rodney, to the island of Martinique, one of the most valuable colonies belonging to France. After some resistance the island passed into the possession of the British. The same fate befell the islands of Grenada, St. Lucia, Tobago,

---

* Similar offers of pecuniary remuneration were made by the King to the Duke of Newcastle; but the Duke replied that "if he could no longer be permitted to serve his country, he was at least determined not to be a burden to it." See *Belsham's Reign of George III.*, Vol. I., p. 45.

† Memoir of the Marquis of Rockingham and his Contemporaries.

and St. Vincents. Another fleet subsequently sailed under the orders of the Earl of Albemarle, which, arriving off the island of Cuba, disembarked a large body of troops in the vicinity of Havana, the capital of the island. The works of that city were valiantly defended by the Spanish governor, Don Louis de Velasco; but in spite of prodigious exertions and unsurpassed valor on his part, he was compelled to capitulate in August 1762; and Havana, together with twelve Spanish line of battle ships then lying in the harbor, and an immense treasure, fell into the hands of the conquerors. Similar success followed the expedition which was sent at this crisis against Manilla, the capital of the island of Luconia, the largest of the Philippines, commanded by Sir William Draper and Admiral Cornish. A ransom of four million dollars was offered and accepted, to save the city from destruction by bombardment; but the port and citadel of Cavite, and all the islands and fortresses connected with the government of Manilla, were included in the capitulation, and remained in the possession of the British.

These triumphs of the armies and navies of England, while they filled the nation with exultation, did not increase the popularity of the young king, or of his new ministry; because it was generally supposed that these various expeditions, which had been crowned with such remarkable success, had originally been planned and suggested by the fallen minister; and to him the credit of their fortunate issue was perversely ascribed. Further changes ensued at this period in the cabinet. The Earl of Hardwicke retired; Lord Halifax took the Seals; and Mr. Grenville was placed at the head of the Admiralty.* The Duke of

---

* Horace Walpole describes this celebrated minister in the following strong but unfair and prejudiced language, in his Memoirs of the Reign of George III.:

"Mr. Grenville had hitherto been known but as a fatiguing orator and indefatigable drudge, more likely to disgust than to offend. Beneath this useful, unpromising outside lay lurking great abilities; courage so confounded with *obstinacy* that there was no drawing a line between them — good intentions to the public without one great view — much economy for that public, which, in truth, was the whole amount of his good intentions — *excessive rapaciousness and parsimony* in himself — *infinite self-conceit, implacability of temper,*

Grafton, Lord Ravensworth, and Lord Ashburnham ranged themselves on the side of the opposition, and served to swell the strength of that formidable combination which was soon to rise, resist, and overwhelm the power of the favorite of the king, and of his scandalous mother, the Princess Dowager.

and a total want of principle. His ingratitude to his benefactor, Bute, and his reproaching Mr. Pitt, were but too often paralleled by the *crimes* of other men; but scarce any man ever wore in his face such outward and visible marks of the *hollow, cruel,* and *rotten* heart within." Vol. iv., p. 271.

"The reversion of Lord Temple's estate could make even the inflexible Grenville stoop; and if his *acrimonious heart* was obliged to pardon his brother [Lord Temple], it was *indemnified by revenge on* his sister's husband [Mr. Pitt]." Vol. ii., p. 174.

Lord Egremont—secretary of state:

"was a composition of *pride, ill-nature, avarice* and strict good breeding, with such infirmity of frame that he *could not speak truth* on the most trivial occasion."

The same spirit is exhibited by Walpole in the following strictures on other members of this cabinet:

"Lords *Gower, (Lord Chamberlain,* afterwards *Lord President,) Weymouth, (Secretary of State,)* and *Sandwich, (First Lord of the Admiralty,)*—all had parts, and never used them to any *good or creditable* purpose. The first had spirit enough to attempt any *crime;* the other two, though *notorious cowards,* were equally fitted to serve a prosperous court. And *Sandwich* had a predilection to guilt, if he could couple it with *artifice and treachery (ib.) Weymouth (Secretary of State)* neither had nor affected any solid virtue. He was too proud to court the people, and *too mean* not to choose to owe his preferments to the favor of the court or the cabals of faction. He wasted the whole night in drinking, and the morning in sleep, even when secretary of state. No kind of *principle* entered into his plan or practice, nor *shame* for want of it. His vanity made him trust that his abilities, by making him necessary, could reconcile intrigue and inactivity. His *timidity* was womanish, and the only thing he did not fear was the ill-opinion of mankind." Vol. iv., p. 240.

CHAPTER II.

Birth of the Prince of Wales—Policy of the Bute Cabinet—Treaty of Peace with Spain—Dissatisfaction of the Nation—Eloquence of Pitt and Fox—Resignation of Lord Bute—His Great Unpopularity—George Grenville becomes Premier—John Wilkes—His Singular Character—His Wit—His Contest with the Court—His Expulsion from Parliament—His Arrest for Libel—His "Essay on Woman"—His Intrepidity—His ultimate Triumph over the Ministers.

On the 12th of August, 1762, the monarch and nation were gratified by the birth of an heir to the throne. The infant prince was he who afterward became the magnificent and miserable George IV. The Archbishop of Canterbury alone was present on the occasion, and the child was baptized a few days afterward by that prelate, whom Horace Walpole wittily termed "the Right Rev. Midwife Thomas Secker."* The coronation of the king had been performed with great pomp and splendor on the 22d of September preceding. A singular and ominous incident occurred on this occasion. As the king was moving about with the crown on his head, the great diamond which formed its chief and most valuable ornament fell to the ground, and was not re-

---

* This singular and witty writer thus describes the incidents connected with the ceremony:

"Our next monarch was christened last night, George Augustus Frederick. The Princess (Dowager of Wales), the Duke of Cumberland and the Duke of Mecklenburgh, sponsors. The queen's bed, magnificent, and they say, in taste, was placed in the drawing-room, though she is not to see company in form, yet it looks as if they had intended people should have been there, as all who presented themselves were admitted, which were very few, for it had not been notified. I suppose to prevent too great a crowd; all I have heard named, beside those in waiting, were the Duchess of Queensberry, Lady Dalkeith, Mrs. Grenville, and about four other ladies." *See Walpole's Letters, &c.*

covered without great difficulty. That diamond might well be supposed to represent the jewel of America, which was soon destined to drop from the chaplet of his possessions. A more pleasing incident was the petition of the king that, while partaking the sacrament, he might be allowed to remove the diadem from his head as an indication of his piety and humility. This act would have been contrary to the established ceremonial of the occasion. The bishops however consulted; were greatly embarassed by the demand of the king; yet they finally concluded that it might be complied with without any detriment to the nation. A similar request on the part of the queen was refused, in consequence of the difficulty of removing the crown from her head without the assistance of her dressers. The various ceremonies of this occasion were exceedingly tedious, and darkness descended upon the gorgeous scene before they were completed. The magnificent Hall of Westminster was crowded by a vast and admiring multitude; and never before had the ancient and opulent nobility of England shone with more splendor. Among the innumerable crowd, it was afterward reported, was the exiled Pretender, who ventured thither *incognito* to witness a gorgeous ceremonial in which he should have been, according to the opinions of a portion of the nation, the principal personage. It is further said that the fallen prince was recognized by a nobleman; that he assured him that "he was present merely out of curiosity, and that the man who was the object of all that pomp and splendor was the one whom least he envied." The festivities continued in the capital during several days; the starving poets sang in fulsome numbers the glories of the youthful sovereign; and the nation seemed to have become a temporary model of satisfied amiability. A few discontents only, unwilling to appreciate the general joy, growled out their intense disgust at the "petticoat government" and the power of the licentious favorite, which then ruled the monarch and his cabinet. But the king was either incapable of perceiving the relation which had long subsisted between his mother and Lord Bute; or he was indifferent to the subject. If the former were the true state of the case, he furnished another evidence of the fact that those who are most deeply injured and disgraced by family outrages or dishonors, are oftentimes the last to discover the existence of the calamity which has befallen them.

It now became the policy of the Bute cabinet to conclude the war by a favorable peace. The prime minister thought it less difficult to retain the slender share of popularity which he possessed amid the tranquil scenes which a general amity would produce, than amid the trying vicissitudes of war. He accordingly gave secret intimations to the enemy that the renewal of negotiations for peace would be acceptable to the British government; and the King of Sardinia was solicited to act as mediator between the hostile powers. The courts of France and Spain were not unwilling to terminate a war in which the arms of Britain had been covered with glory, and in which conquest after conquest had followed in the wake of her victories. The steps of conciliation were so quickly taken that preliminaries of peace were signed and interchanged at Fontainebleau, in November, 1762, between the representatives of England, France, Spain and Portugal.

The proposed peace was utterly distasteful to the nation. They were elated by the victories which their arms had achieved, and the most sanguine hopes had been entertained in regard to the extent and splendor of future triumphs. They indulged in golden dreams in reference to the possession of the realms of Mexico and Peru, whose vast treasures and whose valuable territories they hoped to see united to the British crown. Notwithstanding this state of the public mind, Bute and his confederates persisted in completing the treaty. On the 25th of November parliament met, and the king informed them in a speech from the throne that the arrangements for peace had all been agreed upon, and only awaited the sanction of the Legislature, for their final and complete adoption.

The debate which ensued was one of the most violent which ever shook the British parliament. Lord Bute commenced the deliberations by setting forth in a clear and accurate manner the various provisions of the treaty which had been adopted. These provisions were as follows : The entire province of Canada was ceded to the English; together with all that portion of Louisiana which lay to the east of the Mississippi, the Cape Breton, and all the islands which studded the gulf and river of St. Lawrence. In the West Indies, the islands of Grenada, the Grenadines, Dominique, St. Vincent, and Tobago were also guaranteed to Britain. In Africa they were to possess Senegal, and in the East Indies, the coasts of Coromandel. The French monarch also acknowledged the supremacy of the British in Bengal, in the Carnatic and in the Decan; he agreed to restore Minorca, and demolish the fortifications and harbor of Dunkirk; he stipulated that Hanover and Hesse, and the fortresses of Cleves, Nesil and Guildiers should be evacuated by the French troops which at that time occupied them. The Spanish monarch guaranteed to England the full possession of the Eastern and Western Floridas, and all the Spanish possessions on the North American Continent to the east and south-east of the Mississippi. In return for all these vast and valuable concessions, the British cabinet promised to transfer to France the island of Belleisle; in Africa, the island of Goree; in the West Indies, Guadaloupe, Martinique, and St. Lucia; in the East Indies, Pondicherry and Chandernagore, the islands of St. Pierre and Miguelon; while Cuba, the Havana, and the Manillas were to be restored to the Spanish monarch. The terms of this treaty were in themselves by no means dishonorable or disadvantageous to the British nation.

But it was a sufficient objection to this treaty, both with the people and with the opposition, that it had been negotiated by the Bute cabinet. In order to carry the bill which approved it, it became necessary for the administration to put forth prodigious exertions. After Lord Bute had set forth the provisions of the treaty at length, he was answered and defended by all the great orators who flourished at that time in parliament. Some of these had been bought over by bribes which even Walpole himself would not have ventured to offer. Hundreds of members had been secretly closeted with Henry Fox, the able and unscrupulous Paymaster of the Forces; and had departed from his inner cabinet carrying in their pockets the exorbitant prices at which they had sold their integrity. It has been asserted that in this way the minister disbursed twenty-five thousand pounds in a single morning. Every resource of the government was employed to muster influence, eloquence and votes, on this momentous occasion, in support of the administration. When therefore the debate progressed, some prominent members supported the treaty from whom a different course of action had been anticipated. But still the conflict was manfully maintained by the opposition. Their chief reliance was on the influence and eloquence of Pitt. The discussion had continued several days, when the ex-minister, who was still suffering under a severe attack of gout, rose from his bed, had his limbs swathed in heavy wrappings of flannel, and with crutch in hand reached the chair which usually conveyed him to the house. His progress thither was accompanied by the shouts and acclamations of a great multitude. Having arrived, he was carried by his attendants into the house and placed within the bar. As may well be supposed, his appearance attracted universal attention; for he already began to be but the shadow of his former magnificent self. At the first opportunity he rose to speak. He declaimed three hours and a half against the treaty. But his declamation on this occasion was comparatively feeble, and showed little resemblance to the overwhelming and powerful rhetoric of his prime. His voice was feeble, and several times he was compelled to stop and have recourse to cordials. At length he sat down, and every hearer was convinced that the oratorical glory of the Great Commoner had passed away for ever.

His great rival Henry Fox then rose to reply. He answered the arguments of Pitt in a speech of two hours' duration, and clearly demonstrated the propriety, the profitableness, and the necessity of the treaty. Never had his manly declamation and vigorous, compact logic been better exhibited than on this occasion; and after he had concluded, the vote was taken. The long labors and skilful tactics of the ministry were rewarded by a signal victory. The treaty was sustained by an overwhelming majority.

The king, the court, the cabinet and their partisans, all exhibited the utmost exultation. George III. realized in this instance the fulfilment of the great principle which guided him, sometimes wisely and sometimes blindly, throughout his whole administration; he had preserved the *integrity of the empire.* The Princess Dowager exclaimed as soon as she heard the news: "Now indeed my son is really king." It was generally supposed that this triumph would secure to the favorite minister a long tenure of undisturbed possession of power. But the very next measure proposed by the cabinet, destroyed the popularity which the prestige of this victory had gained them. The expenses of the war had created an immense arrear of debt. It was necessary to devise some new method for reducing the interest; and among the expedients proposed by the Chancellor of the Exchequer was a tax of four shillings upon every hogshead of cider, to be paid by the manufacturer. The opposition eagerly seized this proposition to assail the ministry. The Cider-Land, especially Herefordshire and Worcestershire, were particularly incensed by this attack upon their peculiar interests. The city of London presented a petition against the bill at the bar of the House of Commons. But notwithstanding these and other indications of hostility to the measure, the tax was imposed; though in the House of Lords forty-three peers divided against it. This was destined to be the last triumph of the Bute cabinet; to achieve which, the same extreme processes of bribery and corruption had been adopted, which had been essential to the attainment of all the preceding triumphs of that detested minister. The whole nation was suddenly astounded, immediately after this event, with the news that Lord Bute had resigned.

It is not difficult to discover the reason which led to this unexpected result. It lies upon the surface, although the advocates of the fallen favorite ascribed many other causes for it than the real one. They indeed asserted that all his political purposes had been accomplished; and that by voluntarily retiring to private life he was willing to give his enemies an opportunity to prove and punish any crimes which they might lay to his charge. This was more plausible and complimentary than true. Bute was influenced by much more selfish motives in his retirement. He could not but be conscious that he had become the object of the detestation of the nation. He was the favorite lover of the Princess Dowager, and he was despised as all such creatures deserve to be. He was a Scotchman; and at that time the prejudice which existed in England against the Scotch, resembled in intensity and unreasonableness that which existed during the reign of William III. against the Dutch; and the promotion of Scotchmen to places of emolument and trust by the minister had increased the popular hatred against their name and nation. During Bute's administration, public caricatures, libels and pasquinades had been carried to an extreme of audacity which had never before been seen in England. The uniform symbol by which he was known and ridiculed was a great jack-boot, which was usually accompanied by a petticoat; and these were often hung upon a gallows, or consigned to the flames. Previous to the year 1763, all political libellers confined themselves to giving the initials of the names of their unfortunate victims. During the hated supremacy of Bute, the names of the monarch, of his amorous mother, of her favorite minister, and of his chief supporters were boldly and unscrupulously appended to the most abusive and obnoxious strictures.* It is reasonable to suppose that all this was very distasteful to a man who had lived until his forty-eighth year in the enjoyment of undisturbed repose and of unmingled respect. He was doubtless appalled at the overwhelming torrent of bitter invective and merciless ridicule which was directed upon his head. He found himself suddenly rendered the most unpopular minister who had ever directed the destinies of England. He could not possibly foresee where all this hostility might end. If he persisted in his line of policy, it might conduct him to an impeachment and even to the scaffold. So far as the gratification of

---

* A curious collection of the libels and caricatures of the day will be found in "Wright's History of England under the House of Hanover," Vol. i., *passim*.

his ambition was concerned, he had doubtless become fully satiated with the turbulent and ignominious splendors of place and power. He had ascended the pinnacle of human greatness; he had seated himself upon its most exalted eminence; and he had found that, at that dizzy elevation, tempests raged and whirlwinds blew around him with a degree of fearful violence utterly unknown in the calmer regions below. It is not to be wondered at, therefore, that he hastened to descend from a position, the dangers and miseries of which, could only be conceived of by those who had practically experienced them.

George Grenville succeeded to the post of prime minister. This statesman was the brother of Lord Temple, and the brother-in-law of Pitt. He was a man of narrow intellect, yet industrious, energetic, and perfectly at home amid the most intricate details of business. He was well acquainted with all the resources and the finances of the empire. He was also master of the whole system of the orders and privileges of the House of Commons. His speeches, though always tedious and dull, were often instructive, learned, and impressive. He was honest, but at the same time parsimonious and cautious. The same narrow and prudent thrift which characterized his private dealings, marked all his public measures. He was as unpopular with the multitude as misers generally are; yet he was as indifferent to public censure as was the most obscure and hardened among them. Having attained the first place in the administration, his grasping nature soon rendered him as avaricious of power as he had ever been of money.

An attempt was made at this time by the Duke of Cumberland to unite some of the discordant elements which warred within the bosom of the state, and centre them harmoniously in the administration. A special effort was made to induce Pitt to return to office. These exertions ended in complete failure; and that failure greatly increased the intensity of party rage. The press teemed with the most furious attacks on the government; and among the most offensive of all these, was a journal printed and published by John Wilkes termed the North Briton. Each number of this vile sheet was more scurrilous than its predecessor; until at length the forty-fifth number contained a personal and outrageous attack upon the king, which the court and the ministry thought it necessary to punish by a judicial proceeding. A general warrant was issued under the seal of Lord Halifax for the arrest of John Wilkes under the charge of uttering a seditious libel; and he was arrested late at night at his residence, on the 29th of April, 1763.

The character and history of this man, who was destined to play so distinguished a part in English history, has little to commend him to the admiration of his countrymen or of posterity. He was born at London in 1727, and was the son of a respectable distiller. By a course of unexampled profligacy he had at an early age ruined his fortune and his reputation. He had received a thorough education, he possessed agreeable manners, and had married in 1749 an heiress named Mead, much older than himself, from whom he afterward separated. He was the *habitué* of all the fashionable houses of dissipation in the capital. He associated with men of fortune, without possessing the necessary means to indulge in their expensive pleasures. His wit was remarkable for its originality and its coarseness; and his admirable convivial qualities constantly led him into scenes of ruinous and excessive dissoluteness. To repair his broken fortunes he had applied to the ministers on several occasions for promotion to office. He besought Pitt, when in power, to bestow upon him a seat at the Board of Trade. He afterward endeavored to obtain from Lord Bute, the appointment of ambassador to Constantinople. Later still, his application for the post of Governor of Canada was pressed upon Grenville with great earnestness. In all these ambitious schemes he met with a complete and ignominious failure; a result which was owing chiefly to the desperate degradation of his private character. In his person he was so hideously ugly, that no caricaturist could do justice to his horrible squint and his demoniacal grin. In spite of all these disadvantages, he could boast of many conquests in the field of amorous adventure. Having been defeated in every other effort, he obtained at length a seat in parliament, and sat for the borough of Aylesbury. But he broke down utterly as an orator, and was insignificant and unnoticed among the great statesmen of the nation. In two capacities alone could this desperate and shameless adventurer excel. He ranked as the most unbridled, profane, and agreeable rake in the metropolis. He was also able to render himself the most dangerous and formidable libeller in the country, by using and abusing the then undefined and uncertain license of the press. The former had preeminence he already possessed; and he entertained no fears that that preëminence would be endangered by any successful rival. He therefore determined at this crisis to try what his other, and scarcely more respectable *forte*, might accomplish for the advancement of his ruined interests, and for the elevation of his dishonored name. This was the purpose of the establishment of the North Briton Newspaper, a number of which caused the issue of the warrant against his person.

The only species of talent which Wilkes possessed was that of sarcastic and ribald wit. In this questionable field he was unrivalled; and some of his repartees which have escaped oblivion indicate a high degree of ability. One or two instances will clearly establish this position. Lord Sandwich inquired of him contemptuously, whether he thought he should die by the halter, or by a certain disease. He instantly replied: "That depends upon whether I embrace your Lordship's principles or your mistress." When the profane, selfish, and unprincipled Lord Thurlow exclaimed in parliament, for the purpose of winning the favor of the court: "If I forget my sovereign may my God forget me!" Wilkes, who was seated near him answered, with that horrid squint and demoniac grin directed toward him. "Forget you? No, he will see you damned first." The usual conversation of this unequalled political pimp was made up of blasphemy, indecency, and ribaldry. Every thing which he said and did partook of this foul character. Thus when writing to Junius, he declared that the private letters of the Great Unknown "stirred up his spirits like a kiss from Chloe."*

---

* Woodfall's Junius, i., 325.

Among the many vices of Wilkes cowardice could not be numbered. His arrest furnished him with a most favorable opportunity for commencing, on a grand scale, the role of a demagogue, and defender of the rights of the press and of the people. Accordingly, immediately after his committal to the Tower, he made application by counsel to the Court of Common Pleas for a writ of Habeas Corpus. The writ was granted, directed to the constable of the tower, and made returnable the next day in Westminster Hall. After the pleadings were filed and argument made on both sides, the judges held the case under advisement until the sixth of May. On that day the Lord Chief Justice Pratt, afterwards Lord Camden, gave the opinion of the court, to the effect that the commitment of Wilkes was legal; that the warrant of the Secretary of State, however, was not superior in force to that of a justice of the peace; that it was not necessary to specify in the warrant the particular passages in the North Briton which contained the alleged libel; and that the privilege of parliament *was* violated in the arrest of the person of the defendant, at that time a member of it. The Chief Justice further held that the privilege of Parliament could only be forfeited by the crimes of treason, felony, and breach of the peace. Wilkes was then discharged from arrest; but he was forthwith prosecuted by the Attorney-General, and dismissed from his command as colonel of the Buckinghamshire militia.

These incidents were but the beginning of troubles. Wilkes refused to make an answer to the information filed against him, by the king's Attorney-General; and when Parliament convened in November, 1763, he prepared to enter a formal complaint for the breach of privilege made in his person. He was anticipated in this step by the promptness of Mr. Grenville, who informed the House that he had a message to deliver from the king. The message was immediately read. It set forth that his majesty having received information that Wilkes, a member of the House, was the author of a seditious and dangerous libel, had caused him to be apprehended therefor; that he had been discharged by the Court of Common Pleas on the ground of his privilege as a member of Parliament; and that the king, desirous that public justice should not thus be eluded, had ordered all the papers relating to the matter to be laid on the table of the House, and he invited their attention to the subject. A violent debate ensued. The principle for which Wilkes contended found many able advocates among the members. At last, however, a vote being taken, a great majority decided that number Forty-Five of the North Briton contained a false, scandalous, and malicious libel, manifestly tending to alienate the affections of the people from his Majesty, and excite them to traitorous insurrections. They further ordered the paper to be burnt by the common hangman.

Wilkes was not intimidated in the least by these measures. He boldly brought forward his complaint of breach of privilege by the imprisonment of his person, and the seizure of his papers. Before this subject could be discussed by the House, Wilkes was dangerously wounded in a duel with Mr. Martin, a member for Camelford; and the matter was postponed till his recovery. On the 23d of November the king's message was taken into consideration. The House resolved, after a full discussion, by a majority of a hundred and twenty-five votes, that the privilege of parliament did *not* extend to a case of libel; and the peers addressed a memorial to his majesty setting forth their detestation of the arts of the demagogue, and their devotion to his person. Among the few eminent members who opposed these decisions was Pitt; who contended that they tended to abridge the freedom and independence of parliament, by subjecting every member who did not vote with the minister to the dread of imprisonment.

When the day arrived for the public burning of Wilkes' paper, a great riot occurred; the paper was rescued from the hands of the hangman; the peace officers were attacked; a jack-boot and petticoat were committed to the flames; and the sheriffs placed in great danger of their lives. The parliament immediately resolved that the rioters should be punished as disturbers of the peace; that their conduct was dangerous to public liberty; and that the sheriffs and officers deserved the thanks of the country. Notwithstanding all this adverse influence, Wilkes recovered damages to the amount of a thousand pounds against Lord Halifax for the seizure of his papers, after a trial of fifteen hours' duration. Chief Justice Pratt presided, and in his charge to the jury he instructed them that general warrants, such as that issued in the first instance against Wilkes, were illegal. On the other hand Parliament decreed, on the 29th of January, 1764, after a vehement and protracted debate, that Wilkes should be expelled from his seat in the House. On the same day a singular development was made in the House of Peers. The Earl of Sandwich rose and informed the members that John Wilkes had outraged religion and decency by printing a book of the most scandalous and licentious character, entitled an Essay on Woman; to which notes had been appended which were falsely ascribed to a learned and right reverend prelate, Warburton, Bishop of Gloucester. The facts in reference to this book were curious. Wilkes wrote it, intending it as a parody on Pope's Essay on Man. He had printed it at a private press; only a small number of copies had been struck off; and these were intended for the boon companions of his licentious and dissolute hours. The prime minister had heard of its existence, and had obtained a copy by heavily bribing the printer, which he laid on the table of the House. The instrument used in this trickery was Lord March, one of the most depraved and unscrupulous companions of Wilkes himself.

The unfairness of the means thus employed by the government to injure Wilkes, rendered him what he chiefly desired to become, a persecuted man, and a representative of popular liberty. The steps taken against him by Parliament only added to the popularity of this vile demagogue, who really despised liberty as much as he contemned religion and decency. He was censured by the House, and finally outlawed. Thus after a fierce and protracted struggle, it remained a drawn battle between the combatants. The Parliament declared general warrants to be illegal, and Wilkes had recovered damages for his arrest. But his paper had been stigmatized as a libel, he had been deprived

9*

of his military rank, he had lost his seat in the House, and he was in fact a disgraced and ruined man; to whom the empty adulation of the multitude could be no equivalent for the torrent of execration and contumely from the intelligent and estimable portion of the nation, which overwhelmed him.*

* See *the Correspondence of the late George Wilkes with his Friends, printed from the Original Manuscripts; with a Memoir of his Life. By John Almon.* 6 vols. London, 1805.

CHAPTER III.

Financial Affairs of the Nation—Resolution to impose Stamp Duties on the American Colonies—A Council of Regency Appointed—Death of the Duke of Cumberland—The Rockingham Ministry—Inefficiency of this Cabinet—First appearance of Burke in Parliament—Dispute with the American Colonies—Discussions in reference to their Taxation—Arguments advanced on both sides of the Question—Return of William Pitt to Power.

The financial difficulties of the nation still engaged the attention of the prime minister. The annual revenues were insufficient in the year 1765, to meet the annual expenses of the government. Therefore it was that George Grenville felt the necessity of devising some new sources of income; and his sharp but contracted intellect discovered an expedient, of the real importance of which he had not the remotest conception, but which was the most decisive and momentous in its results ever proposed or executed by any statesman. It occurred to him that the British colonies in America should be taxed in order to increase the home revenue. This was a measure, the boldness of which had appalled even the resolute heart of Robert Walpole, who declared during his ·administration, that it was a project far too hazardous for him to venture upon.

The plan adopted by which such taxation might be imposed upon the subjects of Britain in America, was that of *Stamp Duties*. It required that the innumerable certificates, dockets, clearances, and affidavits, used in the transactions of commerce between the two countries, must, in order to be valid, be printed on stamped paper; and for that stamped paper an exorbitant price was demanded. Nor was the increased expense the only obnoxious feature in this new expedient of the minister. The right therein asserted by England to tax the colonies at her will for her own exclusive benefit, without allowing them the right of representation in the parliament, involved a principle of oppression which would not only be pernicious in itself, but would inevitably lead to other and greater extremes of tyranny, to which no possible limit could be set. As soon as information reached the colonies of this proposed imposition, many petitions and memorials were sent by them to the sovereign, denying the right of the mother-country to levy such a tax, and denouncing the measure as unjust and inexpedient in itself. But all the arguments used were met by the assertion, that it was but proper that the colonies should contribute their share to the general expenses of the empire; that large sums of money had been frequently voted by parliament to the colonies, to indemnify them for the losses which they had sustained in the wars which had been waged against the enemies of Britain on the American continent; and that something was due in return for the protection and assistance which had been received from the mother country.*

While this momentous theme was being agitated in both continents, several domestic incidents of great importance occurred to the person and the family of George III. The king began to give, at this period, the first temporary indications of that mental disease to which he afterward became entirely

* In the month of February, 1756, the sum of £115,000 was voted by Parliament, as a free gift and reward to the colonies of New England, New York, and Jersey, for their past services; and as an encouragement to continue to exert themselves with vigor; May, 1757, £50,000 was in like manner voted to the Carolinas; and in 1758, £41,000 to Massachusetts and Connecticut. April, 1709, £200,000 were voted as a compensation to the respective colonies in North America—March, 1760, £200,000—1761, £200,000—1762, £133,000—in all, one million seventy-two thousand pounds. Exclusive, however, of these indemnifications, and of the extraordinary supplies granted in the different colonial assemblies, a debt of above two millions and a half had been incurred by America during the war; and this debt was far from being as yet liquidated. But it might be inferred from the conduct of the ministry, that the most trivial revenue *extorted* from America was deemed preferable to the largest sums freely and voluntarily granted. *Belsham's Memoirs of George III.*

subject. The heir apparent was still in his minority, being only two years old, and no public provision had been made to carry on the government in case a total aberration of the intellect of the sovereign occurred. In April, 1765, the matter was brought before the House of Peers at the instance of the monarch himself. A bill was accordingly introduced into that body, framed in accordance with the plan of the Regency Act of the Twenty-fourth of George II. empowering the king to appoint the queen or any other member of the royal family resident in Great Britain, as regent until the heir apparent should have attained the age of eighteen years. The *Council* of the Regency were to include the Dukes of York and Gloucester, Princes Henry Frederic and Frederic William, William Augustus, Duke of Cumberland, and the cabinet ministers. By this means the most pressing emergency of the crown was provided for. Subsequently the name of the Princess Dowager was added to the list of the Council, in consequence of the strenuous representations of her friends in the government. The princess was obnoxious to Grenville and to the cabinet which he ruled. The effort which he had made to exclude her from the regency offended the king; and had it been possible to effect an arrangement with Pitt at this crisis, he would have supplanted Grenville in the premiership. But the secret negotiations which were opened on the subject failed.

The other domestic incident of importance was the death of the Duke of Cumberland, uncle of George III. The health of the favorite son of Caroline had long been failing. He had been suffering from a paralytic stroke, and had nearly become blind. On the perilous day of Dettingen, he received a wound which had never been entirely cured. His military talents were respectable; and the triumph of Culloden which he tarnished by unparalleled cruelties to the Scotch had made him the lasting favorite of the English nation. To him had fallen the rare good fortune, to have fought and won on that day one of the decisive battles of the world. He enjoyed the singular lot of receiving from his countrymen the constant and ambiguous title of "the Duke;" a peculiarity which has characterized but three Englishmen—Marlborough, Wellington, and himself. His nature was cruel and fierce; and he was feared much more than he was loved. On one occasion his nephew, afterward George III., entered his apartment, which was so completely hung around with all kinds of deadly weapons, that it very much resembled a miniature arsenal. He took down a sword to exhibit it to his visitor. The latter turned pale, fearing lest the purpose of his rude uncle might be, to dispatch him after the example of a certain Duke of Gloucester, of bloody and savage memory. Yet the Duke possessed some generous traits. Having once lost his pocketbook at the Newmarket races, he remarked to a half-pay officer who had found it, and brought it to him : " Pray keep it, Sir ; if you had not found it, its contents would before this have been in the hands of the blacklegs." On the 31st of October, 1765, when at his town-house in Grosvenor Street, he was suddenly seized with a fit of suffocation. The Duke of Newcastle and Lord Albemarle were present. One of his valets attempted to bleed him. He quietly remarked: "It is all over," and immediately expired. Thus passed away the only member of the House of Hanover in England, who ever possessed the slightest claim to any superiority of intellect or elevation of soul. He died in his forty-sixth year.

One of the last acts performed by the Duke was his introduction of the Rockingham ministry. At the earnest request of the king—who had learned to detest Grenville, his meanness, his narrow-mindedness and his everlasting speeches, beyond endurance—he had undertaken and performed this task. The Marquis of Rockingham was a person of great probity, of respectable talents, of amiable manners, and of excellent character. He was indeed no orator ; and never rose to address the house on any occasion, even after years of experience and practice, without a degree of nervous agitation which he could not conceal. His most eminent qualities were his prudence, and his familiar acquaintance with the wants and resources of the empire. Mr. Dowdeswell was appointed Chancellor of the Exchequer, Lord Egmont became first Lord of the Admiralty, and the Duke of Grafton, a young nobleman afterward destined to an ignoble immortality by the powerful but partial pen of Junius, became Keeper of the Seals. General Conway was made Secretary of State; and to him was intrusted the lead in the House of Commons.

Not one of these ministers possessed any oratorical ability. Every impartial and intelligent observer supposed that a single blow from the powerful arm of the great Pitt, would crush them at once and for ever. The whole of them combined in one, would have been impotent before his tremendous power. They seem to have been aware of this fact; and Rockingham exhibited his usual prudence in providing a protector against the apprehended assaults of the Titan, by enlisting the aid of another giant, younger, more learned, more eloquent, and now more energetic than himself. Some time before this period a young Irishman had arrived in London for the purpose of seeking his fortune. He was poor; and his first resource was very naturally an application for employment to the booksellers. His compositions exhibited such rare superiority, such splendor of diction, such depth of argument, and such richness of imagination, that he escaped the usual fate of applicants both great and small under such circumstances, and his productions were accepted and published. His fame extended widely and rapidly and he became in a short time one of the most eminent men of letters in the metropolis, the associate and rival of Samuel Johnson. Nor were his talents confined to mere literary ability. The young adventurer possessed eloquence of a high order, and all the abilities which were essential to constitute a statesman. He had fortunately become known to the new minister, who fully appreciated his extraordinary merits. As soon as Lord Rockingham entered the cabinet, he appointed this " wild Irishman," named O'Bourke —afterward famous throughout the civilized world as Edmund Burke—as his private secretary, and forthwith secured his election to a seat in Parliament.

The first measure of importance which engaged the attention of the new government was the impending dispute with the American Colonies. The subject was somewhat new to British statesmen, and three opinions prevailed among them in reference to it. One party were in favor of enforcing the Stamp Act by all the rigors of military power. They contended that the government possessed ample authority to impose whatever taxes they decreed necessary, throughout the whole British Empire; and that British subjects everywhere were bound, on pain of treason, to yield implicit obedience to the requisition. They further held that it was in the highest degree expedient to enforce this tax. In America, there were young and vigorous states which had been planted, nurtured, and protected by the mother country. They were increasing day by day in wealth, influence, and prosperity. They were abundantly able to bear the light and easy burden of taxation which had been imposed upon them. England had been greatly embarrassed by the immense expenses of the war which had recently been terminated; and the colonies had derived important advantages from a conflict, from the cost of which they had been exempt. It was high time, therefore, that they should be made to share a portion of the general burdens. This was the opinion of the king and of the court.

Another party held that, though the Act imposing the tax lay within the constitutional competence of parliament, it was most unwise and inexpedient to enforce it. They believed that the British King and his Legislature had power to pass any law they pleased, and that law would be valid. They might, if they chose, abolish the most valuable rights of the subject; they might repeal the Habeas Corpus Act, and the Toleration Act; and such repeal would possess all the force of constitutional law. In this view the taxation of the American Colonies was legal; but they contended that it was at that time inexpedient. The loyalty of the colonists was not as strong as it might be; a powerful party among them was already hostile to British supremacy; it would be impossible to enforce the act upon three millions of subjects against their will; and it was much wiser to repeal it at once with a good grace. These views were held by Lord Rockingham, and defended by his adherents.*

* The debates which occurred in the British Parliament on this question as

A third party, headed by William Pitt, contended that Parliament was not competent to tax the colonies, and that the Act was in itself null and void. This position he defended with great eloquence and force. The chief argument which may be advanced in support of this position, is based on the principle that in justice there can be no taxation without representation. However true the position may be in general, that the British Legislature was competent to pass laws taxing all British subjects, that position is qualified by the single restriction, that those subjects thus taxed should be represented in the national Legislature. They should be permitted to have a voice in reference to the adoption of measures, the expenses and the consequences of which they were expected to share. Having had no part in the councils of the home government, no influence in the adoption or rejection of the policy pursued, either in reference to themselves or to others, they should be free from all responsibility on the subject.

These were the views entertained by the colonists themselves. The Stamp Act was permitted by the British government to retain the force of law; but when the day appointed for its operation to commence arrived, the people displayed the utmost indignation against it. The colors of the ships in the American harbors were hung at half-mast. The muffled bells of the churches sounded forth mournful peals. Copies of the Act were burnt by the populace. Cargoes of the stamped paper were taken from the ships, and consigned to the flames. The houses of those who had been appointed to sell the stamps were assailed by mobs; and justices of the peace gave notice that they would regard the use of such paper in their judicial proceedings as invalid. On the 1st of November, 1768, the day appointed for the use of the stamps to commence throughout the colonies, scarcely a sheet of it could be found. The provincial assemblies met and

---

well as on all others, are to be found in their greatest fulness and accuracy in "The Parliamentary History of England from the Earliest Period to the Year 1803," in thirty-six volumes, octavo, London. For the proceedings in reference to the Stamp Act, and its Repeal, see Vol. xvi., published in 1813, p. 162, *seq.*

passed resolutions condemning the Act, and commanding all good citizens to denounce and resist their introduction. The whole continent had risen in arms against the law.

The administration soon became convinced that it was utterly impossible to enforce the Stamp Act in America, and a bill was eventually introduced by the ministers for its repeal. Both Pitt and Burke, the one the setting, the other the rising, sun of British parliamentary eloquence of that day, exerted themselves in favor of the repeal. The ministers succeeded by a large majority; and the king was constrained reluctantly, and with a very bad grace, to approve the bill, and give it his assent. The repeal of the Stamp Act was the principal measure accomplished by the Rockingham ministry. That upright and estimable nobleman received his dismissal from the cabinet immediately after the adjournment of Parliament. He was succeeded by the "Great Commoner" who had on several former occasions rescued England from disgrace and misfortune. Yet his return to power, and his elevation to the peerage at this crisis, destroyed in a great measure his popularity with the nation; for Lord Chatham never became to them the marvellous hero and unrivalled favorite which William Pitt had so long and so deservedly been.*

* See *A History of the Rt. Hon. William Pitt, Earl of Chatham, containing his Speeches in Parliament, &c., with an account of the Principal Events and Persons of his Time.* By Rev. Francis Thackeray, A. M. 2 vols. 4to. London, 1827. Gerard Hamilton, of "Single Speech" memory, expressed in one admirable sentence the real character of Pitt as a statesman and a minister : "For those who want merely to keep a subordinate employment, Mr. Pitt is certainly the best minister in the world; but for those who wish to have a share in the rule and government of the country, he is the worst." *Correspondence of William Pitt, Earl of Chatham.* Edited by *William Stanhope Taylor, Esq., and Capt. J. H. Pringle.* 3 vols. 8vo. London, 1838.

CHAPTER IV.

Lord Chatham's Inefficiency—His Illness—His Absurd Conduct—His Singular Seclusion—Inflexibility of George III.—Resignation of Lord Chatham—The Parliamentary Election of 1768—Renewal of the Contest with Wilkes—His Repeated Election to, and Expulsion from, Parliament—His Ultimate Defeat—Charter of the British East India Company—The Letters of Junius—Intense Excitement produced by their Appearance.

THE nation was destined to be grievously disappointed in the results produced by the last introduction of Lord Chatham to the highest and most responsible seat in the government. The sagacity, the consistency, and the resistless energy which had formerly rendered him the salvation and glory of England, now appeared to have forsaken him. A new project was set on foot for the taxation of the American Colonies. Charles Townshend, Chancellor of the Exchequer, seems to have been one of the prime movers on this occasion; for he boasted in the House of Commons " that he knew how to draw a revenue from the Colonies without giving them offence." He announced his new project in the cabinet. Mr. Grenville and General Conway, the latter at that time Secretary of State, approved of it. It is probable that Lord Bute, still the favorite of the Princess Dowager, was the secret, yet most active, originator of this new plan of extortion. In March, 1767, its efficiency and expediency were discussed and sustained in the cabinet; but the continued absence of Lord Chatham from their deliberations, which occurred at this period, was the chief reason why the subject was even proposed and entertained. The bill in question imposed duties on glass, tea, paper, and painter's colors, imported from Great

Britain into the colonies. This measure was supposed to be less obnoxious from the fact that port duties had before this period been exacted for the purpose of commercial regulation. This was particularly the case in reference to an act passed in the sixth year of the reign of George II. The same power which enabled Parliament to impose duties in the one case, it was asserted, rendered the act valid in the other; and no objection was apprehended by the home government on the part of the distant colonies. Had Lord Chatham been able or willing at this crisis, to take an active part in the measures of a government of which he was nominally the head, this absurd opinion would have been refuted, and the pernicious measures resulting from it would have been avoided.

But the great minister was afflicted at this period by a singular and a somewhat mysterious disease, which rendered him little more than a mere puppet; and secluded him wholly from the nation, and even from his associates in the cabinet. A difference of opinion has always existed in reference to this subject. Some have asserted that the whole matter was a mere pretence and fraud, intended to excuse him from the labors and the responsibilities of the government at a dangerous and critical crisis; that while he clung to the shadow and the glory of place and power, he meanly avoided its perils and its miseries. Others contended that at this time the great genius of Chatham became shrouded in a total eclipse; that he became utterly deranged; and that he secluded himself, or was secluded, to escape the shame and the disgrace which such a calamity entailed. Neither of these suppositions possessed the least shadow of truth or probability.

The fact was, that the chronic gout with which Lord Chatham had been afflicted during the whole of his life, at this period assumed a wandering and ill-declared condition. It fell upon his nerves, and although it left him in the full possession of his mental powers, it rendered the exercise of them dangerous and pernicious in the highest degree. The effect of this peculiar nervous state has been exhibited in the lives of many other distinguished men of genius. Cowper's muse would only sing at stated intervals and under peculiar influences. Collins and Thompson also suffered under these inequalities of the intellectual faculties; and the immortal strains of Milton never flowed between the autumnal and vernal equinox; but his mind became genial and creative only when the temperature of spring revived all nature, and made the groves and valleys musical with the songs of birds. Thus a temporary inaptitude fell at this period upon the mind of Chatham. Even the writing of an ordinary letter overpowered him. Lady Chatham has herself described his singular condition in a letter to one of his most intimate friends.* "The state of extreme weakness and illness in which my Lord finds himself, from the gout not being fixed, obliges him to beg leave of your Lordship to acknowledge by my hand, the honor of your much obliging letter." He continued in this state during the period of a year and a half. In October, 1768, he had an interview with the Duke of Grafton, after frequent and earnest solicitation. Of that interview, and the impression produced by it, the Duke said: "I must confess, from the length of my Lord's illness, and the manner in which the gout is dispersed upon his habit, that I believe there is but small prospect of his ever being able to enter much into business again.†" The ministry, though deprived of the benefit of his talents, still possessed and valued the influence of his name; but he excluded them totally from personal interviews. Even the ordinary correspondence of the Earl devolved upon Lady Chatham. Both the king and the cabinet regarded the event of his resignation as a great calamity; and hence, though he was a mere cipher in the government, he was nominally at its head. It is curious to observe how earnestly the ministers implored him to grant one of them an interview; and the piteous manner in which he declined. The Duke of Grafton declared in one of his letters: "If I could be allowed but a few minutes to wait on you, it would give me

---

* To Lord Camden, 23d of January, 1768. *Correspondence of William Pitt.* Edited by *Taylor and Pringle.* London, 1838. Vol. iii., p. 317.
† *Correspondence of Lord Chatham*, Vol. iii., p. 337.

great relief; for the moment is too critical for your Lordship's advice and direction not to be necessary." The enfeebled statesman replied by the hand of his wife: "Lord Chatham, still unable to write, begs leave to assure the Duke of Grafton of his best respects, and, at the same time, to lament that the continuation of his illness reduces him to the painful necessity of most earnestly entreating his grace to pardon him, if he begs to be allowed to decline the honor of the visit which the Duke has so kindly proposed." On a subsequent occasion Chatham responded to a similar proposition: "He implores the Duke of Grafton to be persuaded that nothing less than impossibility prevents him from seeing him. The first moment health and strength return, Lord Chatham will humbly request permission to renew, at his majesty's feet, all the sentiments of duty and most devoted attachment."

At length the cabinet became desperate in their inability to extricate themselves from their difficulties, and the king was induced to address an autograph letter to his favorite minister on the state of affairs. The royal writer said: "No one has more cautiously avoided writing to you than myself, during your late indisposition; but the moment is so extremely critical, that I cannot possibly delay it any longer. By the letter you received yesterday from the Duke of Grafton, you must perceive the anxiety he and the President at present labor under. The Chancellor is very much in the same situation. This is equally owing to the majority in the House of Lords, amounting on the Friday only to six and on the Tuesday to three, though I made two of my brothers vote on both those days; and to the great coldness shown those three ministers by Lord Shelburne, whom they as well as myself, imagine to be rather a secret enemy; the avowed enmity of Mr. Townshend; and the resolution of Lieutenant-general Conway to retire, though without any view of entering into faction.

"My firmness is not dismayed by these unpleasant appearances: for, from the hour you entered into office, I have uniformly relied on your firmness to act in defiance to that hydra faction which has never appeared to the height it now does, till within these few weeks. Though your relations, the Bedfords and the Rockinghams are joined, with intention to storm my closet, yet if I was mean enough to submit, they own they would not join in forming an administration; therefore nothing but confusion could be obtained.

"I am strongly of opinion with the answer you sent the Duke of Grafton; but, by a note I have received from him, I fear I cannot keep him above a day, unless you would see him and give him encouragement. Your duty and affection for my person, your own honor, call on you to make an effort: five minutes' conversation with you would raise his spirits, for his heart is good; mine, I thank Heaven, wants no rousing: my love to my country, as well as what I owe to my own character and to my family, prompt me not to yield to faction. Be firm, and you will find me amply ready to take as active a part as the hour seems to require. Though none of my ministers stand by me, I cannot truckle." *

In response to this urgent letter from the royal hand the afflicted statesman answered: " Lord Chatham most humbly begs leave to lay himself with all duty at the king's feet, and fearing, lest he may not have rightly apprehended his Majesty's most gracious commands, humbly entreats his Majesty to permit him to say, that seeing the Duke of Grafton to-morrow morning he understands it not to be his Majesty's pleasure that he should attend his Majesty any part of the day to-morrow. He is unhappily obliged to confess that the honor and weight of such an audience would have been more than he could sustain in his present extreme weakness of nerves and spirit."

One would naturally suppose that such a letter would have excited the royal pity, and that a minister so desperately afflicted

---

* This remarkable letter is inserted at length, because it throws a clear and convincing light not only upon the estimate in which the King held the character and services of Chatham; but also because it reveals the state of the King's mind, the force of faction, the dismay of the ministers, the dissensions of the cabinet, and the miseries which often attend the possession of the most coveted boons of high rank, extensive authority, and illustrious name.

and enervated would have been permitted at last to rest in peace. But such was not the fact. Several days afterward, the difficulties of the cabinet having increased, the king again applied to Chatham, to lay before him a plan by which the government might be extricated from its embarrassments. The persecuted and unhappy statesman answered by the hand of his wife: "Lord Chatham, totally incapable, from an increase of illness, to use his pen, most humbly begs to lay himself with all duty and submission at the king's feet, and with unspeakable affection again to represent to his Majesty the most unhappy and utter disability which his present state of health as yet continues to lay him under; and once more most humbly to implore compassion and pardon from his Majesty for the cruel situation which still deprives him of the possibility of activity, and of proving to his Majesty the truth of an unfeigned zeal, in the present moment rendered useless." This pitiful reply, the spirit of which is so utterly craven, and unworthy of any being possessing the human form, especially of one having the mental superiority of Lord Chatham, seems at last to have melted the heart, and excited the sympathy, of the obdurate and headstrong monarch; who ended his persecutions by prescribing a physician for his afflicted minister.

It is evident, that during this mysterious interval Chatham was not insane, as was generally supposed, for several reasons. His colleagues addressed him letters, as to a perfectly sane person. The answers which they received in reply were evidently the production of a person in the full possession of his faculties. When his illness was greatest he wrote a perfectly rational letter to George III. with his own hand. At the same period he twice held personal interviews with one of his colleagues in the ministry, in which he displayed no evidence whatever of mental derangement.

At length, after nearly two years spent in seclusion and sickness, the health of the prime minister still remained feeble, and his capacity for mental effort utterly suspended. In October, 1768, he delivered himself from the anomalous nature of his position by resigning. The death of Mr. Townshend had taken place some time previous to this event; and Lord North became Chancellor of the Exchequer in his stead. The Duke of Grafton also resigned at a later date, when Lord North was transferred to the post of First Lord of the Treasury. Thomas Townshend succeeded Lord North as Paymaster of the Forces. Thus did the Great Commoner pass away for the last time from that high place which he had once occupied with such unrivalled splendor and celebrity. He survived his last resignation of office for ten years. His release from its burdens and responsibilities seemed to operate as a charm upon his health. He soon began to recover; and in a few months we again behold him in the House of Peers, displaying a degree of eloquence against the measures of a short-sighted and pernicious ministry which, though only the shadow of what his oratorical exhibitions once had been, still surpassed and overwhelmed all his rivals.*

---

* Lord Chatham was the favorite of his countrymen in his own day, and the admiration of succeeding generations; but it is curious to observe the strictures passed upon his character by that sarcastic and sagacious critic, Horace Walpole, who, in his celebrated "Memoirs of the Reign of George III.," has thus expressed himself in reference to different periods of the life of this hero:

"Lord Chatham had already commenced that extraordinary scene of seclusion of himself which he afterwards carried to an excess that passed, and no wonder, for a long access of *frenzy*." P. 342.

"The *mad situation* to which Lord Chatham had reduced himself." *Ib.*, p. 402.

"The *pride* and *folly* of Lord Chatham." *Ib.*, p. 402.

"The *wildness* of Lord Chatham baffled all policy." *Ib.*, p. 416.

"The *madness* or *mad conduct* of Lord Chatham." Vol. iii., p. 67.

"Lord Chatham's wild actions of passion and scorn." *Ib.*, p. 435.

"The Chancellor Camden had given many hints of his friend's *frenzy*." Vol. iii., p. 251.

"As if there were dignity in *folly*, and magic in *perverseness*—as if the way to govern mankind was to insult their understandings—the conduct of Lord Chatham was the *very reverse of common sense*, and made up of such undissembled scorn of all the world, that his friends could not palliate it, nor his enemies be blamed for resolving it into *madness*. He was scarce lame, and even paraded through the town in a morning to take the air; yet he neither went to the king, nor suffered any of the ministers [*his colleagues*] to come to him." Vol. ii., p. 426.

"Lord Chatham might have given firmness and almost tranquillity to the country; might have gone farther towards recruiting our finances than any rea-

The general election which took place in 1768 to supply vacancies in parliament, was characterized by unusual disorder. The current price of boroughs was greatly increased by the profuse expenditure of money exhibited by the ambitious and wealthy *nabobs* who, having returned from Hindostan with vast fortunes, desired to obtain seats and influence in the British Legislature. So desperate were the contests for seats that many opulent candidates were utterly ruined. The abuses which prevailed were carried to their utmost extremes in the county of Middlesex; and from that place the notorious Wilkes was returned, after a contest of unequalled violence and bitterness. This demagogue had been outlawed for his contempt of court, in not appearing to answer a previous charge in Westminster Hall. He had remained on the continent during several years. At length he returned to London, immediately before the election, and appearing publicly at Guildhall, had first offered himself as the popular candidate to the inhabitants of the metropolis. He proclaimed himself the champion of free speech, of a free press, and of the unrestricted rights of the people. In London, however, he was ignominiously defeated. He was not discouraged by this untoward event; but immediately offered himself to the electors of Middlesex. Here he obtained a decisive majority, and the exultation of the populace was unbounded. They paraded the streets, illuminated their houses, and insulted the chief magistrate Harley, in consequence of his known repugnance to the demagogue.

This triumph was at the same time accompanied by a mortifying defeat. On the suits which had been previously instituted against Wilkes he was condemned to suffer two years imprisonment, to pay a fine of a thousand pounds, and give security for his good behavior for seven years. The populace rescued

sonable man could have expected; but, alas! his talents were not adequate to that task. The multiplication-table did not admit of being treated as epic, and Lord Chatham had but that one style. Whether *really out of his senses*, or conscious how much the *mountebank* had concurred to make the great man, he plunged deeper and deeper into retreat, and left the nation a prey to faction and to insufficient persons that he had chosen for his coadjutors." Vol. ii., p. 438.

him from the hands of the officers, as they were conducting him to prison, and then carried him in triumph through the city. Wilkes afterward surrendered himself to the officers of the crown, and went to prison. When Parliament subsequently met, he was expelled from the House by an overwhelming majority; although the demagogue mustered not a few ardent and able advocates among the members. A new writ was issued for the holding of another election in Middlesex, and Wilkes was again returned by a still greater majority. The house was now placed in a critical dilemma. If they persisted in their course they might endanger the tranquillity of the nation, and the security of the government. If they receded, they would incur universal contempt. After considerable deliberation, the House resolved that " Mr. Wilkes having been once expelled, was incapable of sitting in the same Parliament, and that the election was therefore void." A third writ was immediately issued, and Wilkes was a third time chosen. In these proceedings we have a remarkable and amusing illustration of English obstinacy and determination. In this dilemma Colonel Luttrell, a member of the House, resigned his seat, and offered himself as a rival candidate to the electors of Middlesex, being assured by those who controlled the action of the House that, in any case, he would be received by Parliament as the member elect. A fourth election took place; Wilkes was again chosen by a vast majority ; and he was returned by the sheriffs : but Luttrell having presented a petition for the seat to the House, he was declared, after a long and furious debate, to have been duly elected.*

The whole nation was now convulsed with mingled rage and consternation. Never before during the long series of generations in which the British Constitution had existed and flourished, had such a perilous crisis occurred. The occasion was regarded by reflecting persons of all classes as decisive of the future fate of the government. The Commons had thus taken

* See " Parliamentary History of England from the Earliest Period till 1803," Vol. xvi., p. 262. The votes cast for Wilkes on the fourth election were 1,243 ; those given for Luttrell were 296.

high ground, and had consistently adhered to it throughout. The electors of Middlesex had acted with equal resolution and consistency. Other obnoxious persons had been formerly expelled from the house by its own action. Robert Walpole had incurred this fate in 1711, Sergeant Comyns in 1715, and Bedford in 1727. But in all these instances the decision of the Commons had been in accordance with the popular will, and no popular disturbance had been apprehended. The present instance was different in its nature; and great fears were apprehended that the ligatures which bound the nation together, would be severed by the violent struggles through which it might at this crisis be compelled to pass. Nevertheless, the firm position taken by the house eventually prevailed over popular opposition and prevalent fears; and Wilkes having been finally expelled, ventured no longer to intrude into the legislature. His supporters subsided for a time into quiet submission to the will of the Parliament which had been so plainly and so singularly expressed on this memorable occasion.

In 1769 two acts of importance were passed by the legislature. The charter of the East India Company was renewed for five years, and the iniquitous schemes of this gigantic monopoly were again commended and approved by the representatives of the nation. During the same session the private debts of George III. were liquidated by a vote of the house from the resources of the national treasury, to the amount of five hundred thousand pounds. This remarkable act of liberality was performed, even without the formality of a scrutiny having been made into the specific details which swelled the sum total to so enormous an amount.

The restless spirit of the arch-agitator Wilkes did not permit the public mind to repose for any length of time, in reference to his claims as member elect to Parliament for Middlesex; and this subject was again dragged before the public mind by the able and crushing strictures of a powerful but unknown advocate of the interests of the popular favorite. The first letter of the terrible *Junius* bears date January 21st, 1769. The remarkable ability displayed in the compositions which appeared in the Public Advertiser under this name, immediately attracted universal attention. Each number which appeared carried terror into the ranks of the ministry and their supporters; and the appearance of a letter of Junius was heralded in whispers of apprehensive agony from mouth to mouth, as if some insidious, unknown, but deadly foe had invaded their most secure hiding-places, threatening them with destruction. In April, 1769, Junius addressed the Duke of Grafton in reference to the claims of Wilkes, and aroused anew the popular enthusiasm on the subject. The spirit of the people was again aroused. The freeholders of the county of Middlesex presented a petition to the king, in which they set forth their grievances in reference to the election and the expulsion of Wilkes. The city of London presented a petition to the monarch to the same effect, and demanding an immediate dissolution of Parliament. Similar memorials came from fifteen counties of England; setting forth the injustice which had been done to popular rights in the person of Wilkes, and demanding that a proper indemnification should be made therefor.

But these wise and patriotic appeals remained unheard. The Parliament indicated their resolution to persist in their course against Wilkes and his advocates, by commanding the Attorney-General to file a bill in the Court of King's Bench against Woodfall, the publisher of the Public Advertiser, for uttering a false and malicious libel. The case was tried before the learned and famous Lord Mansfield, and the verdict of the jury was *Guilty of printing and publishing only;* which was in effect an acquittal of the defendant. Lord Chatham, who had by this time, after a seclusion of two years, returned to his place in Parliament, endeavored to allay the existing uneasiness of the public mind, by introducing a motion to the effect that the house would take into consideration the causes of the discontents which prevailed in the nation, and especially the late proceedings in the Commons against Mr. Wilkes. But his motion was opposed by Lord Mansfield, and eventually lost. The same measure was subsequently proposed by the Marquis of Rockingham, on the 20th of January, 1770; and the measure, in consequence of the critical state of the public mind, was sustained by a majority of the members. The investigation of the universal discontents which agitated the nation was appointed to commence on the second day of the ensuing February; at which time it was determined that the house should resolve itself into a committee of inquiry. But before the arrival of that momentous day, on the preceding 28th of January, the prime minister, the Duke of Grafton, unexpectedly and suddenly resigned.* This act took the nation by surprise; but its motive was readily divined. The crafty peer endeavored thereby to shield himself from the overwhelming flood of obloquy which would follow his retention of an office, the possession of which on his part, had led to so many and such great popular evils. The vacant office was immediately filled by Lord North; and thus in February, 1770, one of the most memorable administrations presented by the whole range of English history began.

* Horace Walpole, in his "Memoirs of the Reign of George III." thus explains the causes of the resignation of the Duke of Grafton at this crisis. His opinions must always be taken *cum grano salis.*

"His fall was universally ascribed to his *pusillanimity;* but whether betrayed by his fears or his friends, he had certainly been the chief author of his own *disgrace.* His *haughtiness, indolence, reserve, and improvidence,* had conjured up the storm, but his *obstinacy and feebleness*—always *relaying* each other and always *mal-à-propos*—were the radical cause of all the numerous absurdities that discolored his conduct and exposed him to *deserved reproaches;* nor had he depth of understanding to counterbalance the defects of his temper. The details of his conduct were as *weak and preposterous* as the great lines of it." P. 70, vol. iv.

CHAPTER V.

Lord North becomes Premier—Renewal of Wilkes's Case—The Stamp Act—Wilkes elected an Alderman of London—His Contest with the Court—Growing Troubles with the American Colonies—Benjamin Franklin in England—First Convention of the American Congress—Petition presented to George III. by Wilkes as Mayor of London—Commencement of the Revolutionary War—Hostilities between England and France—Disturbances in Ireland—Death of Lord Chatham.

LORD NORTH, by his entrance into the British ministry, inherited a legacy of troubles. The nation was still divided in reference to the conflict between the Court and Wilkes, for such in reality was the nature of the dispute; while the disaffection of the American Colonies remained undiminished. The friends of Wilkes moved in the House of Commons that "the house ought to judge of elections by the law of the land and by the former custom and practice of Parliament." This motion was intended to be followed by others setting forth that the former expulsion of Wilkes by the Commons was illegal and unjust. To avert the long and furious contest which would inevitably have ensued, Lord North adroitly amended this motion, which had been introduced by Mr. Dowdeswell, by adding, "that the judgment formerly passed by the house in the case of Mr. Wilkes *was* agreeable to the law of the land, and in accordance with the usage of Parliament." This amendment was carried by two hundred and twenty-four votes against a hundred and eighty; and thus for a short time the subject was laid over, but not finally settled or disposed of. In May, 1770, Lord Chatham, who, being out of the ministry, was necessarily in opposition, moved in the House of Peers a bill for reversing the judgment of expulsion passed by the Commons in the case of Wilkes. But his proposition was lost by an overwhelming majority, after a protracted and animated debate.

The attention of Parliament was for a time diverted from the case of Wilkes and its attendant difficulties, which seemed to have become perennial and endless, to those connected with the American Colonies. Lord North had readily discerned that the taxes which had been imposed in the colonies, upon the several objects of domestic use already enumerated, could never be collected, and might produce the most disastrous effects upon the unity and peace of the empire. He therefore moved the repeal of the obnoxious taxes on all the articles *except tea*. He supposed it to be proper to retain a duty on something, in order thereby to indicate the still existing supremacy of Britain. It was contended by the ministry and their supporters, that a total repeal could not be made until the dignity of the mother country had been vindicated by the submission of the colonies to her power, as indicated by their obedience in reference to this point. After a long discussion the minister carried his motion; yet only by an insignificant majority of sixty-two. The tax on tea remained; and that tax, though utterly insignificant in itself, afterward became the cause of that revolutionary struggle which produced the dismemberment of the British Empire, and gave existence to the greatest republic of modern times.

During the session of Parliament of 1771, the disturbances made by the arch-demagogue Wilkes again assumed a formidable importance. Two printers, named Thompson and Wheble, were arrested for reporting the speeches delivered in the Commons. A resolution was passed commanding them to appear and answer to this charge at the bar of the house. The printers paid no attention to this summons; when the house resolved that they should be taken into custody by the sergeant-at-arms. The accused absconded, and a reward of fifty pounds was offered for their apprehension. Wheble was soon arrested, and taken before Wilkes, who had been elected an alderman of London, for a hearing. As might have been anticipated, Wilkes discharged the defendant from custody, and further bound him over to prosecute the person who had apprehended him. The impudence of Wilkes even went much further. He addressed a letter to the Earl of Halifax, then Secretary of State, in which he asserted that Wheble had been apprehended in violation of the rights of an Englishman, as well as of the chartered privileges of a citizen of London. Other printers had by this time been arrested for the same offence. They were taken before Crosby the Mayor, and Wilkes and Oliver, Aldermen of London, their cases heard, the warrant of arrest declared illegal, the prisoners discharged, and the messenger of the Commons committed to prison in default of bail, for having made a false arrest.

For this defiance of the authority of Parliament, the offending magistrates were summoned to appear at the bar of the house. Crosby and Oliver obeyed, and after a hearing and argument upon their conduct, they were committed prisoners to the Tower. Wilkes had refused to appear, except in his seat as member for the county of Middlesex. Crosby and Oliver availed themselves of the writ of *Habeas Corpus*, which they obtained from the Court of Common Pleas. But they were remanded after a protracted hearing; and they remained in custody till the end of the session; when, by operation of law, they were discharged. The king was further provoked at this period, by another petition from the city of London, remonstrating against an invasion of their rights in some encroachments which were made upon the river Thames by public embankments. This memorial produced no effect except to irritate the sovereign, who had at this period to endure the additional misfortune of the death of his mother. Augusta, the Princess Dowager of Wales, died on the 8th of February, 1772, in the fifty-third year of her age. Important changes also took place in the cabinet. The Earl of Harcourt became Lord-Lieutenant of Ireland; Charles Jenkinson was appointed vice-treasurer of the same; and Charles James Fox, a young statesman and orator, who afterward filled a place in English parliamentary history second only to that of the Earl of Chatham, appeared upon the scene, and took a seat at the board of the Treasury.

During 1773 and several succeeding years, the peace of the nation was not disturbed at home by any events of importance; nor was the life of George III. signalized by any domestic incident of interest. The subject which occupied the chief attention of the king, the parliament, and the people, was the disaffection of the American Colonies. Lord North, who still retained the post of prime minister, was not unwilling to conciliate. His nature was neither unreasonable nor tyrannical; nor was his intellect narrow and superficial. But events had rapidly transpired in the hostile and restive colonies, which soon placed all possibility of adjustment and reconciliation out of the question. The tea which had been consigned to the merchants of Boston, and upon which a light duty had been imposed, was violently destroyed. A spirit of rebellion against British rule, and a determination to achieve a total independence and separation from the mother country, rapidly pervaded all the colonies. They seemed willing to pay millions for defence, but not a penny for tribute. The assembly of the colony of Massachusetts addressed to the legislatures of the other colonies a circular letter, recommending them to discuss measures which might lead to resistance to the tyranny of Britain, and to freedom from her power. The same assembly voted an address to the king, in which they boldly demanded that he should remove the governor and lieutenant-governor for ever from the province. Benjamin Franklin presented the petition in person to Lord Dartmouth, as the agent of the province of Massachusetts Bay in England. The ultimate result of this step was, that a bill was introduced into Parliament for the purpose of still further encroaching upon the liberties of that colony, which was regarded as the leader in all the rebellious movements which had as yet taken place in America. This bill provided that the nomination of councillors, judges, and magistrates of all kinds should be vested in the British crown, and should be removable at pleasure. It was passed by an overwhelming majority in May, 1774. A military force was sent to

Boston at the same time, under the command of General Gage, to overawe the rebellious descendants of the Pilgrim Fathers into submission to the demands of their tyrants. He conveyed to that city the knowledge of the fact that, as a punishment for past contumacy, the port of Boston had been removed, by an act of Parliament, to the town of Salem.

These outrages rapidly brought matters to a decisive and portentous crisis throughout the colonies. A Congress composed of delegates from all of them convened in September, 1774, at Philadelphia. That Congress passed resolutions sympathizing with the colony of Massachusetts in its conflict with the British monarch. It also prepared an address to the king, and a memorial to the British people, in both of which their alleged grievances were set forth in decisive language. The British monarch and people seemed to turn a deaf ear to these appeals. Petitions presented to Parliament by those subjects who were opposed to the policy of the court, were consigned to the Committee of Oblivion. The Parliament refused to hear evidence in reference to the allegations contained in the petition of Congress to the king. A bill introduced by Lord Chatham for the purpose of settling the troubles in the colonies was rejected by a large majority. The colonies were at last declared to be in a state of open rebellion against the legitimate authority of their gracious sovereign. A petition which was presented to the king by Wilkes in person, who had been elected Lord Mayor of London, and then represented the corporation, expressing the abhorrence of the citizens of the capital of the measures of oppression which had been pursued by the government, to the injury of their fellow-subjects in the colonies, was spurned with contempt from the foot of the throne. The policy adopted by Lord North, and by the court and ministry under his guidance, was intended to uphold the dignity and supremacy of Britain in America; but the results actually produced were vastly different from that proposed. While the British government became more obstinate, the colonists became more resolute and rebellious. Preparations for hostilities were then made throughout the length and breadth of the land. The first blood shed in the great cause of liberty in the New World, flowed at Lexington. Brother had armed against brother, and a conflict had at last begun which could end by no compromise; but which must result either in total subjection or in complete enfranchisement. The battle of Bunker Hill soon followed; and the whole continent was thrown into a frenzy of patriotic ardor and excitement. George Washington—a hero whose glory now overshadows the civilized world with a radiance purer, nobler, and brighter, than that which has been achieved by any other mortal—having taken command of the continental army, drove Lord Howe from the heights of Boston, and released that capital from its perilous position. On the 4th of July, 1776, the colonies proclaimed by their Congress assembled at Philadelphia, their Declaration of Independence; and then ensued all the thrilling and memorable incidents of a seven years' struggle for deliverance from the power of a detested tyrant. General Howe obtained a victory on Long Island. Washington changed the tide of battle at Trenton. And while the respective combatants fought throughout the length and breadth of the thirteen colonies with variable success, the determination of the king and his ministers remained unmoved by calamities and defeats, by popular threatenings, and by the opposition of enlightened patriots in Parliament. In vain did the great Chatham exert his waning powers to their utmost in opposition to the war. In vain, with a degree of pathos and eloquence which in one so aged and feeble has never been equalled, did he condemn not only the principles for which the war was waged, but also the means which were employed to carry it on. In vain did he appeal to the right reverend prelates who sat near him in the hall which witnessed his final efforts, by every consideration of religion and humanity, to oppose some of the measures thus employed. In vain did he invoke the spirit and humanity of his countrymen, appeal to their wisdom and prudence, and urge every consideration which should influence sagacious, profound, and liberal statesmen, in opposition to that unjust and tyrannical crusade against the most sacred rights of man. And it was in vain that the greatest of British statesmen perished at last, in the midst of his exertions in support of a bill which proposed, in the British Parliament, the immediate and complete recognition of the independence of the American colonies.*

While these and other disasters were occurring to the British arms and supremacy in America, defeat followed defeat in other portions of the world. The English flag was dishonored by Admiral Keppel and Sir Hugh Pelissier, in their conflicts with the French, who had become the allies of the rebellious colonies. St. Vincent and Grenada were captured by the fleets of that power. The combined armaments of France and Spain boldly entered the British channel, and haughtily defied the power of the mistress of the seas. The adjacent kingdom of Ireland was disturbed by public discontents, and in the Irish Parliament, an address was voted to the king demanding the obnoxious boon of free trade, as the only means of saving the nation from impending ruin. Thus on every hand was the mind of George III. harassed by the misfortunes which attended his administration of affairs in almost every portion of his dominions. His intentions in most cases were doubtless good, but his policy was short-sighted and imbecile in the extreme; nor is it singular that this long and astonishing series of adverse events should have gradually enfeebled, and should eventually have overthrown, a mind whose powers were never great, and whose obstinacy in adhering to his once-formed purposes, was its most prominent and most pernicious attribute.

* Lord Chatham expired on the 11th of May, 1778, in the seventieth year of his age, at his favorite villa of Hayes, in Kent. The memorable scene connected with his last appearance in the House of Lords has been frequently described, and is familiarly known.

CHAPTER VI.

Domestic Life of George III.—His Public and Private Cares—Repeal of the Laws against Roman Catholics—First Appearance of the second William Pitt in Parliament—Affairs of the British East India Company—The Rise and Progress of that vast Empire—Outrages and Tyranny which disgraced its history—Administration of Warren Hastings—Incidents of the War in America—Second Administration of Lord Rockingham—Proposals of Peace with the Colonies in America—Provisional Articles—Final Adjustment of the Treaty.

THE domestic life of George III. at this period presented but few incidents worthy of notice. There was a total absence in his case, of all those private scandals, personal quarrels, and court intrigues which, in the annals of the majority of princes, constitute no insignificant portion of their history. After the birth of the Prince of Wales, other children were successively added to the royal household. Augustus, Duke of Sussex, was born in 1763; Adolphus, Duke of Cambridge, in 1774; Mary, Duchess of Gloucester, in 1776. The chief attention of the queen was employed in the government and education of her children; and the king and queen both deserve praise for the share of domestic virtue which they possessed, and the example of private excellence which they exhibited both to their family and to the world.

The greatest solicitude of George III. was devoted to the affairs of his government. The nation was in an agitated state. Faction raged at home, and hostilities prevailed abroad. The monarch regarded himself as responsible in a moral sense for the measures adopted by his government; and hence the results of those measures, when pernicious or unfortunate, sorely wounded him. It was the long-continued state of mental excitement into which the untoward current of public affairs threw him, which finally produced the mental disease under which many years of his life were subsequently passed.

In 1780 an effort was made by the Opposition in Parliament to repeal the laws against Roman Catholics. One hundred and twenty thousand persons signed a petition to that effect, which was presented by Sir George Gordon to the House of Commons. Cries of "No Popery" resounded through the streets of London. All the popish chapels in the city were demolished by the mob. Even the private residences of distinguished Catholics were assailed. The aspect of affairs became formidable, and it was at one time apprehended that the capital would become the prey of the flames. In this crisis the king displayed considerable energy. He transmitted general orders to the military to fire on the rioters, and to punish their ringleaders with severity. Many hundreds were slain, and Sir George Gordon was arrested for high treason. A very great number were imprisoned, and their trial was quickly commenced and concluded before Lord Loughborough, the Chief Justice. This energetic magistrate punished the offenders with a degree of severity which had never been equalled in England since the days of the ignominious Jeffreys; and soon all remains of popular turbulence and disorder were obliterated.

On the 1st of September, 1780, the fourteenth Parliament of Great Britain was dissolved by proclamation, and a new Parliament convened on the 31st of October succeeding. It was at this period and during this session that the second William Pitt, second son of the great Earl of Chatham, made his first appearance in that house of Commons, of which he, like his father, became subsequently the most distinguished ornament. He was a person of extraordinary talents, and every way adapted to the achievement of an illustrious figure in the turbulent and perilous history of his times. He soon became the chief personage in the concluding portion of the reign of George III.

Although the events of the American war still continued to occupy a considerable share of the attention of the king and nation, there was another portion of the globe which possessed at this period almost an equal interest in their estimation. During twenty years the affairs of the East India Company gradually increased in importance; their value and profitableness were constantly augmented; and the policy which was pursued by the Company became a matter of great and absorbing concern. The heroism of Lord Clive, then a youthful adventurer, had vanquished the numerous and tumultuous native armies of Bengal and the Carnatic; and a territory more extensive and perhaps more opulent than the British Islands, was in a short time added to the possession of the British crown. After achieving victories, and performing prodigies of valor, which have scarcely a parallel in history, Clive returned to England in 1760. Mr. Vansittart was appointed Governor-General of India in his stead. In 1764 Vansittart returned to England, and Mr. Spencer occupied his place, until Lord Clive revisited the scene of his former glory, and again assumed the supreme command. On the second resignation of Lord Clive, Mr. Veerlst, and after him, Mr. Cartier, became in succession Governors. These were men of comparative insignificance, and added no lustre to British arms or diplomacy during their administrations. But they were succeeded by Warren Hastings, one of the most extraordinary men who ever lived; and whose bold and capacious mind ventured upon the execution of measures which exerted an indelible influence on the destinies of fifty millions of people. The chief aim of the policy pursued by Hastings during the many memorable years of his supremacy in India, was to extort from the inhabitants whom British arms had subjugated, the most incredible sums of money; to grind the unfortunate population into the very dust; to outrage all their religious prejudices and convictions, if they interfered with his purpose; and while he made himself popular with the Company, and its grasping servants and members of high and low degree, to become in substance the curse and scourge of the unhappy and imbecile myriads whom the fortunes of war had placed beneath the iron rod of his power. During his infamous administration, many native princes were deposed without the shadow of an excuse; and the government of the Company was erected in their stead. Their revenues were afterward confiscated; and if the native princes were ever permitted to retain the shadow, without the substance, of their hereditary power, they were compelled to pay enormous tributes; and not a few even of these crowned puppets were reduced, in successive years, from opulence to beggary. There is nothing contained in the whole range of history ancient or modern—not the triumphs of imperial Rome over her subjugated enemies, not the excesses of Spanish tyranny and cupidity upon the vanquished aborigines of Mexico and Peru—which furnish any parallel in infamy to that which was exhibited by the British East India Company, and their favorite agents and emissaries, in their outrages upon India. The record of their deeds is a black and foul blot in English history, which the lapse of ages cannot wipe away. That record displays a long catalogue of the most cruel, insatiable, and unscrupulous encroachments, which were unprincipled, unchristian, and barbarous beyond expression. The Company, authorized and supported by a portion of the nation, invaded the territories of Bengal, the Carnatic, the Decan, and Oude, without the slightest show of reason or justice; and having conquered their inhabitants by the superiority of their arms and their tactics, they tyrannized over their helpless and unresisting victims with a degree of ferocity and cruelty, at which Verres in Sicily or Pizarro in Peru would have blushed and shuddered. And the greatest, the most insatiable, the most unscrupulous of all these civilized savages, was Warren Hastings.*

Deeply interested as a large proportion of the leading men in England were in the vast remittances of money, and other immense profits, which constantly accrued from the British possessions in India, the abuses which had been perpetrated in that fated land during many years under the guidance of Hastings, at

* See *Memoirs of the Life of Warren Hastings, first Governor-General of Bengal. Compiled from Original Papers, by the Rev. G. R. Gleig, M. A.* 3 vols. 8vo. London, 1841. This work, which contains a satisfactory narrative of the incidents of Hastings' life, should be read with caution, inasmuch as very considerable partiality pervades every portion of the work in favor of its celebrated subject.

last became so intolerable, that they forced a solemn utterance; and the wails of afflicted millions reverberating round the globe, were heard in mournful and impressive tones even in the native land of their tyrants. The public attention was aroused on the subject. In 1781 a secret committee was appointed by Parliament to examine into the causes which led to the iniquitous Mahratta war, and into that which had desolated the Carnatic. In the session of 1782 Mr. Dundas, then Lord Advocate of Scotland, made a very able report, as chairman of that committee, in which the policy pursued by Hastings as Governor-General was scrutinized and condemned in the strongest terms; and he remarked truly, that the Governor had no right whatever to imagine himself to be another Alexander or Aurengzebe, and to extend his empire by desperate military exploits, to the ruin of trade, commerce, and the welfare of the people of India. A bill was also introduced recalling Elijah Impey, the Chief Justice, and one of the basest tools of Hastings, to take his trial in England for misdemeanors in office. On the 28th of May, 1782, the Commons passed resolutions, severely condemning the whole system of Indian politics; but the India Company protesting against the measure, and doubtless bribing a necessary portion of the members, succeeded in obtaining a reversal of the resolution. But the unparalleled success of the measures of Hastings, and the abject submission of the inhabitants of India, which their despair had compelled them to make, had rendered the Governor the most unscrupulous of men; and his policy at length became so profound and unfathomable an abyss of mysterious and inexplicable enigmas, that even the members of the council were terrified at it, and negatived his most important measures. When Hastings discovered that his associates at the board, a majority of whom he had always been able previously to control, had become adverse and rebellious, he found himself compelled to resign. He then returned to England, in the possession of a colossal fortune wrung from the wreck and the sufferings of millions, in a far distant and dusky clime, who had been made, by a mysterious and malignant decree of fate, to suffer and to perish beneath the heavy scourge of his superior power and intelligence.* He returned indeed, but it was to meet the anxieties and the indignities of a public prosecution by the Commons of Great Britain, in accordance with the requisitions of the will of the disgraced and incensed nation; the details of which exceed in tragical interest, in the splendors of forensic eloquence, in the importance of the questions involved, in the duration, the acrimony, and the determination of the contest, any trial which ever occurred in England.

Meanwhile the conflict was progressing in America between the English forces and the heroic defenders of liberty. Lord Cornwallis obtained a victory at Camden. Major Ferguson was defeated at King's Mountain. Colonel Tarleton met with an overwhelming defeat at the Cowpens. To reverse the picture, Cornwallis triumphed at Guilford. But all his achievements were sullied by the capture of his whole armament, through the masterly operations of Washington at Yorktown. The effect of these misfortunes to the British arms was, to open the eyes of the British government to the utter impossibility of vanquishing three millions of people, zealously enlisted in the defence of the holy cause of freedom. In February, 1782, General Conway moved in the Commons that an address be sent to the king,

---

* If it be possible to entertain any doubt respecting the effects of the general policy adopted by the English Government in India, it must assuredly vanish when we read the opinion of Lord Cornwallis, the successor of Mr. Hastings, who, in his despatch of August 2, 1789, says: "Independent of all other considerations, I can assure you that it will be of the utmost importance for promoting the solid interests of the Company, that the principal landholders and traders in the interior parts of the country should be restored to such circumstances as to enable them to support their families with *decency*. I am sorry to be *obliged* to say, that agriculture and internal commerce have for many years been gradually declining; and that at present, excepting the class of Shroffs and Banians, who reside almost entirely in great towns, the inhabitants of these provinces were advancing hastily to a general state of poverty and wretchedness. In this description I must even include almost every Zemindar in the Company's territories." In his minute of council, dated September 18, 1789, his lordship asserts, and the assertion is enough to strike men with amazement and horror: "That one-third of the Company's territory is now a jungle inhabited by wild beasts."

earnestly imploring him to listen to the prayer of his faithful Commons, that the war with the American colonies might no longer be pursued, and that their liberties might be acknowledged. This memorable motion was discussed at great length and with much vehemence, and was at last lost by one vote only. Mr. Fox immediately gave notice that in a few days he would revive the question in another form. Accordingly, on the first of March, he introduced a motion to the effect that the king, in pursuance of the advice of the House of Commons, would take such measures without delay as should appear to him most conducive to the restoration of harmony between Great Britain and her revolted colonies. This proposition, after a full debate, was carried by a majority of nineteen. The Opposition were not satisfied with this triumph, but proceeded to move a vote of censure upon the minister, according to whose policy the American war had been begun and conducted; declaring that the chief cause of all the national misfortunes was the want of foresight and ability in his majesty's cabinet. This motion was also carried and immediately after its passage, Lord North, the prime minister, of infamous and unfortunate memory, so far as the American colonies were concerned, resigned his place.

The Marquis of Rockingham now became the head of the cabinet for the second time. Instructions were sent to the commanders of the British forces in America to inform the Continental Congress, that the king and Parliament entertained pacific sentiments toward the colonies; and were ready to treat with them on the basis of their future independence. To this conclusion George III. had been brought with the greatest reluctance. He entertained the strongest aversion to the diminution of the territories over which he ruled; and the great principle to which he most tenaciously but blindly adhered, throughout his whole previous administration, was, under all circumstances, to preserve the integrity of the British Empire. To lose so vast a proportion of the territories which belonged to the British crown, as were contained in the alienated colonies of America, was a misfortune which he deeply felt, and to which he was unconquerably averse. And when, after a protracted and arduous war of seven years, after the expenditure of hundreds of millions, after the loss of thousands of lives, after innumerable cares, anxieties, and vexations, he was compelled to submit to their loss, it was to him as a personal affliction; and he felt it so deeply, that it eventually led, by his own confession, to that imbecility of mind under which he so long and so painfully suffered.*

Provisional articles of peace with America were signed at Paris in November, 1782. Several months previous to this event, the estimable Marquis of Rockingham expired, prematurely, and in the midst of his honorable and useful career. His policy of peace was pursued by the Earl of Shelburne, his successor; but the promotion of this nobleman to the premiership led to fierce dissensions among the Whigs. Mr. Fox resigned as Keeper of the Seals, Lord Cavendish as Chancellor of the Exchequer, the Duke of Portland as Governor of Ireland, and Edmund Burke as Paymaster of the Forces. In their places were substituted the Earl of Grantham, Wm. Townshend, Sir George Young, Colonel Barre, and Earl Temple. But the most remarkable appointment of all was that of the youthful and gifted William Pitt, who, at the early age of twenty-three, became Chancellor of the Exchequer; an office which had always been intrusted to men of great experience, protracted study, and mature years. Yet such was the extraordinary mantle of genius which had fallen upon this descendant of the Great Commoner, that he proved himself quite equal to the performance of the intricate duties of his post.

During the continuance of this ministry in power, but few events of importance occurred. The entire and absolute independence of the American colonies was acknowledged, and all the dangers and expenses of that pernicious and unprincipled war were thus terminated. Minorca was conquered by the Span-

* " I shall never lay my head on my last pillow in peace and quiet as long as I remember the loss of my American Colonies," was the remark of the unfortunate king to Lord Thurlow at a later period. *Doran's Queens of England of the House of Hanover.* Vol. ii., p. 118.

iards; the island of St. Christopher was taken by the French; the Bahamas fell into the power of the Portuguese; but to alleviate these misfortunes, Sir George Rodney gained a great naval victory over the French near the island of Dominique, and a glorious and decisive defence was made by British arms of the fortress of Gibraltar, against the combined fleets of France and Spain by which it was assailed. On the 21st of January, 1783, preliminaries of peace were signed between England, France, and Spain. The terms of this settlement were ultimately approved by the British Parliament; and thus, after many years of uncertain and profitless conflict, both with powers in the Old World and in the New, the British monarch and the British Empire might be said to have obtained the unfamiliar, but inestimable blessings of peace. The hostilities which had been waged between England and Holland, though not adjusted in form until a later date, may also be said at this period to have been suspended; for henceforth a final and satisfactory arrangement was confidently anticipated.

CHAPTER VII.

Joint Ministry of Lord North and Mr. Fox—Renewed Insanity of George III.—Mr. Fox's East India Bill—Dismissal of the Coalition Cabinet—The younger Pitt becomes Premier—The Quality and Effects of his Oratory—Splendid Era of British Eloquence—Mr. Pitt's East India Bill—Troubles in Ireland—Influence of Flood and Grattan—Pitt's Financial Measures—Affairs of India—Administration of Warren Hastings—His Life, Character, and Genius—His Trial before the House of Peers—Unrivalled Displays of Forensic Eloquence — Hastings' final Triumph and Acquittal.

An event of sufficient importance to deserve a place in general history occurred in England during the year 1783, at which period the coalition ministry ruled, headed by Lord North and Mr. Fox, as joint Secretaries of State, the first for the home, the latter for the foreign, department. This administration was exceedingly unpopular with the nation. Mr. Pitt introduced a bill intended to reform the system of parliamentary representation, abolishing a large number of the obnoxious and rotten boroughs; but his efforts were rendered useless by the opposition of the ministry and court, which possessed a large majority in Parliament. Mr. Fox was the author and mover of a bill for the purpose of investigating the affairs of the East India Company; and of placing them in the hands of certain commissioners for the benefit of the proprietary and the public. He contended that the finances of the Company were in a state of total derangement, and that the officers were utterly incapable of governing the vast territories over which, by innumerable acts of violence, fraud and rapine, they had obtained supremacy. This bill, after a long and animated debate, passed the Commons, but was rejected by the Upper House.

At this period the intellect of George III. began to give way beneath the power of the disease which eventually mastered it; and he lost a large share of his usual intelligence and sagacity. A proof of this assertion is to be found in the fact that Lord Temple was not only able to convince him that the India bill of Fox was injurious, pernicious, and wicked; but also to excite the rage and indignation of the monarch in reference to it to an extravagant degree. He persuaded the king to set his hand to a declaration to the effect that whoever supported the India bill was not only not the king's friend, but his direct enemy; and he authorized Lord Temple to put this sentiment in the strongest possible language, and to make it public. Never had George III. perpetrated a more imbecile and silly act since his accession to the throne.

Thee king's hostility to this bill, which had originated with a member of the cabinet, and was approved of by a majority of them, rendered it impossible that they could still act harmoniously together in the conduct of the government. At midnight, on the 18th of December, 1783, a message was sent from the exasperated monarch to the two Secretaries of State, demanding the seals of their respective departments; and early the next morning letters of dismission, signed by Earl Temple, were sent to all the other members of the cabinet. This decisive conduct on the part of George III. clearly showed that, while he had lost a portion of his usual sagacity, he retained more than his ordinary share of stubbornness.

The whole of the coalition cabinet being swept away, William Pitt was chosen to head the government. He was declared First Lord of the Treasury, and Chancellor of the Exchequer. The Marquis of Caermarthen and Thomas Townshend were nominated Secretaries of State. The profane, perfidious, and brutal Thurlow was reinstated as Lord Chancellor. The Duke of Rutland became Privy Seal, and Lord Temple was appointed Governor of Ireland. This new ministry was received by the nation with transports of joy. The powerful charm possessed by the name of *Pitt* had not yet faded away; and the people of Britain, so long harassed by imbecile or by mercenary counsels, confidently hoped to find in the ability and disinterested patriotism of the son of the Great Commoner, a wiser, safer, and better administration of the affairs of the Empire.

The new minister was destined to pass through some of the most violent and desperate struggles which ever tasked the energies of the chief of a government. The talents of the second Pitt were probably as great as those of the first; though they were not as bold, as startling, and as resistless. His eloquence was more polished and courtly; his orations were more elaborate and labored; though the effects of their delivery were less instantaneous and overwhelming. His speeches resembled the firm, steady, onward current of a great and affluent river, which carried a vast body of water at a steady pace toward the capacious bosom of an ocean ready to receive it. The efforts of his illustrious father were very like the tumultuous and powerful plunge of a cataract, which, leaping forward with a rapid and convulsive rush, hurried every opponent down the abyss, and submerged him in ruin. The result of this signal difference between the two Pitts was, that the speeches of the son, inasmuch as they were characterized by a more elaborate and lengthy investigation of subjects, became on that very account more susceptible of reply. His opponents found something in them to combat; and gifted men always met in his orations much that was worthy of their most concentrated and consummate efforts. Hence it was that the parliamentary battles which were fought during the administration of the younger Pitt, were the fiercest, longest, ablest, and most celebrated, which have occurred since the foundation of the British Constitution; for this was the memorable era in which Fox, Burke, Sheridan, Dundas, and Windham flourished, and constituted a galaxy of high and varied genius such as no other age or country ever produced at a single crisis.

The chief subject which engaged the nation, and divided her representatives at this period, appertained to the East India Company. This colossal monopoly had become so notorious for its outrages upon the rights of the millions who were subject to its sway, that it was absolutely impossible for any minister, possessing either honesty, humanity, or patriotism, to ignore the subject. One of the first measures of Mr. Pitt was his India Bill. The terms of this bill were acceptable to the king, but they were rejected by the Commons. He subsequently introduced another, by which a Board of Control, composed of a number of commissioners of the rank of privy counsellors was established, who were to be appointed, and to be removable by the sovereign. Mr. Fox attacked this bill with prodigious eloquence and energy, and showed how it conferred a formidable and dangerous accession of power to the crown. But the splendor of his declamation and the thunder of his invective were all thrown away; and the minister finally carried his proposition in both houses with decisive majorities. It was on this occasion, in August, 1784, that Mr. Burke, for the first time, displayed the full extent of his abilities, and the unfathomable depth of the hostility which he entertained against Warren Hastings, the late Governor-General of India; which was destined afterward to find its culmination in the thrilling scenes and magnificent oratorical displays of a public trial, which is without a parallel in English history, so fruitful of impeachments, persecutions, and judicial assassinations of celebrated statesmen. As soon as the vote was taken on this question, and decided in the minister's favor, Mr. Burke gave notice that he would bring forward a series of resolutions intended as the foundation of an inquiry into the conduct of Hastings as Governor-General of India. Mr. Pitt opposed this measure by moving the order of the day, and for a time the scrutiny was postponed.

In 1785, the kingdom of Ireland became the chief subject of the solicitude of the monarch and the nation. Three great evils produced by British tyranny then afflicted that people. One of these appertained to their restricted commerce. The second referred to their unjust representation. The third resulted from their preposterous ecclesiastical relations. In regard to the first, the Irish through their Parliament, which still existed, and still possessed some trifling show of power and freedom, demanded the removal of those restrictions which so grievously hampered their commerce, and threw all the profits of their industry into the insatiable maw of England. They also demanded universal suffrage, and the abolition of the law which restricted the right of voting to the Protestant freeholders, who were a small proportion of the inhabitants of the country. They also contended for the removal of the iniquitous and ruinous taxes or church rates, which the Roman Catholic population of Ireland were compelled to pay to the support of the clergy of the Established Church. Large popular meetings were held in reference to these reforms at Lisburne, at Dungannon, at Munster; and finally a national convention was held at Dublin. The celebrated Irish orators Grattan and Flood flourished in the deliberations of this convention, and acquired a name and a distinction which have not yet become dim by the lapse of time. They also figured as members of the Irish Parliament; but their patriotic measures were generally resisted and voted down by the decisive majorities which the British ministry, and their agent the Viceroy, were able to command. But the public mind in Ireland was very restless. Fears were entertained of popular disturbances; and several regiments which had been intended for India, were retained to strengthen the garrison of Dublin. The agitation of measures of reform was continued from time to time by Flood and Grattan in the Irish Parliament, but to no purpose; inasmuch as the usual majority of the ministry, in opposition to all proposed changes in the laws and administration of that unfortunate victim of British tyranny, was as a hundred and twelve votes to sixty.

The energies of Mr. Pitt were now employed in the introduction of many measures of minor importance to the national prosperity, which need not here be enumerated. The national revenue at this period amounted to fifteen million pounds; yet even this vast sum was insufficient to meet the current expenses of the government. He proposed to increase the revenue by the imposition of a tax on spirits, imported timber, and perfumery. It was also found necessary to pay the private debts of the monarch, which at this period had, for the *fifth* time, become so great as to have been annoying and burdensome. But these and other minor matters of legislation were all thrown into obscurity, by the absorbing interest which the nation and monarch felt in a great judicial proceeding which, in April, 1786, was commenced by a coalition of the ablest men in the nation, against the most gifted, most unscrupulous, and the most guilty statesman who ever exercised a colossal and dangerous power, in any of the distant appendages of the empire. Warren Hastings, the late Governor-General of Bengal, was impeached at the bar of the House of Commons of high crimes and misdemeanors in his office; at the same time nine articles of accusation were exhibited, which were eventually increased to the number of twenty-two. With Mr. Burke, himself a host, were associated in this memorable prosecution, Mr. Sheridan, Charles James Fox, Mr. Windham, and Charles Grey: Mr. Pitt had refused to take any part in the proceedings.

Warren Hastings, whose life contained a degree of romance far stranger than the strangest of fictions, was born at Daylesford, in 1732. He was descended from a noble but impoverished family, who once flourished with considerable splendor upon an ancestral domain, which had been held by them at that place since the thirteenth century; but of which they had been deprived many years before the birth of their illustrious representative. The boy lived and suffered in poverty at Daylesford until his eighth year, when an uncle who possessed some means, sent him to school. In his tenth year the diminutive Warren was placed under the tuition of the celebrated Dr. Nichols at Westminster; and so extraordinary was his progress in learning, that his generous relative determined to support the talented and ambitious orphan at the university of Oxford. This desirable destiny was thwarted by the premature decease of his benefactor; after which, Hastings fell into the hands of a friend of his family, who gladly released himself of the burden by obtaining for him a writership in the service of the East India Company. Young, friendless, and inexperienced, Hastings was thus thrown adrift upon the wide and stormy ocean of the world, to be wafted by its surging billows either to greatness and glory, or to a speedy and more probable death. He arrived at Calcutta in 1750, in the seventeenth year of his age, and immediately devoted himself to the obscure and irksome duties of his station.

Those were stirring and perilous times in India. The unhappy race who were trodden into the dust by British tyranny, had been for some time on the point of rising upon their oppressors, and wreaking a well-deserved vengeance for their sufferings. The reputation for talent and sagacity which Hastings rapidly gained, rendered him a useful agent in the negotiations which took place between the belligerents, after the horrible sufferings and incidents connected with the Black Hole. After the memorable battle of Plassey, in which the heroic Clive rescued the British Empire in India from impending ruin by unexampled fortitude and skill, Hastings was appointed to reside at the court of the Nabob of Bengal, the obedient puppet of the triumphant Company, as their agent and representative. From this period his importance and influence continually increased. His great talents for intrigue and diplomacy, and his unscrupulous disregard of all the most sacred rights of others, soon elevated him to distinction among the many bold and able men who had resorted to India to advance their fortunes. Many years of toil, adventure, and success passed away; when, in 1769, Hastings was appointed by the Company a member of the Supreme Council at Madras. He still continued his ambitious and crafty career until 1772; when he was promoted, in consequence of his frequent and signal displays of ability in matters of administration and government, to the highest office in the British East Indies, the Governor-Generalship of Bengal. Then followed many thrilling and memorable scenes in the life of this extraordinary man, which scarcely find a parallel in history. His abilities, which were of the highest order, fitted him for the most desperate emergencies. His name became a sound of terror to fifty millions of people over whom he ruled. He obtained from them by rapine and plunder incalculable sums of money, to enrich the coffers of his employers, his associates, and himself. Almost every crime known to the calendar—murder, forgery, extortion, robbery, falsehood, and bribery, the vilest expedients and the blackest villanies—all were put into frequent and repeated operation upon people of every class and every grade, from princes and high priests down to the lowest peasants and the most destitute orphans and widows, to swell the sum of his ungodly gains. These outrages were not unknown in England. After years of success, and the exercise of a dangerous and despotic power on the opposite side of the globe, Hastings, wearied with the toils and sated with the splendors of office, resigned his high place, and returned to his native country. Very soon after his arrival he was officially informed that his conduct would soon be brought to the test of a severe judicial scrutiny. He himself anticipated a very different reception. He expected that the potent influence of the Company whose treasury he had filled with uncounted millions would secure him a peerage, that he would be decorated with stars and garters, and obtain a place in the cabinet of the monarch. These soaring hopes were all destined to be disappointed. He was solemnly impeached, after the necessary lapse of a few months, for high crimes and misdemeanors as Governor-General of Bengal. The chief mover in these bold proceedings was the eloquent Burke; whose ardent imagination had been aroused, and whose sense of justice had been outraged, by the excesses and cruelties of this great criminal, which were a burning disgrace, as he thought, not only to himself, but also to England, and even to human nature.

This celebrated trial commenced in February, 1786. The prosecution was conducted by Burke, Fox, Sheridan, and Grey, the most eloquent and able advocates then existing in the British Empire, and probably in the world. The proceedings were held in Westminster Hall, the most venerable and imposing edifice in England; with which were associated the memories of many of the most important and thrilling events in English history. The audience who crowded that vast space, and gazed with silent wonder on the imposing scene, comprised whatever was noblest, richest, most beautiful, and most illustrious in the realm, including the heir apparent to the throne—the Prince of Wales. The undaunted defendant in this great contest was one of the most distinguished Englishmen of his time; who, possessing talents of the first order, had risen from poverty and obscurity to the government of a distant, powerful, and opulent empire, whose laws, commerce, literature, religion, population, political and social condition, he had controlled, perverted, and cursed. The judges who were appointed to determine this important cause were the Parliament of England, at that time the most able and influential deliberative assembly in the world. The trial may be said to have lasted eight years; for that period of time elapsed between the opening of the case, and the final discharge of the defendant from bail. But the most interesting scenes connected with the trial occurred during the first few days of its progress; when the speeches of Burke, Fox, and Sheridan were delivered, which were masterpieces of unrivalled excellence and splendor in the great art of forensic eloquence. It were vain to attempt any description, in the limited space we here possess, of those prodigious displays of genius, in which the Demosthenes, the Æschines, and the Cicero of modern times put forth their utmost powers upon an occasion so worthy of their fullest exercise. The fortunes of the memorable conflict were varied. After the labors of the accusers and the advocates had been exhausted, Hastings was acquitted on the charge respecting the Rohilla war, and condemned on that in reference to the Rajah of Benares, as well as on the one referring to the Begum Princesses of Oude; whom he had impoverished and despoiled with circumstances of cruelty and horror, which, to this day, stir the indignant blood of the coldest and most indifferent observer. But as the progress of the trial became more protracted, and its ultimate issue seemed to be farther removed in the distant future, the public interest in the subject, which had for a time absorbed the whole attention of the nation, became much diminished; until at last, when the peers voted upon the final question of condemnation or acquittal, their sentence was of so divided and equivocal a nature that it amounted in reality to an acquittal. In the end, Hastings was summoned to the bar of the House of Lords, informed that he had been absolved, and solemnly discharged. Thus ended, after many years of struggle and forensic display, after intense hatreds, animosities, and conflicts, after exposures which kindle the rage, extort tears from the eyes, and execrations from the lips of the wise, humane, and good of every land and creed—thus terminated the most important and remarkable trial, not even excepting that of a beheaded king, which ever occurred on English ground, or absorbed the attention of the British people. Hastings then retired to the secure enjoyment of the luxuries and splendors of his opulent privacy, which had been bought by the sufferings and ruin of millions of his fellow men; and after surviving far beyond the usual extreme of human existence, he quietly disappeared beneath the shadows of the tomb in his eighty-sixth year, at that same Daylesford which had witnessed the sufferings and privations of his hapless infancy.*

* See *Memoirs of the Life of Warren Hastings, first Governor-General of Bengal. Compiled from Original Papers by the Rev. G. R. Gleig, M.A.* 3 vols. London, 1841.

CHAPTER VIII.

Attempt to assassinate the King—State of his Mind—Disgraceful Conduct of the Prince of Wales—The King's Insanity returns—The peculiarities of his Disease—His Successive Attacks—Regency Bill—The King's sudden Recovery—Important Events in France—Their Influence on the Popular Mind in England—Debates in Parliament in reference to these Events—Riots—Recall of the British Ambassador at Paris—Expulsion of the French Ambassador from England—Dangerous Excitement pervading the Nation—The French Republic declares War against the King of England and the Dutch Stadtholder.

THE innumerable cares and vexations attendant upon the royal authority, together with the adverse events which had, from time to time, occurred in different portions of the empire, produced a most pernicious effect upon the intellect of George III.; and in August, 1786, an incident happened which tended to increase his mental irritation. As the king was leaving the palace of St. James by the garden entrance, an insane woman named Margaret Nicholson approached him to present a paper. While he was receiving it, she stabbed him. The blow was not a very violent one, and the weapon did not penetrate much beyond his clothes. He immediately ordered the arrest of the lunatic, and hastened to convey to the queen at Windsor, the first intelligence of the danger to which he had been exposed. As he entered her apartment, he exclaimed with a joyous countenance: "Here I am, safe and well, though I have had a very narrow escape of being stabbed." The queen was at first very much terrified; and while her husband proceeded to describe the circumstances of the event, she burst into tears. She readily appreciated the consequences which would have occurred to herself had the king been slain. Her power and influence, which were second only to

11*

that of her husband, would have been greatly diminished, and her position even rendered unpleasant. When the news of the attempted assassination became known throughout the capital and nation, it increased the king's popularity, as it called forth the popular sympathy. Addresses of congratulation were sent in from every quarter. The papers were filled with strongly loyal articles. Whenever the king appeared in public he was greeted by long and loud acclamations. The first drawing-room which was held at the palace subsequent to the event was more crowded with the rank and splendor of the realm, than any which had occurred during some years.

These pleasing scenes of loyalty and congratulation were destined to be of short duration. Not many months afterward, the mind of the king again became seriously affected. One of the principal causes which led to his derangement in 1788 was the undutiful and disgraceful conduct of his eldest son, the Prince of Wales. As this young person approached manhood, he became the abandoned representative of every vice, and soon earned for himself the unenviable eminence of being the most contemptible of the human race. From this infamy neither his handsome person, his exalted birth, nor the advantages with which he had been favored, rescued him. At the period of which we now speak he had arrived at the twenty-sixth year of his age; and to his other vices had added the disgrace of becoming the political opponent of the measures of his father's administration, while there was neither necessity nor propriety in his mingling in the affairs of government. As the history of this prince will come under minute review in the closing portion of this volume, as George IV., we have abstained from narrating, in this connection, the incidents of his youth, even in their influence upon the conduct and feelings of his royal father. It is necessary here only to observe that his rebellious and reckless conduct had a decisive effect in bringing about the intermediate and also the final derangement of George III.; whose mind, irritated beyond endurance by a thousand public and domestic provocations, at last totally sank beneath the intolerable burden.

One peculiar symptom of the king's illness at this period was a total loss of sleep and great nervous irritation. He had recourse three times to "James's powders," without receiving any soothing influence. He talked continually, incoherently, and gave the clearest evidence that his reason was then dethroned. He was not yet removed from the palace of St. James, or confined in any way. He broke out into his first positive fit of delirium at dinner. The queen, who was present, burst into tears at the sad spectacle, so afflicting in itself, and so humiliating to human nature. The Prince of Wales and the Duke of York were at first frightened; afterward they exhibited unequivocal signs of rejoicing at the near prospect which was thus presented of their acquisition of greater power and consequence in the state.

The first night after the king's attack, he conducted Queen Charlotte to her bed-chamber, as was his uniform custom; but there he repeated the request a hundred times, that she would not disturb him. He concluded by saying affectingly that he needed no physician, as the queen was his best doctor and his most faithful friend. He then became worse, and Dr. Warren was sent for. He refused to see him, and declared that he was only suffering from nervousness, and was otherwise perfectly well. But the physician was enabled by a stratagem to make some scrutiny into the conduct and appearance of the unhappy monarch; and the conclusion to which he came was by no means encouraging. The Prince of Wales now became in reality commander of the palace of Windsor; and soon every thing assumed the disorder and recklessness which marked his own character. Things were done by his orders respecting which an observant courtier justly remarked that, if the king recovered and was informed of them, they would be enough to drive him again into madness.

The king's sons and their intimates sometimes amused themselves by listening in an adjoining chamber, to the hoarse and pitiful ravings of the demented monarch. By some means he had his suspicions aroused on the subject, and he surprised and terrified them one night by suddenly appearing among them, and fiercely demanding what they were doing there. They endeavored to evade the question, and to conciliate him, but they failed. He was not so much deranged as to be unable to penetrate the designs of his worthless offspring. Looking around, the king missed the presence of Prince Frederic, who had succeeded in concealing himself. He then exclaimed: "Freddy is my friend; yes *he* is my friend." Sir George Baker succeeded after a time in inducing the monarch to return to his own chamber; but there, the latter forced Sir George into a corner, and told him he was an old woman, who could not distinguish between a mere nervous malady and any other disease.

The Prince of Wales determined, as the king gave no signs of recovery, to remove him from Windsor to the small palace at Kew. The king declared that he would never go thither. A stratagem was at last resorted to, to overcome his repugnance. He desired very much to be allowed to see his queen and daughters, from whom, for some time, he had been separated. He was informed that they had all removed to Kew, and that if he wished to see them he must follow them. He agreed to do so. Having arrived at Kew he demanded of his attendants the fulfilment of their promise. They refused him; and the unhappy king felt the blow so severely, that he spent the succeeding night in fearful paroxysms of impotent fury and rage.

The malady of the king had commenced with a discharge of humor from the legs. By his imprudence and mental excitement, the affection had been driven from the limbs to the bowels and thence to the head. The physicians endeavored, yet for a long time in vain, to bring the humor back to its original location. Thus the year 1788 wore gloomily away. The Prince of Wales and his friends, of whom Charles James Fox was the ablest and boldest, made preparations to have a regency appointed, and the heir apparent designated to fill the post. Their ambitious and premature plans were destined to be disappointed. On the first day of 1789, the unfortunate monarch was heard in his chamber praying loudly and fervently for his own recovery.

The succeeding third of February had been appointed for the purpose of introducing the proposed Regency Bill, in favor of the Prince of Wales, into Parliament. During this apparent interregnum William Pitt still guided the helm of state with an arm so vigorous and steady, that the empire suffered no injury from the incapacity of the sovereign. Meanwhile the latter gradually began to recover, to the great joy of the queen, and the friends of the monarch, and to the intense mortification of the Prince of Wales, and his unprincipled confederates. Had the Prince attained the regency at this period, he would have instantly expelled the Pitt ministry, abandoned the whole line of policy which they had pursued both as to foreign and domestic affairs, and would have elevated Fox and the ultra-Whig statesmen to power. On the 10th of March, the Lord Chancellor informed the public that the king had perfectly recovered, and that he had ordered a commission to be issued for holding Parliament in the usual manner. The proceeding put an end to the discussion of the iniquitous Regency Bill which had been commenced. The Prince of Wales was greatly disappointed; but the rejoicing of the nation was universal. The restored monarch expressed his determination to make a public expression of thanks to the Supreme Being for the return of his physical and mental health. The cathedral of St. Paul was prepared for that purpose, and on the 25th of June, 1789, one of the most impressive scenes occurred within that stately fane, upon which the eye of man had ever gazed. As the king proceeded from the palace to the temple, he was greeted by the hearty cheers of an immense multitude. He was accompanied by his devoted queen, who shared with him the solemn pleasure of the occasion. As the royal pair entered the cathedral arm in arm, the first effect produced by the preparations which had been made within it was sublime. During the solemn religious service which ensued, in which the vast assemblage seemed to join, and while the sublime melody of the organ reverberated beneath the far ascending vault of the dome, the devout and grateful emotions of the monarch could not be concealed, and were edifying to every beholder. All were pleased and gratified except the selfish and perfidious prince from whose unprincipled grasp the royal sceptre had so suddenly been wrested.

Very soon after his recovery, the king remarked to the Chancellor, Lord Thurlow, that what had already occurred might happen again; and he desired some immediate and permanent provision to be made for such a regency as would settle the government upon a desirable basis, in case he was again rendered unfit to exercise the royal functions. Mr. Pitt and the other members of the cabinet readily admitted the expediency of the measure; but they were divided as to the minor details. It was not until a later period, when the insanity of George III. became hopeless, and the regency became a matter of immediate and absolute necessity, that the full establishment and limitation of its powers and prerogatives were decided upon by Parliament.

During 1789 tranquillity prevailed both at home and with foreign nations. The trial of Warren Hastings still continued to attract a large share of public attention, but some years were still destined to elapse before its conclusion. Mr. Addington was chosen Speaker of the House of Commons, upon the promotion of Mr. Grenville to the office of Secretary of State. The revenues of the year were insufficient to meet the current expenses of the government, and Mr. Pitt was compelled to propose a loan of a million pounds. Yet notwithstanding this incident, the security and prosperity of the nation were such as to give general confidence and joy. The chief source of apprehension arose from the events which were transpiring at this period in France. That mighty revolution which was destined to desolate the fairest kingdom on the continent of Europe, and render it a howling wilderness, had broken forth. Political tempests, such as had never been equalled in fury since the foundation of governments, swept over the land, blasting whatever was fairest and noblest among the monuments of past ages, and filling France with blood and tears. The States-General convened at Versailles, at the command of Louis XVI., who sincerely desired to remedy the existing evils, by the coöperation of the representatives of the nation. Soon this assembly of demagogues and assassins declared their entire independence of the king and court, asserted their superiority over them, and proceeded to excesses, the narrative of which forms the bloodiest and blackest page in the annals of the world. These events are faithfully recorded elsewhere, and do not come within the scope of the present history. They called forth, during their progress, much scrutiny in the British nation, who were able to behold from a safe distance the horrible effects of revolutionary fanaticism. At this period Edmund Burke published his celebrated " Reflections on the French Revolution." Mr. Fox and his friends defended the excesses of that execrable movement by their speeches in Parliament, in answer to those delivered by Burke in that assemblage. He declared " his total dissent from opinions so hostile to the general principles of liberty ; and which he was grieved to hear from the lips of a man whom he loved and revered—by whose precepts he had been taught, by whose example he had been animated to engage in their defence. He vindicated the conduct of the French army, in refusing to act against their fellow-citizens, from the aspersions of Mr. Burke, who had charged them with abetting an abominable sedition by mutiny and desertion—declaring that, if he could view a standing military force with less constitutional jealousy than before, it was owing to the noble spirit manifested by the French army, who, on becoming soldiers, had proved that they did not forfeit their character as citizens, and would not act as the mere instruments of a despot. The scenes of bloodshed and cruelty that had been acted in France, no man, said Mr. Fox, could hear of without lamenting. But when the grievous tyranny that the people had so long groaned under was considered, the excesses they had committed in their efforts to shake off the yoke could not excite our astonishment so much as our regret. And as to the contrast which Mr. Burke had exhibited respecting the mode in which the two revolutions in England and France were conducted, it must be remembered that the situation of the two kingdoms was totally different. In France, a free constitution was to be created. In England, it wanted only to be secured. If the fabric of government in England suffered less alteration, it was because it required less alteration. If a general destruction of the ancient constitution had taken place in France, it was because the whole system was radically hostile to liberty, and that every part of it breathed the direful spirit of despotism."

Sheridan, one of the most gifted, unprincipled, and pitiable of men, advocated the same side in Parliament, with his usually brilliant and sparkling eloquence. Said he: "The people of France, it is true, have committed acts of barbarity and bloodshed which have justly excited indignation and abhorrence. That detestation and abhorrence, however, are still more justly due to the government of France prior to the revolution; the tyranny and oppression of which had deprived the people of the rights of men and of citizens, and driven them to that degree of desperation which could alone have incited those unexampled acts of cruelty and revenge which had been practised in the first agitation and violence of the effort to regain their freedom. Could it be expected, that men in their situation should be capable of acting with the same moderation and the same attention to humanity and sensibility as characterized freemen? Were the mad outrages of a mob an adequate ground for branding the national assembly with the stigma of being a bloody, ferocious, and tyrannical democracy? It was a libel on that illustrious body thus to describe them. A better constitution than that which actually existed, it is allowed that France had a right to expect. From whom were they to receive it? From the bounty of the monarch at the head of his courtiers? or from the patriotism of Marshal Broglio at the head of the army? From the faint and feeble cries emitted from the dark dungeons of the bastile? or from the influence and energy of that spirit which had laid the bastile in ashes? The people, unhappily misguided as they doubtless were in particular instances, had however acted rightly in their great object. They had placed the supreme authority of the community in those hands by whom alone it could be justly exercised, and had reduced their sovereign to the rank which properly belonged to kings—that of administrator of the laws established by the free consent of the community." * The radicals in England attempted at this period to promote the general revolutionary spirit by moving in Parliament the repeal of the Test Act—the great object of the abhorrence of the English Dissenters. The repeal was supported by Fox and Sheridan, but opposed by Burke, with great eloquence and earnestness; and the motion was defeated at last by a vote of nearly three hundred against a hundred and five. This result clearly indicated that, however much the French people might have gone mad with the delirium of political excitement, the sturdy British nation had remained uninfected by their insanity, in any considerable degree, and were unwilling to proceed even to that extent of reform which was consonant with the principles of enlightened and rational liberty.

Although the great abilities of William Pitt were still devoted to the task of conducting the government, it was with the utmost difficulty that its financial necessities could be met. A circumstance occurred at this period which serves to illustrate the truth of this assertion. The minister proposed in Parliament to take from the Bank of England the *unclaimed dividends* which remained in it, and apply them to the payment of the current expenses of the government. These dividends amounted to about five hundred thousand pounds. This proposition, the injustice of which must be apparent to every intelligent observer, immediately incurred a tremendous storm of opposition. It was urged with great propriety, that the measure was dangerous and fraudulent to the utmost degree; that its passage would undermine the confidence and safety of the whole mercantile community; that the charter of the Bank expressly constituted that institution the guardian of the rights of the depositors; that the money when once paid remains private property as much as before; that dividends which 'had not remained unclaimed for *three* years could not properly be termed unclaimed, but only *unreceived;* that the dividends, exclusive of those of the last three

* *Belsham's George III.,* Vol. ii., p. 436.

years, did not amount to a fifth part of the sum proposed by the minister to be seized ; and that the measure was in reality nothing else than an act of public and governmental robbery. Notwithstanding these conclusive arguments, so great was the pressure of the existing necessity, that the minister was enabled to effect a loan from the Bank of five hundred thousand pounds without interest, to remain as such, as long as a floating balance to that amount should remain in the hands of the Bank.

The public tranquillity was, at this period, disturbed by riots which occurred at Birmingham, which were produced by the prevalence of religious excitement on the subject of the Trinity. Joseph Priestley, celebrated both as a philosopher and as a theologian, had advocated, with great learning and ability, the theory that the founder of Christianity was not a divine personage, but merely a great teacher and prophet sent from God, who demonstrated the truth of his doctrines by signs and wonders which the deity performed through him. He also condemned religious establishments as being prejudicial to the progress and power of pure religion ; as well he might, with the overwhelming evidence which the worldliness, selfishness, and profligacy of a great portion of the clergy of the established church at that time presented. Those whose interests were injured, or whose prejudices were shocked, by the views of Dr. Priestley, incited the indignation of the mob to such an extreme, that they attacked and destroyed the chapel at Birmingham in which he officiated, and accomplished a similar outrage upon the private residence, library, philosophical apparatus, and other property of the great Heresiarch. This incident serves as an evidence that George III., his advisers, and his most influential subjects, who gave tone to public sentiment in that day, had been taught no lesson of enlightened charity or liberality by the thrilling and instructive events of the American Revolution.

A significant event of 1792, of a similar nature, as indicative of the conservative feeling which prevailed in England, was the recall of Lord Gower, the British Ambassador at Paris. This act was regarded by the leading revolutionists of France as

an evidence of the enmity of the British court and people to the
new order of things then progressing in that country. Nor can
we wonder at or condemn this step, when we consider the horrible and destructive extremes to which the demagogues and assassins of that fated land were destined ultimately to arrive. Meanwhile, the excesses which were being perpetrated in France so
incensed or terrified the grave and order-loving English nation,
that a great reaction took place among them in favor of conservatism and royalty; and innumerable societies were formed
throughout the kingdom for the purpose of protecting the king,
the throne, and the church. The populace even became excited
on the subject, and their absurd vociferations in favor of what
they neither understood nor appreciated, resounded over the land
from the hills of Cheviot to the cliffs of Dover, from the banks
of the Tamar to those of the Tweed. This feeling was promptly
followed up by the policy adopted by the king and his ministers.
An embargo was placed on vessels freighted for France. The
militia of the kingdom were increased, embodied, and drilled.
Parliament was convened by proclamation before the day appointed in the last prorogation, as if some great public crisis
impended. M. Chauvelin, the French Ambassador, was ordered
to depart the kingdom. These absurd and useless demonstrations soon led to the results which might have been confidently
anticipated. On the 1st of February, 1793, the National Assembly of France unanimously passed a decree declaring war against
the *King* of Great Britain and the *Stadtholder* of Holland. The
object of the convention, and of the desperate assassins who
governed it, in thus declaring war against the *sovereigns* of these
countries, and not against the people or nations themselves, was
to make a false and artificial distinction between the latter and
their rulers, and if possible to create differences and jealousies between them. That those who at that time ruled France did not
possess the sympathy of the nation in their declaration of hostilities against England, was a well-known and incontestible fact.*

* An evidence of this position may be found in the testimony of cotemporary
travellers in France. One of them thus wrote:

"During the whole of our journey (December, 1792,) we remarked that the apprehension of a war with England was peculiarly painful to the French. Though flushed with their late successes, and confident against a world in arms, it was evident there was nothing they dreaded more than such an event; not merely on account of the mischief that might ensue, but because it would force them to regard as enemies the only nation in Europe they considered as their friends. All along the road they anxiously asked us what we thought would be the consequence of the armament in England? We frankly told them we presumed it would be war; and generally observed a moment of silence and dejection follow the delivery of our opinion. The imminence of hostilities, however, in no degree diminished the respect they showed us as Englishmen: and not only we did not meet with any thing like an insult in the whole of our tour, but, on the contrary, we experienced everywhere particular kindness and attention. They seemed eager to court our opinion; and frequently begged us not to ascribe to a whole nation the faults of individuals, and not to charge their government with disorders its present state of vacillation rendered it incompetent to repress. I confess I should never have suspected that I was travelling among a nation of savages, madmen, and assassins—I should rather have wished with Shakespeare,

"——————— That these contending kingdoms,
England and France, whose very shores look pale
With envy of each other's happiness,
May lose their hatred."

Vide " Tour through the Theatre of War, 1792."

CHAPTER IX.

Events of the War with France—Increased Unpopularity of the King—He is assailed by the Populace—He is fired at in the Theatre—The Roman Catholic Bill—Demand of Bonaparte that the French Princes be expelled from England—Incidents of the Hostilities which ensued—Conspiracy of Robert Emmet in Ireland—Its Suppression—Decline of the Addington Ministry—Hostilities with France—Triumph of Nelson at Trafalgar—Exultation of the Nation—Death of William Pitt—He is succeeded by Charles James Fox—His short Administration and Death—Lord Howick—Mr. Canning becomes Foreign Secretary—British Victories in Spain and Portugal—Prodigious Power of Napoleon Bonaparte.

THE events of the war which ensued were not so fortunate as to be adapted to flatter the national pride in any great degree, while the public debts and burdens were thereby vastly augmented. The Duke of York was sent with an English army to join the Dutch in invading France. Partial success at first attended their efforts, and the fortress of Valenciennes was taken. The fortified harbor of Toulon also became the trophy of British prowess. But the events of the second campaign were entirely disastrous to the enemies of France. Toulon was retaken by the exertions of the greatest hero of modern times; for at its siege the name and genius of Napoleon Bonaparte first attained a prominent place in history. At sea Earl Howe subsequently won a victory over the French fleet in the West Indies; and several French colonies were transferred from the jurisdiction of that country to the possession of Britain. Corsica was also subdued, and the Anti-Gallican party, headed by the famous Paschal Paoli, tendered the sovereignty of the island to the British monarch. The English accordingly took possession; but the French faction having subsequently gained the ascendency, the island was evacuated by its new masters, and was again annexed to France.

These and other untoward events served to render the king very unpopular with the nation ; and he was destined to feel the palpable proofs of their disaffection. In October, 1795, as he was proceeding to the House of Lords he was assailed by the seditious cries of the multitude, and was fired at by an assassin among the mob. On his return from the House, his carriage was pelted with stones, rubbish, and other filth ; while the air resounded with shouts of " Bread," " No war," " No king." The unhappy monarch was much alarmed at these displays of popular hostility. Nor were they of short duration. In February, 1796, on the return of the king and queen from Drury Lane theatre, a stone was thrown at their carriage which passed through a glass panel, and struck the queen in the face. Not long afterward a female maniac made her way into the palace with the avowed purpose of assassinating the queen—whom she called Mrs. Guelph—and her mother. In addition to these mortifications, George III. was harassed by the detestable conduct of the heir apparent, the Prince of Wales. This person had been married in 1795, as will be more minutely related hereafter, to the Princess Caroline of Brunswick ; but unhappy differences, which distracted and disgraced the royal family, took place between them shortly after their nuptials. In many ways the Prince of Wales annoyed and afflicted his father, and tended to embitter his existence. These incidents should have won for the king the popular sympathy ; but such was not the case. In May, 1800, another attempt to assassinate him was made by an adventurer named Hatfield. As the king entered his box at the Drury Lane theatre, and was in the act of bowing to the audience, the shot was fired at him from the pit. He remained perfectly cool while the villain was apprehended, and then sat down calmly to witness the performance. Having returned to the palace he remarked to the queen on retiring to rest : " I shall sleep soundly ; and my prayer is, that the unhappy prisoner, who aimed at my life, may rest as quietly as I will."

All these unfortunate incidents gradually tended again to undermine the harassed intellect of the king. Other causes of irritation were added during the years 1801 and 1802. The emancipation of the Romanists from their civil disabilities was a measure very strongly and fiercely urged in Parliament, and by a powerful party in the nation. To this measure the king was earnestly opposed; and he believed that his coronation oath bound him to unyielding resistance to every enlargement of liberty or influence to that dangerous faction. His tendency to mental disease was also aggravated by his disputes with Mr. Pitt, who differed from the monarch widely in reference to the Roman Catholic and other questions. Mr. Pitt at length resigned in consequence of these differences, and Mr. Addington, afterward Lord Sidmouth, became prime minister. Negotiations for peace were immediately commenced with France, which were eventually consummated by the treaty of Amiens in March, 1802; at the terms of which the English nation rejoiced, but of which they had little reason to be proud.

The king, during the mental attack which occurred at this period, remained silent for many hours at a time; but he at length remarked after coming to himself: "I am better now, but will remain true to the church." The meaning of this expression is to be derived from the fact, that the Catholic question had been uppermost in his mind, and that the agitation which had taken place in reference to it, had been the chief cause of his derangement. It produced the same effect upon him which the loss of his American colonies had done upon a former occasion. As soon as the king felt himself conscious of the recovery of his intellect, he sent for the afflicted queen and princesses; and the interview between them was extremely affecting.* The next day he sent for his son, the Duke of York, and held a long conversation with him. For this prince the king entertained con-

* After this attack of insanity had begun, Mr. Addington recommended a *hop pillow* for the king, as being conducive to produce sleep. The suggestion was adopted with the most favorable results, and the repose which the patient thus obtained soon led to his recovery. See *Malmesbury Diaries*, Vol. iv., p. 46.

siderable respect; and with him he spoke freely in reference to what had occurred during the time of his illness. He at length began on the subject of the Catholic question; but the prince, perceiving that his father was becoming painfully excited in reference to it, kindly stopped him, and assured him that Mr. Pitt had abandoned all intention of pressing his views upon the attention of Parliament. George III. afterward remarked in reference to this matter to Dr. Willis, one of his physicians, when speaking of Mr. Pitt's policy : " What has not *he* to answer for, who was the cause of my late illness."* The Duke of Portland subsequently declared, that the king had assured him that he would rather suffer martyrdom than submit to the measure, or approve of it. It was affecting to witness the attachment of the monarch to his wife. He frequently exclaimed : " I am now perfectly well, and my queen, my queen has saved me." † In the fierce and bitter disputes which now took place between the Prince and Princess of Wales, the king uniformly took the side of the latter; and when her husband first endeavored to remove their daughter, the Princess Charlotte, from the keeping of her mother, he declared : " The princess shall have her child ;. and I will speak to Mr. Wyatt about building a wing to her present house." He justly detested and despised the Prince of Wales in his character of husband, as much as in that of a son and a subject.

Napoleon Bonaparte, the ruler of France, entertained at this period the most hostile feelings against the British nation. He only waited for a pretext to recommence hostilities against them ; nor was he long in finding one. Some members of the Bourbon family had escaped the storms of the revolution, and had taken refuge in England. The Count D'Artois and the Dukes of Orleans and Bourbon, were among the number. These persons had been received by George III. and by the principal nobility with courteous hospitality. Mr. Pitt, Mr. Windham, and other leading statesmen had met these princes at the

---

* *Pellew's Life, &c., of Lord Sidmouth,* Vol. i., p. 309.
† *Twiss's Public and Private Life of Lord Eldon,* Vol. i., p. 205.

tables of Lord Grenville, and the Prince Regent. Many of the adherents of the houses of Orleans and Bourbon had also taken up their abode in England, as the only asylum in Europe secure from the destructive rage of the enemies of the old dynasty. The British press, either through their influence, or without it, teemed with the most abusive articles against the French usurper and adventurer. Bonaparte complained that every wind which blew from England wafted to his ears nothing but slander and ridicule of his person and his power. He formally demanded that the Bourbons and their adherents should be expelled from British soil, and that the press be restricted in its allusions to the French ruler.

With this absurd demand the king and his cabinet refused to comply. Angry conferences passed between Bonaparte and Lord Whitworth, the British minister at Paris, which led to no favorable result; and on the 19th of May, 1803, war was declared reciprocally between the hostile powers at the same time, and without concert. Preparations for carrying on the conflict were made on both sides; but the greater energy and success were on the part of the French. General Mortier overran the Electorate of Hanover, and the Hanse towns, Hamburg and Bremen, were laid under heavy contributions. All the English residents in France were detained as prisoners of war. The English, on their part, blockaded with their fleets the mouths of the Elbe and the Weser, and thus inflicted serious injury on the commerce of France and her allies. Another squadron under the command of Commodore Hood attacked the French works on the island of St. Lucie, and compelled them to surrender. Similar results followed at St. Domingo, Demerara, Essequibo, and Berbice.

The congratulation which this series of successes produced, was diminished by the outbreak of a dangerous conspiracy which occurred at this period in Ireland. The leader in the movement was a young and enthusiastic lover of liberty, whose name and eloquence have since justly become historical. Robert Emmet, one of the most gifted men of his age, indulged the sanguine hope that his oppressed countrymen, under his guidance, would be able to elevate their native land from the position of degradation and dependence to which she had been reduced by British tyranny, and place her honorably among the catalogue of independent nations. He proposed to establish a separate Irish republic, by striking a decisive blow in the capital, by obtaining possession of the seat of government, by proclaiming a new and liberal constitution, and by thus completely overturning the detested despotism of Britain in his native land. On the 23d of July, 1803, an assembly of his partisans, forming an immense and tumultuous mob, marched through the streets of Dublin, and proceeded to attack the castle of the viceroy. They were assailed in turn by a hundred and fifty regular troops, and, after a short contest, were entirely vanquished and dispersed. The whole insurrection had been planned and executed with the rash precipitancy and short-sighted enthusiasm, which usually characterize the movements of inexperienced youth. Emmet and his chief associates were taken, tried, convicted, sentenced, and executed. The brightest and best record of his fame and genius is to be found in the thrilling and powerful speech which he delivered in his own defense, in vindication of his unfortunate associates, and in deprecation of the mortal wrongs of his bleeding country, on the occasion of his trial for high treason in Dublin, before a special commission appointed by the king.

The ministry, of which Mr. Addington was the chief, rapidly declined in influence. Various causes led to this result, among which one of the most prominent was the inefficiency with which the war had been conducted on the continent. On the 12th of May, 1804, the nation was gratified with the intelligence that Mr. Addington had resigned, and that the helm of government had been again confided to the skilful and powerful hands of William Pitt. For the last time this great man ascended to the highest dignity in the realm accessible to a subject. Other important changes now took place in the cabinet. Lord Melville became First Lord of the Admiralty, Lord Harborough, Secretary for Foreign Affairs, and Lord Camden, Secretary of War and the Colonies. Immediate steps were taken by the new minister to secure the military defense of the country against the formidable power of Napoleon. By the plan which he proposed, and carried in Parliament, a large standing army was raised, and every citizen of a certain age was transformed to some extent into a soldier, ready at any moment to take up arms against the threatened encroachments of the common foe. In December of this year, the Spanish monarch, under the controlling influence of Napoleon, declared war against England; which event increased the difficulties and dangers which harassed, yet did not intimidate, the country.

The year 1805 was rendered remarkable, among other events, by an autograph letter addressed by Napoleon to George III., in which he set forth the advantages of peace, and professed himself desirous of realizing them. Yet, at the same time, he proposed no definite conditions on which pacific relations could be established.* The answer of the British ministry, which was conveyed through Lord Mulgrave to M. Talleyrand, declared that no positive arrangements could be made on the subject, until the English government had conferred with their allies on the continent, especially with the Emperor Alexander of Russia. This reply terminated the correspondence, and hostilities were resumed. Bonaparte fitted out a powerful fleet in the port of Toulon with the express design of invading England. The fleet set sail, and ultimately steered for the West Indies under the command of

---

* "Your Majesty," said Napoleon, "has gained more, within ten years, both in territory and riches, than the whole extent of Europe. Your nation is at the highest point of prosperity; what can it hope from war? To form a coalition with some powers on the continent? The continent will remain tranquil; a coalition can only increase the preponderance and continental greatness of France. To renew intestine troubles? The times are no longer the same. To destroy our finances? Finances founded on a flourishing agriculture can never be destroyed. To take from France her colonies? The colonies are to France only a secondary object; and does not your majesty already possess more than you know how to preserve? If your majesty would but reflect, you must perceive that the war is without an object, without any presumable result to yourself." See *History of the Reign of George III., by Robert Bissett, LL.D.* Vol. iii., p. 62.

Admiral Villeneuve. His armament consisted of eighteen sail of the line, ten thousand veteran soldiers, beside a full complement of seamen. Lord Nelson had been placed in command of the British fleet intended to meet and attack the French squadron. Subsequently the latter was augmented to twenty-seven sail of the line, by the addition of some Spanish ships. Lord Nelson was still in pursuit of the enemy, when, on the 21st of October, they were descried sailing off Cape Trafalgar on their way to Gibraltar. The English fleet had also been increased to the number of twenty-seven sail. The combatants were thus equal in strength; and that great victory ensued which is perhaps the most brilliant and illustrious in the naval annals of the boasted mistress of the seas. Nineteen French ships of the line, together with their Admiral, were taken by the British, and fifteen hundred of the enemy were slain. The news of this splendid triumph convulsed the nation with joy. No such exultation had been seen throughout the realm, since the memorable day when the victory of Blenheim crushed the prodigious power of Louis XIV. and covered the British arms with fadeless glory. The only restraint upon the universal congratulation was the death of Nelson, who expired from a gun-shot wound two hours after the termination of the conflict.

The triumph of Trafalgar put an end for ever, to all Napoleon's designs in reference to the actual invasion of England. He still continued his marvellous career of conquest on the continent. Battle after battle, and victory after victory, attested the supremacy of his matchless military genius. His triumphant legions entered almost every capital in Europe; and he set up and pulled down kings at his pleasure. A long series of successful engagements, among which those of Ulm and Austerlitz were the most important, won for the Emperor of the French the iron crown of Italy. The British soil remained intact amid the convulsive throes of the nations; for no foreign foe invaded it. While thus exulting in the happy exemption which they enjoyed, the British people were called to mourn the sudden death of the great minister who then guided so ably the helm of state.

William Pitt expired on the 23d of January, 1806, in the forty-seventh year of his age, after having occupied the post of prime minister during a longer period than had fallen to the lot of any previous minister, during the reigns of the Georges. He had labored, and that with eminent success, to increase the maritime power of England; to resist the spread of revolutionary principles; to oppose the encroachments of the great Corsican upon the power and influence of his country; to form continental alliances which would prove serviceable in resisting the common foe, and in advancing the internal prosperity, elevation, and improvement of the nation over whom he ruled. His death was a national calamity; and none felt it more deeply or keenly than the king himself.

On the death of Mr. Pitt, Charles James Fox, his great rival, became Secretary of State for Foreign Affairs. Mr. Windham was appointed Secretary for the Department of War and the Colonies; Lord Grenville, First Lord of the Treasury; Lord Erskine, High Chancellor; and Mr. Sheridan, Treasurer of the Navy. On the accession of Mr. Fox, hopes were entertained that peace might be established with the French Emperor, inasmuch as he was well known to be on terms of personal friendship with that ambitious potentate; nor is it improbable that the negotiations which ensued would have been successful, had not the British minister been compelled by a sense of honor to insist that Russia should be admitted to a share in the deliberations. To this measure Bonaparte was obstinately opposed, and he thus rendered all pacific intentions on the part of the British government utterly abortive.

Mr. Fox was destined to retain the reins of power but a short time, and to follow his celebrated rival to the silence of the tomb a few months after his departure. In August, 1806, he proposed in Parliament the last measure which may be said to have originated with him, and which was worthy of so brilliant and splendid a career. He moved a resolution, asserting that the African slave-trade was contrary to the principles of justice, humanity, and sound policy; that it be abolished, and its practice be deemed piracy throughout the British dominions. The motion was carried in both houses, and at once received the approval of the king. On the 13th of the next month, September, 1806, Mr. Fox expired, in the fifty-seventh year of his age; and his mortal remains, shattered by the prodigious conflicts through which he had passed during twenty-five years of active parliamentary life, were laid, to take their last long slumber, in the same consecrated mould in Westminster Abbey, which contained the forms of his illustrious rival, and of the immortal ancestors of both. Lord Howick was appointed Secretary of Foreign Affairs in the place of the deceased statesman, for whose loss a nation, not much given to the luxury or the weakness of tears, sincerely and universally wept.

The administration of Lord Howick, which proved to be of short duration, was remarkable only for the final abolition of slavery in the British dominions, by the passage of a law which appointed the first of January, 1808, as the latest date at which the inhuman traffic would be permitted in any portion of the land or sea over which the flag of Britain waved. This law received the hearty approbation of the king.

Lord Howick was succeeded by Mr. Canning as Secretary of Foreign Affairs, on the 25th of March, 1807. The chief incident of this year was the war with Denmark, which country had become the ally of Napoleon. A British fleet attacked Copenhagen, which capitulated after a bombardment of three days. The British army took possession of the city, dockyards, arsenals, eighteen ships, and all the naval stores which were found in the capital. The Danes endeavored to retaliate; they harassed the British traders in the Baltic; British property was confiscated throughout the kingdom; and all correspondence with England was prohibited. The Emperor of Russia also became the friend of Denmark, and condemned the precipitate hostilities against that country which had been perpetrated. Bonaparte's retributive decree of Milan, excluding British merchandise from all the ports of the continent subject to his influence, greatly crippled British commerce, and spread a gloomy feeling of apprehension over the nation. The prodigious strides toward universal conquest which Napoleon was making, added intensity to this feeling. During the year 1808 a treaty was negotiated with Spain and Portugal; and a British army was sent under Sir Arthur Wellesley to expel the French forces from those kingdoms. The success which attended the movements of this able General, gradually increased the public confidence.* In January, 1809, Sir John Moore gained a decisive victory over Marshal Soult at Corunna. Subsequently, Wellesley expelled the Marshal from Oporto, and compelled both him and the gallant Ney to retire into Castile. The battle of Talavera added to the lustre of the British arms, by the defeat of Marshal Victor. During the years 1809 and 1810, the attention of the British people and government was chiefly enlisted in the prodigious events which were transpiring on the continent. In Spain, the various vicissitudes of the war of the succession finally resulted in the expulsion of Joseph Bonaparte from Madrid, and the total deliverance of Spain and Portugal from the presence and power of the French. Austria declared war at this period against Napoleon, and the combatants made a trial of their strength at the great battle of Aspern. Both parties claimed the victory. At the battle of Wagram which followed, the result was not so equivocal; and the French gained an overwhelming triumph. The result of the ruin of the Austrian army was the marriage of the conqueror to the daughter of his imperial and vanquished foe, and the elevation of the Archduchess Maria Louisa to the vacant seat of the discarded Josephine upon the throne of France. The hereditary successor of the prince of the apostles at Rome was dragged by the giant arm of the Corsican from his sacred seat, deprived of his secular authority, and conveyed as a prisoner to Avignon. The Ecclesiastical States were then annexed to the swelling bulk of the French Empire. Prussia was prostrated beneath the feet of the con-

---

* See *Considerations on the Causes, Objects, and Consequences of the Present War, and on the Expediency or Danger of Peace with France. By William Roscoe.* London, 1808.

queror; for he had crushed her at the decisive battle of Jena. Holland, Westphalia, and Italy acknowledged the absolute supremacy of this modern Alexander; while the whole continent trembled with the dread of his colossal power. At this period the intellectual life of the British monarch may be said to have terminated for ever. The light of his reason failed at a time when apprehension and gloom oppressed the hearts of his subjects. The attack under which George III. now suffered, and which began in January, 1811, was regarded even by the monarch's friends, as so violent and hopeless, that on the sixth of February, his eldest son, the Prince of Wales, was installed as Regent with regal authority. The death of the amiable Princess Amelia, the favorite daughter of the king, in November, 1810, had been the immediate cause of the final overthrow of his mind, in connection with the disastrous events which had recently occurred in various portions of the Empire.

CHAPTER X.

Renewed and Hopeless Insanity of George III.—Details respecting the Origin, Nature, and Effects of his Mental Disease—His Physicians—His Treatment—His Condition officially communicated to Parliament—A Regency permanently appointed—Gradual Decline of the Health of George III.—War with the United States of America—Growth of the Power and Supremacy of Napoleon—His Overthrow by the European Coalition—His Retirement at Elba.

The insanity of George III. presents one of the most remarkable phenomena contained in psychological history. He was afflicted during his lifetime with five separate attacks of mental disease. The first occurred in 1765, when he was in his twenty-eighth year; the second was in 1788, the third in 1801, the fourth in 1804, and the last in January, 1811. None of these attacks, except the last, exceeded six months in duration. There was nothing in his constitution or mental habits to render such an affection probable. His intellectual faculties, though moderate, were well-proportioned, and no marked deficiency characterized his natural powers. He was possessed of a strong and healthy frame, which had never been enervated by the excesses of passion, or by any sensual indulgences whatever. He took a great deal of exercise, amused himself frequently with the pleasures of music and the drama; and was so fond of inspecting the useful and healthful operations of agriculture, that he deservedly received the epithet of "Farmer George." He was, moreover, extremely abstemious in eating and drinking, and observed with great strictness all the rules of propriety in thought, word, and deed. That such a man, whose reign extended nominally during the unparalleled period of sixty years, and none of whose ancestors or family had been similarly diseased, should be afflicted with insanity, and that eventually in an incurable form, was singular indeed.

The king's first physicians when thus attacked, were Sir George Baker, Dr. Warren, Sir Lucas Pepys, Drs. Reynolds, Addington, and Gisborne. None of these persons possessed any peculiar skill or experience in the treatment of mental diseases; and therefore the Rev. Francis Willis was added to their number. He was a clergyman of the established church, who had charge of a parish in Lincolnshire; but he had carefully studied the subject of insanity, had practised a great deal in that department of medical science, and had attained wonderful success and great repute. He had provided an establishment for the treatment of the insane at Gretford, which was filled with patients, many of whom had greatly benefited by his treatment. At the period when he undertook the care of the insane king, he was an aged man, and a person of great cheerfulness, firmness and benevolence.* His first introduction to his patient was marked by an amusing incident. The latter asked him " whether he, as a clergyman, was not ashamed to exercise the profession of a doctor." Willis answered: " Sir, our Saviour himself went about healing the sick." " Yes," replied the king, " but he did not get seven hundred pounds a year for it."† Dr. Willis associated his son John with him in his treatment of their august patient, who was confined to his apartments in the palace. One attendant and one page were constantly required to remain in his room. The remedies which were given him were chiefly bark and saline medicines, and sometimes blisters were applied to his legs. He was secluded in a great measure from his family, his ministers and his friends; and sometimes he was even placed in a straight jacket, when his paroxysms became violent. This extreme was resorted to by way of discipline, perhaps oftener than was necessary; and it was a sad spectacle to behold the monarch of a great empire thus subjected to the most degrading

---

* See *Wraxall's Posthumous Memoirs of his Own Time.* Philadelphia Edition, p. 447.

† *Lord Malmesbury's Diaries, &c.* Vol. iv., p. 317.

of indignities.* The mastery which the elder Willis obtained over the mind or the instinct of his patient, may be illustrated by an incident which occurred on the occasion of the examination of the physician before a committee of Parliament, of which Edmund Burke was a member. Willis had allowed the king to have a razor and a penknife in his hands, at a time when every other observer regarded the act as perilous in the extreme. Burke asked him how he would have controlled the king had he suddenly become violent while these instruments were in his possession, and had attempted harm to himself or to others. Willis placed the candle near his face, and answered: "There, sir, by the *eye;* I would have looked at him *thus,* sir," at the same time assuming a basilisk expression which compelled Burke instantly to avert his view from the spectacle. It is also asserted that Willis confounded Sheridan, a member of the same committee, in a similar manner, on the same occasion. Said he: "Pray, sir, before you begin, be so good as to snuff the candles, that we may see clear, for I always like to see the face of the man I am speaking to." Sheridan, the most impudent and brazen-faced of men, was so overcome by this salute, that he was utterly unable to proceed.†

The last attack under which the king suffered, was more violent than the others which had preceded it, and was more nearly allied to delirium than to insanity or mere derangement. The incidents, therefore, connected with his life were more painful and affecting, as his case became more desperate and hopeless. These incidents became gradually known, and elicited the sympathy of the nation. The state of the king was officially communicated to Parliament from time to time, and became the subject of lengthy public discussions.‡ A difference of opinion existed among his physicians as to the possibility of his recovery, some indulging the hope that the attack might end favorably, and some regarding the disease as incurable. His feelings were of a varied character; at times he was elated, frivolous and extravagant, while at others he was gloomy, silent and depressed.

* *Wraxall's Posthumous Memoirs,* p. 520.
† *Swinburne's Courts of Europe.* Vol. ii., p. 75.
‡ *Hansard's Parliamentary Debates, First Series,* xix.

Some of his delusions were singular, exhibiting a mixture of simplicity and shrewdness. On one occasion he appeared to be addressing his conversation to two of his personal friends who had long been dead. Sir Henry Halford, who was present, remarked to him, that the persons to whom he spoke had been deceased many years. The king replied: "True, dead to you and to the world in general; but not dead to me. You forget that I have the power of holding converse with those whom you call dead, and it is in vain for you, so far as I am concerned, to kill some of your patients."*

For some years the last attack to which the king was subjected, merely unfitted him for the performance of his high and responsible regal functions, and was not an entire overthrow of the powers of reason. During this period he enjoyed short intervals which might almost be termed lucid. He sometimes took a deep interest in politics; his perception was tolerably clear, his memory very accurate, but his judgment was fallacious and unreliable. On one occasion the queen entered his apartment while he was singing a hymn, and accompanying himself on the harpsichord. He then knelt down, prayed for his family, his subjects, and for his own recovery to health and saneness. On another occasion he heard the church bell toll, and inquired of his attendant for whom it was rung. Being answered, he replied: "She was a good woman, has gone to heaven, and I hope soon to follow her." With the progress of time, however, the unfortunate monarch became worse, both mentally and physically. In 1819 his appetite failed him; in 1820 it was with difficulty that he was kept warm; he was reduced to a skeleton; and remained scarcely conscious of existence until, on the 29th of January, 1820, he quietly sank into the arms of death, in the eighty-second year of his age, and in the sixtieth year of his reign.

While the British monarch was thus removed from the exercise of his royal functions after October, 1810, the attention of the nation was chiefly enlisted in the momentous events which were transpiring on the continent, in the issue of which their

* *Campbell's Lives of the Lord Chancellors.* Vol. vii., p. 221.

own security was deeply involved. Napoleon still continued his career of triumph, and with the exception of Spain, Portugal, and Russia, may be said to have laid the whole continent at his feet. The interest of the English people was for a time divided between these momentous events, and those connected with the hostilities which were then waged with the United States. On the 18th of June, 1812, the latter power declared war against Great Britain, and brilliant victories were gained by the fleet of the young republic over the ships of the mother country. On land, General Hull surrendered Fort Detroit and twenty-five hundred men with thirty pieces of ordnance to the British General Brock. On Lake Erie, six British vessels were destroyed or taken by an equal squadron of the Americans. The capitol of the Confederacy at Washington was attacked, taken, and the public buildings of the Federal Government burnt. The contest was honorable and profitable to neither party; and peace was at length proclaimed between the belligerents, by the establishment of the treaty of Ghent, on the 24th of December, 1814.

Meanwhile the insatiable ambition of Bonaparte was overreaching itself on the continent of Europe. He determined to invade the Russian dominions with a vast army, and subject them also to his sway. Five hundred thousand men, fully equipped, with a prodigious array of artillery, passed the Niemen, and directed their march towards the walls of Moscow. Then followed an expedition which has no parallel in history. The Russians defended their territory with a degree of heroism which rivalled that of the Spartans at Thermopylæ. Great battles were fought, in which the proud Corsican was humbled, and the most fearful slaughter made of his veteran heroes, who had been triumphant on a hundred fields of blood; for the carnage of Borodino has no equal in the annals of war. The invader was expelled with ignominy from the hostile territory; his power broken, his army buried beneath the frozen snows of Russia, and his throne shaken to its very foundations. Twenty-five thousand regular troops recrossed the Niemen, the wrecks of the myriads who had proudly passed over it six months before, with all the glorious pomp and majesty of war. Thus weakened, the usurper was soon compelled to confront a formidable conspiracy of nations, who combined to crush him, and tear him from his throne. He confronted them at Lutzen, Bautzen, Dresden, Leipsic, and on other immortal fields, sometimes obtaining triumphs, sometimes suffering defeats, but always remaining heroic and undaunted. Destiny seemed to turn against her favorite child; and he was compelled to obey her firm behest in adversity as well as in prosperity. England, united with her continental allies, at length achieved the overthrow of the most fierce and formidable enemy who had ever assailed her power or her existence; and Napoleon at last abdicated the throne which he had usurped, but which he had adorned with such matchless splendor. He accepted the diminutive diadem of Elba, and there for a short period reposed the energies which had shaken and well nigh subdued a continent. But the great task of England, of her prince, her statesmen, and her people, was not yet completed. Another contest, the brightest, bloodiest, fiercest, and most important, yet remained to be fought, before the security, prosperity and glory of Great Britain would be placed upon a secure and permanent basis, exempt from all peril or mutability, and the details of these events still appropriately belong to the history of the era of George III.

CHAPTER XI.

Napoleon's Escape from Elba—His Arrival at Paris—Combination of the Great Powers of Europe against him—His Prodigious Efforts to Confront them—Immense Resources of the Allies—Conflict at Charleroi—At Ligny—At Quatre Bras—Preparation for a Decisive Battle—The Field of Waterloo—Incidents of this Memorable Battle—Heroism of the Combatants—Defeat of Napoleon—Gratitude of the British Nation to the British Generals and Soldiers—Pacification of the Continent—State of the Finances—Commotions in Ireland—Domestic Legislation—The Regency—Death of George III.—State of the British Empire at this Period.

On the 26th of February, 1815, Bonaparte sailed from Elba, in command of nine hundred men, with the determination of recovering the throne of France, and if necessary of again convulsing the continent of Europe by the storms of war. He landed at Cannes on the 1st of March; he disembarked and immediately commenced his approach to the French capital. The successive triumphs of this strange and adventurous journey, whose thrilling incidents were worthy of the unparalleled career of the great conqueror, began at Grenoble, whose garrison threw down their arms and shouted " *Vive l'Empereur,*" the moment he appeared to their view. Here his troops swelled to the number of three thousand; and he took the line of march thence to the more important city of Lyons. The Bourbon princes and Marshal Macdonald attempted here to stem the swelling tide of the invader's popularity, but in vain. The same magic spell which everywhere gained the conqueror of Austerlitz and Jena the hearts of the French soldiery, effected the same result here, and Napoleon entered Lyons in triumph. At Besançon he first met his old comrade Ney, who had rashly promised Louis XVIII. to bring Napoleon to him captive in an iron cage; and after a short interview, so powerful was the spell which the Corsican threw over the impulsive marshal, that he re-entered his service, and assisted in swelling Napoleon's triumphant *cortege* as it neared the capital. On the 20th of March the ex-emperor entered Paris, from which the Bourbon and Orleans princes had previously taken their flight.

On regaining possession of the throne, Bonaparte immediately despatched letters to all the sovereigns of Europe, informing them that he had been restored to supreme power by the unanimous will of the French nation; and that he was willing to maintain the existing peace on the same terms as those which had been settled with the Bourbons. These letters were referred by their several recipients to the Congress of Vienna, which still continued its deliberations in the Austrian capital. But that assemblage decreed that no answer should be returned to the letter; and they further issued a manifesto declaring that Napoleon, by his desertion of Elba and his invasion of the French territory, had placed himself beyond the pale of all civil and social relations; that he had forfeited the only title to life which he yet retained; that he was a disturber of the tranquillity of Europe; and that he had become obnoxious to public vengeance. The great powers of Europe, England, Austria, Prussia, and Russia, entered into a treaty on the 25th of March, by which they bound themselves to unite their entire military resources, and not to lay down their arms or to conclude peace, until Napoleon, the common enemy of mankind, had been finally and completely crushed.

Unterrified by this formidable proclamation, the French emperor instantly commenced to made preparations to confront a continent which was rising in arms against him. He displayed prodigious energy and inexhaustible activity in every department of administrative duty. New levies were ordered throughout France, already exhausted by the loss of her best and most vigorous blood. Ammunition, arms, and artillery were fabricated by every possible means, and with the most urgent haste. As many of Napoleon's former marshals as he could influence, he regained from their sworn allegiance to the Bourbons; but of these eminent soldiers, Macdonald, Augereau, Oudinot, Victor, Marmont, and St. Cyr refused to violate their oaths and rejoin his standards. On the 1st of June he proclaimed a new constitution on the Champ de Mai, by which visionary and delusive fabric he hoped to gain the doubtful hearts of the French people. A showy and gorgeous pageant was exhibited on that occasion, such as was well calculated to attract and fascinate the nation; but the ultimate decision in this great conflict was dependent, not on imposing and glittering shows, but on the stern and bloody fortunes of war.

The armies of the allies were hastening toward the frontiers of France. A hundred and fifty thousand Austrian troops, commanded by Prince Schwartzenberg, were marching toward the Rhine; two hundred thousand Russians were gathering on the confines of Alsace; a hundred and fifty thousand Prussians, under the orders of Blücher, and burning with unquenchable fury to avenge the horrors and outrages of Jena, occupied Flanders; while eighty thousand British troops, led on by Wellington, were assembled in Belgium. The smaller contingents of the secondary German principalities, were preparing to take the field; and the whole of these combined together, would swell the number of men in arms against Napoleon during the Hundred Days to nearly a million. Against this vast armament, the French emperor, by the exercise of exertions which no mortal had ever before or since exhibited, in any great crisis of human destiny, could muster only four hundred thousand men, and a large proportion of these were raw recruits and youths who had practised no military training, nor had ever witnessed the horrors of a battle-field.

Napoleon commenced operations on the 15th of June, by attacking the Prussians posted at Charleroi. In this movement he was successful, and compelled the latter to retire to Ligny. At this place the combatants again encountered each other on the 16th. A furious conflict ensued, for Blücher himself now commanded the Prussians. Here, for the last time, the star of Napoleon's glory was triumphant, and that great warrior who had been the victor on so many fields of blood, who seemed to have chained the goddess Fortune to his car during so many adventurous and memorable years, gained the last laurels which were destined to decorate his imperial brow. Though Blücher fought with the ferocity of a lion, and repeatedly led on his broken ranks to the charge, he was eventually vanquished, and compelled to retreat. But he left the field, though not the victor, yet unconquered; and reserved his chief energies for the great battle of the age which was soon to ensue.

While Napoleon was thus earning his last laurels at Ligny, Ney was combatting the English army at Quatre-Bras. Here the "Bravest of the Brave" strove in vain to make any impression upon the adamantine ranks of that stern race, whose military prowess he and his haughty master had never yet fully tested, but with which they were destined soon to become familiar. The French were repulsed in all their attacks, and the British remained masters of all their positions. The shades of darkness alone put an end to the bloody conflict, and five thousand dead and wounded on each side attested the degree of fury which had characterized it. Yet these engagements were all merely preparatory to that more decisive combat which was about to occur, in which was involved the future destiny not only of the British empire, but also of every country and throne in Europe.

During the 17th of June, the French and allied armies approached from different directions the immortal field of Waterloo. The rain fell in torrents; and few even of the bravest slept during the solemn hours of the night which succeeded. The awful grandeur and importance of the approaching conflict, impressed even the most thoughtless. Never before since the beginning of time, had men contended for stakes of such prodigious magnitude. Upon the uncertain issue of the coming battle depended the fate of that mighty hero, whose achievements far transcended the achievements of all other men. A battle was about to be fought more decisive than that of Marathon, Cannæ, or Blenheim. The destiny of a greater hero than either Miltiades, Hannibal, or Marlborough then hung trembling in the uncertain balance. And now for the first time the two ablest generals of that age were about to measure their swords together; and the future fate of each entirely depended upon the issue. If the British were defeated, retreat even from the battle field would be impossible; for the dense forest of Soignies in their rear would cut off every means of escape. If Napoleon were vanquished, his fortunes would be ruined forever, and he would thenceforth become a fugitive and vagabond on the earth; and those who were about to engage in this struggle, were fully conscious of the supreme importance of the occasion.

At length the tedious hours of night wore away. The busy sounds of hurried preparation, the confused and multitudinous hum which betokened the near presence of mighty armaments, and which had echoed from both camps during the night, gradually subsided. The morning of the 18th of June, 1815, arose upon the world; and with its cheerful light there came that hour, pregnant with the fate of so many millions of human beings; that hour to which the events of preceding centuries had long converged; that hour to which many ages yet to come will point as the great decisive epoch which gave tone and color to the history of succeeding generations. The last grand act in the stupendous drama of Napoleon's career was now about to commence, ere the curtain fell upon it in darkness and gloom forever.

When the day dawned, a hundred and seventy-five thousand men sprang from their dripping beds, and arrayed themselves for the last time for the shock and the carnage of battle. Soon the various regiments of both armies began to deploy into their assigned positions. The battle-field extended two miles in length from the chateau of Hugomont on the extreme right, to that of La Haye Sainte on the left. Through the centre of this line the great high road or *chaussée* from Brussels to Charleroi passed, nearly a mile from the village of Waterloo. Both armies were arrayed on the crest of gentle eminences somewhat semi-circular in form, and opposite to each other, between which a natural slope or glacis intervened. The two armies presented a magnificent appearance. The French numbered eighty thousand, the English and Belgians seventy-two thousand. Like huge serpents the long, dark masses wound around the eminences to the thrilling sound of martial music, and gradually formed into line. Napoleon had two hundred and fifty cannon; the English a hundred and fifty-six. The French troops were formed in three lines, each flanked by dense masses of cavalry. Their brilliant uniforms and dazzling arms presented a gorgeous and imposing spectacle. The English troops were drawn up for the most part in solid squares, supported by cavalry in the rear. In front of their whole position their artillery was skilfully arrayed, directly facing the formidable number of guns displayed by the French. Appearances were certainly in favor of Napoleon before the battle began, both as to the number, the equipment, and the arrangement of his troops. On that great day, each of the opposing commanders had exerted his utmost skill, and had exhausted the whole military art, in the disposition of their respective armies, so as to increase their effectiveness to the fullest degree.

Just as the village clock at Nivelles struck eleven, Napoleon gave the order to commence the combat from the centre of his lines. The column of Jerome, six thousand strong, first attacked the English posted in the chateau of Hugomont. A vigorous contest here took place which resulted in the dislodgement of the English troops, and the conflagration of the edifice. This conflict, however, was only intended by Napoleon to conceal the main point of attack, which was in the right centre. The cannonade had now become general along the whole line. Ney was ordered to attack the British stationed along the hedge, and in the chateau of La Haye Sainte. This was the strongest position held by Wellington. As soon as the latter perceived the large masses of troops which were marching against this portion of his line, he drew up the splendid and powerful regiment of the Scotch Greys, the Enniskillens, and the Queen's Bays in its support. The French columns steadily pressed up the slope till within twenty yards of the British guns. Here a furious conflict ensued. The heroic Picton fell at the head of his regiment, as he waved forward his troops with his sword. The Scotch Greys attacked their foes with prodigious energy and effect. The French columns then hesitated. The Scotch, shouting "Scotland forever," rushed on to the attack. They carried a battery of twenty guns; charged the second line, routed it, and assailed the third. The last line of the French even began to yield, when Napoleon, perceiving the greatness of the disaster, ordered Milhaud's cuirassiers to charge the advancing foe. In this collision the brave Ponsonby died a heroic death; and so desperate was the conflict that the returning Scotch brought back with them scarcely a fifth part of their original number. As Napoleon gazed from the eminence on which he stood while he surveyed the battle, at the splendid and effective charge of the brave Scotch cavalry he exclaimed: *Ces terribles chevaux gris; comme ils travaillent!* But before the Scotch had completed their charge, they had broken and dispersed a column of five thousand men; had taken two thousand prisoners; and had either captured or spiked eighty pieces of cannon, which comprised the whole of Ney's artillery.

Undismayed by this disaster, Napoleon ordered twenty thousand cuirassiers under the command of Milhaud, to advance to the support of Ney in the centre. Soon La Haye Sainte was taken. An entire battalion of Hanoverian troops was almost destroyed by the French, but their tide of conquest was terminated by Wellington ordering up the Life Guards, the Royal Horse Guards, and the 1st Dragoon Guards to the defence. The advance of the French was then stopped; but Napoleon being determined to carry the important post of La Haye Sainte, brought up his whole body of light cavalry to the attack. Wellington still resisted these furious and repeated onslaughts on his lines, by ordering up to their support his whole reserve, and the Belgian regiments which were stationed in the rear.

Thus for three hours the uncertain conflict raged throughout the whole length of the tumultuous lines, with the most desperate fury. Prodigious acts of heroism were performed by many whose names have long since descended with them to their gory and forgotten graves, on that ensanguined field. The dead and dying lay piled in immense heaps, and the whole of the contending armies were involved in the dense smoke and the thundering uproar of battle. Neither host appeared willing to yield. Both seemed determined to conquer or to perish. As evening approached, Napoleon saw the necessity of combining his energies, and by one prodigious effort to carry the day. All along the line, two miles in length, the awful conflict raged; but it was now destined to become more furious, more deadly, more destructive still. Suddenly at half-past four o'clock, a dark mass appeared in the distance, moving in the direction of Frischermont. It was a Prussian corps, sixteen thousand strong, who were hastening toward the scene of conflict. Napoleon immediately detached Lobun with seven thousand men to arrest their progress; while he himself determined, at that critical moment, to put into execution his last and greatest resource, the one which had rarely failed to win the victory to his standards, and to crush the most powerful, enthusiastic, and formidable foes. This was to bring forward the grand attack of the Old Imperial Guard. It was this veteran corps which had decided the fate of Europe on many great battle-fields. It was this corps which had made the best troops of Russia and Austria quail and flee at Friedland and Wagram; which had broken the power of the Prussian columns at Jena and Lutzen; which had overwhelmed the Russian lines at Borodino and Austerlitz. Napoleon himself now rode through the ranks of these grim and dauntless warriors, and harangued them with a few words of burning eloquence. He briefly told them that the fate of the day, his own fate, and the fate of France and Europe, now depended upon themselves. Loud shouts of *Vive l'Empereur* in reply echoed far and wide over the plain, and drowned for a moment, even the mighty thunder of the cannon. Napoleon accompanied his veteran heroes a considerable way down the slope on their advance; and as each column defiled before him, he addressed them words of stirring eulogy and hope, which revived or increased their courage. They advanced to the final attack of the British centre in two great masses, one of which was led by Marshal Ney, the other by General Reille.

Never before, in the memorable annals of warfare, had there been such a shock as that which took place when the Old Guard, having approached with solemn and steady tread within forty feet of the English lines, commenced with their ancient heroism and resolution the task of vanquishing their desperate and powerful foes. The very earth shook beneath their terrific onset. They were met by the English Foot Guards, and the 73d and 30th regiments, with a heroism equal to their own. The eyes of all the combatants were turned toward the spot where that deadly conflict was taking place. Quickly and with desperate energy all the most destructive evolutions of warfare were executed. Immortal deeds were then achieved, which find no superior in all the blood-stained annals of military glory and ambition. But Wellington had made admirable dispositions to meet this last grand attack of the Old Guard, which had also been anticipated. He had stationed his artillery so as completely to sweep their lines; and as they approached near to his position, his batteries were unmasked, and they poured into the advancing host a prodigious storm of iron hail. The first lines of the Imperial Guards melted like frostwork as they came within range of the terrible guns; and though those in the rear resolutely pressed on to the attack, they made no further advance. They still crumbled away. A dead mass of soldiers rose higher and higher above the earth; but the head of the living column was unable to approach nearer than before, to the object of their attack.

At length the Imperial Guard recoiled. Napoleon, who had intently watched their progress, turned deadly pale, when he witnessed their useless heroism and their slow and ignominious retreat. Soon the horrid cry was repeated along the French lines: "*Tout est perdue, la Guarde recuile!*" and the enormous mass, broken and in confusion, fled in headlong retreat down the hill.

At this instant the rest of the Prussian army under Blücher and Ziethen came within range of the field, and opened a battery of a hundred guns upon the tumultuous masses of the French. It was now nearly eight o'clock. Soon the Prussians, thirty-six thousand in number, reached the French lines, and commenced a furious attack upon the exhausted and disordered multitude. At that moment the star of Napoleon's glory, after having for twenty years shone in unequalled splendor near the zenith, trembled, flickered, and then descended in ominous gloom, never to rise again. In vain the desperate and ruined adventurer strove to rally his discomfited warriors. In vain he swept on his noble charger over the plain, recalling his faltering troops to return once more to the attack. Terror now pervaded every breast. The retreat became general; and though Napoleon exposed himself in the most dangerous positions, and seemed even to seek for death, in restoring courage and order, all was in vain; and the ruin of his army, his fortunes, and his hopes was complete and irremediable. At last exclaiming: "All is lost! let us save ourselves!" he turned his horse and fled from the field of battle. The Prussians pursued the helpless fugitives with a rancor which only the memory of the horrors of the battle of Jena, and the unequalled outrages then committed by Napoleon on Prussia, could have excited. Multitudes of the retreating French were slain. The whole of Napoleon's artillery fell into the hands of the pursuers. For miles the earth was completely covered with an innumerable number of broken carriages, wagons, baggage, arms and wrecks of every kind. Forty thousand men only escaped of that vast and splendid armament of eighty thousand, who on the morning of that very day, full of martial pomp and pride, had marched under the French eagles. Nearly forty thousand men had either been slain, wounded, or taken prisoners. The loss of the Allies was sixteen thousand killed and wounded. The loss of the Prussians in the battles of the 16th and 18th of June amounted to thirty-three thousand.*

The fallen hero reached Paris during the night of the 20th, and the two Chambers were immediately summoned. The deliberations which ensued resulted in the abdication of Napoleon, his departure for Rochefort, his reception on board the Bellerophon, his transfer to the distant island of St. Helena, the reinstatement of Louis XVIII. upon the throne of his ancestors, and the general establishment of peace throughout a continent so long convulsed and distracted by the innumerable horrors of war.

One of the first acts of the British Parliament, after the conclusion of hostilities in 1815, was to pass votes of thanks to the Duke of Wellington and Marshal Blücher; while more substantial, and therefore more valuable, evidences of public regard and gratitude than votes of thanks were bestowed upon the great English commander and his troops. All the regiments of cavalry and infantry which had been engaged in the battle, were permitted to inscribe the word *Waterloo* upon their colors; and the soldiers were allowed to count two years for that victory in reckoning their future claims for an increase of their pay, or for a pension when discharged. Half a million pounds were raised for the relief of the wounded, and for the relatives of those who had fallen on that bloody field. A grant of two hundred thousand pounds was voted by Parliament to the Duke of Wellington, in addition to the considerable emoluments which he had received for his previous services, as an evidence of the appreciation and gratitude of the nation and their representatives.

Meanwhile the plenipotentiaries of Great Britain were actively engaged in the conventions of Vienna and Chaumont, which were delegated by the powers of Europe to settle the affairs of France, and her relations to surrounding countries. The French

---

* See *Memorable Scenes in French History, from the Era of Cardinal Richelieu until the Present Time; Embracing the Prominent Events of the Last Three Centuries.* New York: Miller, Orton & Co., 1858, p. 820.

territory was reduced to the same limits as those which existed previous to the commencement of the first revolution; and an indemnity of seven hundred millions of francs was demanded, and conceded by the government of Louis XVIII., to reimburse the Allies for the expenses incurred during the war; nor can this vast sum be deemed exorbitant when the events of the past were impartially considered. During the year 1815, the territorial importance of Great Britain was farther increased by the addition of the island of Ceylon to her dominions. This result was produced by a native revolution. The subjects of the King of Candy, who governed the interior, rose in rebellion against his insufferable tyranny, overthrew the despot, and finally took him prisoner. The native Chiefs then conferred together, and resolved to offer the supremacy of the island to the British monarch. A treaty was adopted between the Chiefs and the representatives of the English government then present at Ceylon, by which it was agreed that the Candian Empire should be vested in the British sovereign, reserving to the native Chiefs and to their subjects their rights and immunities. The family of the deposed king was forever excluded from the throne; many cruel laws were at once abrogated, and beneficial regulations introduced; while the administration of justice and the religion of Buddha were allowed to remain unaltered and inviolable. This new accession of territory may justly be regarded as having been a desirable event, both for the inhabitants of Ceylon themselves, and for that colossal empire to whose enlightened laws and influence they thenceforth became subject.

When the British Parliament assembled in February, 1816, the prosperous state of the affairs of the nation excited general congratulation. The various documents having reference to the several treaties which had been recently adopted, by which the peace of Europe had been consolidated, were laid before Parliament, and approved. The Chancellor of the Exchequer gave a full exposition of the financial state of the Empire; and his report set forth that provision should be made for the outstanding bills of the years 1814 and 1815, which he estimated at thirty five million pounds. He also stated that the nation was then laboring under great financial embarrassments, which chiefly arose from the depreciation of agricultural produce, and the immense burdens imposed by the recent wars. He proposed, as a remedy, to renew the property tax, but at a diminished rate of one-half its preceding proportion, at five, instead of ten, per cent. The ordinary annual revenues were estimated at twenty-seven million pounds, the five per cent. property tax at six millions; and an advance from the Bank of England of six millions at four per cent. was recommended by the Chancellor as a necessary addition. But the renewal of the property tax was resisted by the vociferous opposition of the community, and it was therefore eventually abandoned. Parliament was prorogued on the 2d of July, after having effected various measures which tended to promote the prosperity of the nation. Yet these efforts were not entirely successful; for the first year of peace proved to be almost as disastrous to the domestic trade and interests of the people as the preceding years of war had been. This circumstance arose from the fact that, by the establishment of peace, all those sources of industrial profit which had been opened by the exigencies of nations at war, were at once dried up; and men no longer possessed the means of indulging in those commodities and luxuries from the production of which vast numbers derived their subsistence.

These evils were greatly increased by an inclement season which ensued, and which destroyed in a great measure the agricultural resources of the kingdom. Serious riots ensued in the counties of Norfolk, Suffolk, and Huntingdon. The colliers of Staffordshire, and the iron founders of South Wales, suffered greatly from being thrown out of employment; for men had learned to turn their spears into pruning hooks, and their swords into ploughshares, and no longer needed the accumulation of iron for the fabrication of the murderous weapons of war. Other riots occurred in the metropolis, which at first threatened to produce dangerous consequences; but these and all other indications were eventually put down by military force, and ameliorated by the reactionary power of increasing industry and thrift.

During the parliamentary session of 1817, several important measures were passed by the British Legislature. Bills were passed to compensate for civil services; to abolish the office of Wardens and Justices in Eyre; to issue Exchequer bills to the amount of half a million pounds to complete the public works then in progress; while a motion, introduced by the eloquent Irish patriot, Mr. Grattan, to remove the disabilities which unjustly impeded the introduction of Roman Catholics into Parliament, was rejected by a small majority. Mr. Wilberforce, the great opponent of the foreign slave trade, again proposed his beneficent reforms in reference to that infamous traffic; and demanded that Portugal, Spain, and Holland, who had agreed by solemn treaties to abolish it entirely within their dominions, but who had failed to execute their obligations in the premises, might be compelled to do so. The motion was passed in Parliament; without however any specific means having been authorized, by which the beneficent end contemplated might be practically realized. During this year three persons, Brandreth, Turner, and Ludlaw, who had taken a prominent and dangerous part in the popular tumults which occurred in different portions of the kingdom, were tried for high treason at Derby by a special commission, were found guilty, and were executed. Many others who were implicated with them in a less degree, received more lenient punishments; and some who had been led astray by ignorance rather than by wickedness into revolt, were pardoned by the royal clemency.

In 1818 acts were passed by Parliament appropriating the sum of a million pounds sterling for the purpose of erecting new places of worship for the use of congregations of the Established Church; for dividing parishes into two or more parochial districts, each of which was to be provided with a church and minister; to authorize the building of chapels of ease, the clergymen of which were to be nominated by the rectors of the parishes in which they were situated, subject to the approval of the diocesan.

An Alien Act was passed, to continue in force during two years, for the purpose of excluding from the British territory those persons who might use their vicinity to France in order to plot against the permanency of the throne of Louis XVIII., or any other of the allies of Great Britain. Changes were also made in the powers and prerogatives of the Regency, by which the queen was empowered to appoint additional members of the council to whose care the person of George III. had been intrusted. In pursuance of this act, the Earl of Macclesfield, the Bishop of London, the Lord St. Helen, and Lord Henley, were added to the existing members of the council. Mr. Brougham introduced his famous bill respecting the education of the poor of the realm during the session of 1818, and supported its passage with great eloquence and ability. After being subjected to various amendments in the jealous House of Lords—a body of men which has been, during many generations, only a dead weight and a pernicious obstacle to the advance of British legislation, resisting every measure, however beneficent and enlightened, which might tend in any way to increase the importance and to enlarge the influence of the masses of the people—the bill, after being mutilated, emasculated, and deformed by their lordships, eventually passed both houses.

During 1819 the care of the person of the invalid king was entrusted to the Duke of York, subject to the assistance of a council. This measure became necessary in consequence of the death of his consort, Queen Charlotte, who expired on the 17th of November preceding, after having spent many years in mournful yet assiduous attendance upon the wants of her unfortunate husband. By her death the treatment which was applied to the king became less tender and considerate; and had he still retained a glimmer of intellectual light, he would have been able to perceive that in Charlotte's death he had lost his most faithful and devoted friend.

In 1819 Sir James Macintosh introduced into the British Parliament a subject which had long demanded their corrective and reformatory agency. This subject was the Criminal Jurisprudence of the realm, which was based upon a barbarous and cruel code, which has been the disgrace of England during many ages. As the law then existed, the penalty of death was affixed to three classes or *genera* of crimes. The first included murder, and all other malicious acts which were directly intended to destroy human life. The second comprehended arson, robbery, piracy, and crimes of similar character which usually tended to the loss of life, as a concomitant of their chief purpose in the unlawful acquisition of property. The third class related to a hundred and fifty different offences which were of much less magnitude, and which were punished in all other civilized countries, by a much lighter penalty. Sir James proposed that in reference to all crimes which were included in the third class, the death penalty should be abolished; and after a long and arduous contest, in which he was sustained by all the statesmen distinguished for enlightened views in the realm, he succeeded in carrying his proposition, by the appointment of a select committee, through whose agency the proposed reforms were eventually consummated.

During this session of Parliament Sir Francis Burdett moved his famous bill proposing that the House of Commons should take into consideration the subject of the representation of the people in Parliament. The great curse of British legislation was the want of a fair and equitable representation; and the proposed measure, if properly carried out, would result in the amelioration of the existing evil. A very spirited debate ensued; but eventually, by the artful management of the Tory leaders, the issue was evaded through a vote by which the house passed to the order of the day. This result did not crush the spirit of disaffection which was gradually increasing throughout a portion of the kingdom; and public meetings, in which the subject of parliamentary reform was discussed in a bold and seditious manner, were held at Birmingham, Smithfield, Manchester and Leeds. Riots ensued, which were eventually suppressed only by the interference of the military, and by the effusion of blood. The public discontents afterward became the subject of discussion in Parliament, and acts were passed for suppressing seditious libels, for subjecting cheap popular tracts to a duty, for preventing seditious meetings of all kinds, for the seizure of arms intended for seditious purposes, and to prohibit military training. By the rigid enforcement of these provisions, the danger which seemed to threaten the internal peace of the kingdom was successfully averted.

At the period of the death of George III., the vast empire of which he was the nominal head may be said to have attained a degree of harmony, prosperity, and splendor, which it never before possessed. All its colonies and appendages, including those of the Eastern and Western Indies, were loyal and united; Ireland for the time being was tranquil and appeased; education, commerce, and manufactures flourished at home; and intimate alliances firmly bound the British government in amity with the great powers of the continent. In May, 1819, a short time previous to the death of the king, Mr. Tiernay moved in the House of Commons for the appointment of a committee to take into consideration the state of the nation, alleging at the same time that the conduct of ministers had been unwise, pernicious, and censurable; and demanding their immediate removal from office. What opinion the British Parliament entertained in reference to the condition of the British people at that moment, may be clearly inferred from the significant fact, that the motion of Mr. Tiernay was lost by an overwhelming vote of three hundred and fifty-seven against a hundred and seventy-eight.[*]

---

[*] The supplies for the year were stated at £20,477,000. Of the ways and means, the annual malt, and temporary excise duties added to the minor sums arising from the lottery and the sale of old naval stores, amounted to £7,074,000; a loan of twelve millions by competition, and another of the same amount derived from the sinking fund, joined to the above sum, produced a total of £31,974,000, leaving a surplus of £10,597,000 to be applied to the reduction of the unfunded debt, of which five millions would be payable to the Bank of England, and the remaining $5,597,000 to the individual holders of Exchequer bills. *Bissett's History of the Reign of George III.*, Vol. iii., p. 359.

CHAPTER XII.

Importance of the Era of George III.—Historic Portraits of its most Distinguished Personages—William Pitt, Earl of Chatham—His Appearance—Character of his Eloquence—His high sense of Honor—His Enlarged and Enlightened Views—Lord North—His Character and Talents—The Difficulties of his Position—Splendid array of Parliamentary Orators of this Era—Varied Talents of Edmund Burke—His Imagination—His Erudition—His Conservative Opinions—Charles James Fox—His Contrast in every Respect to Burke—His prodigious Power as a Parliamentary Debater—His Efforts as an Author—The Younger Pitt the sole Rival of Fox as a Debater—Sheridan—His Merits and Defects—William Windham—Junius—Distinguished Jurists—Horace Walpole—Eminent Historians, Poets, and Prelates of the Reign of George III.

THE protracted reign of George III. may justly be regarded as the most remarkable which has occurred in English history. This distinction did not result from any peculiar quality or superiority of the sovereign ; for, like every other monarch of his race who ever swayed a sceptre, he was in every respect a most ordinary and common-place person. But the importance of his era, and of the events which occurred during its continuance, arose from the splendid abilities of the statesmen to whom he successively confided the government ; from the commanding talents of those who acted in opposition to his administration ; from the matchless skill and fortitude of many of his generals ; and from the peculiar combination of causes and effects, of influences and counter-influences, which happened to combine and to culminate during the progress of his reign. We will conclude our survey of the life and times of George III., by presenting historic portraits of some of the most distinguished personages who then lived and flourished.

William Pitt, the first Earl of Chatham, is the great colossal figure of this epoch. His importance has rendered it necessary for us to refer to him so frequently in the previous history, that a very extended notice of him is less requisite here. His grandfather had been Governor of Madras, and had amassed a fortune in India. His father was member of the House of Commons for Oakhampton. Pitt's elder brother inherited the family estates; he himself was the possessor of a matchless genius, far more valuable than any estate. His education was completed at Oxford University; and at the early age of twenty-four, by the assistance of the family influence, he was elected to a seat in Parliament for Old Sarum. Then began his splendid Parliamentary career which continued during thirty years, and which no Englishman has ever surpassed or even emulated.

At the period of Pitt's entrance into Parliament, and for many years afterward, the art of reporting speeches was in a most imperfect state; and consequently many of the most magnificent displays of his eloquence were lost to posterity. For many years it was even illegal to publish pretended reports of the proceedings of the Legislature; but notwithstanding these disadvantages, the superiority of Pitt as an orator soon commanded the admiration of the nation. His person was tall and stately. His features were prominent and expressive. His eye was the eye of an eagle; and its mere defiant or derisive glances struck many a hostile orator dumb with confusion and dismay. When he spoke he did not disdain to use every art which could give effect to his eloquence. His gestures, his attitudes, his attire, all were duly arranged and disposed so as to render them most impressive and effective. His speeches were never prepared beforehand, and delivered from memory. On a single occasion he attempted this plan, and signally failed. He uniformly spoke from the impulse of the moment; and his speeches, if not remarkable for length, for close consecutive reasoning, for long-drawn and elaborate deductions and processes of illustration and argument, were characterized by a rapidity, a force, a concentration of oratorical and declamatory power, which, without stopping to overturn his adversaries in detail, blasted the whole assemblage of them by a few overwhelming and resistless blows.

He resembled a Titan who obliterated a generation of pigmies not by many, but by a single stroke of his powerful arm.

Lord Chatham possessed great firmness and fixedness of purpose. Nothing could move him after he had once taken his position. He was disinterested, and scorned money and all the other mercenary considerations which govern the conduct of the majority of men. His immense popularity with the nation arose from his supposed integrity and incorruptibility of character; which seemed to be more astonishing in a day when even Robert Walpole declared that every man had his price. No one knew the statesmen of England better than Walpole; for his potent bribes had corrupted all of them, save Pitt alone. He too had his price; but it was not money which influenced him. His was a nobler passion. He loved power with the same insatiable greediness with which Marlborough, the most avaricious of statesmen, loved money. After power, Pitt loved fame; and he desired to be known and esteemed by his countrymen as a celebrity. But he was also a true patriot. An injury or a disgrace inflicted on his country, he felt deeply as a grievous misfortune inflicted upon himself. Hence, when he at last attained supreme power, his measures, which were wise and sagacious, were executed with such prodigious energy, and with such single reference to the honor, glory, and power of Great Britain, that he soon rendered her the first nation on the globe. His views were much in advance of those of his age and generation. This was clearly illustrated by the policy which he pursued in reference to the American Colonies. The stupid king was obstinately bent on preserving the integrity of the empire at all hazards, and without making any sacrifice. His fawning favorites commended and applauded his perverse ignorance. Pitt alone clearly saw that it was impossible to retain the colonies in base dependence upon, and subjection to, the mother country; that there were growing and resistless energies lodged in the heart of those colonies, which must be expanded and developed freely without constraint; and that if any attempt were made to repress them or confine them, an explosion would inevitably occur which would shatter the empire into fragments. Consequently he recommended that the cords should be relaxed, that the young restive giants should be governed loosely, that they should be permitted to expend their pent-up powers freely, and that, while they should be retained in nominal connection with the mother country, the home government should scarcely seem to control them at all; but should hope to derive their greatest revenue and profit from the increased and extended commerce which would rapidly arise between the two countries. These views seemed absurd to the short-sighted contemporaries of Pitt; and acting on an opposite line of policy, the cords broke which were too tightly drawn, and America became a free, a hostile, and even now, a rival empire. One of his declarations on this subject was as follows: " I rejoice that America has resisted. Three millions of people, so dead to all the feelings of liberty, as voluntarily to let themselves be made slaves, would have been fit instruments to make slaves of all the rest. America, if she fell, would fall like a strong man; she would embrace the pillars of the state, and pull down the constitution along with her." Pitt was great in the ministry and out of it; and was trusted by the nation more heartily than any other statesman before and since. His acceptance of a pension for his family and of a peerage for himself rendered him unpopular for a time, as his enemies intended it should; but he soon recovered his place in the inmost heart of the nation; and at last his death enshrined him there with a security and permanence, which no lapse of time or vicissitude of events can ever diminish.

Lord North remained for some years the favorite minister of George III., and the regard which the obstinate yet conscientious monarch entertained for him was very great. His disposition was amiable, agreeable, and conciliatory. He rendered a great service to the king, by accepting the labors and perils of office at a time of considerable danger, when the Duke of Grafton suddenly resigned the post of premier, and retired to the ebmraces of his mistress at Newmarket, and left the king almost helpless. North was a man of noble birth and liberal education, and spoke the principal modern languages of Europe fluently. Madame de

Staël asserted that he possessed *l'Esprit Européen* which made him perfectly at home in the saloons of Paris, Naples, Vienna, and London. Before his promotion to the premiership, he had held several important offices; he had been one of the Lords of the Treasury, Paymaster of the Forces, and Chancellor of the Exchequer. He retained his highest trust during thirteen years; and that period was rendered memorable by the progress and conclusion of the war in the United States. No minister was ever surrounded by greater difficulties than Lord North. He was compelled to support the war by the express command and determination of the king. The nation at home was soured and incensed by the ultimate defeat which justly met the line of policy pursued toward the resisting and restive colonies. A powerful opposition in Parliament crippled his movements, and hindered him in the attainment of his most cherished purposes. The eloquence of Burke, Fox, Barre, and Dunning, was hurled at his head. Chatham aimed his vast oratorical thunderbolts at his exposed principles and measures. And yet, without claiming or possessing any of the qualities of a great speaker, he succeeded in maintaining his position, in spite of them all, for some years. His mental powers consisted chiefly in his clear, excellent good sense, his natural adroitness and tact, his ever ready fluency of speech, his undaunted and unflinching courage, his enlivening and playful wit, and a perfect self-possession, and control of temper, which was never disconcerted or disturbed. On one occasion, a fierce declaimer in Parliament demanded his head as a penalty for his treason; and looking round to see what effect this terrific onslaught would produce upon his victim, was overwhelmed to see him asleep; and when the orator at length awoke him by his increased vociferations, Lord North complained how cruel it was to deprive him of the solace which all other criminals enjoyed, of having a night's rest before their execution.

The most splendid intellectual phase of the reign of George III. was the combination of parliamentary talents which the union of Burke, Fox, Sheridan, and Pitt presented at one and the same time, in the National Legislature. Four such men were never associated together before or since, in any legislative assembly. Burke was an Irishman by birth, and came over to England at an early age, to advance his slender and insufficient fortunes. His first occupation was literature, and he devoted his superior powers to the elaboration of several works—one on the Sublime and Beautiful—which hold a permanent place in English literature. It is probable that his early habits of scholastic thinking exerted a strong influence on his subsequent career as an orator, and gave him that stately and elaborate unfitness for a popular assembly which characterized him, and which rendered him, when discussing a dry and abstruse theme of finance or political philosophy, one of the most tedious and insufferable of men.* He possessed an imagination of the richest and most luxuriant affluence; which was stored with the varied learning which he had gathered from the literature and the history of all nations, climes, and ages. This peculiarity was illustrated in his speeches against Warren Hastings, during which he proved himself to be perfectly familiar with all that appertained to the vast and diversified communities of India. He described with the minuteness and accuracy of which a native or a resident of that distant zone might alone be supposed to be capable, the gorgeous and exquisite temples of the Hindoo faith, the worship and forms of gaudy and hideous idols, the repulsive usages and sufferings of religious devotees, the magnificence of oriental courts and palaces, the bright array of Indian armies, the bewitching loveliness of Eastern female beauty, the mingled and miscellaneous scenes of canopied elephants, showy horsemen, turbaned slaves, and barbaric pageants of every kind, which constantly attract and astonish the traveller; he depicted with unrivalled power, the ancient laws, institutions, and customs, both religious, literary, and political, of that vast realm, which contains within its limits the crumbling

---

* Thus Goldsmith very properly describes him on these occasions as being—
  "Too deep for his hearers: he went on refining,
  And thought of convincing, while they thought of *dining*."
Samuel Johnson declared that no man could meet Burke under a gateway, in a shower, without discovering that he was a great man.

empire of the Great Mogul, the palaces of Aladdin, Ackbar, and Arungzebe, the splendors of Delhi, Lucknow, and Benares, and the matchless marvels of art, wealth, and luxury which there exist, of which peacock thrones, crystal halls, perfumed fountains, and royal tombs decorated with massive gold and priceless gems, are frequent and familiar ingredients.

But Burke possessed talents of a more practical character than a gorgeous imagination. He was a safe and sagacious statesman. His powerful intellect probed to the bottom of every subject. He was shocked at the excesses of the French Revolution, as well as by its theoretic principles, and he remained its fierce traducer till the last day of his existence. His mind was so constituted that, with the best intentions, if his prejudices and conscientious convictions were once fixed against a principle or a person, he was their unflinching opponent under all circumstances, and at every risk. In his prosecution of Warren Hastings, he was evidently justified by the facts of the case. The same remark is applicable to his condemnation of the French Revolution. But he sometimes carried his ardor to unwarrantable lengths. An illustration of this fact is furnished by his treatment of his intimate friend Mr. Fox in 1791, when discussing the bill for establishing a constitution in Canada. During the debate, the French Revolution was alluded to by Mr. Fox, and commended; though the latter contended that remarks in reference to the state of France were, in that discussion, totally out of order. Mr. Burke replied that he and Mr. Fox had often differed, and with no loss of friendship; but that there was something in the "accursed French Constitution" which envenomed every thing. Mr. Fox interrupted him and said, that there was no loss of friendship, as he hoped, even in that dispute. Mr. Burke replied that there was an end to their friendship, and he knew the price of his conduct.* Mr. Fox hearing this declaration, immediately burst into tears at the thought of being thus remorselessly whirled away by his ancient friend, in the wild tumultuous vortex of his passion. He was undoubtedly honest and conscien-

* *Belsham's Life of George III.*, Vol. iii., p. 475.

tious in all his opinions and measures. He was incorruptible in regard to pecuniary affairs; and in 1782, while Paymaster of the Forces, he voluntarily diminished his own emoluments in order to increase the revenue of Chelsea Hospital. He positively refused a pension until after his retirement from political life in 1795; although he had been pressed by his friends in the government to accept one at a much earlier period.

As an orator, Mr. Burke stands unrivalled as the head and representative of a great class. He belonged to the elaborate, gorgeous, and somewhat artificial school, each of whose orations, like those of Demosthenes, may be regarded as a finished and complete masterpiece. The same highly-wrought style of composition which is exhibited in his writings—in his Thoughts on the Causes of the Present Discontents, in his Reflections on the French Revolution, in his Discourses on Taste—is displayed in his speeches. They all evince a mastery over a wide range of intellectual accomplishment, and are richly stored with argument, pathos, epigram, metaphor, logic, and illustrations from every department of human science. He was greatly the superior in the profundity and diversity of his attainments to Fox, Pitt, or Sheridan. Throughout life he was a conservative in sentiment, and always opposed and condemned the supremacy of the mob. He undervalued the rights and interests of the people, and did not give due credit to their influence and importance in the body politic. This was the sole error under which he labored, the solitary delusion which misled him. As an orator he is deservedly placed in the front rank of British statesmen; as the worthy rival and associate of Fox and Pitt, and as being the greatest representative of a class of men whose mental and moral qualities differ *toto cælo* from those of the illustrious men we have just named.

Charles James Fox was the chief of these. No greater contrast could possibly be imagined than that which existed between him and Burke. He was the son of Henry Fox, the distinguished rival of the first William Pitt. He was deficient in those vast and varied attainments which Burke possessed. His acquisitions did not extend even beyond the ordinary range of English and classical learning, modern languages, and history. Of the sciences, natural, metaphysical, and mathematical, he was generally ignorant; but he was the greatest master of a close, clear, conclusive, declamatory logic that ever appeared in the British Parliament. The structure of all his faculties was robust and vigorous. He was careless of ornament, and never sought to embellish his speeches with any of the beauteous accessions which taste, poetry, fancy, or art might bestow. He always followed closely and tenaciously the main point under discussion; met and overthrew with the strokes of his logic every argument which opposed his advance; and delivered his speeches with the fervid, rapid, abounding fluency which indicated both the richness of his mental resources and his lavish expenditure of them. His delivery was ungraceful. His features were coarse, heavy, and repulsive, with a dark complexion and beetle-brow. He was fond of pleasure, and his morals were of the worst description.* Yet his temper was sweet and amiable beyond all comparison; and it rendered him the idol of those who were admitted to his society. There was little of dissimulation or duplicity in his character, and his impulsive candor sometimes rendered him the victim of the designing. It was singular that a man so given to a life of pleasure and business, whose scholastic attainments were so limited, and whose mental habits were so discursive, should have undertaken the task of authorship. His worst speech was the only one which he ever wrote,† and his "History," which remains merely as a fragment, clearly indicates that it is the production of a great mind, but one unused to the task of composition, and unskilled in the acquisition and disposition

---

* On one occasion he was travelling with his mistress, Mrs. Armstead, on the Continent, when a renewed attack of the king's insanity gave hopes of the immediate accession of the Prince of Wales to the regency, and Fox's promotion to the premiership. Though he hastened back rapidly to London, he was doomed at that time to be disappointed. One of his chief vices was his desperate devotion to gambling.

† Against Francis, Duke of Bedford. See *Brougham's Lives of Statesmen of the Time of George III.*, Vol. i., p. 157.

of the proper materials. The style is indeed correct, because it is polished with anxious care; but it is lifeless, because the artist in the desire to polish, has subdued all the salient points which indicate the presence and power of intellectual life. His sole glory in truth was as a debater. In opposition and in reply he was the most formidable antagonist whom the younger Pitt, himself a giant, was compelled to encounter. His political opinions or standpoint was that of the genuine Whigs; and he adhered to these views throughout his chequered life. He attained the premiership only a few months previous to his decease; and the garland for which he had toiled during many laborious and tempestuous years, withered on his brow almost before time permitted it to settle securely there. His highest merit as a statesman probably was, that he supported and promoted the abolition of the African Slave Trade, and aided to wipe out that crimson blot from the escutcheon of England. As the *leader* of a great party in the House of Commons he was a model, and has since had no equal; for his potent eloquence was connected with other qualities equally essential, of which many distinguished party leaders have been destitute: his lax moral principles made him willing to adopt unscrupulously all possible expedients; his sweetness of temper gained over and retained the most arrogant and irascible of men; his placability healed the wounds of every fierce dispute; his firmness and courage made him reliable in every emergency, while they rendered him undismayed by any peril. One singular ground of his immense popularity with the nation, was the fact that he was the most perfect specimen of an Englishman, in every respect; and a model of English taste as an orator and as a man, both as to the faculties of his mind and his peculiar social qualities. Even his fastidious disregard of all redundant ornament in his speeches commended him to the admiration of his countrymen; for they regarded him as the honest, hearty, and sturdy champion of English freedom, English laws, English commerce, and English tastes, in opposition to all that was foreign, transplanted, or corrupted.

The first position in the affection of the British people was

long contested with Mr. Fox by William Pitt, the son of the
"Great Commoner." He appeared in Parliament at a very early
age, and exhibited the abilities of an able orator and a mature
politician, at a period of life when others are acquiring the very
rudiments of eloquence and political science. He passed through
his studies at Cambridge with credit, and there became familiar
with classical, scientific, and mathematical knowledge. He afterward studied the law, with ultimate reference to his admission
to the bar. He was very soon transferred by the interest of his
family and by his own growing fame, from the courts of justice
to the more ample and distinguished arena of the Senate; and
from the day of his entrance there, he assumed a place in the first
rank of British orators. After several years spent in this position he was promoted to the cabinet of George III., and subsequently, as has appeared from the preceding history, to the
premiership.

Pitt's fame as an orator was well deserved. He was not
florid or ornate in his style; he rarely called in the use of
tropes and figures to aid his purpose; he had little variety of
manner, and less gracefulness of delivery. But he possessed extraordinary fluency; he never hesitated, as Fox sometimes did,
for the appropriate word; and there was a magical and harmonious
flow of his utterance from the beginning to the end of the speech,
which resembled the ample and affluent current of a great river—
rushing onward to its termination with confidence and exultation.
His orations were characterized by a lucid arrangement, which
rendered his discussion of the most intricate financial questions
clear and intelligible; while the correctness and elegance of his
diction, his perfect self-possession, his strong and sonorous voice,
his commanding attitude, and his significant and natural ges-
ticulation, free from all surreptitious arts or assumed affecta-
tions, contributed to make him one of the most impressive
speakers who ever graced the British Parliament. So undeni-
able was his merit in this respect, that it extorted unqualified
praise from his opponents and rivals, even from the most distinguished; for Mr. Fox himself, when replying to Pitt's great

speech on the war in 1803, candidly declared that "the orators of antiquity would have admired, probably would have envied it." This encomium would have applied with greater propriety to Pitt's speech in 1791 against the African Slave Trade, which presented, during several hours, an uninterrupted torrent of the most majestic, pathetic, and impressive declamation; respecting which effort William Windham, one of the most capable of judges, remarked that, as he thoughtfully returned to his home after hearing it, he was lost in a reverie at the amazing compass and power which human eloquence could possess, and which, till then, he had never fully witnessed.

The spirit of this illustrious statesman was bold and enterprising. The measures which he proposed and adopted were of this description; and Napoleon himself had no abler or more formidable opponent in his ambitious schemes than he. His judgment was singularly sagacious, and was rarely deluded by the most specious or attractive chimeras which solicited his attention. His favorite department was that of commerce and finance; in the elaboration of its details he was perfectly at home; and he loved to associate with men who were addicted to similar studies and pursuits. He was eminently industrious, laborious, and painstaking. His patriotism was of the purest and highest order. When invited by his father to marry the rich and illustrious Mademoiselle Necker, afterward Madame de Staël, he replied, with some truth, that he was already married to his country; and he never had any other spouse. To her he devoted his undivided affections, and all the gigantic energies of his nature. He was incorruptible; and during his long tenure of the highest office in the realm, he reformed many of the worst abuses which cursed the administration of the government, and added nothing to his private fortune. He was more scientific and accurate than his father; but he was less colossal in his intellectual bulk. He did not possess the majestic and imposing countenance of the elder Pitt, nor his marvellous grace and power of delivery. His features were shorter, and less expressive; and his person, though tall, was meagre. In advocating great measures of domestic policy or foreign war, he cared little for the expense which attended them. Accordingly, the result of his administration uniformly was to increase the public debt to a prodigious extent. He was fertile in expedients, and devised a multiplicity of new taxes. His love of power was so insatiable, that he could bear no aspiring person near the throne. Accordingly, his chief associates and agents in the administration were Dundas, Rose, Jenkinson, and Benfield—all men of secondary abilities. The great authority with Mr. Pitt in the science of political economy and philosophy, was Adam Smith, whose able work, The Wealth of Nations, was his constant companion and text-book. In private life Pitt was amiable and blameless; but he had no domestic ties. His high office, he justly described as the pride of his heart and the pleasure of his existence. His chief glory is that, during many stormy and tempestuous years, he fought the whole battle of his government, single-handed, against a host of the most fierce and gifted adversaries who ever assailed a minister, including such master spirits as Burke, Fox, Sheridan, Windham, North, Erskine, and Barre.

But England, so fertile in men of superior genius, has produced but one Sheridan—the most remarkable combination of high faculties and contemptible weaknesses which the checkered page of history exhibits. In his youth he was idle and indolent beyond measure. He was sent to school at Harrow, where he might have profited by the instructions of the learned Parr; but he paid no attention to his books, and till the day of his death, remained so deficient in acquired stores of learning, that he never knew any thing of so ordinary an attainment as French, and he frequently misspelt words in his native language. After leaving Harrow, Sheridan being without the means of attending a university, took to literature, the usual starving refuge of dependent and impoverished genius. He wrote poetry and novels—all of which, happily for the fame of the author, have long since descended to oblivion. He resided at this period of his early manhood at Bath, and there became acquainted with a distinguished songstress, Miss Linley, whom he afterward married. She was remarkable for her beauty, intelligence, and wit, and shared the subsequent fate of her husband with mingled pride, sorrow, and patience.

Though Sheridan entered himself as a student of law on the books of the Inner Temple, he never seriously prosecuted his legal studies. Shortly after his marriage, he obtained a share in Drury Lane Theatre, and began to write plays. His convivial qualities were so remarkable that they rendered him popular in the highest circles of the metropolis; and he soon obtained sufficient influence to be elected to a seat in Parliament from the borough of Stafford. In early manhood this remarkable man was surrounded by all the splendors of genius, fame, fashion, and popularity. He attached himself to the Whig party, and displayed in Parliament a degree of popular eloquence which was, for its kind, unequalled and unrivalled, and made him one of the most valuable of those allies who aided the opposition which assailed George III. during many years.

Sheridan was a man without principle, who lived only for popularity, and for the emoluments of office. He deserted his party and his friends whenever his interests dictated such a course. This assertion is proved by his conduct on two memorable occasions; in 1802 and in 1806. He himself urged as an excuse for his perfidy, the pecuniary necessities of his position; but with a man of principle such an argument can have no weight.* His political and parliamentary career continued till

---

* " I have seen Sheridan weep two or three times (says Lord Byron): it may be that he was maudlin, but this only rendered it more affecting, for who would see

'From Marlborough's eyes the tears of dotage flow,
And Swift expire a driveller and a show?'

" Once I saw him cry at Robins, the auctioneer's, after a splendid dinner full of great names and high spirits. I had the honor of sitting next to Sheridan. The occasion of his tears was some observation on the stanchness of the Whigs in resisting office and keeping to their principles. Sheridan turned round: 'Sir, it is easy for my Lord G., or Earl G., or Marquis B., or Lord H., with thousands upon thousands a year, some of it either directly derived or inherited in sinecures or acquisitions from the public money, to boast of their patriotism and keep aloof from temptation; but they do not know from what temptations those

1812, when he was defeated in his attempt to be returned again from Stafford; after that period he was but a lonely and helpless wreck upon the tempestuous sea of life. He continued to decline in public favor, overwhelmed with debt and misery, until at last his career was closed by death in 1816.

Sheridan's talents were of a multifarious character. Several of his plays, the Rivals, and the School for Scandal, are among the best in English comedy. This was nothing extraordinary, inasmuch as he was the son of an actor, had early been made familiar with the stage, and had himself been the manager of a theatre. But that such a man should possess talents of the first order in the Parliament of a great nation, among many other gifted and illustrious men, was one of the intellectual phenomena of modern times. He possessed a warm imagination, a bold and intrepid spirit, an intimate acquaintance with human nature, a brilliant and pungent wit, an unrivalled quickness of repartee, which, though often prepared beforehand, and kept, cut and dried in readiness for the first suitable occasion which might offer for its use, was always introduced with the best effect, and with excellent taste; a style of impassioned, fervid declamation, which charmed the ear and led captive the judgment, a sweet and sonorous voice, a graceful and appropriate delivery, and an inventive genius which enabled him to turn the arguments and authorities of his opponents to his own use, and to their discomfiture—these were the intellectual and physical resources which rendered this weak, vacillating, and miserable man one of the most distinguished ornaments of the British Parliament. He was not a great statesman, nor any statesman at all; for he originated no measure of importance. He was not adapted to exercise the supreme command of a party; but was admirably fitted to fill the post of a lieutenant-general under such able leaders as Fox and Burke.* He was to these men what Murat and Ney were

---

have kept aloof who had equal pride, at least equal talent, and not unequal passions, and nevertheless knew not, in the course of their lives, what it was to have a shilling of their own; and in saying this *he wept*." *Manuscript Diary of Lord Byron*, p. 57.

* "When Fox was asked what he thought the best speech he had ever heard,

to Napoleon : perhaps he might even claim such eminent relation to them as that which Davoust and Massena bore to the triumphant Corsican. His most splendid displays of eloquence were those made in connection with the trial of Warren Hastings. His sparkling and brilliant declamation on that memorable occasion charmed and delighted the vast audience which crowded Westminster Hall, and bore a favorable comparison even with the speeches of Burke. This is the bright side of this strange picture. The personal habits of this versatile and gifted man were exceedingly gross and low. He was greatly addicted to intemperance ; and his pecuniary embarrassments, and the ridiculous or dishonest expedients to which they led him, rendered him the laughing stock of a nation who willingly admired his brilliant genius, and praised his stupendous abilities.

Having thus dwelt at some length upon the most eminent statesmen of the reign of George III., a shorter notice will suffice for those of inferior abilities and importance. William Windham ranked next after those already considered. His mind was remarkable for its shrewd and crafty tendency, which made him cautious and prudent, and deprived him of the boldness and self-reliance necessary to a great party leader. He was exceedingly handsome in his person, singularly chivalrous and courtly in his manners, and his speeches were marked by a superior degree of ability. Their prevalent tone was that of familiar conversation ; which of course deprived them of the power and ardor which fervid declamation always gives even to orations of inferior merit. His mental *calibre* was secondary ; and his fondness for paradox sometimes rendered his opinions dangerous and unreliable. His political career achieved for him the esteem of his countrymen : neither his talents nor their praise ascended to the highest range, or placed him in the loftiest niche.

One other man deserves to be ranked in this bright and select

he replied—Sheridan's on the impeachment of Hastings, in the House of Commons, (not that in Westminster Hall.) When asked what he thought of his own speech on the breaking out of the war, he replied, ' That was a d——d good speech too.' I heard this from Lord Holland." *Lord Byron's MS.*

category, over a part of whose fame a singular mystery hangs: *Stat nominis umbra.* Sir Philip Francis was a man of superior ability; though not of a popular or brilliant description. He first distinguished himself in India as the ablest and most unyielding enemy of Warren Hastings; and after his return to England his influence in Parliament, and his concealed power as the author of the famous "Letters of Junius," rendered him still more important. Francis possessed a wide range of thought, a retentive memory, a classical taste, and great force and energy of expression. His chief defect was his bitter acrimony of spirit, which characterized every thing he said and did. He was tall and thin in person, and his somewhat repulsive and sharp features seemed a fitting indication of the quality of his spirit. An intimate acquaintance of the man, for friends he had none, declared that he never saw him smile. As a speaker he was quick and awkward in his gestures, but forcible, unadorned, and effective. "I am not an old man," said he, when opposing Pitt's famous India Bill, "yet I remember the time when such a proposition would have roused the whole country into a flame. Had the experiment been made when the illustrious statesman, the late Earl of Chatham, enjoyed a seat in this assembly, he would have sprung from the bed of sickness, he would have solicited some friendly hand to lay him on the floor, and thence with a monarch's voice he would have called the whole kingdom to arms to oppose it. *But he is dead,* and has left nothing in the world that resembles him. *He is dead,* and the sense, the honor, the character, and the understanding of the nation are dead with him." The effect of this passage is said to have been prodigious and lasting.

One of the great enigmas of English history is the question whether Francis was Junius? There is a flood of preponderating evidence in favor of the supposition which, in the absence of direct proof on either side, is almost conclusive. Every sentiment contained in the Letters corresponds with what were known to be the opinions of Francis. The style, which is so peculiar, is precisely his own—that polished, condensed, epigrammatic style, which has elicited so much praise which it does not deserve.

For the reader who carefully scrutinizes those celebrated productions will readily discover that the author has only one way of treating all subjects; that he uniformly constructs his sentences so that they may be most expressive and telling, without any regard to the question whether truth will in all cases justify the superlative phrases which he uses; that his savage invectives would be just as appropriate to one bad minister as to another; and that, on the whole, a hard, malicious, vindictive spirit filled with *inimicitia contra omnes homines*, lurks beneath his polished yet virulent periods. Some writers have asserted that the only objection to the supposition that Francis was Junius, is to be found in the fact that his vanity would not have allowed him to conceal his authorship of so celebrated a production.* But the author had ample reasons for keeping the secret till his dying day. He had libelled some of the best men of his time, and even some of the worst. He had shamefully slandered Lord Mansfield, the brightest ornament of the British judiciary; he had almost broken the heart of the amiable and learned Blackstone; he had trampled the Duke of Grafton, Sir William Draper, and Horne Tooke in the very dust.† All the public men of England regarded the issue of a new number of the "Public Advertiser" as the advent of a thunderbolt which might strike, no one could foretell whom. Though Junius was the professed advocate of popular rights, and was a defender of that vile and filthy baboon George Wilkes, he was feared and detested by the nation; and had his identity become known, he would never have died in his bed. Apprehensions so well founded overbalanced the vanity of Francis, and constrained him to bury the secret of Junius with him in the eternal silence of the tomb.‡

---

* Wraxall, in his Posthumous Memoirs, makes this assertion.

† Sir William Draper died with only one ardent wish ungratified; that he might discover who Junius was, and then bathe his sword in his heart's blood. Nor did he keep this purpose by any means a secret.

‡ One of the contemporary journals charged Francis with being the author of Junius; and he denied the charge in so ambiguous a manner as in effect to give strength to the suspicion: "Sir, you have attributed to me the writing of Junius's letters. If you choose to propagate a false and malicious report, you

The other prominent statesmen who adorned the reign of George III. were Wilberforce, the great opponent of the slave trade, Lord Grenville, Mr. Dundas, Mr. Perceval, and Mr. Canning; though the last and Wilberforce belong more properly to the era of George IV. The reign of George III. was prolific of great jurists; for then flourished the matchless Mansfield, the strong-minded but profane Thurlow, the coarse and uneducated yet indefatigable Kenyon, the stern and unbending Loughborough, the precise and accurate Chief Justice Gibbs, the logical Sir William Grant, and last, but among the greatest, the eloquent and graceful Lord Erskine. Another remarkable character belongs to this era, who was neither statesman, lawyer, judge, nor orator, yet holds no obscure place among the celebrities of his time. This was Horace Walpole, the author of the "Castle of Otranto," and the witty, elegant, gossipping writer of Letters which have not lost their value or their attractiveness even in our own time. He was born in 1717, and was the third and youngest son of Robert Walpole. He was educated at Eton and Cambridge. After leaving the university he travelled over Europe, accompanied during part of his tour by the poet Gray. In Italy he gratified his love of art and of antiquarian literature by the study and inspection of the great monuments of both, which there exist. He returned home, and possessing an ample fortune, he entered Parliament in his twenty-fourth year. He soon wearied of the rude storms of parliamentary life, and retired, determined to spend his days in elegant and intellectual trifling. He purchased a mansion named Strawberry Hill, and proceeded to alter and adorn the building according to his fanciful and eccentric taste. He crowded the grounds with grottoes, statuary, and miniature temples. He filled the house with nick-

may. Yours, &c." Burke never wrote the letters of Junius, because he had more amplitude and variety of style. It was not Wilkes, for he had less ability than the letters display. It was not Dunning, for *he* would not have made the blunders in law which Junius committed. Single-Speech Hamilton had not the necessary energy and courage. Horne Tooke is himself assailed by Junius, and himself replies to him. Every probability and every argument cluster around Sir Philip Francis, and fix on *him* the indelible brand.

nacks, gimcracks, rarities, and curiosities of every description. He collected specimens in every department of art; missals illuminated with great care; sculptures and vases by Benvenuto Cellini; portraits of distinguished people of all ages and countries; marbles and bronzes of every style; collections of coins, crockery, all kinds of *bijouterie* from every country under heaven; and a handsome and rare collection of books, plates, old and odd furniture, and antique armor. He devoted his life to the perfection of this strange assortment, and to the several literary works which he published. In 1791 he succeeded his nephew in the Earldom of Orford; and he died at last in 1797, in the eightieth year of his age, after a long career of pleasure, cheerfulness and amusement.* His talents were such that, in spite of his strange eccentricities, his name occupies no insignificant place in the contemporary history of George III.

The era of this monarch was rendered remarkable by the many eminent men in literature who then flourished. Though he himself furnished but little patronage to that department of intellectual endeavor, it advanced and produced abundant fruits without his aid, and in spite of his apathy. The most eminent *historians* of this period were Gibbon, Hume and Robertson. Gibbon was born at Putney in Surrey, in 1737. His father was a man of affluence and a member of Parliament. In his fifteenth year he went to Oxford university, where he was distinguished for his discursive reading and his habits of dissipation. This career was

---

* At his Strawberry Hill press were printed his "Anecdotes of Painting Engraving, and the Arts in England;" "Historic Doubts of the Life and Reign of Richard III.," a work that excited in its time much attention; "The Mysterious Mother," a tragedy; "A Catalogue of the Royal and Noble Authors of England;" "Ædes Walpoliana, or a Description of the House of Sir Robert Walpole, at Houghton;" with others of less importance, but still sought after with avidity by bibliomaniacs, for the peculiarity of their contents.

But it is upon his Letters chiefly that the posthumous fame of Horace Walpole rests. He was a gossip of the first order. "His epistolary talents," as Miss Berry has said, "have shown our language to be capable of all the grace and all the charms of the French of Madame de Sévigné;" and if to *tittle-tattle* upon paper gracefully, be a merit, Horace Walpole cannot be denied to have attained that flattering distinction.

soon ended by his becoming a papist, and his removal from the university by his incensed father. To rid him of his Catholic tendencies he was sent to reside at Lausanne, in the family of a Protestant clergyman, who became his tutor in classical and historical studies. In 1758 his father permitted him to return to England. In 1761 he published his first work, an *Essai sur l'Etude de la Litterature*. In 1763 he again returned to the continent, visited Rome, and there, while seated meditatively amid the crumbling ruins of the Capitol, he first conceived the idea of writing the work which has since rendered his name immortal. He revisited England in 1770, and was even a member of Parliament for several years before he published the first volume of his Decline and Fall of the Roman Empire. His attention was wholly occupied in the completion of this immense and elaborate production from 1768 till 1787, during the greater part of which interval he resided on the continent at Lausanne. He returned to England to visit his intimate friend Lord Sheffield, in 1793, and died in London in the commencement of the following year. This celebrated writer was characterized by a cold and phlegmatic temperament, and was induced to labor only by the overwhelming pressure of his vanity and ambition. He was one of the most learned men of his time; his intellectual treasures were rich, vast and varied; and his literary sagacity enabled him to use his resources to the best advantage. In sentiment he was an infidel, and had imbibed the opinion that sincere belief in any form of religion was an impossibility to the enlightened and untrammelled human mind. His great history is the ablest and most dangerous opponent to Christianity, because an indirect and an undeclared one, which modern literature presents. It is rich and elaborate with various learning, and filled with acute and sagacious observations. It is polished with scrupulous care, and loaded with excessive ornament. One of its defects is that it labors to degrade and deride whatever is noblest and most heroic in human conduct and character; and places the worst aspects of humanity in the boldest prominence. It teaches no great ethical lessons, or dogmatic truths; but endeavors to confound and obliterate the distinction between virtue and vice, and thereby create contempt for all religion and moral principle. Gibbon himself was a disciple of Voltaire, and entertained the same opinions in morals, literature, philosophy and religion, which characterized that gifted and witty Frenchman. The subject of his history was an admirable one, and had it been executed with virtue, honesty and benevolence, equal to the genius and erudition which it evinces, it would have been a monument to his fame and reputation nobler than that possessed by any modern writer. In tracing the progress and fortunes of the Christian church he divests the noblest and best institution which the world has ever seen, of all its sublimer attributes, renders every thing commonplace and mean, infuses the deadly poison of doubt, ridicule, and unbelief into every event and development; and while he paints the beastly and voluptuous Mahomet with all the luxuriance of Italian art, and exalts the weak and perfidious Julian to the highest niche in the temple of glory, he degrades Constantine and Theodosius into ridiculous, short-sighted and imbecile personages. But in spite of all its great defects, the unquestionable merits of an intellectual kind which the Decline and Fall of Rome contains, will secure it a permanent place in the first rank of the achievements in English literature.

Hume chose a less gorgeous and brilliant theme as the subject of his labors; and his mental qualities were well adapted to the nature of his task. With competent learning he possessed a deep knowledge of the old philosophical systems, had studied the relations between the ideal and the material world, the laws of testimony and historical authority; and he wrote therefore, not for technical readers or verbal critics, but for statesmen, for intelligent observers of men and events, who desired to probe to the real foundation and causes of things, and not to be satisfied with the mere surface. His style is unadorned, clear, strong and forcible. Though belonging to the school of philosophical infidels he did not obtrude his sentiments continually throughout his history; and though he did not admire the Puritans, or the early defenders of the Protestant faith in the north of Europe, he never follows them and the cause which they supported with the perpetual sneer and the insatiable enmity which Gibbon displays on every page against the Christian cause and name.

Robertson's characteristics were different from those of both his rivals. His History of Charles V. indicates that laborious mediocrity which elicits no new ideas, or considers human conduct and opinion under any new or original aspect. He wrote, not for the thinking few, who closely scrutinize and examine, but for the great mass and multitude of men, who, though educated, are never thorough or profound in their researches or reflections. His style is smooth and correct, his opinions are always moderate, and cautious of trenching on extravagances or extremes of any kind, and he writes and thinks with the mechanical accuracy and uniformity of a practised advocate or preacher. He was nominally a believer in the Christian faith, and was a distinguished member of the Scotch Church; but in reality he was an infidel or at least skeptical, as a passage in one of his letters to Gibbon clearly indicates.* He was probably more eminent as a pulpit orator and a controversialist in the Scottish General Assembly, than as a historian.

During the reign of George III. the most eminent writer in political economy and philosophy of modern times lived and flourished. Adam Smith, the author of the Wealth of Nations, was a Scotchman by birth. He was stolen by gypsies in his third year, but was fortunately recovered before the captors had escaped with their prey. He passed three years at the university of Glasgow, and thence proceeded to Oxford. At eighteen years of age he published his "Colonial Policy," which, for so young an author, exhibited remarkable abilities. In 1748 he settled in Edinburgh, and during three years read a course of lectures on Rhetoric. His associates at this period were Hume, Robertson, and Wedderburne. In 1751 he was elected to the professorship of Logic in the university of Glasgow, which was afterward exchanged for that of Moral Philosophy. In 1759 he published his Theory of Moral Sentiments, which never obtained

* See *Westminster Review*, September, 1845, p. 52.

much influence or celebrity. The rest of his life was devoted to the elaboration of the chief monument of his fame, his work on Political Economy. During its composition he corresponded with Turgot, D'Alembert, Necker, and other French philosophers, in reference to the principles involved in the work. He even visited France to facilitate his researches. On his return he shut himself up for ten years in his study at Kirkaldy, and in 1776 he published as the perfected fruit of his labors his "Inquiry into the Causes and Nature of the Wealth of Nations." The immediate and subsequent success of the work was very great; and it still remains an undisputed classic in that important and abstruse branch of literature.

Some eminent poets flourished during this protracted reign, the most distinguished of whom were Johnson, Shenstone, Churchill, Young, Akenside, Gray, Goldsmith and Cowper. The Task, the Night Thoughts, the Elegy, the Deserted Village, and the Vanity of Human Wishes, are gems in English literature of unsurpassed beauty and value, which have gained the admiration and familiar knowledge of reading persons of both sexes throughout the civilized world. To expatiate further upon their merits were a superfluous labor.

George III. was the patron of good morals, and during his reign he endeavored to repress the boldness and the prevalence of vice ; but the state of the Established Church was not such as to indicate the existence of much piety among its members. A few incidents will prove the truth of this assertion. Dr. Cornwallis, Archbishop of Canterbury, gave great offense to the few pious persons in the Church by his worldliness and love of pleasure. He frequently entertained fashionable and dissipated company in the palace of Lambeth, at which times excesses of frivolity and indecorum were permitted, which were scandalous in a churchman of his rank and office. The wife of the Archbishop, an elegant and magnificent woman, and the leader of the fashionable circle, aided and perhaps tempted to the occurrence of these events. Lady Huntingdon, a person of true piety and reforming zeal, conveyed intelligence of these scandalous proceedings to the king ;

and the latter was so incensed at details which, upon further inquiry, he found to be true, that he wrote the Right Reverend offender a letter condemning his conduct, and giving him very plainly to understand that a reformation was indispensably necessary.* Even Queen Charlotte censured the conduct of the prelate, and remarked, that it was a pity that Lady Huntingdon could not be made a bishop, for if she were, her piety and zeal would reprove more than one incumbent on the bench.

As were the prelates, such in a great measure were the inferior clergy. At a drawing room held by the queen in 1777, Cumberland, who was present, asserts that a nobleman had his order, which was encircled with diamonds worth seven hundred pounds snatched from his ribbon; and he believed the theft to have been committed by a clergyman who stood near him, but one of such high position that he did not dare to charge him with it. A similar attempt was made on a similar occasion to tear off the diamond guard of the sword of the Prince of Wales, which was of great value; and in this instance the known but unpunished offender was a clergyman of the Established Church. Dr. Dodd received no mercy from the king when convicted of forgery and condemned to death, inasmuch as the monarch was resolved to make an impressive example of him to the recreant order of men to whom he belonged. Their notorious vices and unworthiness led to the beneficent reforms introduced by Wesley

---

"MY GOOD LORD PRIMATE,—I could not delay giving you the notification of the grief and concern with which my breast was affected at receiving authentic information that routs had made their way into your palace. At the same time, I must signify to you my sentiments on this subject, which hold these levities and vain dissipations as utterly inexpedient, if not unlawful, to pass in a residence for many centuries devoted to divine studies, religious retirement, and the extensive exercise of charity and benevolence; I add, in a place where so many of your predecessors have led their lives in such sanctity as has thrown lustre on the pure religion they professed. and adorned. From the dissatisfaction with which you must perceive I behold these improprieties, not to speak in harsher terms, and in still more pious principles, I trust you will suppress them immediately; so that I may not have occasion to show any further marks of my displeasure, or to interpose in a different manner. May God take your grace into his almighty protection! I remain, my lord primate, your gracious friend.

"G. R."

and Whitefield; the monuments of whose innovating zeal remain until this day, and will be coeval with the duration of the British empire.

Having thus concluded our survey of the events of the reign of George III., we may sum up the review by saying, that this monarch exhibited many serious defects of character; that he was narrow-minded, prejudiced, and obstinate beyond measure; that this peculiarity led him sometimes to adhere to ill-advised measures with a perseverance and pertinacity which injured his popularity, sometimes even endangered his throne, and cursed his subjects; but that, on the other hand, he possessed some very great merits, more of the heart than of the head; that he was ever disposed to govern his dominions in accordance with constitutional law, and while he asserted the full extent of his prerogatives, never wishing to transcend them; that he was virtuous in an age of prevalent vice; that he was pious and devout at a period when even priests and bishops threw scandal on their profession by their worldliness and profligacy; and that generally, it was his conscientious desire, but not always his realized end, to act with honesty, consistency and justice.

14*

PART IV.

LIFE AND REIGN OF GEORGE THE FOURTH.

CHAPTER I.

Birth of George IV.—Congratulations on the Event—His Early Education—His Talents—His Disposition—His Connection with Miss Darby—Her History—Frantic Admiration of the Prince—Incidents of their Attachment—The Prince removes to Carlton House—His Peculiar Manner of Making Love—His Connection with Mrs. Crouch—He becomes the Admirer of Mrs. Fitzherbert—Her Origin and History—Her Extraordinary Beauty—She is privately Married to the Prince—Their Residence together—Unprincipled denial of their Marriage in Parliament by orders of the Prince—Mrs. Fitzherbert's Indignation at his Perfidy—Immense Debts of the Prince—They are paid by an Appropriation of Parliament.

GEORGE, Prince of Wales, afterward George IV., was born on the 12th of August, 1762. The great officers of state were present, according to the established etiquette of courts, when an heir to the throne appeared. Immediately after the birth the propitious event was announced to the inmates of the palace. The multitude who then thronged all the avenues to St. James's, eager with expectation, received the news with the utmost enthusiasm; and in an hour it flew over the whole capital, and travelled with the rapidity of the wind to the extremities of the island. The popularity of George III., which had for some months been strangely on the wane, was immensely increased, and general congratulation gave expression to the universal joy; which was increased by the significant accident that the heir apparent first saw the light on the anniversary of the accession of the House of Hanover to the British sceptre. Before the nation were delivered from this prince, they had ample time and reason to moderate the ardor of their felicitations at his advent.*

Innumerable letters and speeches of congratulation were addressed to the father of the august child, by all the corporations in the kingdom, which were filled with the rhapsodic flattery and absurd adulation which usually characterize such productions. The public life of the young prince began at a very early age; for when only three years old, he received a deputation from the Society of Ancient Britons on St. David's Day. In the same year he was invested with the Order of the Garter.

In 1771 the education of the Prince of Wales began. He was placed under the control of Lord Holdernesse as governor, Dr. Markham as preceptor, and Cyril Jackson as sub-preceptor. Markham was at that time at the head of the celebrated School at Westminster. His first inquiry of the king when he accepted his office as tutor to the prince was, "How would your Majesty have him treated?" George III. answered, "Like the sons of any private English gentleman. If he deserves it, let him be flogged, just as you used to do at Westminster." This order was obeyed to the letter, and the princely back of the young student was made to smart more than once by the energetic and conscientious discipline of the tutor. But after the lapse of some time the governor and preceptors of the prince resigned, in consequence of the adverse influence exerted by the paramour and favorite of the Dowager Princess of Wales; whose purpose was to instil into the mind of the child more absolute and conservative ideas than accorded with the will of the king and his most

---

* The infant was created Prince of Wales a few days after his birth; for the eldest son of the British monarch does not possess that title by inheritance but by creation. This ancient title was one of the trophies connected with the conquest of Llewellyn, and was first conferred by the first Edward upon his eldest son and heir, in 1284, with the usual ceremonies of investiture by cap, coronet, verge and ring. The eldest son of the king becomes, by inheritance, Steward of Scotland, Duke of Rothsay, Earl of Carrick, and Baron of Renfrew. These titles belonged, before the union of England and Scotland, to the heir apparent of the latter kingdom. The Prince of Wales is born Duke of Cornwall, and possessor of the revenues of that duchy. *Hume's History of England*, Vol. ii., p. 141.

trusted advisers. The Duke of Montague was then appointed governor of the prince; Bishop Hurd and the Rev. Mr. Arnold, preceptor and sub-preceptor. The Bishop was a man of feeble character, who permitted his pupil to study and to do whatever he pleased. On one occasion he attempted to administer much needed discipline after the manner of Dr. Markham. But the prince and his brother the Duke of York, who was also a pupil of the Bishop, conspired together, and by a vigorous and united *coup-de-main* wrested the rod from his grasp, turned on him, and laid it upon his own back so effectively that bodily punishment was never afterward attempted.* But the education of the heir apparent was accurate and thorough. Few princes attained the same degree of familiarity with classical learning, or the same extent of proficiency in mathematical and natural sciences. On one occasion, at a much later period, he quoted half a page of Homer's Iliad in the original, correctly and without premeditation; and he understood Latin, French, and German with the facility of a mother tongue. These accomplishments were absolutely necessary to complete the character of the "first Gentleman in Europe," to which dignity he always aspired, and which he undoubtedly attained.

In 1791, when at the age of nineteen, the prince was released from the control of his instructors. He was one of the handsomest and most graceful youths to be found in the kingdom. He was tall, vigorous and well proportioned. His figure possessed a combination of beauty, intelligence and good health, which was highly attractive and pleasing; and it may readily be supposed that his exalted rank, and his brilliant prospects as the heir apparent to one of the greatest monarchies on the globe, surrounded him with flatterers, temptations and seductions of every imaginable description. In due time the subject of his separate provision was brought before Parliament, and after considerable discussion, fifty thousand pounds were voted him as an income, and one hundred thousand for an outfit. Thus amply provided with means, the young man, whose passions were of

* See *Croly's Life and Times of George IV.*, p. 59.

the most vehement nature, commenced one of the most remarkable careers recorded in the checkered annals of princes. In three short years, which were passed in the whirlpool of London vice and sensual pleasure, his ruin was completed. He plunged into every sort of dissipation; and before long the virtuous Queen Charlotte, his mother, was astonished and horrified at the information that he had taken Miss Darby or Mrs. Robinson, the most beautiful actress of the day, as his acknowledged mistress.

This young lady was born at Bristol in 1758, and would have been rich had not her father wasted his large fortune in an insane speculation, one essential ingredient of which was the civilization of the Esquimaux Indians. She had been a pupil of Hannah More; and had devoted some time to the laborious and thankless labors of an instructress. She was singularly handsome, and among her other attractions, she was a most graceful dancer. By some accident she crossed the path of Garrick; she pleased the modern Roscius, and he gave her some instructions in the dramatic art. Her first appearance was under his auspices, at the Covent Garden Theatre, in the character of Cordelia. In her sixteenth year she married Mr. Robinson, a clerk in an attorney's office, who possessed a handsome fortune. But this was soon wasted by extravagance and mismanagement. The husband was arrested for debt, and his wife spent fifteen months with him in prison. At length the stern demands of necessity again drove her to the stage. Her great beauty and her considerable talents soon rendered her the favorite actress of the day. During some time she permitted her husband to live in luxury on the earnings of her labors; and refused many offers from opulent and princely admirers on condition that she would separate from him. All these she refused, until in December, 1779, the young Prince of Wales first saw her. She played the part of *Perdita*, in the Winter's Tale, on that occasion, in the presence of the whole royal family. Her appearance and manner are represented as having been bewitching; and the young prince became frantically enamored of her. He sent a note to the fair charmer, signed

Florizel, by the hand of the Earl of Essex, containing the most rapturous flatteries; which was delivered her the moment she reached her dressing room. So brilliant a conquest it was scarcely in the heart of woman to refuse. An interview was contrived between them in the gardens of the palace at Kew, by moonlight; of which interview there was but one other witness, the brother of the prince. The consequence, as might have been expected, was an intrigue of some duration, of intense devotion on the part of the lovers, and of considerable scandal on the side of the public. Among other acts of folly the prince gave the young lady a bond for twenty thousand pounds, to be paid when he came of age. But when that period arrived the ardor of the lover had cooled, other flames consumed his inflammable and inconstant breast, and he refused to liquidate the sum nominated in the bond. The lady flew into paroxysms of rage and despair; and to avoid further disgrace and exposure, an annuity of five hundred pounds a year was eventually settled upon her. With this sum she retired to Paris, lived in some splendor there, and even attracted the notice of Marie Antoinette, who honored her with the epithet of *La belle Anglaise*, and presented her with a purse knit by the hand of the daughter of the Cæsars. She devoted some of her time to literature, and produced several novels and romances, all of which now quietly slumber in oblivion. She subsequently undertook to superintend the poetical department of the Morning Post, but died after a few months, in 1800. Such was the history of the first notorious connection of the Prince of Wales; which was but the beginning of a long series of similar offences, which continued with greater or less publicity until an advanced period of his life.

When the prince received his separate income from Parliament, in 1783, he took possession of Carlton House as his residence. This palace had been the abode of Frederic, his grandfather. It had originally been built in 1709 by Lord Carlton, and had been embellished and enlarged at various subsequent periods. The prince employed the architect Holland to effect other changes and improvements. Ionic screens, Corinthian porticoes, and various ornaments were added; and an air of great luxury, so consonant with the tastes of the possessor at that time, was thrown over the whole. In 1783 the prince first took his seat in the House of Lords. He was attended on this occasion by the Dukes of Cumberland, Portland and Richmond, and was regarded as the friend and patron, from the day of his entrance into Parliament, of Fox, Sheridan and the opposition. His seat in the house was, however, rarely occupied. More attractive pursuits drew him elsewhere. He hunted the phantom pleasure in every possible form, and squandered immense sums of money in his pursuit of it. Gaming, horse-racing, and every imaginable species of dissipation were indulged in; and soon the public were astonished and amused to learn, that the heir apparent supported in magnificent style at least two acknowledged mistresses; and that many casual and temporary attachments claimed and received his attention. The two recognized sultanas were Mrs. Crouch, an actress of beauty and talent, and the well-known Mrs. Fitzherbert.

The manner and demeanor of the prince in his intercourse with women, and in making love, were so peculiar as to deserve narration. He became silly and contemptible. When refused he proclaimed himself to be in despair, and wept in the most ridiculous and farcical manner, rolling on the floor, striking his forehead, tearing his hair, and using other excesses of the same description. When he first declared his passion to Mrs. Fitzherbert, and was courteously repelled, he pretended to go frantic, swore that he would abandon the country, that he would renounce the succession, that he would sell every thing and fly to America. To get rid of his absurdities and importunities, Mrs. Fitzherbert fled to the continent. After a short absence she returned. The desperate passion of her lover had lost none of its intensity. He again did his best to win her favor. To render his person more interesting and attractive he phlebotomized himself; and then asserted that the pangs of an unquenchable and unrequited passion had made him pale and thin. At length, when he found that

* See *Doran's Queens of the House of Hanover*, Vol. ii., p. 87.

nothing else would influence the really attractive and beautiful woman of whom he was so desperately enamored, he proposed to marry her secretly, though he well knew that as Mrs. Fitzherbert was a Roman Catholic, such a marriage was illegal according to one of the statutes of the realm; and also because the union would take place, if at all, without the king's consent, and before the prince had attained the age of twenty-five. The lady, it appears, was not influenced by any such scruples, and she finally consented to become the morganitic wife of her enamored and frantic admirer. The ceremony was performed secretly by a clergyman of the Established Church, whose name, and those of two attending witnesses, were attached to the certificate which still remains in the possession of the lady's family.

Mrs. Fitzherbert was the daughter of William Smythe of Tonge Castle. Her family were connected with the nobility, and were all highly esteemed. When very young she married Mr. Weld, of Lulworth Castle. After his death she was united to Fitzherbert of Swinnerton, who died in 1780. She was educated in the Roman Catholic faith. Her reputation was unblemished until her connection with the prince began. She was one of the most beautiful women of her time. Her appearance was majestic, and her form and features were faultless. She retained her hold on the affections of her unprincipled and worthless lover longer than any other woman; and he always treated her, even after their separation, with courtesy and respect. After the subsequent marriage of the prince to the unfortunate Caroline of Brunswick, a pension of six thousand pounds a year was settled on her; and she survived to enjoy it long after the death of the prince, until she had nearly reached the age of eighty years. Even after her husband had carried on a notorious and disgraceful intrigue with Lady Jersey, he still regarded "Mrs. Prince," as she was usually called, with the greatest deference; and spoke of her in terms very different from those which he applied to all the other women, whose name indeed was legion, with whom he had been connected.*

* See *Diary Illustrative of the Court of George IV.; with Letters of*

The expensive habits of living in which the prince indulged, soon involved him deeply in debt. In 1787, notwithstanding the liberal allowance made by Parliament for his support, his obligations amounted to a hundred and fifty thousand pounds. At a later period, in 1792, they reached the prodigious sum of four hundred thousand pounds. The subject became one of public scandal and scrutiny. Carlton House was known to be the continual scene of the most lavish and reckless luxury. In April, 1787, the matter of the prince's debts was for the first time introduced into Parliament. The Opposition contended that his income should be increased and the accumulated debts paid. The minister, Mr. Pitt, responded that he had received no commands from the king on the subject. In the course of the subsequent debate, the minister made some allusion to the marriage which, it was commonly rumored, had taken place between the prince and Mrs. Fitzherbert, as being one of the guilty and censurable causes of the prince's embarrassments. Mr. Fox responded by denying in the most positive manner, and as by authority from the prince himself, that any marriage had taken place between him and the lady in question. This denial was supported by Sheridan and other leading members of the Opposition. Yet these assertions could not overturn the reality of truth ; for the marriage itself, though perhaps illegal and invalid, had actually and infallibly taken place. After the discussion had continued for several days, a compromise was effected between the ministry and the friends of the prince. The king addressed a message to Parliament, in which having set forth the pecuniary difficulties of his son, he proposed that the sum of ten thousand pounds should be paid yearly out of the civil list, in addition to the fifty thousand already allowed ; and that his existing debts should be liquidated by an appropriation. The Parliament generously concurred in the royal proposition, and suggested that twenty thousand pounds should be granted in addition, to pay for necessary repairs on Carlton House. Thus, for a time at

Queen Caroline, Princess Charlotte, &c. London : 4 vols., 1839. Vol. iii., p. 174.

least, the self-caused embarrassments of this lavish voluptuary were removed.*

* The following statement of the private affairs of the prince was officially presented to Parliament on this occasion:

Debts.

Bonds and debts	£13,000
Purchase of houses	4,000
Expenses of Carlton House	53,000
Tradesmen's bills	90,504
	£160,504

Expenditure from July, 1783, to July, 1786.

Household, &c.	£29,276
Privy purse	16,050
Payments made by Col. Hotham, particulars delivered in to his Majesty	37,203
Other extraordinaries	11,406
	£93,636
Salaries	54,734
Stables	37,919
Mr. Robinson's	7,059
	£193,643

CHAPTER II.

Removal of the Prince of Wales to Brighton—His Attachment to Mrs. Fitzherbert—His Extravagance—His Marriage proposed to a German Princess—Alleged Invalidity of his Marriage with Mrs. Fitzherbert—His Match with Caroline of Brunswick Consummated—Her Character and Appearance—Arrival of the Princess in England—Her first Interview with her future Husband—Its Unhappy Result—The Marriage Ceremony—Disgraceful Conduct of the Bridegroom—His Removal to Carlton House—Liquidation of the enormous Debts of the Prince—Domestic Quarrels between the Prince and Princess of Wales—Birth of the Princess Charlotte—Final Separation of her Parents.

In 1787 the prince erected his celebrated country residence at Brighton. At that period this spot was nothing more than an obscure fishing village; but the situation was magnificent, commanding a full view of the rolling ocean, being within half a day's rapid drive from London, and possessing all the advantages of a fertile and pleasing circumjacent country. The location was also agreeable to Mrs. Fitzherbert, and of this lady the prince at that time was intensely enamored. Whatever she desired was attained, even if heaven and earth were moved to accomplish it. The prince therefore bought a few acres and began to build. At first he intended to construct only a cottage, surrounded by shrubbery. This was soon found to be inadequate to the wishes of the imperial Sultana, and numerous additions were therefore made from time to time. These finally culminated in the edifice known as the Pavilion, exhibiting the peculiar and heterogeneous style of architecture which has excited the critical humor of hundreds of tourists. In the comparative seclusion of this peaceful abode, the prince, by his own confession, spent some of the happiest years of his life. The society which graced the sumptuous saloons of the Pavilion was among the most intellectual and distinguished which Europe afforded. Here were frequently found such men as Fox, Sheridan, Erskine, Hare and Fitzpatrick, the Duchess of Devonshire, the Duchess of Gordon, Curran, the wittiest of Irishmen, the chivalrous Ponsonby, and many other celebrities of the day were habitual visitors there; while no distinguished foreigner who came to England failed to pay his respects to the splendid and accomplished heir apparent of the Empire. The intellectual feasts which such society afforded, no less than the exquisite entertainment of a more gross and sensual nature which characterized the Pavilion, rendered the privilege of an introduction there highly prized and earnestly coveted by all classes, not excepting the greatest and noblest in the realm.

During some years the prince continued to live in comparative repose and retirement with the attractive and congenial partner of his existence, either at Brighton or at Carlton House. When the first serious attack of insanity overturned for a time the intellect of his father, and the Regency question became one of paramount prominence and importance, he was drawn from his peaceful seclusion to take an active part in the contest which ensued between his friends and the partisans of the demented monarch. The result of that contest was highly disagreeable to the prince; for, notwithstanding the utmost endeavors of his confederates and supporters in Parliament, he was obliged to be content with an arrangement by which, in case of the future repeated insanity of the monarch, he would be invested with a regency shorn of its powers, hampered in its functions, and restricted in its prerogatives. The consequence was, that the prince abandoned politics in disgust, and gave himself up more completely to every vicious and expensive indulgence. Several years thus spent, again involved him in overwhelming pecuniary embarrassments. His creditors soon became importunate for payment. The aggregate of these obligations amounted to the prodigious sum of six hundred thousand pounds. It was absolutely necessary both for the safety of the princely debtor, and for the credit and dignity of the royal family, that some provision should be made to liquidate this enormous load of indebtedness, and also that some decisive steps should be taken, by means of which a similar dilemma might be avoided in future.

It was at this crisis in the history of the prince, that his father conceived the idea of his marriage, and devised the most absurd and unfortunate match which has ever occurred in the history of royal miseries and infamies. The young lady whom the king proposed as a wife to his already mated and enamored son, was the Princess Caroline Amelia Elizabeth, the daughter of his brother-in-law, the Hereditary Prince of Brunswick. She was born in 1768, and was therefore six years younger than her intended husband. In every other respect except the matter of age alone, she was wholly unfit for the proposed alliance. Yet the king promised that, if his son would marry his cousin, his debts should be paid, and he be furnished with a more liberal and extensive establishment. To this proposal the prince at length agreed, harassed and annoyed, as he constantly was, by the importunities of his creditors, and the indignities to which he was frequently subjected. But before we narrate the events connected with this marriage, it will be proper to dispose of the lady who already claimed to possess the hand as well as the heart of the illustrious bridegroom.

The prince had overcome Mrs. Fitzherbert's repugnance to him in the first instance by a contemptible trick. Edward Bouverie, his friend, arrived at her residence in great haste and consternation, declaring that he had stabbed himself, and that her presence alone could save his life. The young widow immediately hastened to his bedside, to rescue the hope of a great nation from self-murder. When she arrived she found him pale and covered with blood; and he solemnly declared, that unless she promised to become his wife, he would destroy himself. She could resist no longer; the Duchess of Devonshire furnished the ring; and the frantic lover placed it upon her fair finger, as a sacred pledge of marriage. The wounding in this case was said to be really genuine; and Mrs. Fitzherbert frequently declared to her friends subsequently, that she often saw the mark of it. Nevertheless she became terrified at the act which she had committed, and fled to the continent. But her lover only became more desperate, and his couriers rapidly traversed France, Switzerland, and Holland, bearing letter after letter filled with the most rhapsodic declarations of adoration and devotion. These couriers were so frequent, and so urgent in their pace, that they excited the suspicion of the French government, as if they carried missions pregnant with the future destinies of empires; and three of them were arrested. But soon after, when the real nature of their commission was ascertained, they were discharged with a general roar of laughter from the guard house. When the lady returned to England, the marriage ceremony already alluded to, took place. The uncle of the bride, Henry Errington, and her brother, John Smythe, were present. The certificate of marriage was written in the hand of the prince himself, and signed by him and by the lady. The names of the witnesses were added, but they were subsequently removed, to avert from their heads any possible punishment. The performance of the ceremony by a Protestant clergyman did not render it less valid in the estimation of the bride; because the presence of a Roman Catholic priest, according to the theory of the Romish Church, would not have increased its validity; and the fact that a minister of the church established by law in England officiated, may have been regarded by her as an additional reason why she should esteem the ceremony binding and efficacious according to the laws of the realm.

And this was the view generally taken of the matter by the public at that day. Horne Tooke spoke of the lady as "legally, really, worthily, and happily for the country, Her Royal Highness the Princess of Wales." The statute which forbade the heir apparent of the British Empire to marry a Roman Catholic, or a subject, was regarded as a nullity, morally speaking, by the vast majority of the populace; and Mrs. Fitzherbert was by them esteemed as the lawful wife of the prince. The first coolness which arose between the lovers was produced by his pecuniary embarrassments. But they were soon reconciled; and, as is uusal in such cases, they became more devoted than before. In the course of time, however, the malignant star of the handsome and intriguing Lady Jersey crossed Mrs. Fitzherbert's path; and soon she discovered that her talented rival had succeeded in making an impression on her lover's heart. Until this period she had always received the greatest kindness and courtesy from the royal family; and the Duke of York was her especial friend. When the ascendency of Lady Jersey over the mind of the prince had attained a considerable degree of absoluteness, the marriage with Caroline of Brunswick was proposed and consummated. After the occurrence of this event, Mrs. Fitzherbert separated herself entirely from her supposed husband. When the quarrel commenced between the prince and princess, the former desired to renew his intercourse secretly with his first wife; but she peremptorily repelled him. He commenced a desperate pursuit after her, and placed her in a most delicate situation. In this dilemma she had recourse to the advice of the highest authority in the Catholic Church. The Rev. Mr. Nassau was sent to Rome to request the guidance of the Holy Father in the matter; and he returned with a Brief in which the Pope gave an answer favorable to the suit of the prince, alleging that the marriage with the Princess of Brunswick was null and void, in consequence of her own prior and indefeasible claims. Assured by this supreme authority, she again permitted the society of her impassioned admirer, and continued to reside with him during eight years, which she always termed the happiest of their union. She was accustomed to declare that they were very poor, but very merry; that sometimes they could not muster five pounds between them; but that the pleasure of each other's society made ample amends for the embarrassments which they were compelled to endure.

But it was not in the nature of the prince to remain faithful to any human being in any relation. The beautiful Marchioness of Hertford at length supplanted Mrs. Fitzherbert in the affections of her volatile lover. Yet notwithstanding the fact that this lady, and even others, attracted the amorous regard of this voluptuous and unprincipled man at different periods of his subsequent life, they never wholly effaced his kindly remembrance and regard for Mrs. Fitzherbert. She seemed to be, till the close of his life, the woman with whom his most tender and pleasing recollections were associated. When he lay on his death-bed, she addressed him a letter full of affection, by which his callous heart was deeply impressed. He retained her miniature during his whole lifetime; it was attached to his person when he expired; and when at last that once graceful and stately form was wrapped in cerecloth, and arrayed in the gorgeous mockery of funereal trappings for the tomb, the Bishop of Worcester, who was present, saw that miniature still fastened around the neck of the departed king, by a small silver chain; and with the corpse it descended to the grave.* After the accession of William IV. Mrs. Fitzherbert presented herself before that monarch; exhibited to him the evidences of her marriage with the former Prince of Wales; and was duly authorized by him to assume the royal livery, and wear the weeds of the widows of the sovereigns of England. He invited her to visit him at the familiar palace at Brighton, and on her arrival there, handed her out of her carriage, and introduced her to the royal family as one of their own number. At a subsequent period all the letters and papers which related to the connection of this remarkable woman with the prince, were by her destroyed; except a few which were deposited for safe keeping in the bank of the Messrs. Coutts, and several others which she retained in her own possession. The latter were her mortgage on the palace at Brighton for six thousand pounds, which she had received from the prince, and on the interest of which she chiefly subsisted; the certificate of her marriage; † a letter from the prince when king, acknowledging their relation as husband and wife; a will written by him at a later period of his life; and a letter of the clergyman who performed

---

* See *Memoirs of Mrs. Fitzherbert; with an Account of her Marriage with H. R. H. the Prince of Wales, afterward George IV. By the Hon. Charles Langdale.* London: Bentley.
† Dated December 21st, 1785.

15

the ceremony, with her own memorandum endorsed upon it. The concluding years of her long and romantic career were spent in dignified retirement at Brighton, the scene of her happiest days, and at that place her life terminated in 1837. Very few incidents connected with the existence of George IV. place his character in a more disgraceful light, or indicate more clearly the perfidy of his heart, and his total want of moral principle, than his treatment of this remarkable woman whose greatest error seems to have been, that she loved her *soi-disant* husband not wisely but too well.

Although George III. was totally unacquainted with the personal character of Caroline of Brunswick, he despatched Lord Malmesbury to the court of her father, not to scrutinize her appearance and disposition, and report the result of his observations, but to make an immediate and positive demand of her hand in marriage for the Prince of Wales. He arrived at Brunswick in November, 1794, and was received with a most cordial welcome. Being introduced to the Princess Caroline, he found her to possess a pretty face, fine eyes, good hair, tolerable teeth, and a well-proportioned figure. She was witty and sprightly in her conversation; her laugh was hearty and satirical; but her manners were too undignified and free.* Even the courtly and gallant diplomatist could not fail to notice that the princess exhibited one of the most repulsive weaknesses of which women can be guilty. She was not addicted to superfluous cleanliness; and if the truth must be known, this defect, together with the results which naturally and inevitably flowed from it, were the chief causes of her subsequent misfortunes. She was to be united to one of the most fastidious and voluptuous men of the age;

---

* A few specimens of her girlish wit remain. Being asked by her instructor in natural history "in what country the lion is to be found," she replied: "Well, you may find him in the heart of a Brunswicker." Her father having asked her, when twelve years old, "how she would define time and space," she answered: "Space is in the mouth of Madame von L., and time is in her face." A woman possessed of so great a disposition to sarcasm would not be harmless or inoffensive in such a melancholy contest as afterward ensued between herself and her husband.

and yet she was one of the least endurable of women to such a man. Had the Prince of Wales been permitted to see his intended bride previous to the ceremony, no power on earth could have induced him to accept her. Had the Duke of York, when visiting the Prince of Brunswick several years before, made a more critical examination of the appearance and qualities of the princess than he did, he would never have recommended the match, or have been the means of bringing it eventually to a completion. The representations of the Duke of York seem to have excited the curious ardor of the intended bridegroom to the highest pitch; for Lord Malmesbury was followed to Brunswick by Major Hislop, who brought with him a portrait of the prince, and a letter to the former vehemently urging him to hasten homeward with the princess.

Accordingly Malmesbury was married to Caroline vicariously on the eighth of December, 1794. Several months elapsed before the journey to England was commenced. During this interval the English envoy endeavored to infuse into the mind of the princess more correct views of decorum; for of this matter she appeared to him to be strangely ignorant. Her father, the old Duke of Brunswick, said of her, perhaps cruelly, yet enigmatically: "She is no fool; but she has no judgment." Her greatest fault was her everlasting loquacity. Her tongue seemed never to repose; and when people are eternally talking, even the wisest must needs utter a vast quantity and variety of nonsense. This was precisely the misfortune and the error of Caroline of Brunswick. Malmesbury endeavored in vain, in his frequent and confidential conversations with her, to correct her conduct, and to impress upon her mind the conviction that the Princess of Wales should be a model of dignity and propriety He counselled her to avoid familiarity with any one, and to have no confidants. She promised to obey his advice, and instantly broke her promise by asking him questions in reference to Lady Jersey and Mrs. Fitzherbert, of whom she spoke as the two mistresses of her intended husband. Malmesbury wisely advised her never to seem conscious of the existence of these persons, and assured her that appearances of jealousy on the part of a wife are always unpleasant, generally useless, and frequently injurious to the injured wife in the highest degree. He also urged her to attend divine service regularly, and to seem to be, if she even were not, devoutly attached to religion and the established church. The admonitions which the subtle diplomatist imparted to his ward might be fitly condensed into a single word, and a single precept; but this was the word which, throughout her whole life, she constantly ignored, and the precept which she invariably violated—be prudent. He even thought it necessary from the indications of frivolity which he observed in the princess to caution her against the slightest disposition to flirt with the handsome courtiers who would surround her in her new residence; and while he informed her that, by the laws of England, the penalty of death was inflicted on any man who dared to solicit the favors of a Princess of Wales, he added with prudent boldness, that it would be high treason in her to accede to any such approaches, and that the penalty of high treason in all cases was death. This novel and startling announcement caused the princess to fall into a profound reverie; after which, however, her usual excessive gaiety returned.

The young bride left Brunswick on the 29th of December, 1795. The party stopped at Hanover on their way. Several months were occupied in accomplishing the journey to England. Rather singular developments were made to Lord Malmesbury during this interval in reference to the personal peculiarities of the future Queen of England. His olfactories convinced him, in spite of his repugnance to such a conclusion, that the princess was very careless in regard to her person, that she made her toilette with excessive haste, that she rarely paid much attention to cleanliness, and that she was even offensive from this neglect. This discovery was a stunning blow to the diplomatist, who well knew the fastidious and exquisite taste of the intended bridegroom; and he anticipated results as unpropitious as those which actually occurred.

Caroline of Brunswick arrived at Greenwich on the 4th of

April, 1796. The news of her arrival rapidly spread through the vicinity, and the whole populace gave utterance to their hearty welcome. In a short time the royal carriages arrived to convey her to the capital. A large company of lords and ladies were sent to escort her, and among the latter was Lady Jersey, the crafty and malignant star of the princess's future destiny. Lady Jersey commenced to ridicule her dress, appearance, and manners; and began a series of persecutions which ended only in the grave of the unfortunate woman who was thus unwillingly dragged up to greatness by the stupidity of George III. Having arrived at St. James's Palace, the royal family were officially informed of her presence. The Prince of Wales immediately hastened to greet his bride and cousin; and this was the beginning, the opening scene of that melancholy, disgusting, and disgraceful tragedy, which has cast such eternal infamy over the House of Hanover, and especially upon the Prince of Wales. The princess had not been allowed leisure to pay any attention to her person or her toilette after her long and tedious journey, before her intended husband rushed into her presence with the eager curiosity and uncourteous rudeness of an overgrown boy. Lord Malmesbury alone was the witness of this first interview. He instantly introduced the princess to the prince. She then attempted to kneel, according to the usual etiquette; but the prince approaching, prevented her, embraced her, and instantly retired to a remote corner of the room, exclaiming: "I am not well, Harris, get me a glass of brandy." The astonished Malmesbury was confounded at this singular deportment, and replied, "Sir, had you not better have a glass of water?" The prince, apparently much offended, said, "No, I will go directly to the queen," and then rushed from the apartment. During this scene, the princess remained standing, and in amazement. At length she exclaimed to the attendant, "My God, does the prince always behave in this way? He is very coarse, and not near as handsome as his portrait." Malmesbury was greatly perplexed, and stammered out, that the prince was naturally much confused at this first interview, and that she must excuse his rudeness; but the real cause of the catastrophe which thus attended the commencement of this unpropitious union, was, that the nostrils of the bridegroom were offended beyond endurance by the odor which proceeded from the person of the unwashed and slovenly princess.

The unfavorable impression already produced on the mind of the bridegroom, was soon increased by the deportment of the princess at the royal table. She affected flippancy, raillery, and wit, and endeavored to irritate Lady Jersey, the mistress of her husband, by her sarcastic allusions. Such conduct would have been at all times indecorous, but so soon after her arrival in England it was doubly improper. The prince was heartily disgusted with his matrimonial bargain; and he declared to Malmesbury, his great regret that he had not been permitted to see, or at least to know, the peculiarities of the princess before her arrival in England. The truth is, that her defects both of person and character were of so trivial and so remediable a nature, that they might have all been cured and removed, and the union which could not then be easily dissolved, might have been made agreeable and propitious, had not the husband himself been one of the most worthless and contemptible of men. He possessed not a single quality which enabled him, or disposed him, to exercise a favorable influence upon her mind. A prudent and sagacious partner might have moulded the tastes and converted the character of the princess to admirable qualities and uses; but he was himself a volatile and unprincipled voluptuary, who scarcely, during his whole existence, conceived a useful thought or accomplished a desirable end.

The ceremony of this most unfortunate marriage in modern times was performed on the 8th of April, 1795, in the Royal Chapel of the palace of St James. Nothing which has ever been described in the exaggerated pages of romance, or in the sterner realities of the history of princes, equals the disgraceful and lamentable scenes which took place on this occasion, the real importance of which to the future happiness of millions cannot well be estimated. Then a connection was to be formed which would mould in future years by the direct and indirect influence which would inevitably proceed from it, the fate of a vast empire, the future relations of princes and kingdoms, and all the various interests of countless multitudes of human beings. Assuredly on such an occasion, the chief actor would entertain some appreciation of its importance; and would deport himself in some degree worthy of the responsibilities which he assumed. The fact was widely different. The bridal party assembled in the apartments of the queen, and proceeded thence to the royal chapel, which was crowded. The ceremony was performed by Dr. Moore, the Archbishop of Canterbury; but the scene was most repulsive. The bridegroom was so completely intoxicated, as to be unable to stand. During the ceremony he was supported on each side by the attendant groomsmen. After he knelt, he rose again before the proper time; the Archbishop paused, the service was interrupted, universal confusion prevailed among the royal circle; and the prince could only be brought to his knees again, almost unconsciously, by the decisive action of George III., who rose from his seat, briskly walked to his bewildered son, whispered in his ear, and assisted or compelled him again to kneel. After this incident the ceremony was concluded with the aid of the groomsmen, who, on this occasion, were compelled to perform a service which never fell to the lot of princely attendants before. During the ceremony the unhappy bride, who was unprepared for so mortifying a scene, could not conceal her well-founded sorrow. A supper followed at Buckingham palace, at which the unlucky pair took no notice of each other. At midnight they retired to their own residence at Carlton House, and quarrelled with each other on the road. Such was indeed a fitting commencement of this unfortunate and unpropitious marriage.*

* *Doran's Queens of England of the House of Hanover*, Vol. ii., p. 238. It is difficult to assign a reason for the conduct of the Prince of Wales on this occasion, or to explain why he should have had recourse to the pernicious influence of intoxicating liquors. Probably he was filled with remorse at the consciousness of his previously existing marriage with Mrs. Fitzherbert, and regret at the thought of resigning her; for he apprehended that she would thenceforth

Carlton House had been furnished for the reception of the prince and his bride with regal magnificence. The dressing-room of the princess alone cost twenty-five thousand pounds. Many valuable presents had been prepared for her by the several members of the royal family. But all these indications of courtesy and esteem, as well as the countless effusions of loyalty and admiration which filled the newspapers of the day were falsified by the event. One of these asserted that "the Princess of Wales was one of the best harpsicord players among the royal families on the continent: the prince being passionately fond of music, *harmony* will of course be the order of the day!" It was asserted in the same quarter that the princess was always dressed in a simple but elegant style; that her taste in every part of her attire was equally exquisite, and that she would doubtless become the standard of fashionable taste and elegance; whereas a deficiency in this very respect was the most glaring and invincible defect in her character.

After the hateful pageantry of the marriage of the prince, came the irksome and repulsive task of paying his enormous debts. These now amounted to the sum of six hundred and forty-two thousand nine hundred pounds. The prince had consented to the match only on condition that these obligations should be liquidated; he had performed his part of the contract and George III. was expected to do the same. On the 27th of April, 1795, Mr. Pitt introduced the subject to the attention of the Commons in a very able speech. The king sent in a message in which he set forth the necessity of providing a suitable establishment for the heir apparent, and added that the first point preparatory to all others, was to liquidate his debts. One expedient by which he proposed to accomplish this result was to appropriate a portion of the prince's

---

repel him. In addition to this he was doubtless disgusted with the offensiveness of the person of the princess. A third reason might have been the fact that the princess had herself acknowledged, that her affections were already preoccupied by an attachment to a member of her father's diminutive court at Brunswick; which circumstance, with her usual carelessness and imprudence, she had communicated to her worst enemy, Lady Jersey.

intended income, and the yearly revenues of the Duchy of Cornwall to the payment of his obligations. Mr. Pitt proposed that the annual income of the prince should be fixed at a hundred and twenty-five thousand pounds, that twenty-eight thousand should be allowed for jewels and plate for the marriage, and twenty-six thousand be allowed for the finishing and enlarging of Carlton House. The revenues of the Duchy of Cornwall were thirteen thousand pounds. The accumulation during the prince's minority from 1763 to 1783 were two hundred and thirty-three thousand pounds. The minister proposed that seventy-eight thousand pounds of this sum should be appropriated to this purpose; and that the princess should have a yearly income of fifty thousand pounds, independently of her husband.

The discussion on the proposition of the minister continued during nearly three months. Fox and Sheridan greatly distinguished themselves during its progress, by the ability and fierceness with which they attacked the king and his cabinet. The mind of the nation was hostile to the prince. It was at that very period sore and fretted, in consequence of the disastrous results of the French war, and the splendid triumphs which clustered around the eagles of the rising young Republic. The taxes which the nation paid were already enormous; and when they heard of a farrier's bill for forty thousand pounds, and an annuity to his cast-off mistress, Mrs. Crouch, being among the obligations of the voluptuous and lavish prince, they became intensely and not unjustly incensed. Mrs. Fitzherbert was at this period residing in a magnificent mansion in Park Lane, at the rate of ten thousand pounds a year; while Lady Jersey succeeded in extracting from the purse of her unprincipled paramour of no inconsiderable sum.

What might eventually have been the result of the debate in Parliament on the subject, it would be impossible to assert, had not the prince himself, by Mr. Anstruther, his solicitor-general, proposed a compromise. The proceedings eventually terminated by the passage of three bills; the first, for preventing future Princes of Wales from incurring debts; the second granting an establishment to the prince; the third providing a jointure for the princess. Commissioners were also appointed to examine into the nature and justice of his debts. Some of the claims were rejected as utterly groundless; many were reduced in a great degree as exorbitant; and a per centage was taken off from the whole of them. The creditors whose demands were allowed, were to be paid by debentures bearing interest, and the term of nine years was allowed for the final settlement of the entire amount. By this means, this most lavish and expensive of human beings was again relieved for a time from the pecuniary embarrassments by which for some years, he had been annoyed.

The domestic quarrels of the prince and princess began immediately after their marriage, and never ended until the death of the latter. The prince soon succeeded in winning back the society of Mrs. Fitzherbert—from that of Lady Jersey he had never separated himself. On more than one occasion, both of these women, by the contrivance of the prince, dined at the same table in order to mortify the princess. On the 7th of January, 1796, the Princess Charlotte, the ill-starred fruit of this untoward match, was born; but her advent brought no joy to the heart of the unfortunate mother. The father, when presented with the infant, coldly remarked that it was a fine girl, and never approached the bedside of the mother. He refused all public demonstrations of congratulation from the various corporations of the realm, which courteously tendered them; and the reason was, that he had already determined upon a total and final separation from his wife. As soon as she had partially recovered from the effects of her confinement, her husband's purpose was conveyed to her by Lady Cholmondeley. She replied, with as much composure as she could assume, that such an intention should be conveyed to her directly from her husband in writing; and that, should a separation then take place, their intercourse should never under any circumstances be again resumed.

In accordance with the intention thus expressed, the prince wrote a letter in which he said that " our inclinations are not in our power; nor should either of us be held answerable to the other, because nature has not made us suitable to each other. Tranquillity and comfortable society are, however, in our power; let our intercourse therefore be restricted to that." He expressed his hearty concurrence in the determination of the princess, that if they separated at all it should be forever; and even went so far as to contemplate remote and possible contingencies by adding, that should any accident happen to their daughter, by which her life would be terminated, he would never propose to remedy the calamity by resuming "a connection of a more particular nature."

The princess was compelled to acquiesce in the purpose of her husband; and after precisely one year's experience of domestic life, they separated forever. Her allowance was at first fixed at twenty thousand pounds; but she finally refused to accept this sum, and held her husband responsible for her expenses. She retired to a small residence at Charlton near Woolwich; but subsequently she removed to Montague House on Blackheath. She still retained possession of her daughter, and was occasionally visited by her royal father-in-law and uncle. At Montague House, the princess entertained her friends in a handsome manner; and among her frequent visitors were Lord Chancellor Eldon and George Canning. The young Princess Charlotte was placed, when at the proper age, under the superintendence of Lady Elgin, in a mansion in the vicinity; though the visits of the unhappy mother to her child were generally restricted to one a week.

The matter of the pecuniary support of the princess was finally settled by an annual allowance of about twenty thousand pounds—the sum which she previously refused. Her husband now retired for some years from the public gaze, and spent his obscurity in the indulgence of all his luxurious and voluptuous tastes. Those eight happiest years of his life in the society of Mrs. Fitzherbert then ensued, to which reference has already been made; and while the continent was convulsed with the great events attendant upon the meteoric ambition of Napoleon Bonaparte, the prince luxuriated in the enjoyment of the choicest

felicities which earth can bestow, except one and the greatest—
an easy conscience.*

* The reply of the Princess of Wales to the communication of her husband, in which he expressed his desire and determination to have a permanent separation, was as follows:

"Sir,—The avowal of your conversation with Lord Cholmondeley neither surprises nor offends me; it merely confirmed what you have tacitly insinuated for this twelvemonth. But after this, it would be a want of delicacy, or rather an unworthy meanness, in me, were I to complain of those conditions which you impose upon yourself. I should have returned no answer to your letter, if it had not been conceived in terms to make it doubtful whether this arrangement proceeds from you or from me. You are aware that the honor of it belongs to you alone. The letter which you announce to me as the last, obliges me to communicate to the king, as to my sovereign and my father, both your avowal and my answer. You will find inclosed a copy of my letter to the king. I apprise you of it, that I may not incur the slightest reproach of duplicity from you. As I have at this moment no protector but his majesty, I refer myself solely to him on this subject; and if my conduct meet his approbation, I shall be, in some degree at least, consoled. I retain every sentiment of gratitude for the situation in which I find myself, as Princess of Wales, enabled by your means to indulge in the free exercise of a virtue dear to my heart—charity. It will be my duty, likewise, to act upon another motive—that of giving an example of patience and resignation under every trial.

"Do me the justice to believe that I shall never cease to pray for your happiness, and to be, your much devoted, Caroline." *Croly's Life and Times of George IV.*, p. 202.

CHAPTER III.

Defects of the Prince of Wales—The Inconsistency of his Political Conduct—The Situation of the Princess of Wales—Lord and Lady Douglas—Malicious Charges of the latter against the Princess—Trial of the Princess for Adultery—Evidence in her favor—Her Acquittal—The Sympathy of the Nation in her behalf—The Prince of Wales takes a new Mistress—Lady Hertford—Financial Embarrassments of the Princess of Wales—Death of Mr. Percival—Duke of Wellington—The Prince of Wales obtains an unrestricted Regency.

PERFIDY and want of consistency were among the most glaring defects in the character of the Prince of Wales; and he displayed them in every stage of his career. In his early manhood, when he first entered political life, his rebellious hatred to his father induced him to form an intimate alliance with his father's fiercest enemies, the liberal Whigs. When the French Revolution broke forth, and threatened to prostrate to the earth every throne in Europe, he deserted the Whig party, which admired and commended that remarkable movement, and publicly avowed his hostility to the sentiments and measures of his former associates. After the alarm of the terrified monarchs subsided, and they recovered their usual repose and confidence, the prince gradually returned to his deserted friends, for the purpose of using them as tools with which to embarrass his father's government. When the confirmed insanity of George III. placed the regency in the hands of the prince, he again shamefully abandoned the Whigs, patronized the Tory faction, and even persecuted his former confederates with that malignant rancor which he only can exhibit, who is conscious that he has so deeply injured, that he can neither forgive nor be forgiven. The same pernicious and unprincipled policy characterized his conduct toward his wives and mistresses. He promised to marry Caroline of Brunswick only that he might obtain money. He knew that he had already entered into a most solemn obligation to "love, cherish and protect" another lady, who was indeed not unworthy of his affection, and no sooner was the second marriage consummated than he abandoned the unfortunate woman whom he had induced by the false offer of an unappropriated hand and heart, to leave her paternal roof and accept a shelter under his own. He then commenced a series of persecutions and indignities against her which has scarcely a parallel in history; placing tempters in her way, and spies to hover around her steps, so that he might eventually ruin her reputation, blast her happiness, and inflict upon her those miseries which, to the female spirit, are most calamitous and crushing.

The solitude in which the desertion of her husband, and the removal of her daughter, left the Princess of Wales, induced her to seek an alleviation in the society of children. She had heard that Sir John and Lady Douglas, who resided in the vicinity of her own abode, possessed a child of rare beauty, and she called in person to see it. Previous to this event she had no acquaintance with the family, but after the first interview, their intercourse rapidly ripened into the closest intimacy. Lady Douglas was an intriguing woman, and her reputation was not spotless. She was a most dangerous person to be the associate of a woman so bold and imprudent in her speech as the Princess of Wales; for she was capable of turning all that she heard, in moments of unsuspicious freedom, to the worst account. The princess soon became aware of this painful circumstance, and then she suddenly broke off the acquaintance. This course greatly incensed the discarded family; and their indignation was increased when they received an anonymous letter of an insulting character, which they falsely ascribed to the princess as its author.

Lady Douglas determined to revenge the supposed insult. In 1802 the princess had taken a fancy to an infant whose parents were named Austin, and which had been born in a hospital. She had it removed to her own residence, and there tended with the utmost care. Lady Douglas took advantage of this circumstance, to base upon it the most gigantic and formidable pyramid of lies which ever yet crushed a woman's reputation. She informed the Duke of Kent that she was in possession of important facts which closely concerned the honor of the Prince of Wales, and was prepared to communicate them. The Duke had an interview with the lady; and afterward scrupulously detailed to the prince of the substance of her information. The latter welcomed the intelligence, and requested that Lady Douglas might prepare a written statement of all the facts within her knowledge; with which request she eagerly complied. She declared that during her close and confidential intercourse with the princess, she discovered that she was coarse in conversation, vulgar in behavior, and vicious in conduct; that she attempted to seduce even Lady Douglas herself from the path of virtue; and that she had laughed at her supposed scruples. She asserted that the princess had acknowledged to her that she was about to become a mother; that to avoid suspicion she had resolved to pretend to adopt a child, and call it Austin; and that the person of the princess, immediately before the appearance of that child, indicated by every infallible evidence the existence of her pregnancy. Various other details followed, so indelicate in their character that they cannot be here repeated.

On the strength of this statement a commission was formed in 1805, to take the testimony of some corroborating witnesses to whom Lady Douglas referred. These were chiefly servants in the household of the princess. Accordingly, John Cole was examined, whom the princess had recently discarded, as he asserted, for no greater offense than having accidentally observed some improper conduct between her and Sir Sidney Smith. He added that he had seen immoral proceedings between the princess and Captain Manby of the Royal Navy, and between her and Lawrence the painter. Bidgood, another servant, was also examined. He testified that he had seen Captain Manby kiss the princess, and had observed her to weep at his departure from her residence. He deposed to similar improprieties between his mistress and Captain Hood. All these witnesses had been placed in the household of the princess, in the first instance, not by her own selection, but by that of her husband.

In consequence of this additional evidence, the king issued his warrant in May, 1806, to Lords Erskine, Grenville, Spencer, and Ellenborough, directing them to inquire into the truth or falsehood of the accusations made against the princess, and report the results of their investigations. They examined all the witnesses under oath. These testified before the royal commissioners to the same effect as when first interrogated. Lady Douglas, Sir John Douglas, Cole, Fanny Floyd, and Bidgood, were the principal witnesses to the improper and guilty behaviour of the accused; but their declarations were afterward contradicted in the most positive and conclusive manner by other witnesses far more credible and competent than themselves. The evidence to show that young Austin was not the child of the princess, but was born of a poor and humble mother in Brownlow Street Hospital, was complete and overwhelming. It became equally clear that the princess had taken charge of it from motives of charity and benevolence. It was also established by more honest witnesses who were in the service of the princess, that she had never exhibited the slightest indications of pregnancy. Captain Manby swore positively, that the assertion of Bidgood, that he had seen him kiss the princess, was totally and absolutely false; and that he had never on any occasion or in any manner approached her person. The painter Lawrence testified that he had never been alone with the princess in his life, save once, and that only for a moment, when he turned back from the company which was retiring from her presence, to answer a question put to him by the princess in reference to her portrait which he was then painting; and he solemnly averred that he had never touched her person in any manner. Mr. Edmondes, whom one of the witnesses against the princess had accused of having said, that he knew facts which would convict and condemn her, deposed that he had never uttered a word tending in any way to criminate or degrade her. Mr. Mills, the medical attendant of the princess, declared under oath, that the witness who asserted that he had intimated that the princess was pregnant in 1802, swore falsely; and that the princess had never shown the least evidence of pregnancy since his acquaintance with her. Other witnesses testified that they had seen Lady Douglas and Bidgood in secret conversation together, evidently hatching between them the minute details of these infamous slanders. Sir Sidney Smith also testified that, though he had been intimately acquainted with the princess, and had frequently visited her in the morning, which was a usual custom at that time even in the highest ranks of English society, there had never passed the slightest impropriety between him and the accused.*

The evidence in favor of the princess was in truth overwhelming. Every charge was triumphantly refuted. The written and verified testimony taken before the royal commissioners was then submitted to the scrutiny of the king, who carefully examined it, and was completely satisfied in regard to the innocence of his daughter-in-law. Yet nine weeks elapsed before she received any communication which could alleviate her suspense on the subject. She then addressed a courteous letter to the king, requesting that he would hasten his final judgment in the matter, inasmuch as such delay caused her to sink in the estimation of his majesty's subjects, and gave a temporary and unfair triumph to her enemies. Yet some months passed away after this appeal, before the king rendered his opinion of the innocence or the guilt of the accused. In January, 1807, the cabinet, at the command of the monarch, gave utterance to the conclusion to which he had arrived; and they set forth that the evidence did not justify further proceedings against the accused. They however did not acquit her formally and absolutely, as they should have done; but set forth that the princess had evidently been guilty of great imprudence and impropriety; and concluded

* See *Diary Illustrative of the Times of George IV., with Letters of Queen Caroline, Princess Charlotte, and other Distinguished Persons. Edited by John Galt.* 4 vols. London: Colburn, 1839. Vol. iii., p. 240.

with administering to her a reproof and a caution as to her conduct in future. This last was indeed not undeserved; but the absence of a total acquittal, in a case where the evidence did not, in the eyes of the commissioners, justify a conviction, was an outrage upon English law and natural justice. After the termination of the whole affair, the king formally informed Caroline that "his Majesty was convinced that it was no longer necessary for him to decline receiving her into the royal presence." Thus terminated this memorable and infamous scrutiny, which was in itself an object of popular disgust and reprobation. The nation at large exulted in the vindication of the princess which resulted from it; for she then possessed, as she did until the day of her death, their confidence and sympathy; but they condemned the inquest because it did not give to approved innocence that signal triumph to which it is entitled, when it overwhelms the false accuser with a resistless flood of vindicatory evidence. The English nation readily discerned that, behind the solemn and majestic form of justice, the shadow of the real prosecutor, the recreant husband, hovered; and that his pernicious influence prevented the full and equitable performance of the behests of truth and righteousness toward the accused. This conviction greatly injured the prince in the estimation of the people, and augmented that load of censure and execration under which he already so ignominiously labored.

Shortly after the termination of this "delicate investigation," as it was courteously termed, the prince consoled himself for his disappointed vengeance by taking a new mistress. The person in question was Lady Hertford. He made her acquaintance in consequence of wishing to gratify Mrs. Fitzherbert in obtaining a niece of the former lady, Miss Seymour, as a companion for her. During the progress of the negotiation the prince was charmed with the beauty, intelligence, and amiability of Lady Hertford, and fell desperately in love with her. At first his offers and his person were repelled. He then betook himself to his former ridiculous expedients to win female pity and sympathy, bled himself excessively, became in consequence very pale and interesting, and ended by adding the obdurate beauty to the already extensive and varied list of his female conquests.

The purpose of George III. to admit the Princess of Wales to a personal interview was postponed for a time by the interposition of her husband, who informed the king that he was not satisfied with the result of the late inquiry, but intended to refer the charges back again to the action of his legal advisers. But in March, 1807, the Grenville administration, who were hostile to the princess were compelled to resign, and a new ministry were appointed, the leading members of which were favorable to her. Among their number were Lord President Camden, Lord Chancellor Eldon, Lord Privy Seal Westmoreland, the Duke of Portland, Mr. Canning, and Viscount Castlereagh. These statesmen suggested to the monarch the propriety of doing tardy justice to the princess; and accordingly in the succeeding May she was invited to the queen's drawing-room. A large and brilliant company were present. During the course of the evening the prince and princess accidentally met in the centre of the apartment. The collision must have been most unwelcome to the former, but he was compelled to assume a degree of courtesy which was greatly foreign to his feelings. He bowed to the princess, stood face to face for a few moments, exchanged some words which the eager bystanders were unable to hear, and then passed on. His manner was cold, repulsive, and stately; hers, was a melancholy and feeble assumption of gaiety, which clearly indicated that her heart was heavily oppressed with anguish. They never met again during the course of their subsequent lives.

Another misfortune now overtook the princess. She was burdened with debts, and embarrassed for means. One of her chief defects was her total inability to financier, and an utter ignorance of the value of money. In 1809, she was compelled to apply to the ministers for relief, to liquidate debts which had accumulated to the sum of fifty thousand pounds. The Prince of Wales embraced the opportunity to effect a formal separation from his detested and injured wife. On this condition he agreed to pay her obligations, with the proviso that he should be released from all future pecuniary responsibility on her behalf; and an income of twenty-two thousand pounds per year was allowed her, to be disbursed under the control of a treasurer, who was to superintend her expenses. Such was the relation which was established between this unhappy and unenviable pair, when in 1810, the prince, in consequence of the king's temporary insanity, obtained a restricted regency. The princess continued to reside quietly at Kensington Palace; the prince at Carlton House. An intense feeling of hostility mutually embittered their lives. Meanwhile their daughter, the Princess Charlotte, increased in years and graces, and was hastening forward to the completion of that melancholy career which fate had allotted her. She was permitted occasionally to see her mother, but she continued to reside at Carlton House. She was a beautiful, graceful, and intelligent girl. She is described as having been large for her age, with a full bosom, ample and well-rounded shoulders, hands and arms of faultless symmetry, with a sweet and musical voice.* Her personal charms and accomplishments improved with the progress of time, until her marriage subsequently consummated her transient felicity.

At length in 1812 the insanity of George III. appearing to have become confirmed and hopeless, the restrictions which had been placed upon the Regency were removed, and the Prince of Wales virtually became the monarch of the British Empire. The brilliant talents of Mr. Percival then guided the destinies of the nation as prime minister; but the sudden blow of the assassin terminated his eminent career, and deprived the Prince Regent of the invaluable aid of his services. On the 11th of May, he was shot when passing through the lobby of the House of Commons, by an obscure person named Bellingham, who was doubtless insane. The prince, on being informed of this great calamity, sent a message to the house, condoling with them on the general loss, and proposing an annuity for the family of the

---

* See *Diary Illustrative of the Times of George IV., comprising the Secret History of the Court, &c. By Lady Charlotte Bury, Maid of Honor to Queen Caroline.* 4 vols. London, 1839. Vol. i., p. 65.

murdered statesman ; which was readily acceded to by the members. The Marquis of Wellesley was then commissioned by the prince to form a new ministry. Many difficulties obstructed the way. Lords Grey and Grenville were invited to share in the administration, and both refused, unless they obtained possession of the whole of the patronage of the government. This demand was regarded as exorbitant beyond sufferance, and the deliberations terminated on the 8th of June, 1812, by the appointment of the Earl of Liverpool as the First Lord of the Treasury. At the time of the accession of the prince to the unrestricted Regency, he was one of the most unpopular sovereigns who ever wielded the sceptre of England.

CHAPTER IV.

Unpleasant Position of the Princess Charlotte—Published Letter of the Princess of Wales—Flight of the Princess Charlotte from her Father's Residence—She is compelled to return—Rage of the Prince Regent at her Flight—Persecutions of her Mother—The Princess of Wales resolves to travel on the Continent—Marriage of the Princess Charlotte—Her Subsequent Death—General Grief of the Nation—Conduct of the Princess of Wales during her Travels—The Milan Commission—Resolution of the Princess to return to England—Her Second Trial for Adultery is resolved upon.

As the Princess Charlotte advanced in years, and comprehended more clearly the unfortunate relations which existed between her parents, she very naturally became the partisan of her mother. The Prince Regent was not slow to discover this unwelcome fact, and his treatment of his daughter became in consequence extremely tyrannical and harsh. He endeavored to restrict their intercourse still more than it had previously been; but the two ladies, though watched by the agents of their father, eluded their vigilance, and corresponded repeatedly and continually. But the epistolary labors of the Princess of Wales were not confined to her daughter. In 1813, she wrote a long and feeling letter to her husband in which she asserted her innocence of all guilt, condemned the restrictions which were placed upon her intercourse with her daughter, and demanded that an end should be put to the numerous and unjust persecutions which she was compelled to endure. The letter was returned unopened. It was again sent to the prince, and again returned with an intimation that the prince would enter into no correspondence with its author. Legal advice was taken and the letter was again despatched to the prince. An answer was returned by Lord Liverpool, to the effect that the prince had been informed of its contents but had no reply to make to it. The princess then published the letter in the Morning journals, and its appearance excited the wrath of the regent to an extent which almost overturned his reason. The nation eagerly perused this document, containing the story of the writer's wrongs; one voice of indignation against the prince resounded throughout the length and breadth of the land; and the strongest popular sympathy was excited in behalf of an innocent woman, who was persecuted and outraged by a notorious libertine, an unprincipled sensualist, a lavish and unscrupulous tyrant, for no fault whatever, except that her person and disposition did not please his fastidious and prurient taste.

The popular sympathy only impelled the prince to treat his discarded wife with more unjustifiable cruelty. When in 1815, the allied sovereigns of Europe, who had triumphantly placed their feet upon the neck of Napoleon, congregated in London, and when the absolute etiquette of courts demanded that all the royal visitors should pay their respects to the wife of the Regent, he prevented them, by the most peremptory requests, from giving the least indication that they were conscious of her existence. His antipathy even extended to interfering with her appearance in the theatres, and to prohibiting invitations to be sent to her to be present at the banquets given by the great corporations of the realm in the capital. Sometimes, however, in spite of all his efforts, the princess confronted her husband in public, and divided with him, to his infinite annoyance, the applauses of the multitude. Such triumphs very naturally afforded her exquisite pleasure; at other times, the indignities inflicted on her by her husband and his emissaries, drew tears from her eyes. On the other hand, the abuse with which the populace sometimes avenged her wrongs upon the Regent extorted curses from his lips; for as he once proceeded from Temple Bar to a public banquet in Guildhall, they rent the air with insulting cries of "Where's your wife?"—the most unwelcome and repugnant question which could possibly have been propounded to his Royal Highness under any circumstances, but especially on so public and notorious an occasion.

In July, 1814, the Princess Charlotte indicated the boldness of her spirit, and her preference for her mother, by an act of great resolution. She was informed that her father had determined to remove her from Carlton House to the remote and secluded residence of Cranbourne Lodge, in Windsor Forest. The purpose of the Prince Regent in so doing was to place her at a greater distance, and in more complete separation, from her mother. As soon as the princess was informed of this intention, she dressed herself, silently and quickly descended the stairs of the palace, and reached the pavement of Cockspur street. It was seven o'clock in the evening. She instantly summoned a coach, and drove unattended to the residence of her mother in Connaught Place. Having arrived there she found her mother absent at Blackheath. She dispatched a message thither to request her return; and her mother's legal advisers, Messrs. Brougham and Whitbread, were also sent for. After a short interval all these parties arrived at Connaught House, when the young princess explained to them the causes and the purpose of her flight. But Mr. Brougham was compelled to inform her that, by the laws of the realm, the King or Regent had absolute power to dispose of the persons of all the royal family while under age, and that it would be impossible for her to resist the authority of her father. This information greatly distressed the princess. Other eminent personages soon afterward arrived: the Archbishop of Canterbury, Lord Chancellor Eldon, the Duke of Sussex being among the number; and they all concurred in confirming the opinion of Mr. Brougham. At length, after a conference of some hours, the princess was prevailed upon, with great difficulty, to return to her father's residence, though she expressed her willingness so to do, amid a flood of tears. She was accompanied thither by the Duke of York and her governess; and she arrived between four and five o'clock in the morning.* The rage of the

---

* There was a Westminster election then in progress in consequence of Lord Cochrane's expulsion from Parliament, and it is said that on her complaining to Mr. Brougham that he too was deserting her in the hour of her need, and leaving her in her father's power when the people would have stood by her—he

Prince Regent, when informed of this defeated *escapade*, was boundless, and the princess was immediately removed to the hateful seclusion of Cranbourne Lodge. Previous to this incident, she had declined the matrimonial offers of the eldest son of the King of Holland. Her father was greatly in favor of the match; but the repugnance of the princess to it was insuperable. After her removal to Windsor Forest she persisted in this feeling with such invincible earnestness that the project was eventually abandoned. Said she : " I am resolved never to marry the Prince of Orange. If it shall be seen that such a match is announced, I wish this my declaration to be borne in mind, that it will be a marriage without my consent and against my will ; and I desire the Duke of Sussex and Mr. Brougham to take particular notice of this." The determination of the princess, which was in part ascribed by her father to the adverse influence of her mother, irritated his haughty and unprincipled spirit beyond measure.

The bitter persecutions which the Princess of Wales had endured, rendered her weary of the land in which she had experienced so many sorrows ; and she now adopted the resolution to spend some time in travel on the continent. Her best advisers warned her against this course. Mr. Brougham, foreseeing the fatal consequences of a foreign residence to such a woman placed in such peculiar circumstances, assured her that he would willingly answer by his head for her safety both of person and reputation if she remained in England ; but that, if she journeyed abroad, he

---

took her to the window, when the morning had just dawned, and, pointing to the Park and the spacious streets which extended before her, said that he had only to show her a few hours later, on the spot where she now stood, and all the people of that vast metropolis would be gathered together, with one common feeling in her behalf; but that the triumph of one hour would be dearly purchased by the pernicious consequences which must assuredly follow in the next, when the troops poured in and quelled all resistance to the clear and undoubted law of the land, with an immense effusion of blood ; nay, that through the rest of her life she never would escape the odium which, in this country, always attends those who, by breaking the law, occasion such calamities. This consideration, much more than any quailing of her dauntless spirit, or faltering of her filial affection, is believed to have weighed upon her mind, and induced her to return home. *Edinburg Review* for April, 1838, p. 220.

would not answer for either for an hour. But Caroline never listened to good counsel when she had once made up her mind, although all her wisest friends, excepting Mr. Canning, united in an opinion adverse to her own. Accordingly she addressed a letter to Lord Liverpool informing him of her purpose, and inquiring whether there would be any opposition on the part of the government to its realization. He replied by order of the Regent that there would be none whatever; and that amiable prince on the day of her subsequent embarkation honored the event by a toast at his table, which was unequivocally expressive of his gratification at her departure.* On the 9th of August, 1816, the princess went on board the *Jason* frigate, commanded by Captain King, accompanied by her suite. A vast multitude lined the beach, who extended to the unfortunate traveller a subdued but respectful farewell. Her first destination was Hamburg, thence she proceeded to her native Brunswick. She assumed the less imposing title of Countess of Cornwall, and passed some weeks in Switzerland in the society of the Ex-Empress, Maria Louisa. Thence she journeyed to Milan. It was at this city that a portion of her English suite, having become disgusted with the excessive freedom and improprieties of her behavior, deserted her; and here, in substituting others in their stead, she first made the acquaintance of Bartholomew Bergami, an impoverished Italian nobleman, with whom she was afterwards charged with having committed repeated and habitual adultery. And it must be admitted that, if merely indecorous and imprudent conduct can be regarded as a conclusive evidence of guilt in a woman, the princess furnished ample cause for conviction.

The wandering and uneasy princess visited all the principal cities of Italy. She purchased a villa on the flowery and umbrageous banks of the placid Lake of Como, which was built of red and white marble, with gilded apartments and ceilings painted by the skilful pencils of Italian artists. Here she spent some months in the enjoyment of luxurious ease, and perhaps finding

* "To the Princess of Wales, damnation; and may she never return to England." *Doran's Queens of England*, ii., p. 297.

in the society of her chamberlain, the handsome and amiable Bergami, that pleasure which she had hoped to find in the marriage relation, but to which she had ever been a stranger. Soon all her English attendants deserted her, and she substituted others in their stead who were natives of the land of her sojourn. After some months spent at Como, she continued her travels, visiting Sicily, Palestine, Tunis, Greece. and Turkey. From inspecting the antique wonders of the romantic and historic East she returned to Europe. Passing through Vienna she reached Carlsruhe. She was sojourning at Trieste, still enamored of the graceful Bergami, and devoted to his person, when, in January, 1820, the death of the aged monarch George III. elevated her to the rank of Queen Consort of the British realms.

During this unpropitious absence of the princess on the continent, several important incidents had occurred in which both herself and her husband were deeply interested. Their daughter, the Princess Charlotte, having absolutely refused to marry the Prince of Orange, had subsequently become the wife of Prince Leopold, of Saxe-Cobourg. This match was one of real affection, and the few months of married life which the princess enjoyed were by far the happiest period of her life. But this halcyon interval of love and bliss was destined to be of short duration. She expired in childbed, after having given birth to a still-born infant, on the 6th of November, 1817. The unexpected intelligence of her death was received by the nation with universal sorrow. Before the orders for mourning could be issued to the populace, every rank and grade had already and spontaneously anticipated them. All public places of amusement were voluntarily closed; the churches were hung with black; domestic entertainments and marriages were suspended; business was postponed; and the unparalleled spectacle was presented of a whole community being bowed to the earth by the crushing weight of a real, incalculable, universal sorrow. The pulpits resounded with funereal eulogies on the departed princess; and the occasion was rendered memorable, among other minor incidents, by the delivery of that matchless and magnificent discourse by Robert

Hall, which will remain to the end of time one of the great masterpieces of British eloquence and genius.

During the absence of the Princess of Wales on the continent, exaggerated reports of the indelicacy and even the guilt of her behavior had reached England; and the Prince Regent, eager to find causes of offense against his unhappy wife, had sent a commission to Milan, composed of men of respectability, whose duty it was to inquire into the conduct of the princess, to take evidence of her former and present behavior, and report the results of their researches. Caroline was not aware of the existence of these spies, or of the scrutiny and *surveillance* which they exercised over her daily life; and never did her habitual want of caution lead her to a greater degree of imprudence, and disregard of decorous appearances. The commissioners returned to England furnished with sufficient real and fabricated evidence to place the conduct and character of the nomade princess in no very favorable light. On the strength of their representations the prince would have taken the necessary steps to procure a divorce, had he not been assured by the friends and representatives of the princess, that she never intended to return to England. In 1819 some negotiations had taken place between the hostile pair, by which it was understood that, as long as the princess received her annuity of fifty thousand pounds, she cared not to assume the title of queen. But no sooner was George III. dead, and quietly inurned, than the princess announced her determination to return to England and demand the rank, appointments, and dignities of queen. When this purpose became known to the Prince Regent, who had become, by the death of his father, King *de jure*, though for some years he had already been King *de facto*, he expressed his determination to bring the princess to trial for high crimes and misdemeanors. She met Mr. Brougham and Lord Hutchinson at St. Omer, on her rapid journey to England, and there again rejected an offer from her husband not to enter his dominions on condition of receiving fifty thousand pounds during the remainder of her life. She hastened on to Calais, and embarked at that port for Dover. During her progress from Dover to London, the populace poured forth by myriads to welcome a woman whose persecutions they believed to be unparalleled. She took up her residence in London, in the house of Alderman Wood. Immediately after her arrival a message was delivered from the King to both Houses of Parliament to the effect that some information would be laid before them containing facts of great importance to the future welfare of the country, on which a Bill of Pains and Penalties against the queen would be based. This message was accompanied by documents which set forth the results of the labors of the Milan Commission, which had been composed of three persons; a chancery lawyer, who had never examined a witness in his life; a colonel in the army, who knew no more of evidence than a lunatic; and a shrewd attorney, who, though sharp and sagacious, was totally devoid of integrity.

The advisers of the king in these proceedings were Lord Liverpool, a cautious, unpretending and prudent official hack; Lord Castlereagh, a cunning, cold, and circumspect courtier; Lord Eldon, a far-sighted, learned, and profound jurist, and the Duke of Wellington, a firm, bold, and resolute soldier. The defenders of the queen were Henry Brougham, one of the most eloquent and powerful advocates of his time; and Mr. Denman, a lawyer of eminence, who united greater learning and legal acquirements to less oratorical ability, than his associate.* An effort was made in Parliament by Mr. Wilberforce, to compromise the chronic difficulties between the parties; but with no avail. Caroline boldly demanded that she should receive the appointments and prerogatives of Queen of England; that her name should be inserted in the liturgy and read in the churches; and that, in all respects, the usual formalities should be observed toward her, and in the maintenance of her court, which appertained of right to the Queen Consort. All these demands were abhor-

* The other counsel of the queen who played a less distinguished part were Dr. Lushington, Mr. Justice Williams, and Mr. Sergeant Wilde. See *The Trial at Large of Her Majesty Caroline Amelia Elizabeth, Queen of Great Britain, in the House of Lords, &c.* 2 vols. Manchester: J. Gleave, 1821.

rent to the mind of the indignant and hostile king. It became perfectly evident that the day of conciliation had forever passed by; and that this domestic feud, of such long standing, of such intense bitterness, and of such universal notoriety, could only be terminated by the vexatious vicissitudes and revolting details of a public and protracted prosecution. Mr. Brougham, on the part of the queen, requested a postponement of two months from the House of Lords, in order that the accused might have time to prepare her defense. The request was granted. The interest which the nation felt in the approaching scrutiny was intense and universal; yet all their sympathies were in behalf of the defendant. After the designated interval had elapsed the hostile parties —the most illustrious personages in rank in the realm—prepared to confront each other; and then ensued one of those great historical " trials of princes " which have marked important epochs in human history, which have elicited the noblest displays of human genius, and which have proved to the satisfaction of the common herd of mankind, that the greatest are often the meanest and most miserable of their race.

CHAPTER V.

Commencement of the Scrutiny—The Famous Bill of Pains and Penalties—The Queen's Accusers and Defenders—Imposing Scene in the House of Lords—Distinguished Rank of the Judges, Accuser, Defendant, and Counsel—Examination of the Witnesses—Learning and Acuteness of Messrs. Denman and Brougham—Overwhelming Power of their Eloquence—The Virtual Triumph of the Queen—The Withdrawal of the Bill—Exultation of her Friends—Popular Rejoicings and Processions—Mortification and Malignity of the King.

THE peers determined to commence the proceedings in this memorable cause by appointing a secret committee to examine the report of the Milan Commission, in order that they might be guided thereby in the adoption of their subsequent course. The queen by her counsel protested against any *secret* proceedings in the case whatever; and demanded that she should be represented by her legal advisers before any inquisition which should appertain to the trial. The peers refused to acquiesce in this demand, and the secret committee proceeded to the performance of their duty. They made their report to the House on the first day of July, 1820; and they therein set forth that the documents denominated the Milan papers contained charges affecting the honor and tarnishing the character of the queen, which amounted in substance to the allegation of adultery; and that these charges were accompanied by concurrent and corroborative testimony. After this report had been officially made, Lord Liverpool, on the part of the king, introduced his famous Bill of Pains and Penalties against the queen, involving the punishment of degradation and divorce. This event occurred in the British House of Peers, on the 5th of July, 1820.

The first step of the defendant was to demand that she should be furnished with a statement of the specific charges made against her, together with the names of the intended witnesses, and the dates and places of the alleged offences. To this reasonable request the lords refused to accede. The utmost minuteness of detail which was allowed the accused was a declaration that she was charged with scandalous and vicious conduct with one Bartholomew Bergami. A copy of the bill was served upon her by Sir Thomas Tyrwhitt. She received it with a degree of emotion which she was unable to conceal; and remarked that, had the prosecution been commenced a quarter of a century earlier, it had served the purpose of her royal husband better. She added that the injustice of the course adopted by the ministers was apparent, because they first condemned her by this bill without proof, and then proceeded to inquire what evidence might be obtained to justify the condemnation.

The trial began in the House of Lords on the 17th of August. The queen had expressed her determination to be present during its progress; and to aid in the fulfilment of this purpose she obtained permission from the widow of Sir Philip Francis to occupy her residence in St. James's Square during the continuance of the proceedings. She therefore left Brandenburgh House, which was her stated residence, and removed temporarily to the quarters offered her. Her next door neighbor was her most zealous adversary, Lord Castlereagh. In her passage to and from the House of Lords she passed by Carlton House, the residence of her husband; and she enjoyed the gratification of presenting to his detesting eyes each day the spectacle of the vast multitudes of the populace who escorted her carriage, and of saluting his ears with the unequivocal plaudits with which they greeted her. She was attended on these occasions by Lady Hamilton, by Alderman Wood, and by her chamberlains Sir William Gell and Mr. Keppel Craven. On her arrival at the House she was received by Mr. Brougham and Sir Thomas Tyrwhitt, and conducted by them to the apartment assigned to her use, or to her seat in the House, each holding her by the hand.

The scene presented on this memorable occasion was not devoid of that imposing splendor and magnificence which usually attend the great state trials which have occurred in the history of Britain. There were not indeed the same vast assemblage, the same collection of all that was noble, beautiful, and distinguished in the realm, the same impressive ceremony and stately pageantry which attended the trial of Warren Hastings; nor the same universal deluge of popular execration and fury which marked the hour when Charles I. and Lord Strafford defended their honor and their lives against the most malignant and unrelenting of persecutors: nor were the interests at stake of such extensive moment and such vital importance to a great community, involving the destinies of millions in the issue, as when that unhappy monarch vainly sought to stem the tide of death which was surging resistlessly around him, and eventually submerged him beneath its billows. But there were other interests involved in this case which called forth intenser sympathy from every dispassionate heart in the empire. There was a woman, well advanced in years, a discarded wife and bereaved mother, who, after many years of sorrow and persecution from her husband, was compelled at last to confront the worst and most degrading calamity which his malignity could inflict. In one respect she was a stranger in a strange land. The monarch himself was her bitterest foe, and an obsequious nobility cringed at his feet ready to do his bidding against her. But she remained undaunted; and declared that she felt secure in the consciousness of her innocence, and under the broad protection of a higher power than that of her husband—the protection of the British Constitution—yet in her case, even that Constitution was about to be violated, as it had never before been violated. She was to be tried for high crimes and misdemeanors, and was, when defending herself against a charge of adultery, to be deprived of the immemorial privilege, so ancient indeed that the memory of man ran not to the contrary, of being permitted to recriminate, and to hurl back upon the guilty head of the man who falsely accused her, and strove to drag her down to ruin, the same charge which he himself preferred against her; and prove to the world that, while she was innocent, he was one of the most licentious and libertine of men. Though thus shorn of the rights which the humblest subject possessed—though her accuser was the highest in the realm, she boldly came forward to the scrutiny, and defied the combined power of her enemies.* Her character thus assumed an heroic attitude, and challenged not only sympathy but admiration. Other elements of greatness marked the scene. The tribunal before which this dauntless woman thus appeared, comprised the most ancient, opulent, and illustrious nobility in the world. Among them were the descendants of men who had assisted at the laying of the foundation of the British Constitution, and of some who had extorted from the brutal but overborne King John the Magna Charta. There were others present whose ancestors had taken a part in the most brilliant and the most tragical events which had characterized English history during the long lapse of a thousand years; and there were some who had themselves played a distinguished part in those great events which, during the opening years of the nineteenth century, had convulsed Europe, and had shattered all the thrones, dominions, and empires in the civilized world.

The accused in this grand inquest was not unworthy of such judges. She was the descendant of an ancient line of princes, who, though not kings in rank, had been in some instances more illustrious for their genius and achievements than any contemporary king. She represented in her own person a portion of the highest dignity, in perhaps the greatest empire then existing. She belonged to that illustrious line of personages which included the stately Elizabeth, and the beautiful and fascinating Mary Queen of Scotts; and she exhibited a dauntless spirit which would have ennobled either of them. If men possessing the matchless power of Fox, Sheridan, and Burke no longer figured on the scene, and threw over it the splendid and gorgeous halo of their genius, there were other actors there, who were worthy

* *Letter of Queen Caroline to the King on the subject of the Proceedings against her, with a Letter from Sir G. Noel.* Edinburg, 1820.

to occupy their places, and inherit no inconsiderable portion of their fame. The injured queen was to be defended by the fervid and declamatory eloquence, the keen and penetrating logic, the bold and scathing sarcasm of Brougham, her attorney, and by the accurate learning, the professional skill, and the clear, conclusive reasoning of Mr. Denman, her solicitor. And that stately hall which had in former generations so often resounded with the overwhelming bursts of a Chatham, a Mansfield, and a Somers, was now destined to witness, for the last time, at least in that generation, a display of forensic genius which would compare favorably with the most renowned exhibitions of a similar description in preceding times.

On the morning on which the trial commenced, the queen proceeded in state to the House, and entered while the roll of the peers was being called. She was plainly but elegantly attired in a black satin dress, with a white veil thrown over a plain laced hat. As she entered, all the peers rose to receive her, and she acknowledged the courtesy with that graceful dignity, in which she excelled all women when she chose to assume it. She was conducted to the handsome throne-like chair and cushion provided for her, near her counsel, but within the bar. Several days were occupied in preliminary proceedings. On the 19th the attorney for the crown opened his case, setting forth the charges preferred against the accused. At the conclusion of his speech the examination of witnesses commenced. The first of these was the most important of all. He was Theodore Majocci, an Italian, who had been employed in the service of the queen during her continental tour. As soon as his ominous name was called, the queen exclaimed, "Oh! the traitor!" and withdrew instantly to her apartment adjacent to the hall. Majocci swore in substance that on the deck of the vessel in which the queen sailed a tent had been erected; that the queen slept within that tent; that Bergami her chamberlain also reposed there; and that he frequently attended her when in the bath. The remainder of his evidence amounted to but little; yet the impression produced by his testimony was at first deep and powerful. The adversaries of the queen began to exult, and her friends to be less confident. The populace, who believed Majoccito have been bribed and therefore unworthy of credence, became intensely irritated, which feeling extended even to the troops who formed the garrison; and it has been asserted by authorities worthy of belief that, had the Duke of Kent, the most popular and most resolute prince of the royal family, been then alive, a revolution in his favor would have broken forth which would have shaken if it did not overturn the throne of George IV. But the next day the tide of victory turned. Majocci was subjected by Mr. Brougham to one of the most thorough and searching cross-examinations recorded in judicial annals. He tore his evidence to pieces with the power and facility of a giant. He overwhelmed the witness with confusion, and even with terror. He dragged from him one contradiction after another, so that one portion of his testimony, completely rebutted the other. He proved by the witness himself that, though Bergami slept under the same tent with the queen, the tent itself was constantly open on all sides; that the intense heat of the climate rendered such a usage necessary, as well as universally customary; and that the prevalent light of an Italian sky made it easy for any intruder at any hour to see all that transpired beneath the loose folds of the tent. He proved that, though Bergami had attended the queen in the bath, she uniformly on such occasions wore a bathing dress which prevented the least indecorous exposure of the person. Every other point of this witness's testimony was rebutted and invalidated in the same effective manner.*

The examination of other witnesses followed, all of whose testimony only proved that, encouraged by the greater licence of continental manners, the queen had been guilty of what, according to English views of decorum, would be stigmatized as gross impropriety and very great imprudence, both in language and in conduct. But of satisfactory and competent evidence of

* See *the Trial at Large of Her Majesty Caroline Amelia Elizabeth, Queen of Great Britain, in the House of Lords, &c.* 2 vols. Manchester: Gleave, 1821. Vol. ii., p. 210, *et seq.*

actual guilt, or of evidence which, by a fair and reasonable inference, would conclusively prove to an impartial mind that positive guilt had been in any case incurred, there was absolutely none. The testimony was all concluded by the 7th of September. The house adjourned till the 3d of October. Mr. Brougham then entered on the defense of his client in a speech of extraordinary power, which in turn exhibited magnificent displays of oratorical ability, of resistless logic, of bold and scathing sarcasm, of tender and affecting pathos. That speech is immortal in English history. He was followed by his associate, in an oration which, if not quite equal to that of Mr. Brougham, was still worthy of the occasion. During its delivery he gave utterance to one burst which for impressiveness and effect reminded the hearer of some of the best passages of the great masters of English rhetoric and forensic genius. Turning his eagle eye toward the Duke of Clarence, who had once been the ardent friend of the queen, but had become her bitterest enemy, he raised his sonorous voice and exclaimed in a tone of thunder : *" Come forth, thou slanderer !"* in allusion to the earnest activity exhibited by the Duke in the prosecution of the accused. The orator's power was evinced by the terror which racked the spirit of the princely personage, who was thus made the deserving victim of his overwhelming bolt.*

The testimony which was produced in behalf of the queen proved, that some of her English attendants who had deserted her when abroad, had not discovered any improprieties in her conduct, and had left her only on account of ill-health. Others declared that all the acts of impropriety charged and proved in her conduct in Italy, were permitted by the universally prevalent customs of that country, and in themselves involved no guilt, nor even any impropriety. Mr. Craven proved that he himself had selected Bergami as the chamberlain of the queen, and that he brought most excellent testimonials of character with him. After the evidence for the defense closed, the deliberations of the peers commenced. Contrary to their usual custom their debates were stormy. When at last the vote was taken on one clause of the

* See *Richard Rush's Residence at the Court of St. James.*

Bill, the majority against the queen was twenty-eight. When the clause touching the divorce was voted upon, their majority was only nine against the defendant. As this was the precise number of peers who composed the cabinet, this ballot instead of being a victory was in reality a defeat. In this emergency the ministers resolved to make a virtue of necessity, and abandon the prosecution, while they seemed to have the *eclat* of at least a nominal triumph. But that triumph was only nominal. In the opinion of the nation, the accused had at last conquered the most formidable combination which was ever arrayed against a British queen; and she was yet, in spite of the utmost exertions of the haughty monarch of the British empire, his lawful wife, and the partner of his power. The exultation of the populace at this result was intense beyond all parallel; and their joy was exhibited in a variety of ways which must have been as annoying to the king, as they were grateful to his discarded wife.

Immediately after the withdrawal of the Bill the queen applied to Lord Liverpool to be furnished with a suitable residence and provision as Queen Consort. He replied that, though the king would not permit her to reside in any of the royal palaces, she should regularly receive the fifty thousand pounds per year which was her present allowance. About the same period she received the communion in the parish church at Hammersmith; and on the 29th of November she proceeded in as much state as she could muster to the cathedral of St. Paul, to return thanks to God for her escape from the assaults of her enemies. The indignant king did his utmost to render this event insignificant and abortive. To some extent he succeeded. No change took place in the appointed service of the day; her whole court consisted of her vice-chancellor Mr. Craven; but her attendance comprised a vast multitude of the populace of London, some on foot, on horseback, and in vehicles. Conspicuous in the procession were the various trades; among whom the braziers distinguished themselves by perpetrating a significant pun. On their banner were inscribed the words: "The Queen's Guards are Men of Metal." The day passed by without tumult or accident; and the queen returned to Brandenburgh House to the enjoyment of that seclusion and quiet which she imperatively needed.*

* It was a significant circumstance, which exhibited the intensity with which George IV. hated his unhappy spouse, and which at the same time displayed the despicable subserviency of some of the clergy of the Establishment to the behests of those in high places, even though they were the most infamous of men, that the parenthetical clause in the prayer of general thanksgiving, which is intended for any individual who desires to offer thanks and gratitude to God, and which was very appropriate to the purpose of the queen on this occasion, and was intended to be used by her, was *omitted*, contrary to the established custom and obligation, by the officiating priest, while the queen was upon her knees on the floor of the cathedral! It would be difficult to discover a more disgraceful instance of the want of Christian feeling, even in the annals of ecclesiastical bigotry and perfidy.

CHAPTER VI.

Preparations for the Coronation of George IV.—Intense interest felt by him in the Ceremony—Determination of Queen Caroline to be present—Efforts made to dissuade her from so doing—Her Unconquerable Obstinacy—Splendor and Magnificence of the Ceremony—Effort of the Queen to gain admission to the Abbey—Her Ignominious Failure—Her Dreadful Mortification—The effect produced by it upon her Health—Her immediate and rapid Decline—Her Death—Her Character—Malignant Hatred of her Husband—His Joy at her Death—Removal of her Remains to Brunswick—Her Burial.

A DISTINGUISHED event in the life of so commonplace a personage as George IV., was the ceremony of his coronation, which took place on the 19th of July, 1821. He had set his heart upon rendering this celebration of the most ancient of the stately pomps and pageantries of England, unequalled for its imposing magnificence. The necessary preparations had been in progress during many months. All the resources of mechanical art, of antiquarian learning, and of heraldic skill in the realm, were called into requisition and tasked to the utmost. A million pounds were expended by an unwilling people, whose national debt already exceeded the debts of all other nations on the globe, in order to increase the eclat and the splendors of one of the most undeserving of mankind. George IV. employed the labor of entire days in rehearsing his part; and he displayed the childish ardor of an overgrown boy, in enacting that portion of the gorgeous mummeries which would fall to his share. The costume which he was destined to wear on the occasion, became a matter of insatiable and absorbing interest to his mind; he entered into long discussions with his friends in reference to the most puerile questions of colors, fashions, contrasts, and effects; and when at last the jewelled robes which were to deck his stately person were completed, he had no rest until one of his servants was arrayed in their ample and glittering folds, and paraded up and down before him with an assumed and fictitious air of kingly dignity, such as he himself exhibited on all public occasions.

The unhappy and injured wife of the man who was to be the chief figure in these expensive but transient grandeurs, was not invited to take the least share in them. In May, preceding the event, she addressed a letter to Lord Liverpool, setting forth that, as Queen Consort, it was her right and intention to partici pate with her husband in the ceremonial. The prime minister replied that his majesty had determined, for various conclusive reasons, that she should not be recognized in any way in the proceedings, and that consequently she could not even be permitted to be present. Her legal advisers, Messrs. Brougham and Denman, then demanded a hearing in her behalf, before the Privy Council. Their request was complied with, as a matter of form; but after an elaborate argument had been made on both sides, that tribunal decided that the Queen Consort of England was not entitled of right to be crowned at any time; much less could she claim to be crowned at any particular period which she might designate; and that the presence of the queen on the approaching occasion, as it must be irregular and unauthorized, and as it might lead to serious difficulties, must be absolutely forbidden and prevented.

But the resolute Caroline was not to be thus satisfied and quieted. She determined with her usual imprudence and obstinacy to disturb and tarnish the splendor of a pageant in which she could have no honorable share; and thus to mortify the man whom of all others she most intensely and most reasonably hated. She formally notified the Duke of Norfolk, the Earl Marshal of the realm, of her intention to be present; and requested that his grace would make proper preparations to receive her. This demand the earl civilly evaded, and declared that it was impossible for him to obey her command. She then addressed a letter to the Archbishop of Canterbury, setting forth her desire to be crowned either on the same day and in the same ceremony with her husband, or very soon afterward. But the crafty churchman answered that he was ready at any moment to obey any commands which he might receive from his majesty. The queen terminated these futile and vexatious preliminaries by sending the king a sarcastic protest, declaring his proposed coronation informal, unjust and invalid. Thus far indeed the conduct of the unfortunate princess was consistent, defiant, and not undignified; and had she stopped at this point, it had been well for her future happiness and reputation. But such a degree of prudence and moderation was not to be found among the characteristics of Caroline of Brunswick. She resolved to go much further, and was eventually guilty of extremes of impropriety and violence, which deprived her of the sympathy of the nation, and rendered her conduct and character repulsive and ridiculous in the highest degree.

At length the memorable coronation day of George IV. dawned upon the world in serene brightness and splendor. Five hundred thousand people crowded the streets of the metropolis, to become witnesses of different portions of the proceedings. Westminster Abbey, the most venerable and imposing edifice in the kingdom, was fitted up with gorgeous hangings and glittering canopies, to add impressive effect to the ceremonies. The far-extending galleries which occupy a portion of the stately pile, were crowded, at an early hour, with all that was most noble, beautiful, and distinguished in the realm. The central space in front of the chief altar was graced by a platform, supporting a throne of imposing splendor, which was surrounded by a host of illustrious personages who were to enact a part on the memorable occasion. The body of the building, and the capacious aisles were appropriated to a miscellaneous and martial host, whose waving plumes, military costumes, and polished arms added to the grandeur and majesty of the scene. The king proceeded in great state from Carlton House to the Abbey; and there, after being robed, he took his seat on the throne, and the ceremonies began. So far as outward appearance was concerned, he looked indeed like a monarch. The proceedings were long, and the ceremonial tedious. Many distinguished noblemen figured in the pageant. Lord Londonderry, who was arrayed in the magnificent robes of the Garter, was a splendid representation of the Order established by Edward III., among whose members so many illustrious persons had been enrolled. The Marquis of Anglesea, though he had left a severed leg to moulder on the blood-stained plain of Waterloo, still exhibited unrivalled skill in the management of his horse, and was especially admired; and in this respect the animal divided equally with his courtly rider the enthusiastic praise of the brilliant assemblage, by retiring backward from the hall, easily, decorously, and without any accident. The Champion of England was represented by the youthful Dymoke; who threw down his gauntlet with a very imposing air of defiance to all the world. But the most interesting personage who appeared on the occasion, and to whom all eyes were directed with intense curiosity, because he was a real, and not merely a scenic hero, was the Duke of Wellington. He took a prominent part in the ceremonies; and no one could look upon his rigid features, battered by the storms of a hundred conflicts, without reflecting how, in the stern presence of the great master spirits of the world, those whom birth and accident have pushed forward and upward into prominence, dwindle into their native and genuine insignificance. The evidence of this fact was specially seen in the box which was assigned to the foreign ambassadors; which itself contained many personages who had played a distinguished part in the events of their time. That box glittered as if in a blaze of light, in consequence of the profusion of jewels which were worn by its occupants. Prince Esterhazy, the Austrian ambassador, was arrayed in a dress, the value of which was a hundred thousand pounds. Other representatives of foreign potentates almost equalled the magnificence which he displayed. Yet the interest of all these high and great personages was constantly centred on the person and the proceedings of the conqueror of the Corsican. He bore himself proudly throughout the imposing mummery; and even the king, who enjoyed such stately scenes with exquisits relish, expressed his unqualified admiration of the immortal Duke. The declining sun cast his mellowed rays through the stained windows of the vast Gothic edifice, throwing a golden radiance over the whole majestic scene, before the lengthy ceremonies were terminated. During one day at least, George IV. was satiated with glory—with that species of grandeur of which alone he was capable. At length all was over; the crowned king and his crowd of nobles returned in state to the royal palace; the vast assemblage retired from the abbey; and the inhabitants of the capital celebrated the occasion in their myriad homes, during the ensuing night, by festivals, bonfires, and every species of popular exultation.

But a single incident occurred on this day which threatened to mar its pomp and splendor. At six o'clock in the morning, Queen Caroline, burning with indignation and eager in her obstinacy, proceeded from her residence in a carriage drawn by six horses to Westminster Abbey. She was accompanied by Lord and Lady Hood, and Lady Anne Hamilton, her most intimate friends, who in fact then constituted her whole suit. She took this desperate step in defiance of the earnest solicitations of Mr. Brougham, her chief legal adviser, who readily perceived the unfortunate results which would inevitably ensue from it. But no power on earth could change her purpose; and she hastened to execute it. As she passed along the streets, she was greeted by the noisy acclamations of the multitude. Having arrived at the Abbey, she descended from her carriage amid long and deafening shouts. She advanced between the lines of soldiery to the chief door, followed by her three friends. Her manner was stately, self-possessed, and resolute. Having reached the door, she approached the officer on guard, stated that she was the queen, and demanded admission to the interior. The officer declined to let her pass, on the ground that his orders were to admit no one who was not provided with a ticket. Lord Hood then spoke, and claimed exemption for her in consequence of her rank. The officer nevertheless refused to admit her, even though she were, as she said, the Queen of England. During the progress of this parley, the multitude which surrounded the edifice maintained unbroken silence, anxious to see what would be the issue of the strange and doubtful crisis. Caroline then addressed the officer sternly, and exclaimed : " I am your queen ; permit me to enter ; it is my right." In vain she repeated the demand ; the obstinate official refused to comply ; and the company of soldiers who stood at his back were ready to enforce obedience to his orders. Perceiving at length that it would be impossible to succeed at the chief entrance, the discomfited queen hurried along the platform from one side door to another, repeating at each of them her demand for admittance, and receiving at each a positive, and even an insulting denial. At last, having exhausted every means of solicitation and intimidation in vain, she was rudely turned off the platform by several of the attendant soldiery. Here her resolute heart failed her, as well it might; for she now stood in the curious and derisive gaze of the multitude, attempting to laugh, while in reality the tears of mortification and rage were forcing their way to her eyes, and rolling down her cheeks. She looked around her, as she moved irresolutely, sometimes appealing by her troubled glances to the people who had so shortly before applauded her, but who now remained dumb and indifferent in the moment of her greatest necessity ; and sometimes looking at the edifice which she had so unwisely endeavored to enter, but from which she had been so ignominiously excluded. As she stood in this painful reverie, the distant sounds of the approach of her huband's gorgeous *cortège* reached her ears. In a few moments he would pass along that same platform arrayed in the extreme of human pomp. Even the determined and inflexible spirit of Caroline quailed at suffering *such* an encounter as that would have been ; and she had but time to hasten to her carriage, followed by her three friends, and drive rapidly away, before the head of the procession which escorted the exultant king appeared in sight. The unfortunate queen retired to her residence, but she carried back with her a poisoned barb which was destined to rankle and fester in her heart, until the agony of life became unendurable. She was conscious that she had lost the applause of the populace; that she had incurred the derision of the nation; and that her hostile and malignant husband had at last, in consequence of her own imprudence, gained a decisive victory over her, in which he would rejoice, and over which she would mourn, as long as the bitter drama of her existence continued.

A few days after the coronation, the king celebrated the event by giving a sumptuous banquet at Carlton House. The royal family were all in attendance, except the queen, and the Duke of Sussex, who entertained friendly sentiments toward her. The chief nobility of the realm, the foreign ambassadors, and many eminent statesmen were also present. The company arrived at seven in the evening, and remained till two o'clock the next morning. The entire dinner service was of gold; and its magnificence was unsurpassed by any previous display of royal or imperial opulence in Europe. In a festive scene, George IV. was in his element, as much as on any occasion of pompous parade; and he presided at this dinner with more than his usual dignity and grace. Here also the Duke of Wellington was in reality the chief personage present, and was the object of general attention to the most brilliant assemblage in the world.

While these joyful scenes were progressing at the Carlton Palace, the heart of Queen Caroline was breaking in the seclusion of her own home at Brandenburg House. The agitation and excitement to which she had been subject for many months, together with the deep chagrin and mortification with which she had been afflicted on the coronation day, produced a diseased state of her system which proved to be beyond the reach of human remedy. Her physicians were Doctors Maten, Warren, and Holland. From the beginning the royal patient seemed to be conscious that her case was hopeless, and that her malady was incurable. Her mind was diseased. A deadly canker gnawed at her very heart. She felt that she had not established the entire innocence of her conduct in the estimation of the nation; that the abandonment of the Bill of Pains and Penalties by her enemies had not rescued her character from moral degradation; and that her unfortunate attempt to participate in the ceremonies of the coronation, and her baffled efforts to disturb and defeat them, both by her own conduct, and by the anticipated co-operation and violence of her friends, had deprived her of the popular sympathy, and overwhelmed her with universal ridicule. She henceforth furnished one of the most memorable examples on record, of the truth of those oracular words uttered by the great bard of Avon in reference to another queen, more gifted, more guilty, but not more miserable than she:

> "Thou canst not minister to a mind diseased;
> Pluck from the memory a rooted sorrow;
> Raze out the written troubles of the brain;
> And with some sweet oblivious antidote,
> Cleanse the stuffed bosom of that perilous stuff
> Which weighs upon the heart."

The queen's illness assumed a serious aspect on the second of August. A bulletin was issued on that day, which announced that she was suffering severely from internal inflammation and obstruction. Having from the first attack anticipated a fatal issue, she declared herself willing and ready to terminate an existence which to her had long been one of unmingled sorrow and misery. She calmly executed her will; gave many directions to her attendants in reference to her personal affairs; ordered the private diary which she had kept for many years to be destroyed; spoke charitably of all her enemies; gave express directions that her body should be transported after her death to her native Brunswick; and that upon her tomb should be inscribed the following words: "Here lies Caroline of Brunswick, the injured Queen of England." Having given these last commands she rapidly grew worse. During five days her sufferings were intense. At length, on the morning of the 7th of August, 1821, this unfortunate woman, whose life had been one of singular vicissitude, and of wonderful extremes, sank into the arms of death, without a struggle. In her last moments she was surrounded by Lord and Lady Hood, and by Lady Hamilton. Alderman Wood, one of her best friends, and all her legal advisers and physicians, were also in attendance in an adjoining apartment. The queen expired in her fifty-fourth year. She had spent eighteen years in England, in a state of hostility against her husband; and some additional years she had passed in travelling over the continent, mingling in scenes which, if not guilty and culpable, were at least indecorous, imprudent, and suspicious in the highest degree.* Yet many excuses may be urged in her behalf. She had been reared without any particular moral instruction; and her parents had never permitted her to unite with any church, in order that she might be the more free to accept any desirable match which would in subsequent life be offered; and that she might more easily espouse the religion of her husband, whether it were Roman Catholic, Greek, or Protestant. Her mother had been a vain, frivolous, and unprincipled woman; her father, a vicious, reckless, and daring adventurer. She passed from the moral influence and example of such questionable persons, to the society of the most licentious and debauched prince of his age; a man who entertained no respect for women; who was governed by no moral principles whatever; whose passions were fierce and uncontrollable; whose pride and arrogance were unbounded; and who was totally unfit in every respect to render her happy, virtuous, or useful. And after their mutual hostilities began, the indignities which her husband heaped upon her, and the innumerable provocations with which he irritated her, necessarily provoked her to acts of imprudence and violence from which, under other circumstances, she might have recoiled. And even in the worst view which can be taken of her conduct, she must ever appear as an angel of light when compared with the individual who traduced, and attempted to ruin her. Had she been even a Messalina, her husband would have had no right to have condemned her; for he consigned her directly to the society

---

* See *Gynecocracy; with an Essay on Fornication, Adultery, and Incest.* By the Author of "*Rumors of Treason*" (*Richard Carlyle*). London: Stockdale, 1821. 8vo. This work, which is rarely accessible, was written by a violent partisan; but while some of its statements may seem to be of doubtful veracity, its contents are in general interesting and valuable.

of his own paramours and prostitutes; and these rivals gratified their jealousy by rendering her hateful and repulsive to her husband, and by finally driving her, through their spiteful persecutions, to leave his residence. All these indignities were palliations of her faults, and should diminish the censure which the severest critic of human conduct and character could inflict upon her memory.

The vengeance and malignity of George IV. pursued even the lifeless corpse of his unfortunate queen. She had expressed the desire that not till after a delay of three days should her remains be carried to Brunswick for interment. The king ordered that they should be immediately conveyed to Harwich for embarkation. Lady Hood was justly shocked, as were indeed all the friends of the deceased princess, at this disgraceful haste; and she addressed a letter to Lord Liverpool, declaring that it would be impossible for the ladies of the queen to make the necessary preparations for travelling in so short a time. The reply stated that no alteration could be made in the arrangements which had been designated; and that if the queen's ladies were not furnished in time with the appropriate mourning apparel, they might remain behind. The most direct route to Harwich passed through the city of London; but as the metropolitan populace might make some demonstration favorable to the deceased, the king ordered that the *cortège* should proceed by a circuitous route to Romford, and thence to Harwich. The preparations which were made for the funeral were mean and contemptible in the extreme. Never before had any Queen of England been buried with such a beggarly display. The rain fell in torrents and added to the dismal aspect of the scene. When the government officials entered the room where the body lay, in order to remove it, Dr. Lushington and Mr. Wilde, the executors of the queen, protested formally against the indecent haste and insufficient preparations which characterized the whole proceedings. They protested in vain; and the unconscious and dishonored corpse commenced its last mournful journey. It was attended by a meagre array of cavalry; and its progress was marked by no incident of importance till it reached Kensington Church. Here the direct route through the capital was deserted, and the line of march was taken through Church street into Baywater Road; but a wild burst of indignation from the immense crowd assailed the *cortége;* and as soon as it was perceived that this protest produced no effect, the highway was dug up, barricades were erected, and further progress in that direction was rendered impossible. The guards and the police at first indicated a disposition to force their passage; but the determined manner of the populace soon convinced them of the impossibility of accomplishing their purpose. The order was then given to proceed directly through London; and then a yell of triumph arose from myriads of throats, which might almost have waked the departed queen from the icy slumber of death. When the procession arrived at Park Lane, another conflict ensued between the populace and the military, which ended more seriously. The latter were assailed with missiles, and many of them were seriously wounded. They fired a volley in return into the serried mass, and two persons were killed, and several others were dangerously injured. This decisive conduct on the part of the troops diminished the ardor of the people only for a time; for when the corpse arrived at Tottenham Court Road, an impenetrable multitude compelled its bearers to turn again southward toward the city, and to pass through Drury Lane into the Strand. The friends of the unfortunate woman thus triumphed at last, after a conflict of seven hours; during which the unhonored remains of a British queen had been dragged sometimes slowly, sometimes at an indecent pace, through the rain and mud, toward their distant destination. During the intervening night, the corpse was placed in St. Peter's Church in Colchester; and while the silent hours were wearing away, a silver plate, bearing upon its front the chosen words of the dying Caroline—"The injured Queen of England"—was mysteriously affixed to the lid of the coffin. But this plate was removed as soon as the morning light revealed its unwelcome presence to the agents and servants of the king. When the corpse reached the port of Harwich, it was transferred on board the frigate Glasgow, which was accompanied by several other vessels. A small group of silent mourners attended the remains as they were thus dispatched to their last resting place. The faithful friends who had adhered to the varying fortunes of the queen during life and in death, did not desert her clay tenement in that hour of sad and melancholy loneliness. These were Lord and Lady Hood, Lady Hamilton, Mr. Austin, Dr. Lushington and his wife, and Count Vasali. Having safely crossed the channel, the squadron sailed up the Elbe, and landed its burden at Stade. Thence it was conveyed by land to Brunswick, the natal spot of her who had experienced such strange vicissitudes of fate and fortune. At the solemn hour of midnight, on the 24th of August, the remains were deposited in the vault of the ducal family, beneath the Cathedral of St. Blaize, in the capital of the Duchy; on her coffin was placed a plate which set forth her age and several of the prominent incidents of her life; and she was laid at last to repose between the coffins of two remarkable men, her father and her brother, the former of whom fell at Jena, vainly resisting the colossal power of Napoleon, the latter at Waterloo, in the hour of exultant victory and glory. The ceremonies which attended the burial of this unhappy princess were not such as decency demanded; because the Duchy of Brunswick was at that period an appendage to the British crown, the hereditary Duke being yet a minor; and George IV. carried the gratification of his insatiable hatred to the last recorded incident of his wife's earthly career, and scarcely permitted her inanimate remains to escape ignominy and persecution even amid the ghastly solitude and gloom of the grave. Thus ended in sadness and shame the memorable career of Caroline Amelia Elizabeth of Brunswick. Her character was one of a mixed and an equivocal nature. Her intellectual powers were above the ordinary range; she was intelligent, witty, and sagacious. She was strong and firm in her friendships; bitter, yet not implacable, in her hatreds. Her nature was generous, liberal, and completely devoid of that quality which is the most requisite attribute of courtiers, and of those who have to deal with them—she was entirely free from guile and perfidy. Her chief fault was her reckless imprudence, and her contempt of female delicacy. Nevertheless, as these defects appeared only at a later period of her career, after she had suffered years of persecution and ignominy from her husband, it is probable that, had her heart not been soured and her mind alienated by unmerited suffering, she would have remained through life an estimable woman, not destitute of woman's greatest jewel.

CHAPTER VII.

Death of the Duke of Kent—Historic Portrait of his Life—His early Education—His Residence at Geneva—His Sudden Flight to England—Tyranny of George III.—The Duke is ordered to Gibraltar—His Poverty—His Campaign in the West Indies—His Residence in Canada—He is appointed Governor of Gibraltar—Character of his Administration—He returns to England—His Debts—His Marriage with the Princess of Leinengen—His Residence at Amoorback—Birth of the Princess Victoria—The Duke of Clarence—George IV. visits Ireland, Scotland, and Hanover—Abilities of Mr. Huskisson—Financial state of the Empire—Valuable services of Mr. Canning.

GEORGE IV. received the news of the death of the queen with a joy which he could not conceal. The great plague of his existence was at last removed; and that notorious and infamous scandal which his domestic vices and family feuds had engendered throughout the world would thenceforth be diminished. A short time previous to this event other incidents had occurred in the royal family which possessed a public interest, and demand a place in our history. On the 23d of January, 1820, Edward Augustus, Duke of Kent, expired, in the fifty-third year of his age. He was the fourth son of George III., and was born in 1767. His life had been an unhappy and gloomy one, for he was always disliked by his parents, hated by his brothers, and persecuted by his enemies; yet, in spite of them all, he subsequently became the father of a young princess who inherited, under the name of Victoria, that very sceptre whose repulsive and hostile influence had so much afflicted him.

The first preceptor of the young Duke of Kent was Dr. Fisher, afterward Bishop of Exeter and Salisbury. In his eighteenth year he was sent to Luneburg, in Hanover, to pursue his military studies under Baron Wangenheim. He here commenced to feel the miseries of that parsimonious allowance of money, which was one of his greatest calamities through life. His father gave him only a thousand pounds a year; and the half of this sum stuck to the adhesive fingers of his preceptor, before the balance reached his own. Coeval in point of time with his poverty, the chief defect of the prince was developed. This was a great disposition to extravagance. None of the sons of George III. ever appeared to possess the least conception of the value of money; and all of them were annoyed by the misfortunes which such ignorance inevitably entails. In May, 1786, the prince was promoted to the rank of Colonel in the army by brevet; and soon after, he was chosen Knight of the Garter. In 1787 he removed to Geneva, in accordance with the command of his royal father. He was still under the authority of the stern Wangenheim, who plundered him as usual of one-half of his allowance. Here his Royal Highness began to comprehend the indescribable pertinacity and infelicity which are involved in the idea of a *dun*; and he never became practically free from a familiar acquaintance with that disgusting knowledge till the day of his death. While he dwelt at Geneva, he began the habit of borrowing money at immense interest; and thus loaded himself with burdens which adhered to him pertinaciously during life. It is true that, like all princes of the blood, he was subjected to innumerable appeals for aid, and to potent temptations to vice; and this circumstance constitutes his chief excuse. He was also afflicted by other unseemly annoyances. His valet was in reality a spy upon his conduct, and was in his father's pay; while Wangenheim, one of the most inflexible and unendurable of men, was still in authority over him.

The prince became of age in 1788; yet he endeavored to endure his disagreeable position some time longer. At length it became insupportable; and in January, 1790, he suddenly determined, in spite of the positive prohibition of his father, to return to England, and lay his grievances in person before him. Accordingly he arrived at night unheralded in London, took lodgings at a hotel in King Street, and sent word to his brother, the

Prince of Wales, of his unexpected presence. The prince immediately visited him, and brought him to Carlton House. Here he was joined by the Duke of York, and the three consulted together in terror as to what was then best to be done. It was finally agreed that the Duke of York, who stood best with George III., should inform him of the arrival of the Duke of Kent, and should obtain for him an audience. He did so, but the wrath of the monarch at the disobedience of his unhappy son was overwhelming. He would listen to no excuse; he would accept no palliation of his crime; and his presence in London was an act of the most daring and deliberate defiance of his royal authority. In vain, during thirteen successive days, did the young Duke of Kent endeavor to propitiate his father by every possible expedient. On the fourteenth, he received a sealed official paper. It contained an order for him to embark for Gibraltar within twenty-four hours. Immediately before his departure, he was allowed an audience of five minutes' duration, and then received an outfit of five hundred pounds.

At Gibraltar the Duke was placed under the care of General Symes, a man of some intelligence and feeling; and thus the unhappy prince was at last released from the surveillance of the detested Wangenheim. While residing at Gibraltar, he became interested in military tactics, and became something of a disciplinarian, both over himself and over those whom he was permitted to command. His rank was then Colonel of the Royal Fusileers; and from Gibraltar he and his regiment were ordered to Quebec. At this period he was already greatly in debt; and his residence at Gibraltar had increased their aggregate to twenty thousand pounds. His position at Quebec was rendered unpleasant in many respects, chiefly from want of adequate support; and he endeavored to release himself from the intricate coil of entanglements which enveloped him, by removing to a distant scene of military service. He requested and obtained an appointment under Sir Charles Grey, who was at that time engaged in hostilities against the French in the West Indies.

The Duke of Kent was not deficient in personal bravery. At

the capture of Guadaloupe in April, 1794, he led on the first division to the attack, and he exhibited such gallantry as to extort unqualified praise from the Commander-in-Chief, in his official report to the government. Thus, at the age of twenty-seven, he obtained distinction in an honorable profession. When the British nation received information of the intrepidity which the prince had displayed, the unusual spectacle excited their warmest applause, and their representatives in Parliament passed a vote of thanks for his " gallant conduct and meritorious exertions." Similar honors were bestowed upon him by the Irish Parliament. But as philosophy cannot make a Juliet, neither can public honors liquidate debts ; and the mortifications and difficulties of the lavish and generous prince increased constantly in every position in which he was placed. During his residence at Martinique, he was destitute of every thing except the clothes upon his person.* It is indeed difficult to account for the indifference which George III. exhibited to the wants and the troubles of his son, which sometimes were so great as to render his royal relationship contemptible, and the subject of popular derision. It is presumed that the prince had incurred the inveterate repugnance of his narrow-minded and inflexible father, by his extremely liberal principles ; and that all his calamities were to be attributed to that cause. The prince himself declared, in a letter written from the West Indies, that "the wish entertained about him, in certain quarters, when serving here, was that he might fall."

At the end of his campaign in the West Indies, the Duke was ordered to return to Canada. At this period his allowance was raised by Parliament to the sum of twelve thousand pounds per year; and soon after he received the appointment of Commander-in-chief of the forces in British North America. Ill health soon compelled him to resign this difficult post ; but as if to remove him as far and as continually as was possible from his relatives

---

* See *Life of Field Marshal His Royal Highness, Edward, Duke of Kent. By the Rev. Erskine Neale, M. A., Rector of Kirton.* London : Bentley, 1850, p. 149.

and his country, he was ordered to assume the vacant Governorship of Gibraltar—a position still more onerous and undesirable than that which he had deserted, in consequence of the extreme insubordination and disaffection which at that time pervaded the whole garrison. The Duke arrived at Gibraltar in May, 1802; and he immediately discovered that he had undertaken a repulsive, and even a dangerous task. Discipline was entirely relaxed; drunkenness universally prevailed, both among officers and privates; hostility existed between the soldiery and the inhabitants of the town; and every possible species of abuse and vice was openly indulged. The fortress might very properly be compared to an Augean stable, whose vast and foul pollutions none but a modern Hercules could cleanse. At first, the new governor looked on the spectacle in silent disgust. After some reflection, he resolved to undertake the removal, or the cure, of the evils which pervaded every branch of the service. He stopped the retail of spirituous liquors, in a very great measure, as being the chief cause of all the existing vices; and he carried forward his reforms in every possible direction, and with the most unflinching rigor. So extreme did that rigor become, that several of the regiments mutinied; and for a short time, the Duke was in imminent danger of assassination. But he displayed remarkable intrepidity in the midst of great personal peril, and put down the insurrection with an iron hand. The ringleaders were taken, tried, convicted, and executed. Other offenders of less degree were punished in proportion to their guilt. The Duke did his duty inexorably, but he became very unpopular; and three months after the restoration of order, he was directed by George III. to return to England.

Several years of retirement ensued in the life of the Duke, during which he seems to have performed nothing worthy of note, except that he added vastly to the accumulation of his debts. These again became so burdensome, that in 1816, he removed to the continent, and took up his residence, for the sake of greater cheapness, at Brussels. In visiting the several branches of his family in Germany, he became acquainted with the

Princess of Leiningen, the sister of Prince Leopold of Saxe Cobourg. This young lady had been married at the age of sixteen to the hereditary Prince of Leiningen, a venerable and dilapidated suitor, who was twenty-eight years her senior. It was her calamitous fate to endure this partner during twelve years. To the handsome and amiable widow of this ancient husband, the Duke of Kent was married in May, 1818, at Cobourg. Both parties were poor, but both seemed happy. They resided at Amorbach, the petty capital of the small principality of Leiningen. Soon it became evident that the Duchess of Kent was pregnant, and it was a matter of the first importance to her and to her husband that their child should be born in England. Yet so impoverished were the parents of the future powerful queen of the British Empire at that time, that they had not even the means necessary to convey them across the channel. The Duke in vain appealed for aid to his eldest brother, the Prince of Wales. The luxurious and unprincipled sybarite of Carlton House turned a deaf ear to his appeals. Other members of the royal family refused their aid; and it was at last through the contributions raised by a few obscure and untitled friends of the Duke of Kent in London, that the necessary means of travelling were procured. This assistance came none too soon. Scarcely had he and his wife reached Kensington Palace, when, on the 24th of May, 1819, their daughter, the future inheritress of the British crown, was born. A few months afterward the royal pair returned to their former residence at Amorbach; and here the Duke suddenly expired from inflammation of the lungs, several weeks after his arrival. Had he lived, the lapse of time and the demise of intervening claimants would have invested this most persecuted and unfortunate member of the family of George III. with that sceptre, under whose partial and perverted power he had himself so often and so severely suffered. The Duke of Kent possessed one pre-eminent excellence over all the other members of the royal family, which deserved to embalm his memory in the judgment of posterity. He alone of that exalted circle, was a man of principle; and his principles were such as all enlightened men must approve and commend. His brothers had no principles whatever; but were time-serving, vascillating, hypocritical, and perfidious; and uniformly governed their conduct in accordance with their interests, their impulses, and their passions. The general unpopularity of the Duke of Kent with all his relations, and especially with those whose heads were successively decorated with the diadem, resulted from his liberal views, and from his disposition to enlarge and secure the franchises of the British subject.

Another member of the royal family whose personal history deserves a passing notice in this connection, was William Henry, Duke of Clarence, the third son of George III., who afterward succeeded George IV. upon the throne. This prince was born in August, 1765. From his youth he was destined for the naval service, and accordingly, when fourteen years of age, he was placed on board the "Prince George" as midshipman, commanded by Lord Digby. He subsequently saw some active service under Admirals Rodney, Hood, and Nelson. At the termination of the war in 1782, he determined to qualify himself for command, and continued in active employment visiting Cape Francois and the Havana. He rapidly passed through all the ascending grades of rank; became lieutenant and captain; and in 1790 was appointed Rear Admiral of the Blue. His talents were by no means remarkable, yet in 1818 he was promoted to the important post of Lord High Admiral of England. In the performance of the duties which this responsible station involved; he visited all the naval depots of the realm; examined into abuses; corrected errors; made necessary promotions; and effected some judicious reforms. His chief adviser and assistant in these achievements was Mr. Canning, whose sudden and premature death cut short the brief career of his own official usefulness and fame. After the resignation of his office as Lord High Admiral, the life of the Duke of Clarence became one of retirement and obscurity, until his final elevation to the highest seat in the empire. The character of this prince presented no salient points which were in themselves commendable. He was a great spendthrift; and if the declaration of Lord Nelson is to be believed, he was in his early manhood, an incorrigible liar. His most solemn assertions could rarely or never be relied upon. An idea may be formed of the prodigality usually displayed by this prince, from the fact that, during the fifteen months in which he commanded at the Admiralty, his expenses there incurred were twenty-five thousand pounds; although it must be admitted, as some extenuation of this lavish waste, that a portion of this sum was spent in the munificent hospitality which he exercised toward the profession. In his intercourse with women the Duke of Clarence was indeed less promiscuous and less unscrupulous than his brother, the Prince of Wales; but this circumstance resulted more from his sated inclination than from his purer principles. He maintained a *liaison* during many years with the celebrated comic actress, Mrs. Jordan; by her he had a numerous family of children; and her he cruelly and brutally deserted when he had attained his fiftieth year, to unite himself in marriage with the Princess Adelaide of Saxe-Meiningen. If he was not notoriously vagrant and versatile in his amours, the credit is due, not to his superior virtue, but to Mrs. Jordan's transcendant charms.

Of the other members of the family of George IV. it is unnecessary here to speak; and we have digressed thus far from the main current of our history, to glance only at the personal career of two relatives of the king, who were remarkable and worthy of note; the one, because he became the father of the princess who, to the infinite chagrin of some of her connections, afterward wielded the sceptre of the British Empire, and the other, because he himself eventually ascended the throne.

Scarcely had the imposing pomps, the festivities and the congratulations which attended the coronation of George IV. terminated, when he resolved to visit several important portions of his empire, to which till then he had remained personally a stranger. In August, 1821, he journeyed to Ireland; in the following September to Hanover; and in August of the next year to Scotland. It would be difficult to discover any practical good which was effected by these expensive travels; their only result was to flatter the vanity and gratify the curiosity of the sated and listless monarch; while the outward shows of respect and esteem which attended his progress were but additional evidences of the false and delusive flatteries which usually surround the possessors of supreme power. For at that very moment the financial and commercial interests of his subjects were rapidly approaching a perilous and complicated climax. Universal bankruptcy threatened the nation. During the long prevalence of the war from 1797 till 1815, paper money had been made the substitute of the precious metals in a very great degree; and thereby the price of all the articles of commerce was nearly doubled. By the continuance of peace throughout Europe, and by the revolutionary and disturbed condition of the South American countries, whence the largest supplies of gold and silver had for many years been derived, the circulating medium of the nation became vastly reduced. This circumstance diminished by one-half the price of all the articles of production and commerce. To remedy this evil, therefore, as far as possible, the British Parliament passed a bill in 1822, extending to ten years the period during which small bank notes were to be retained in circulation. The currency immediately became greatly expanded; the nation was amply provided with paper money of small and large denominations; the general prosperity of every branch of industry seemed to increase immensely; and all this apparent good fortune was attributable to the prodigious financial ability of Mr. Huskisson, who in January, 1823, was appointed President of the Board of Trade, with a seat in the Cabinet. This remarkable man was the confederate of another statesman of equally valuable, but of more brilliant qualities. In August, 1822, after the death of Lord Londonderry, Mr. Canning had been invited to fill the office of Minister for Foreign Affairs. He was already one of the most popular ministers who ever guided the destinies of England. He co-operated heartily in his high place with the plans and measures of Mr. Huskisson, and introduced into the Cabinet the ascendancy of the commercial, manufacturing, and trading interests of the nation; inasmuch as these were regarded by the leading states-

men as the paramount interests in the empire. Mr. Huskisson may justly be denominated as the most consummate master of the science of finance who has ever held a seat in the British Cabinet. His statistical and commercial information was vast, diversified, and accurate, and merchants and manufacturers discovered in him a more profound acquaintance with all the details of their respective interests and pursuits than they themselves possessed. His talents indeed were all of the solid, useful, and practical description; he was totally destitute of every showy and glittering quality, yet on financial questions he was an able debater; his judgment was slow but sure and safe; and the influence which he exerted over the men of weight and substance in parliament was deservedly absolute. He was in general the advocate of liberal measures. During many years he had been the associate of Pitt and Dundas in the cabinet; and after the accession of Mr. Canning to power became his most able and powerful coadjutor. He directed special attention to the British Navigation Laws; and having devised, he proposed and carried through, the commercial policy known as the Reciprocity system, which may be more properly designated as the law of commercial retaliation, a pacific war of tariffs. Other nations allowed a premium of ten per cent. on all articles imported into them by their own vessels, thus in substance imposing a similar duty on the cargoes of all foreign vessels. By the Reciprocity system of Mr. Huskisson the same enactment was passed and observed by the British government in reference to all the goods imported into British ports. Thus, in 1823, reciprocity treaties based on this principle were established with all the chief commercial communities on the globe; and soon the most beneficial results were found to accrue to the pecuniary interests of the nation.

When the year 1825 opened, the financial condition of the empire was in the highest degree prosperous; before its close, a dark cloud overhung the political heavens and an imminent crisis occurred in its fate. The leading members of the Cabinet, of which Mr. Canning was the gifted head, successively proposed measures of a liberal and enlightened nature, and even went so far as to lay themselves open to the taunt of the extreme Whigs, that they had, while openly retaining the name of Tory, espoused opinions to which Tories had ever been absolutely hostile. This insinuation was even boldly made by Mr. Brougham, the leader of the Whig opposition in Parliament; and he declared that the chief credit of the liberal measures of the government was due to the radicals, who had in reality themselves devised and first proposed them. This singular assertion drew from Mr. Canning a retort, the mingled wit and severity of which has rendered it historical. He said that this claim of the Whig leader reminded him of a certain dramatic writer named Dennis, who flourished in the reign of Queen Anne; and who unfortunately labored under the insane delusion that he was himself the author of all the popular plays of the time. Thus when a new and successful tragedy was produced in which a prodigious quantity of hail and thunder abounded, the incensed Dennis exclaimed from the pit: "They have stolen my thunder!" Thus, said Mr. Canning, did his eloquent opponent assert, when any new measure was proposed by any party whatever for the promotion of the prosperity of the nation; he claimed it for his thunder!*

The conclusion of 1825 was marked by a terrible commercial panic, which greatly crippled the energies of the empire. Vast quantities of the precious metals had been extracted from the realm and exported to foreign countries. In a few months the bullion in the Bank of England sank from twelve millions to less than two millions. The existing paper currency, whose value depended solely upon the actual pressure of that treasure which it was intended to represent, became comparatively worthless; confidence was lost; commerce, both domestic and foreign, was greatly circumscribed; and consternation and distress pervaded every class of the community. In the midst of this great peril, the resources of Mr. Canning and his associates did not fail them; and after some deliberation, a measure of relief was devised which proved efficacious in averting coming evils, and in remedying those which already existed. The Bank of England was authorized

* *Parliamentary Debates*, Vol. xii., p. 25.

by Act of Parliament to issue notes for country circulation of the denomination of one and two pounds; and these notes, immediately passing into universal use, supplied the place in a great measure of the real though absent currency of the country. By this means the threatened crisis was averted; money, or that which possessed all the omnific attributes and prerogatives of money, become accessible to all classes of the community; and the circulation of the Bank of England increased during the lapse of four weeks in the month of December, 1825, from seventeen million pounds to twenty-five and a half millions. In the accomplishment of all these results, so far as George IV. was concerned, he acted merely as the supple and compliant tool of the sagacious statesmen, who, happily for the welfare of the empire, then firmly held the potent wand of power.

CHAPTER VIII.

Disturbed state of Ireland—Miseries endured by the Laboring Classes—Establishment of Secret Societies—The Catholic Association—The Talents and Influence of Daniel O'Connell—Agitation in favor of Irish Emancipation—Repeal of the Corn Laws Proposed—Death of Lord Liverpool—Dilemma of George IV.—Mr. Canning becomes Premier—His Death—Lord Goderich succeeds him and resigns—Duke of Wellington becomes Prime Minister—Opposition of George IV. to Catholic Emancipation—Passage of the Catholic Relief Bill—English antipathy to Papists and Jesuits—Parliamentary Reform Bill introduced—Illness of George IV.—His Death—His Character.

THE unfortunate and disturbed condition of Ireland constituted for some years the source of much uneasiness to the government of George IV. During many generations the English rulers of that fertile and once prosperous island tyrannized over its unfortunate inhabitants in every imaginable way; and the laws by which the latter were governed were a blot on justice, and a disgrace to Anglo-Saxon legislation. The constant effect produced by these laws was the diffusion of poverty, distress, outrages without number, disaffection toward the government, internal feuds, and every species of misfortune which man can inflict or suffer. The pampered proprietors of the land, after extorting the utmost farthing from the despairing and starving wretches who tilled their fields, wasted their revenues in the expensive pleasures and luxurious vices of European capitals, and rarely resided in their native country. At length a proposition was made by the Irish land-owners to introduce Scotch and English husbandmen into the occupancy of their lands, as being more thrifty and more profitable, to the exclusion of the native farmers. This infamous proposal immediately led to outbursts of violence and indignation from those unfortunate men; and they attempted to avert so ruinous a result by the formation of secret societies, which were known by the epithet of *Ribbonmen*. To oppose the threatened purposes of these organizations all of whose members were Roman Catholics, the Protestant residents and land-owners established hostile associations under the name of Orange Lodges, which were also secret in their measures and regulations. The frequent conflicts which subsequently occurred between these two organizations, form the bloodiest page in the vexed and disastrous annals of Ireland; and innumerable crimes and reciprocal wrongs were perpetrated by them, which have scarcely a parallel in the domestic history of nations.*

Evils so great as these naturally forced themselves upon the attention of English and Irish statesmen, and various remedies for them were proposed. Thirteen million pounds sterling were yearly extorted from the Irish peasantry by the land-owners; and facts like these goaded the sufferers on at length to the adoption of active measures of relief. The Catholic Association was established at Dublin in 1824. The avowed purposes of this association were to petition Parliament for a redress of grievances; to resist the operations of the Orange Lodges; to establish and support a free Irish press; to obtain the repeal of the Union between England and Ireland; and until that event was realized, to secure the admission of Roman Catholic peers into the British House of Lords, and Roman Catholic representatives into the British House of Commons. Meantime the advocates of the interests of Ireland in the English legislature were not silent. A long and violent contest ensued throughout both countries in reference to the heavy grievances and the plundered rights of Ireland. A bill was brought forward in the Commons in 1825, by Mr. Goulburn, providing for the suppression of the Catholic Association in Ireland, and its tributary branches in England. This bill was strenuously supported by the ministry and government, but was fiercely opposed by the whole Whig party, and by the Catholic interest in parliament. It was eventually passed

* *Porter's Progress of the Nation*, 658, 667.

after a prodigious contest; but its effects were immediately paralyzed by the instant dissolution of the Association, and by the establishment of a new society having in view the same ultimate purposes, but evading those features which would have rendered it obnoxious to the bill.*

At this period Daniel O'Connell, the ablest statesman whom Ireland has ever produced, and who was singularly adapted for the crisis by his great talents, by his unconquerable perseverance, by his superior skill, and by his dauntless intrepidity, appeared upon the stage. The elective franchise had been extended in some measure to the Irish Catholics by a bill introduced by Mr. Pitt in 1793; and under the operation of this law, Mr. O'Connell was chosen to represent the county of Clare in parliament. From that moment he became one of the master spirits in the British Legislature. His first triumph, which was in substance an evasion, appertained to his right to a seat in parliament without taking the test oaths; and the effect produced by it upon his partisans throughout Ireland was so immense, that universal rejoicings and tumultuous exultations pervaded every extremity of that land, where mourning and tears had been during so many generations the unvarying portion of the unhappy people.

Meanwhile other public interests demanded the attention and excited the solicitude of British statesmen. During 1826 all classes of the nation were depressed and afflicted by the pecuniary difficulties in which they were involved. The manufacturers found that their orders decreased. The banks refused to lend money on any conditions. An infinite number of workmen were thrown out of employment; and another scene of general bankruptcy seemed to be impending. The ministers deliberated anxiously upon the measures which should be adopted to restore financial confidence; and they at length resolved upon the expedient of suppressing the use of all paper money at and under the denomination of one pound. It was supposed that, by the introduction of gold and silver into the small circulation of the country, the existing evils would be removed. And when we

* *Parliamentary Debates*, Vol. xii., 214, 229.

remember that such sagacious statesmen as Lord Liverpool, then Chancellor of the Exchequer, Mr. Huskisson, and Mr. Canning, approved of the measure, we must admit its wisdom and expediency. The bill to abolish small bank notes was carried in both Houses of Parliament by a large majority. The effects produced by this measure were such as its authors had anticipated; and by the immediate rise in the price of various commodities, and by the remuneration earned by operatives of every description, a better condition of the finances and the currency was attained.

The year 1826 rendered the reign of George IV. remarkable as being the period when the repeal of the Corn Laws was first proposed and introduced into the discussions of Parliament. The object of this repeal was the removal of those duties and restrictions which then impeded the importation of foreign grain into England, and which increased the price of breadstuffs by the exorbitant duties which were levied upon them. This repeal was strenuously resisted by the ministerial party at this period; and it was negatived when finally pressed to a vote in the Commons, to be renewed however at a subsequent period with a different and more desirable result. During 1827 the financial state of the nation greatly improved. At the opening of the year several events of importance occurred which were calculated to produce a permanent effect, both upon the feelings of the monarch and upon the destiny of the nation. On the 5th of January the Duke of York, the heir apparent to the throne, expired; and a few days afterward he was followed to the tomb by Lord Liverpool, who, since 1812, had occupied the chief posts of influence and power in the government of the country. By the death of the first personage the king was left without the counsel and sympathy of his most intimate and trusted friend; by the death of the second he was deprived of the services, not of one of the ablest, but of one of the most prudent, adroit, and conservative ministers, who ever controlled the destinies of England.

On the death of this experienced statesman George IV. was placed in a painful dilemma. The Whig or Liberal party ruled in the House of Commons with almost absolute majorities. It would have been vain for the king to call to his counsels a Tory Cabinet; for advisers of that party would have been unable to carry a single measure through either House of Parliament. He was at last compelled to have recourse to the services of the very men whom he had often betrayed, and whom he therefore most intensely hated. But of the great Whig leaders, several were personally obnoxious to him beyond all endurance; and an accommodation with them was utterly impossible. The chief of these was Mr. Brougham, the bold, fearless, and gifted advocate, who had defended the injured queen against the formidable conspiracy which her husband had organized against her; and who, in the performance of his professional duty on that memorable occasion, had savagely, though not unjustly, slaughtered the character and principles of the august prosecutor. He must necessarily be excluded from the Cabinet. Mr. Canning, the next in genius and in influence to Mr. Brougham, was also distasteful to the haughty monarch; for he too had been one of the advisers of the detested queen. Nevertheless there was eventually no other alternative left for the harrassed monarch; he must accept Whig ministers, and not even obscure or second-rate politicians, but those who occupied the leading positions in the government of their party. Mr. Canning therefore became first Lord of the Treasury and Chancellor of the Exchequer; Lord Lyndhurst was appointed Lord Chancellor; the Duke of Portland to the Privy Seal; Mr. Huskisson was made President of the Board of Trade, and the Duke of Wellington was succeeded by the Marquis of Anglesea as Grand Master of the Ordnance.

The administration of Mr. Canning proved to be a brilliant but a short one. During his supremacy the subject of parliamentary reform became the paramount theme of agitation in the nation. The shocking extremes of bribery which had been repeatedly perpetrated in the election of members of Parliament; and especially the fearful degree of corruption which was practised, and which had been suddenly exposed, in the boroughs of East Retford and Penryn, attracted the attention of the whole nation to the subject. A bill was immediately introduced into parliament and passed by large majorities disfranchising both of these boroughs. This was one of the last triumphs which Mr. Canning was destined to achieve. He expired, after a very sudden and brief illness, in August, 1827, to the great regret of a nation which admired his talents, commended his principles, and supported his measures. The sensation produced by the death of this illustrious man was universal and profound. The most extravagant expectations had been formed in reference to his future usefulness, all of which were blighted by his premature death.

Lord Goderich succeeded Mr. Canning in the premiership; and the resemblance which existed between these two men was very much like the similitude of Hyperion to a satyr. During the short period of the troubled existence of this administration, the inefficiency and the pernicious blunders which characterized it rendered it the object of universal contempt; and it terminated ignominiously in January, 1828. Lord Wellington was then invited by the distracted and now enfeebled monarch to assume the chief direction of affairs. The liberal Tories who were already in the cabinet retained their seats, but all the stringent Whigs resigned. Mr. Peel was appointed Home Secretary; Earl Bathurst, President of the Councils; while Messrs. Huskisson, Palmerston, and Lord Dudley remained in their former offices. The last three statesmen resigned in the following May, and the Wellington cabinet underwent a reconstruction, by which Sir George Murray succeeded Mr. Huskisson, Lord Aberdeen took the post of Lord Dudley, and Sir Henry Hardinge replaced Lord Palmerston.

This cabinet was called upon at the opening of its career to dispose of two measures of vital importance to the nation: the Repeal of the Corn Laws, and the abolition of the Test and Corporation Acts. The latter of these was but a preparatory step to the final triumph of Catholic emancipation. Both measures passed through both Houses of Parliament during the winter of 1828; and thus clearly indicated the gigantic strides which enlightened principles were then making, in what had formerly been one of the most conservative and illiberal communities which existed in the civilized world, in which the antiquated prerogatives of a privileged class had ever been guarded with unparalleled jealousy and pertinacity. George IV. was at this period of his life hostile to any movement of reform, and especially to any advancement of the interests, or enlargment of the liberties of the Roman Catholics. He complained to Lord Eldon that every thing had taken a revolutionary turn; that he had frequently and vainly suggested to his ministers the necessity of crushing the Roman Catholic Association, and of even suspending the Habeas Corpus Act; that he himself was in the perilous position of a person with a pistol presented to his breast; and that even the aristocracy of the realm, which had ever been characterized by its opposition to popular movements, seemed to have deserted him and to have joined his adversaries. It was scarcely possible for George IV. to entertain any settled principles on any subject, except such as were exclusively dictated by a regard to his own interests; and this attribute of his character clearly appears even in his apparently pious antagonism to the Roman Catholics. He was bitterly opposed to Catholic emancipation because he believed that his title to the throne, the security of his claims, and the undiminished amplitude of his power, all depended upon his firm and unbending devotion to the Protestant interests. He well knew that the Protestantism of the house of Hanover was the only quality which had elevated them to the British throne in the first instance; that their Protestantism was the single feature of their character which still recommended them to the favor of the British nation; and that the moment their Protestanism seemed to diminish in its intensity and fervor, that moment they loosened their grasp of an unmerited sceptre. Therefore it was that the king felt the necessity of exhibiting the utmost hostility to every thing which bore the impress of Romanism; and the circumstances of the case clearly evince that he would have been opposed to any measure, had it been the most reasonable and equitable in the world, if its support would have thrown the least suspicion on the purity and excess of his adhesion to the Protestant interests.*

This assertion is clearly proved by the fact that, though all the members of the existing cabinet had been formerly opposed to Catholic emancipation, their enlightened and sagacious appreciation of the state of the kingdom convinced them of the falsity of their first position, and induced them to support and approve the measure. The Duke of Wellington had formerly resisted any such movement. Sir Robert Peel had spoken violently against it in parliament. Lord Lyndhurst, Mr. Goulburn, Mr. Dawson, had acted prominently in opposition to the Romanists. They all now veered round suddenly and unanimously to the opposite policy; and gave the king plainly to understand that the period for the triumph of Catholic emancipation could no longer be resisted or postponed.

To accelerate a result which was now considered inevitable, the champions of the Irish Catholics also continued their agitation of the subject. On this potent hobby Mr. O'Connell rose to the summit of popular fame and adulation. He kindled a conflagration throughout Ireland which could be suppressed by no human power; and every possible expedient was used to inflame the minds and excite the enthusiasm of the Irish Catholics in favor of their own speedy and complete emancipation from those unjust inflictions under which they and their ancestors had so long suffered. When Parliament met in February, 1829, the moral power wielded by their leaders, and especially by Mr. O'Connell, was prodigious; yet in his speech from the throne the king

---

* Another motive has been assigned as the cause of the intense opposition of George IV. to Catholic emancipation. It is well known that while Prince of Wales, and even while Regent, he had publicly declared himself to be the friend of that measure, and had promised that, when invested with the full prerogatives of the Crown, he would effectively promote its consummation. After his accession he became bitterly opposed to it; and it is asserted that one cause of this change in his feelings was the influence exerted upon his mind by Lady Yarmouth, Marchioness of Hertford, one of his mistresses, who entertained a deep aversion to the Church of Rome. See *Chambers' Papers for the People*, Vol. iv., *ad fin.*

gave utterance for the last time to his opposition to the claims of the Romanists; and he lamented that an association still existed in Ireland which was dangerous to the public peace; which was inconsistent with the spirit of the constitution; which produced discord and ill-will among his subjects; and which in reality only impeded the improvement of the condition of Ireland. Soon after the opening of the session Mr. Peel moved for permission to introduce a bill granting all the demands of the Catholics. This proposition, and the subsequent introduction of the bill itself, opened wide the field of discussion; and all the bearings of the case were fully and amply investigated in the deliberations which ensued. The bill was eventually carried in the house of Peers by a majority of a hundred and four votes, and in the Commons by a plurality of a hundred and seventy-eight.*

The passage of the Catholic Relief Bill by the British Parliament was one of the most significant events of modern times. It illustrated the triumphant progress of free principles. The arguments urged in favor of it were conclusive and powerful. The whole measure was based upon the broad and comprehensive principle of the natural rights of man, one of the fundamental and most indefeasible of which is that of thinking and acting freely on the subject of religion, and being exempt from all penalties, personal or political, in consequence of the exercise of that freedom. Nor could any government claim to be a free or enlightened government which did not recognize this cardinal doctrine and act according to it. Five millions out of seven millions of Irishmen were Catholics by conviction; they regarded the Church of Rome as the only source of religious truth; they believed themselves to be under moral obligations to obey the mandates and the precepts of that church, on the peril of the loss of their souls; meanwhile they bore a portion of the burdens of the general government under which they lived; they were for the most part industrious and valuable citizens; they constituted a most important integral part of the empire; and in addition to all these considerations, they had already been compelled to en-

* *Parliamentary Debates*, xx., 893, 1631.

18

dure the most infamous and tyrannical abuses from the class whom an unpropitious fortune had placed in a dominant position over them. It was high time that such tyranny should terminate; and that a too tardy justice should be done to the political and religious rights of the Catholic inhabitants of Ireland.

Nor was the other side of this great question devoid of potent and seemingly conclusive arguments. It was urged by the opponents of Catholic emancipation that the constitution of Great Britain was essentially a Protestant constitution; that it was formed by Protestants for the promotion of the interests of Protestants; that it was one of the dogmas of the Roman Catholic Church, that its members should obey any foreign potentate who was a Catholic, in preference to a native prince who was a heretic; and that therefore the Irish Catholics did not deserve the protection of a Protestant government. In addition to this it might be urged, that the past history of the Romanists in England had not been such as to commend them to the acquisition of greater power in the state. They had often proved themselves to be dangerous and ambitious subjects. They had exhibited an appalling degree of cruelty and ferocity on many critical occasions when their religion came in question, which had threatened entirely to overturn the fabric of the government. The chilling memory of Gunpowder Plots and Rye House Plots came over the minds of some; and others remembered how the intrigues and machinations of Romish priests and emissaries, during the reign of Queen Mary and even of James II., had well nigh brought the kingdom to the verge of ruin. The experience of the past had taught them, that of all the organizations on this earth which were most to be feared and dreaded, that of the Jesuits was the most formidable; and they inferred that with the removal of the disabilities from the Roman Catholics, this hated order would again be introduced, and would overflow a country from which they had long been excluded at the peril of their lives. Nor was this dread of the order of Jesus unfounded or unreasonable. The history of modern times presents no organization of men so powerful, compact, untiring, and unscrupulous as it is. We may contemplate the daring exploits and reckless intrepidity of the legions of Imperial Rome, selling the diadem of the world's dominion to the highest bidder, sometimes on the plains of Gaul, sometimes amid the snows of Parthia; we may peruse the deeds of the terrible Janissaries, for so many ages the bulwark of the Ottoman Empire, whose unyielding valor has been conspicuous in some of the greatest of conquests; we may trace the career of the Imperial Guard of Napoleon, rudely battered yet invincible on a hundred fields of blood, whose eagles soared in martial glory beneath the burning sun of Egypt, as amid the wintry storms of Russia, and who remained faithful to the last to the marvellous fortunes of their illustrious chief; yet all these illustrations would fail to convey an adequate conception of the real character of this wonderful order. With them, all personal and individual interests, the claims of ease or of ambition, are alike buried in oblivion, or merged in their absorbing devotion to the progress and triumphs of the Romish church. It is a joy to them to forsake all the endearments of early association, to cross wide oceans, to penetrate remote climes, to sacrifice the strongest ties of human existence, to labor, to teach, to preach, to intrigue, to suffer, and at last to perish, either in the crowded capital, or as solitary exiles in the most distant recesses of human abode, for the aggrandizement of the church, for the extension of her power, and for the enlargement of her supremacy. Nor does the dreaded agency of the Jesuit terminate here. He is most to be feared in the domestic circle, and in the confessional. There he extorts revelations from female lips which the husband and father never hear. Like an insidious viper he stealthily crawls into the inmost sanctuary of a man's home; and with subtle power he dispenses discord, disaffection, and treachery to which there is no possible antidote. He exerts a mysterious and baleful influence which neither parental, fraternal, nor conjugal authority can counterbalance. The Protestant father will exercise but little control over children whose mother is one of the passive victims of Jesuitical enchantment. His offspring will scorn him; the partner of his bosom will distrust him ; her spiritual adviser will know all his affairs ; while living he will thwart his purposes, and when dead he will control his property ; and he is a mere tool in the hands of an unknown foe, who secretly and perniciously directs the main current of his destiny, and of those most intimately connected with him.*

The past experience of the English people had amply taught them the perilous nature of this order, so justly termed the *Janissaries de l'église*; and some of them naturally apprehended that, by the passage of the Catholic Relief Bill, the door would be opened for the reintroduction of the evils and calamities of the past ; perhaps for the eventual triumphs of Popery throughout the kingdom ; and even for the return of the exiled Stuarts. They supposed that the Church of Rome never changes in its character and principles with the lapse of time ; and that the same events would probably be brought about in the nineteenth century, which had occurred in the seventeenth, if the Romanists regained the possession of power.† Hence they entertained the utmost horror and dread of any reform which might by any possibility lead to so disastrous a result.

Yet, singular as it may appear, that party in the nation who then held these sentiments proved to be greatly in the minority. The bill having passed both Houses of Parliament, was presented to George IV. for his approval. He seems on this occasion to have been exercised and disturbed, much more than his selfish nature was usually capable. Every member of his cabinet was arrayed against him ; and in his distress he sent for Lord Eldon, the aged adviser who had so long possessed his confidence. He declared to him the painful dilemma in which he was placed ; how he detested and feared the passage of this bill ; how all his

---

* In proof of this see "*Instructions Secrètes des Jésuites, ou Monita Secreta Societatis Jesu.*" Blois et Paris, 1845.

† This is affirmed, in so many words, by many of the Romish standards. See *Catechism of Council of Trent*, p. 85, Ques. 16. Sed quam admodum hæc una ecclesia errare non potest in fidei, ac morum disciplina tradenda, quum a Spiritu Sancto gubernatur : ita ceteras omnes, quæ sibi ecclesiæ nomen arrogant, ut quæ diaboli spiritu ducantur, in doctrinæ, et morum perniciosissimus erroribus versari necesse est.

ministers threatened to resign if he did not sign it; how he was deserted by the nobility; how he was hated by the people; and how, if he was compelled at last to yield, he could abandon the throne, and retreat to the repose of his kingdom of Hanover. Finally he fell upon the neck of the venerable Chancellor, and gave vent to his grief in a flood of tears.* But Lord Eldon clearly perceived the position in which the king was placed; that it would be impossible for him to resist the overwhelming flood of popular determination, or to carry on the functions of the government; and he also advised the monarch to accede to the popular will. George IV. was at last subdued; and with an unwilling heart he gave the bill the royal assent on the 13th of April, 1829, *by commission*; thereby indicating to the world that the approval was that of the cabinet rather than of the sovereign.

But another humiliation almost equally great, was soon in store for the unfortunate monarch. Progress and reform now became the detested watchword of the leading parties and statesmen of the day, and it was impossible for the conservative king to predict, or even to conjecture, where these things would terminate. The radical movement took the shape of the celebrated Reform Bill; and although this great and beneficent measure did not reach a final triumph until 1832, after George IV. had been laid in the tomb, its vigorous and resolute agitation had already commenced, and the successes which the progressive party had already attained, stimulated them only to the accomplishment of greater. Financial difficulties now occurred, which furnished a convenient topic for agitation and declamation. The manufacturing classes of England in 1829, were greatly depressed by the diminution of the circulating medium, which was the necessary result of the abolition of the small note paper currency. The results which usually attend financial distress followed. Riots occurred at Coventry, Nuneaton, and Bedworth; strikes for higher wages were made by the operatives at Macclesfield and Barnesley; and in Ireland, the old feuds between the Roman

---

* *Alison's History of Europe, Second Series*, Vol. ii., p. 308.

Catholics and the Orangemen were revived. Collisions took place in Armagh, Benauglen, and Tipperary, in which many were wounded and slain. In the midst of these troubles, Parliament met in February, 1830. The king in his speech from the throne adverted to the existing evils, and suggested several desirable measures to alleviate them. A long debate ensued in the House of Commons, upon the state of the country. The Duke of Wellington was still premier; but his position was becoming one of great difficulty. He proposed measures of relief, which were not approved by the House of Commons. Mr. Hume, so celebrated for his pertinacious adherence during many years to all measures of retrenchment, moved for a reduction of the army and navy as an incipient step of relief; but his motion was lost. Mr. Thompson then moved for a revision of the system of taxation; and his proposal met with a similar fate. Mr. Attwood subsequently proposed a bill repealing the law which abolished the use of bank notes under the value of five pounds. But the House was equally impracticable in this case, and this measure was also voted down. At length the cabinet resolved to reduce the taxes, as being the most direct and efficacious remedy of the existing evils. Accordingly the imposts on beer, leather, and cider were remitted, which annually amounted to the sum of three million and a half pounds sterling.* This measure for a time was highly successful; and greatly augmented the popularity of the ministers; though in the end the results produced by it were quite insignificant and inadequate. The next expedient of relief adopted, was the abandonment of the sinking fund, by which means the sum of five million pounds, which had been appropriated yearly to the diminution of the national debt, would be employed in paying the current expenses of the government. This measure was rendered partially necessary in consequence of the diminution of the taxes; and it was triumphantly carried through both Houses of Parliament. It quickly received the royal approval; for George IV., with the

* *Parliamentary Debates*, xxiii, 124.

advance of age, and the increase of physical weakness, no longer possessed the mental power to resist any influence which might be brought to bear upon him. The end of his long, voluptuous, yet troubled existence had at length arrived.

The king's health had been gradually declining during the last two years of his life. He was afflicted severely with the gout, but the ossification of the heart had begun, and was rapidly progressing. The severe winter of 1829 prevented him from taking his usual exercise, and thus hastened the fatal termination. At this period he resided in his Lodge at Windsor; and whenever the weather permitted, he indulged himself in his favorite drives through the ancient and magnificent forests which adorn that domain. He was particularly averse to being seen by any of the populace; and to prevent such an annoyance, servants were stationed at the corners of the roads which he traversed, extending fifteen and tweny miles in length, for the purpose of warning off all intruders at the approach of his Majesty. He still continued to hope that his disease might not prove fatal; and he undertook some repairs upon the royal lodge but a few days before his death. He was intensely anxious that a new dining hall would have been completed before his approaching birthday. When that day arrived, the king had been slumbering for a month in the unwelcome embrace of the tomb. So inveterate had the habit of ostentatious trifling become with that pampered and superficial spirit! The king rode out in his open carriage for the last time on the 12th of April; he then passed an hour in his menagerie. Here he was attacked by faintness, by a dry cough, and by wheezing respiration. It became apparent, from an examination which was subsequently made of the respiratory and circulating organs, that the ossification of the heart had proceeded a great length, and that the vital functions could not much longer continue. On the 15th of April the first bulletin was issued to the public, stating the perilous condition of the king. He continued to sink rapidly from day to day, notwithstanding the utmost efforts of medical skill; and on the morning of the 26th of June, 1830, the final hour of his existence arrived. A severe fit of coughing coming on, he was taken by his physician into his arms; when the king suddenly exclaimed: "Oh God, I am dying!" In a few moments afterward he expired, in the sixty-eighth year of his age, and in the eleventh year of his reign.

The royal remains lay in state during some days, after which they were deposited with imposing ceremonies in the mausoleum built by George III., in which already reposed the bodies of that monarch and his queen, the Princesses Charlotte and Amelia, the Dukes of Kent and York, and the infant princes Octavius and Alfred.

Thus passed away for ever, the most stately, magnificent, voluptuous, and censurable monarch of the House of Hanover, who has occupied the English throne. The character of George IV. lay upon the surface, and was easily discernible to the most casual observer. His intellectual powers were good, though by no means remarkable. He was well-informed, sagacious, and intelligent; but at the same time he possessed all the stubbornness and selfish capriciousness of his family. He was regardless of every principle or duty which interfered with the gratification of his passions. He was exceedingly sensual in his nature; he had not the slightest appreciation of female virtue; like the serpent in Paradise, he seduced all who attracted his desires, fascinating them, and glittering with azure, purple and gold; and having accomplished their ruin, he turned heartlessly away to achieve other and equally villanous conquests. He paid no regard to truth; and had he not been restrained by the adamantine and immovable barriers of the British constitution, he would have carried his tyranny to an unparalleled extreme. His desertion of "Perdita," his conduct toward Mrs. Fitzherbert, his cruelty to Queen Caroline, his perfidy toward the numerous undistinguished victims of his amorous passions, all attest that his heart was one of rare rottenness and corruption. He was an admirer of the fine arts; he himself performed with some skill upon several musical instruments; and he possessed very considerable appreciation of the productions of genius in its varied departments of endeavor. Whatever was noble and brilliant in his administration, was due to the superior talents and patriotism of his ministers; whatever was pernicious and bad, was as clearly attributable to his own personal defects and vices.

CHAPTER IX.

Survey of Distinguished Personages during the Reign of George IV.—Mr. Canning—Mr. Brougham—Details of their Lives and Labors—Estimate of their Talents—William Wilberforce—Charles Earl Grey—Eminent Men of Letters—Sir Walter Scott—Lord Byron—Thomas Campbell—Thomas Moore—Metaphysicians—The School of Modern British Essayists—Her Historians—Artists—Tragedians and Preachers of the era of George IV.—Conclusion.

THE era of George IV. both when regent and when king, was prolific of great men in every department of intellectual excellence. Commencing with that class of persons whose talents and position are confessedly the most influential and important in the empire—the statesmen who wielded the destinies of England, the first who attracts our attention is Mr. Canning.

George Canning was born in London in 1770. His father was a man of aristocratic connections, belonging to the Irish gentry; but having offended his family by a disgraceful amour, he was discarded and cut off with a hundred and fifty pounds a year. In 1757 he came to London, and commenced the study of the law; which however he soon relinquished for the purpose of entering into the more attractive pursuits of literature and politics. At the period of the birth of his celebrated son, he was overwhelmed by pecuniary embarrassments, which continued to increase until his death. This event occurred when the younger Canning was but twelve months old. After this event the small sum which the deceased had still received from his relatives was withdrawn; and Mrs. Canning was reduced to the utmost distress. To avert impending starvation for herself and her child, she made her appearance on the stage in 1773. She seems to have been a woman of considerable talent and of remarkable beauty; although the latter was her chief qualification for the dramatic profession. She was but partially successful, and soon followed the fate which generally awaits beautiful, but not very brilliant actresses—she was married to a profligate player. This person was named Reddish. It has been, however, asserted that no marriage ceremony took place between the parties, and that their connection was merely a *liaison*; nor was any proof ever presented, or known to exist, to establish the contrary statement. Reddish, who was a drunkard, soon became a lunatic, and afterward died in a madhouse. Mrs. Canning subsequently married again. Her last husband, after failing in business and breaking down on the stage, also died, leaving his widow and several children to the usual vicissitudes of poverty and distress. She continued to buffet these calamities as best she could, until the rising fortunes of her talented son surrounded her with the means of comfort, and even of luxury.

The very unfavorable and singular circumstances which thus surrounded the youth of Canning, would have inevitably conducted him to ruin instead of the premiership, had he not been rescued by a fortunate accident. The beauty and sprightliness of the lad, who was employed in carrying the theatrical wardrobe of Reddish and his mother to and from the theatre, attracted the benevolent regard of an old actor named Moody, who determined to interfere in his behalf. He went to Canning's paternal uncle, a rich merchant of London, the father of Sir Stratford Canning, and so forcibly represented the case to him, that he prevailed upon him to send the boy to school. The uncle first placed him under Mr. Richards at Winchester. Thence he sent his *protégé* to Eton. At this noble institution, the brilliant talents of young Canning soon gained him, child as he was, a high reputation. In his fifteenth year he became the senior scholar. Soon afterward he projected a periodical entitled the "Microcosm," in the pages of which he exhibited his superior talents both for poetical and prose composition. In 1787 he went to Oxford, carrying with him thither a brilliant reputation. In the following year his generous uncle died, and Canning was compelled to leave the university without a degree. He then entered himself at Lincoln's Inn as a student of law; but soon his acquaintance with Sheridan, Burke, and other distinguished men of genius with whom he became familiar, induced him to abandon his legal studies, and devote himself to political life. By the assistance of Mr. Pitt he succeeded in being elected to Parliament in 1793, as a member for Newport, in the Isle of Wight; and thenceforth he commenced that career of political distinction which has few parallels in British history.

Canning's first speech was made in support of the subsidy which the ministers had granted to the King of Sardinia. It was, for so young a man, a powerful effort; and it at once established his reputation as one of the ablest and most promising members of the House. He was now pitted against Fox, and the great leaders of the opposition; and he treated them from the start of his career with a facile and masterly power which clearly indicated his own consciousness of equal ability. The defence of the ministerial measures was now intrusted in a great measure to Canning, and he was regarded as the ablest ally on whom Pitt could depend. As a reward for his services he was appointed Under Secretary of State in 1795. In 1801, when Mr. Pitt resigned, he followed his fortunes; and taking his seat on the benches of the Opposition, he assailed the Addington ministry with a sarcastic and ferocious power, which had never been witnessed in the British Parliament; and exhibited his versatility of talent in no very pleasing or amiable light.

When Mr. Pitt returned to office in 1804, Mr. Canning again accompanied him as Treasurer of the Navy. In this position he was reconciled to Mr. Addington, who had been created Lord Sidmouth, and co-operated with him as President of the Council. When Mr. Pitt put forth all his prodigious powers to avert the impeachment of Lord Melville, Mr. Canning gave him his utmost assistance. Their united efforts were unavailing, and the discomfited premier hid his mortification and shame in the grave. After the death of Mr Pitt, Mr. Canning began to act with more independence of purpose and character than he had previously exhibited. Under the Portland ministry he held the office of Foreign Secretary. In 1809 he retired in consequence of his duel with Lord Castlereagh. In 1814 he accepted the embassy to Lisbon; in 1816 he became President of the Board of Control; in 1822 he was appointed Governor-General of India; in 1827 he reached the dizzy eminence which crowns the vaulting ambition of British statesmen, and became prime minister. Four months afterward, a sudden attack of illness, produced by accidental causes, terminated prematurely the earthly career of this brilliant and powerful intellect.

Mr. Canning belonged to the party known by the epithet of liberal Tories, and as one of these he was called upon to oppose many measures which were regarded by wise and good men as desirable in themselves, and as being adapted to promote the welfare of the British Empire. The chief measure of reform which he advocated was that of Catholic Emancipation, but his endeavors led to no important results, inasmuch as the bill which he introduced on the subject, and which was ably supported by Grattan and Plunkett, was shorn of its most valuable clauses before it came to a final vote, and was consequently abandoned by its author. When the movements of the Radicals in 1817 and 1819 became so violent as to strike terror into the hearts of the landed gentry throughout the realm, Mr. Canning placed himself in the van of the fierce conflict, assailed their principles and purposes with intense severity and scathing power, and was mainly instrumental in resisting the advancing tide of social and political reform. The suicide of Lord Castlereagh prevented his proceeding to India as Governor-General, and restored him to the domestic service of his country. As premier, his measures were inefficient and feeble; but the fault of his failure in this high place was not attributable to any defect of his own, but to the peculiarly unfavorable combination of adverse circumstances by which he was surrounded. Had his life been prolonged, it is probable that he would have amply realized the brilliant expectations which had been entertained respecting him.

As an orator, Mr. Canning had few equals in the British

Parliament. He was a match, even when quite young, for Mr. Fox; and when afterward, at the death of Pitt, a ministry nicknamed "*All the Talents*" was formed, composed of leading men from the three parties, of whom Mr. Fox, Lord Grenville, and Lord Sidmouth were the chiefs, Mr. Canning's attacks on them were so formidable and overwhelming that they hastened the death of Fox, and considerably shortened the career of that eminent statesman. His eloquence was masterly in its character and effect. No British orator of his time equalled him in his power to satisfy his own adherents, to puzzle and confound his opponents, to persuade and charm the indifferent. His speeches displayed comprehensive logic, great critical acumen, superior rhetorical art in marshalling his arguments and retorts, so as to produce the greatest impression; while vivid and striking images, clear and forcible illustrations were introduced into every discussion. His style was habitually and uniformly elegant; and though his orations were always extemporaneous, so perfect and consummate was his forensic skill that each effort displayed the same freedom from all blemish, as if it had been carefully elaborated in the closet. Sometimes, indeed, he seemed to forget the maxim, that *ars est celare artem*, and his fastidious elegance was rendered purposely visible. His excessive polish of style and manner was not unfrequently overdone. This peculiarity resulted from his natural refinement of mind, and from his sedulous literary culture. In this respect he resembled Burke; and like him he had mastered not only all the departments of *belle lettre* literature, but he had also probed to the bottom the intricacies of philosophical and metaphysical science. His leading arguments often contained the enunciation of profound general principles, whose invention and utterance clearly proved the presence of an original and comprehensive mind. He possessed a ready and retentive memory, so that all his intellectual acquisitions were at his command in the most sudden and pressing emergencies. His sarcasm was scathing and destructive; and some of the forensic combats in which he took a prominent share were terrible. His wit resembled that of Sheridan; his learning that of Huskisson; his logic that of Fox; his declamation that of Pitt; his imagination that of Burke; and his invective that of Brougham. He was the just pride and glory of the liberal Tory party; and had his career not been prematurely terminated by death, the ragged and penniless child of an unfortunate actress, who, in his boyhood, had timidly skulked behind the scenes of a provincial theatre uncertain of the morrow's food and shelter, would in all respects have achieved as brilliant a fame, and wielded as absolute a power, as William Pitt himself.

The only worthy rival to Mr. Canning in the British Parliament, during the latter portion of his career, was Mr. Brougham. This extraordinary man, whose intellectual qualities were so peculiar and so varied as to render him a complete anomaly in the history of British statesmen, was born in Edinburgh in 1779, and was related to the family of Dr. Robertson the historian. He was educated in his native city, whence after completing his academical career with great distinction, he removed to London, and commenced the study of the law. Already at an early age he had contributed many articles to the Edinburgh Review, then recently established, which exhibited superior talent; and which held an honorable place among the most elaborate compositions of such men as Jeffrey, Sidney Smith, Mackintosh, Playfair, and Malthus.

Having been admitted to the English bar, Brougham soon distinguished himself as an advocate and *nisi prius* pleader. His genius was bold, self-confident and acute; these being the very qualities most essential to the attainment of success in the profession of a popular advocate. But his ambition was by no means confined to one, or even to several departments of mental superiority. In 1810 he was elected a member of Parliament; and in that year his name first appeared in the debates of the British Legislature. In this new sphere, his great abilities enabled him at once to assume a distinguished rank. Very soon, Mr. Canning, then the leading orator in the house, discovered that Brougham was a complete and equal match for him. All the elder forensic giants had passed away. Fox, Burke, Pitt, and even Sheridan had disappeared from the brilliant stage upon which they had played so magnificent a part. The combat now lay between Canning and Brougham alone; and rarely had two more gifted and consummate intellectual gladiators entered the arena. In the senate, the eloquence of Brougham obtained a more suitable and enlarged field of operation than at the bar. Compared with Canning, his mind was more athletic and powerful, less polished and beautiful. He was not equally accomplished with the elegance and ornaments of eloquence. But he possessed a ruder and more gigantic intellect; he was furnished with more ample intellectual resources; and indeed there was scarcely any branch of knowledge from the history and the principles of a great revolution, down to the scientific analysis of a ray of light, of which he was not master. His delivery was energetic, rapid, and impressive; to which his personal appearance added its favorable accessories. His genius was essentially constituted and armed for attack; his powers of invective, sarcasm, and obliterative logic were overwhelming. Among other peculiarities which he exhibited, he was capable of uttering original aphorisms, which were pregnant with such suggestive and sententious truths, that they at once flew over the land, crossed oceans and seas, and became household and familiar maxims wherever the English language was known. An illustration of this may be found in his phrase: "the schoolmaster is abroad," which was uttered by him in 1828, in a speech in reference to the appointment of the Duke of Wellington as prime minister, and as successor to Mr. Canning. Said he: "Field Marshal the Duke of Wellington may take the army—he may take the navy —he may take the great seal—he may take the mitre. I make him a present of them all. Let him come on with his whole force sword in hand against the constitution; and the English people will not only beat him back, but laugh at his assaults. In other times the country may have heard with dismay that the soldier was abroad. It will not be so now. Let the soldier be abroad if he will; he can do nothing in this age. There is another personage abroad—a personage less imposing, in the eyes of some perhaps insignificant. The *Schoolmaster is abroad;* and I trust to him, armed with his primer, against the soldier in full military array." Other instances of the utterance of oracular thoughts are found in his performances in the senate, which added greatly to the popular effect which they produced. Among his parliamentary orations, that delivered in 1817 on the state of the nation was preëminent for its lucid statements, its methodical order, its varied knowledge, its masculine power, its originality, beauty and force. His speech on law-reform in 1828 was another instance of similar nature; and though its great length rendered six hours necessary for its delivery, the assembly to which it was uttered exhibited no signs of tedium or fatigue.

Mr. Brougham was most successful as an orator, when he was called upon to attack an adverse party, to break opposing ranks, or to carry a stronghold by storm. His dialectical skill, his vigorous and adroit logic, his facility in exposing a fallacy, or crushing a weak pretence, his galling irony, his flaying sarcasm, his varied learning, his rushing resistless declamation, his boldness and self-confidence, and his ability to wrest a weapon from the hands of an adversary, and then either break it over his own head, or turn it fatally against his own bosom—all these rare powers came into full play when their possessor was employed as an assailant. Canning was the only British statesman who could withstand Brougham under such circumstances, and some of the encounters which took place between them were imposing exhibitions of the fearful formidableness of two great minds, supremely endowed and accomplished, marshalling their resources in hostile array against each other, in conflicts in which even a defeat would not have been inglorious to either.

From the year 1810 till 1830 Brougham was constantly engaged in advocating large and fundamental principles of liberty, either in the senate or in the popular assemblage. He contended for the freedom of the press against the arbitrary purposes of Ellenborough, and the keen legal acumen of Gibbs. He assailed the rampant and insolent Toryism which, rendered arrogant by the military triumphs of that party on the continent, and by the downfall of Napoleon; which, supported by the courage of Castlereagh, by the eloquence of Canning, by the official skill of Huskisson, and by the unscrupulous knavery of Sidmouth, seemed determined to arrogate to itself all the influence and the prerogatives of power in the empire; that great party Brougham assaulted with fearless courage, and did much to meliorate the ultra-tendency of their measures. After this service he plunged boldly into the gap which yawned between the unfortunate Queen Caroline and her husband, and defended her heroically against the malignant and brutal tyranny of George IV. Some of his speeches for the queen were masterpieces of reasoning and dialectics. The rank and sex of his client, her persecutions and misfortunes, the exalted position of the assailing party, the intense interest felt by the nation in the result, the odiousness of the oppression which his client had endured, and the sympathy which was universally felt in her behalf; all these circumstances called forth his utmost powers. He proved himself worthy of the memorable occasion; and no sudden emergency, no unexpected narrowing by the judges of the grounds allowed to the defense, no hostile array of learning, talent and influence, sufficed for a moment to daunt or confound him. When, however, in 1830, he accepted the Lord Chancellorship, he took the most unfortunate step of his life. On this occasion he was first offered the Attorney-Generalship; but this post he indignantly spurned. He demanded something higher; and the Chancellorship was at last tendered him by Lord Grey, the new Whig premier. He remained in this office till 1835; and during all this period he occupied a false and dishonorable position. He who had been the most able and zealous advocate of progress and reform, suddenly assumed the attitude, and uttered the sentiments, of a conservative Tory. He condemned the measures of his former associates as revolutionary and disorganizing. He eulogized the constitutional spirit and the legislative wisdom of the House of Lords; and spoke of that inert and pernicious body, as the great and salutary corrective of the evils produced by the radical legislation of the Commons. The inevitable consequences of such perfidy and inconsistency was, that Lord Brougham fell from his exalted place in the estimation of the nation; nor did his success as a judge compensate him for his unpopularity as a trimmer. His legal learning was scarcely sufficient for the post. He had never been a mere *leguleius* in the technical meaning of that term; and his judgments as Chancellor never ranked with those of Eldon, Camden, or Hardwicke. During the period of Lord Grey's ministry, Lord Brougham defended the most unjustifiable acts of the premier. After the fall of that minister in 1835, Lord Brougham remained during some years in retirement. His moral influence in the nation was lost; and it was supposed to have been irretrievably forfeited. In the progress of time, however, he emerged, and gradually succeeded in regaining the popularity which he had alienated, by the advocacy of wise measures, and by his bold and vigorous defense of principles which were consistent with those in the support of which he had expended the masterly energies of his earlier manhood.

But Lord Brougham's sole distinction was not as a lawyer, as an advocate, as a judge, or as a parliamentary orator. He was the most versatile of men. His great abilities shone as a historical and philosophical writer with equal splendor. His Discourse on Natural Theology deserves to be called the tenth Bridgewater treatise, and is the rival of the great work of Paley on that subject. His treatise on the Objects and Pleasures of Science is another literary masterpiece. His Historical Sketches of Statesmen in the time of George III., as well as of Men of Science and Letters, exhibit varied learning, and familiar acquaintance with almost every department of knowledge. They are written with a clear and vigorous style, though they exhibit a want of polish, and of proper attention to the *labor limæ*. His scientific researches were even carried so far, that, amid the anxious turmoil of professional life, and the nervous agitation of the senate, he could engage in investigations in reference to the polarization of light, and furnish an elaborate discussion on that or kindred subjects, to the Royal Philosophical Society, which the first savans of the age regarded as worthy of their attention. Add to all these attainments, a competent knowledge of classical literature, both of Greece and Rome, an acquaintance with the principal languages of modern Europe, a familiarity with political, moral, and intellectual philosophy, rare conversational powers, and a perfect insight into human nature in all its phases and positions, and the reader will then be able to form an accurate idea of the vast and multiform powers with which Lord Brougham was gifted; and he will cease to wonder at the exalted position which he attained in the history and the evolutions of the age in which he lived.

Among the statesmen who flourished in the era of George IV., William Wilberforce stood pre-eminent for a rare combination of moral worth, benevolent influence, and intellectual power. He was born at Hull, and descended from an ancient and opulent family. His early mental training was combined with rigorous religious instruction; and this circumstance served to impart a peculiar tinge to his whole subsequent career. He was educated at Cambridge, where he formed a close and confidential intimacy with William Pitt. He was noted for his piety not only in his boyhood, but during his youth, manhood, and riper age. Accident threw him into the society of Thomas Clarkson, by whom his attention was first directed to the subject of African slavery—a theme which became the chief and all-absorbing interest of his subsequent existence.

In 1783 he was elected to Parliament from his native city. It was his determination from the moment he entered the Legislature of his country, to devote all his energies to the suppression of Negro slavery in every form, and in every clime in which the power or the influence of Britain extended. He gathered around him a small party of philanthropists possessing sympathies kindred to his own. At that period the project of abolishing the African slave-trade was regarded with hostility by all classes of the nation. The monarch, George III., condemned it, chiefly for the sagacious reason, which suited his calibre of intellect, that it was an innovation. Other classes of the people resisted it because it conflicted either with their prejudices, their interests, or their antipathies. Wilberforce remained at first alone, and yet undaunted. He introduced his first motion bearing on the subject into Parliament in 1789. He succeeded in having a commission appointed to take testimony, and report the result of their labors to the House. Several years were worn away by the necessary and the unnecessary delays which took place in the performance of this task. Nevertheless he persevered until in 1794, after prodigious exertions, he obtained the passage of a bill in the Commons, requiring immediate abolition of the African slave-trade. The Guinea and Congo merchants, whose vast gains from human blood would have been terminated had Mr. Wilberforce been triumphant in the House of Peers, exerted every nerve, and eventually succeeded in crushing the bill in that enlightened and philanthropic assembly. Nevertheless he renewed his motion in 1795, with no better result. Ten successive efforts did this philanthropic statesman make in ten successive years, to gain the support of both Houses of the British Parliament, and in all of these he failed. He then attempted other tactics. He proposed the future abolition of the slave-trade after the termination of five years. In various forms the great measure was suggested by its author in Parliament, meeting uniformly and ultimately with defeat until 1807; when at last, after twenty years of unremitting toil and anxiety, he accomplished the great purpose of his life in the abolition of the African slave-trade throughout the British Empire.

This glorious result was accomplished through the endeavors of a man who stands in the foremost rank of the British states men of his era without possessing any of those qualities which usually characterize that class of men. He was totally destitute of their craft, of their versatility, of their oratorical ability, of their accurate statistical information, and their familiarity with the details and the *data* of political economy. His speeches were not enriched by valuable historical knowledge; his style was parenthetical and obscure; he possessed none of the graces of elocution, none of the splendors of forensic oratory. His manner of speaking was chiefly of the colloquial kind; yet by this quality he succeeded in pleasing, interesting, and charming his auditors, while other men astonished, overwhelmed, and enraptured them. But the result was often equally felicitous and favorable. The colloquial style of Mr. Wilberforce was pleasing in itself, and it was new and rare. But the chief motive power which he wielded, was the vast weight of his moral character. This quality, so rare among statesmen, exerted a prodigious influence in favor of the measures which he advocated. There was a simple majesty in the honesty and benevolence of his purposes, in the purity and consistency of his principles, in the virtue and morality of his life. So pre-eminent was this feature in his character and position, that one of the most startling practical jokes which Sheridan—the antipode of Wilberforce in every imaginable respect—ever perpetrated, had reference to him. One night a watchman of London found an intoxicated man lying in the gutter. He approached him and demanded his name. "I am Mr. Wilberforce," replied Sheridan, and rolled over again in the mire. The influence of this excellent man was greatly increased by the fact that he was no partisan. Though personally attached to Mr. Pitt, he dissented from him on many important questions of national policy. His career was a long, and eventually an honored one. He represented the county of York in Parliament during forty years. He advocated the great measure of Catholic Emancipation and assisted in its consummation. His benevolent labors were not confined to those of political life. His "Practical View of Christianity" is a work of deep thought and evangelical piety; and has exerted a powerful influence in promoting the cause of morality and religion. He died at an advanced age in 1833. He was buried in Westminster Abbey, and his funeral train was graced by the presence of thirty peers, a hundred and thirty members of the House of Commons, and a vast concourse of citizens.

Charles, Earl Grey, held no inconsiderable or secondary place among the statesmen of the era of George IV. He was born in 1764, and entered Parliament in 1785. He at once joined the

Whig party, being seduced thereto, as it has been confidently asserted, by the potent though virtuous fascinations of the beautiful Duchess of Devonshire. At first he took no part in the debates of Parliament. He passed three years in forensic silence. His first speech exhibited clear evidence of his superior oratorical ability. He took a bold stand against the measures of Mr. Pitt, and soon became one of the most formidable members of the Opposition, which was headed by the powerful genius of Charles James Fox. Mr. Grey distinguished himself in the memorable trial of Warren Hastings; and amid an array of varied and brilliant talent such as has scarcely ever before or since been enlisted in the assault or the defence of a great criminal, whose successive and rival displays astonished, delighted, and overwhelmed the most cultivated and fastidious audience which has convened in modern times—amid such a galaxy of genius, that of Mr. Grey held a prominent place. He was a man of chivalrous honor; and when George IV., yet Prince of Wales, desired him to contradict in an equivocal and dishonorable way, the statement of Mr. Fox in Parliament, that the prince was married to Mrs. Fitzherbert, he spurned the base office, and thereby forever offended the unprincipled and unscrupulous prince.

When Mr. Fox became prime minister in 1806, Mr. Grey took the office of First Lord of the Admiralty, and the title of Lord Howick. On the death of Mr. Fox, he became Foreign Secretary and leader of the House of Commons. Soon afterward, on the death of his father, he was called to the Upper House as Earl Grey, and became the leader of the Opposition among the peers. He retained this position during eighteen years. In public life he displayed the stern severity of a censor; in private, he was a model of rigorous virtue, propriety and purity. He contributed greatly in 1820, to defeat the prosecution against the queen, not that he defended the weaknesses of the lady, so much as that he abhorred the unfathomable vices and perfidy of her husband. At length, after the fall of the Wellington ministry in 1831, he became prime minister; and one of his chief measures was the celebrated Reform Bill. He retained office until 1834, when, at the age of seventy he resigned. He reached the patriarchal age of eighty-one, and then expired full of years and honors. Earl Grey was a man of high talent, of inflexible virtue, of scrupulous honor; a noble specimen of an English peer and statesman; whose antipathies, if they were strong and lasting, were generally based on justice and reason; and who amply deserved the high position which he held during so many years, in the estimation of his friends, of his country, and of the civilized world.

From the eminent statesmen of this era, we turn to the most distinguished men of letters who adorned it. The chief of these beyond all controversy was Sir Walter Scott. This prolific and powerful writer was born at Edinburgh in 1771. He was educated in his native city, and in 1786 he became an apprentice to the profession of an attorney in the office of his father. In 1792 he was admitted to practise as an advocate at the Scottish bar; but the dry and repulsive drudgery of the legal profession had few charms for a mind so genial and so rich as his. By a natural and resistless impulse he gradually reverted to literary pursuits. His first publication was a translation of some of the wild romantic ballads of the German Bürger, which had captivated his youthful imagination. As yet the great Magician of the North remained unconscious of the prodigious powers with which nature had gifted him; and his literary labors were for some time confined to the elaboration of inferior works. At length, in 1802 the appearance of his "Border Minstrelsy" indicated the opening of a purer and richer vein within him. This work was followed by the "Lay of the Last Minstrel" and "Marmion," and the "Lady of the Lake," the chief of his poetical productions. These labors were but preparatory to those greater and more illustrious works which he was destined to achieve. Having accidentally discovered an unfinished romance among the old lumber of a garret, he completed it, and published it anonymously under the title of "Waverly." Its success was prodigious, and the impression produced by it almost without a parallel. He now conceived the resolution of continuing his literary labors, not for the purpose of acquiring literary fame, but wealth, in order that he might become a large landowner. Accordingly he produced in rapid succession a long list of novels, beginning with "Guy Mannering," all of which, being published anonymously and exhibiting great power, increased the curiosity and mystification of the public to an intense degree. But his secret soon became divulged; and with its proclamation his fame widely extended. In 1820 he was created a baronet, in acknowledgment of his rare literary and intellectual pre-eminence. Then followed a series of the most able and valuable novels which enrich the English language: the "Bride of Lammermoor," the "Legend of Montrose," and especially "Ivanhoe," taking the pre-eminence for masterly powers of diction, of imagery, of familiarity with the human character, of acquaintance with antiquarian lore, and of every quality which characterizes the consummate romancer. At this period Sir Walter resided at his stately seat of Abbotsford. In 1826 by the failure of his publishers, the Messrs. Constable, he became involved in the enormous sum of a hundred and twenty thousand pounds. He bore calamities so great as this with heroic fortitude, and immediately addressed himself to the herculean task of liquidating his obligations by the labors of his pen. During the five succeeding years until 1831, he produced eight or ten new works of fiction, beside his "Life of Napoleon," "History of Scotland," the "Tales of a Grandfather," and several other elaborate works. By this means fifty-four thousand pounds of his vast indebtedness were liquidated; but his exertions proved to be too great for his physical strength. He became prematurely old; and in 1831 his health rapidly and seriously declined. To avert or postpone impending dissolution, he journeyed to Rome and Naples; and though he enjoyed the usual felicities attendant upon foreign travel, he returned in July, 1832, to his favorite Abbotsford, only to sink rapidly into the grave. He expired six weeks after his return. The genius of Sir Walter Scott was the richest of all those British writers who have labored in the department of romance. The coinage of his prolific and powerful brain are masterpieces in that difficult department of literature, which will retain their undisputed pre-eminence as long as the language in which they are written endures. One of the most commendable acts of the reign of George IV. was the compliment which he paid to virtue and genius in the person of Sir Walter, by creating him a baronet of the United Kingdom in 1820, as a testimony of his personal favor, and his appreciation of his genius.

Second in greatness to Walter Scott among the literary men of this era was George Gordon Byron. This gifted poet was born in London in 1788. His father was a profligate person, who, shortly after his birth, abandoned his mother and himself, proceeded to Valenciennes and there died. The youth of Byron was spent at Aberdeen. In his fourteenth year he was removed to Harrow, where he received the rudiments of academic and classical knowledge. From Harrow he proceeded to Cambridge. During his residence there, his studies were desultory in the extreme; and in 1807 he published his first work entitled Hours of Idleness. This production, which exhibited in exaggeration all the defects with few of the merits of his genius, elicited the famous criticism in the Edinburgh Review, which was penned by Mr. Brougham. The severity of this criticism, falsely attributed to Jeffrey, excited the wrath of the young poet to frenzy, and he wrote in reply his " English Bards and Scotch Reviewers," in which he hurled defiance upon the heads of his literary foes and rivals. In 1809 he entered the British House of Peers, but made no figure in the discussions which took place. He now visited the Levant, Greece, Syria, and Asia Minor, during the progress of which journey he wrote portions of his greatest and best work—" Childe Harold." He returned to England in July, 1811. He immediately published the product of his nomadic labors; and the success of the work was immense. As he himself declared: " he awoke one morning and found himself famous." This was the period of the climax of his popularity. The beauty and splendor of that production were fully appreciated by the public, and many editions of it were rapidly sold. The " Giaour," the " Bride of

Abydos," and the "Corsair," successively followed; and so great had the fame of the writer become that fourteen thousand copies of the last were sold in a single day.

In 1815 this brilliant and successful author was united by marriage to Miss Milbanke; but the match proved to be an unhappy one almost from the day of the nuptials. A year afterward the parties permanently separated. The chief cause of this unfortunate result was to be found in the licentious habits of the poet, whose excesses were beyond all endurance on the part even of the most amiable and complacent of wives. His domestic troubles and ungoverned dissipations did not entirely prevent him from producing some works not unworthy of his genius. "Lara," the "Siege of Corinth," and "Parisina" were successively written and published. Meanwhile his domestic troubles and disputes became more annoying, the public interested themselves provokingly and officiously in his private affairs, they decided, as might have been expected, against him, and the most flattered and adulated poet of modern times fell suddenly and fatally from the dizzy eminence of his popularity, into the depths of general odium and contempt. Driven to despair and frenzy by this experience of the changeableness and injustice of popular praise, the poet determined to abandon his detested country for ever. He passed through France and Switzerland to Italy. At Venice he completed the third and fourth cantos of "Childe Harold," the "Prisoner of Chillon," "Beppo," "Manfred," the "Lament of Tasso," and some minor poems. Between the years 1819 and 1822 he produced, while living at Venice in oriental luxury, his chief dramatic works, including "Sardanapalus," "Werner," the "Deformed Transformed," and "Marino Faliero." But neither his literary fame which continued to increase from year to year, nor his licentious indulgences which were curbed by no restraints, satiated his powerful but diseased mind; and he hoped for relief and an unfelt happiness in plunging with the heroic Greeks into the surges of that revolution which was then raging in their fair and classic land. He arrived at Missilonghi in January, 1824; but his vital powers had been too far exhausted, he survived only a few months, and that magnificent wreck expired in the succeeding April, in the thirty-sixth year of his age. No man in English history ever achieved at so early a period of life so brilliant and so enduring a fame; and had those stupendous talents not been united to one of the most depraved and corrupt spirits which ever animated the human form, they would have achieved monuments of their power, perhaps greater, nobler, and more wondrous than those even of Shakespeare.

Other poets of exalted talent graced the era of George IV.; among whom belong Campbell, the greatest lyric writer whom England has produced, but who also excels in other species of poetic composition. He may justly be denominated the Peerless Bard of Hope; for his poem on that subject contains stanzas of matchless beauty. His "Mariners of England," "Hohenlinden," "Battle of the Baltic," and "Last Man," all possess a kind of lurid, meteoric, unearthly grandeur, which, while it delights, also appalls the reader, and retains a deathless grasp upon his memory and imagination. Thomas Moore was essentially the poet of Love, both Oriental and Hibernian; the Ovid of modern times both in genius and in morals. His images are often brilliant, and generally pleasing; he is the favorite chiefly of women and youth. Yet a few of his minor productions, such as "Oft in the stilly night," "The Last Rose of Summer," and "Love's Young Dream," find a welcome echo in every human breast, and will ever be cherished as among the brightest and purest gems of genius. Secondary and inferior to these poetic master-spirits were Rogers, the author of the "Pleasures of Memory;" Southey, the writer of "Thalaba;" Wordsworth, the poet of nature and the poor; Coleridge, the erratic, philosophical, unhappy metaphysician and bard, who might have accomplished anything, and effected almost nothing; the pathetic and polished Hemans; Crabbe, the unimaginative, and Tennyson, the eccentric; these constitute the chief stars in that rare galaxy of gifted minds, which render the era of George IV. an Augustan age of British poetry.

Nor was that age deficient in the production of able and profound thinkers. Dugald Stewart, Thomas Brown, Malthus, Paley, Bentham, were all men of vast depth and originality as thinkers and writers in the several departments of Mental Philosophy, Natural Theology, and Political Economy. This was the era of the birth of that keen and powerful class of critics whose abilities founded and built up the Edinburgh Review and Blackwood's Magazine, and introduced a new, more just, and more startling style of criticism than had ever been known in the history of British literature. Jeffrey, Brougham, Mackintosh, Sidney Smith, Alison, Macaulay, Lockhart, and Wilson, constituted this remarkable assemblage of writers, whose essays rival in beauty, while they excel in profundity and thoroughness, the productions of the elder school of British essayists, of whom Addison and Steele were the chief. Turner, Lingard, Tytler, Hallam, Mitford and Grote, were the most eminent historians of this period; Marryatt, Miss Edgeworth, Bulwer, and D'Israeli were its chief novelists; Sir Thomas Lawrence, Turner, Copley, Landseer, Wilkie, and Flaxman, were its most distinguished artists; Mrs. Siddons, Miss O'Niell, John Kemble, and Edmund Kean, were its most accomplished tragedians; Chalmers, Robert Hall, John Foster and Edward Irving were the most eloquent and popular of its pulpit orators. The details of the lives and labors of all these illustrious persons are necessarily excluded from a general survey such as the present; but every reader in any degree familiar with the literary history of the era of George IV. will at once recognize the varied power, richness, and splendor of the intellectual wealth which was lavished by British genius, upon British law, letters and art, during its continuance. It may therefore be truly said, that all these high spheres of intellectual effort flourished with more than ordinary vigor at this propitious period; for though we have here enumerated but the greatest names of the time, and though these be comparatively few, the general spirit of improvement prevailed; the "schoolmaster was abroad," thought, action, hope, were vigorous, and progress in every branch of human endeavor and improvement was steady and decisive. This statement applies with peculiar force after the wars which had desolated Europe had been terminated; after the nations had recovered from the collapse which the unaccustomed repose of peace had produced; and after the conclusion of the regency, and the commencement of the sovereignty of George IV. Prolific as are many eras of British history in the production of events of vast importance and of thrilling interest, the period of The Four Georges, the survey of which we here terminate, must be regarded as possessing no secondary consequence. During its stormy and adventurous progress, the principles of constitutional freedom, which are the great boast of the British nation, were clearly defined and permanently established; the limits of the empire in the East were vastly enlarged and aggrandized; those in the Western World were indeed lopped off and curtailed; but this apparent calamity led to the consummation of events most glorious for humanity, if they were pernicious to Great Britain, inasmuch as it secured the establishment of a numerous cluster of powerful republics which are now the refuge and the shrine of the oppressed of all nations : while the Georges held rule, the European continent was upheaved by the throes of revolution and of warfare; that continent was again in turn pacified and rendered stable; and when the last monarch of that name descended to the tomb, he left behind him, without any merit on his part, an Empire more extensive, more powerful, more enlightened, and more opulent, than that which had, in any previous age, acknowledged the supremacy of the British sceptre.

APPENDIX.

No. I.

REPORT OF THE ROYAL COMMISSIONERS ON THE CHARGES PRE-
FERRED AGAINST QUEEN CAROLINE.

May it please Your Majesty.

Your Majesty having been graciously pleased by an instrument under your Majesty's Royal Sign Manual, a copy of which is annexed to this Report, to "authorize, empower, and direct us to inquire into the truth "of certain written declarations, touching the conduct of Her Royal "Highness the Princess of Wales, an abstract of which had been laid "before Your Majesty, and to examine upon oath such persons as we "should see fit, touching and concerning the same, and to report to "Your Majesty the result of such examinations." We have, in dutiful obedience to Your Majesty's commands, proceeded to examine the several witnesses, the copies of whose depositions we have hereunto annexed; and, in further execution of the said commands, we now most respectfully submit to Your Majesty the report of these examinations as it has appeared to us: But we beg leave at the same time humbly to refer Your Majesty, for more complete information, to the examinations themselves, in order to correct any error of judgment, into which we may have unintentionally fallen, with respect to any part of this business. On a reference to the above mentioned declarations, as the necessary foundation of all our proceedings, we found that they consisted in certain statements, which had been laid before His Royal Highness the Prince of Wales, respecting the conduct of Her Royal Highness the Princess. That these statements not only imputed to

Her Royal Highness great impropriety and indecency of behavior, but expressly asserted, partly on the ground of certain alleged declarations from the Princess's own mouth, and partly on the personal observation of the informants, the following most important facts; viz. That Her Royal Highness had been pregnant in the year 1802, in consequence of an illicit intercourse, and that she had in the same year been secretly delivered of a male child, which child ever since that period had been brought up by Her Royal Highness in her own house, and under her immediate inspection.

These allegations thus made, had, as we found, been followed by declarations from other persons, who had not indeed spoken to the important facts of the pregnancy or delivery of Her Royal Highness, but had related other particulars, in themselves extremely suspicious, and still more so when connected with the assertions already mentioned.

In the painful situation, in which His Royal Highness was placed, by these communications, we learnt that His Royal Highness had adopted the only course which could in our judgment, with propriety be followed. When informations such as these, had been thus confidently alleged, and particularly detailed, and had been in some degree supported by collateral evidence, applying to other points of the same nature (though going to a far less extent,) one line only could be pursued.

Every sentiment of duty to Your Majesty, and of concern for the public welfare, required that these particulars should not be withheld from Your Majesty, to whom more particularly belonged the cognizance of a matter of State, so nearly touching the honour of Your Majesty's Royal Family, and by possibility, affecting the Succession of Your Majesty's crown.

Your Majesty had been pleased, on your part, to view the subject in the same light. Considering it as a matter which on every account, demanded the most immediate investigation, Your Majesty had thought fit to commit into our hands the duty of ascertaining, in the first instance, what degree of credit was due to the informations, and thereby enabling Your Majesty to decide what further conduct to adopt concerning them.

On this review, therefore, of the matters thus alleged, and of the course hitherto pursued upon them, we deemed it proper in the first place to examine those persons in whose declarations the occasion for this inquiry had originated. Because if they, on being examined upon oath, had retracted or varied their assertions, all necessity for further investigation might possibly have been precluded.

We accordingly first examined on oath the principal informants, Sir John Douglas, and Charlotte his wife: who both positively swore, the former to his having observed the fact of the pregnancy of Her Royal Highness, and the latter to all the important particulars contained in her former declaration and above referred to. Their examinations are annexed to this Report, and are circumstantial and positive.

The most material of those allegations, into the truth of which he had been directed to inquire, being thus far supported by the oath of the parties from whom they had proceeded, we then felt it our duty to follow up the Inquiry by the examination of such other persons as we judged best able to afford us information, as to the facts in question.

We thought it beyond all doubt that, in this course of inquiry, many particulars must be learnt which would be necessarily conclusive on the truth or falsehood of these declarations. So many persons must have been witnesses to the appearances of an actually existing pregnancy; so many circumstances must have been attendant upon a real delivery; and difficulties so numerous and insurmountable must have been involved in any attempt to account for the infant in question, as the child of another woman, if it had been in fact the child of the Princess; that we entertained a full and confident expectation of arriving at complete proof, either in the affirmative, or negative, on this part of the subject.

This expectation was not disappointed. We are happy to declare to Your Majesty our perfect conviction that there is no foundation whatever for believing that the child now with the Princess is the child of Her Royal Highness, or that she was delivered of any child in the year 1802; nor has any thing appeared to us which would warrant the belief that she was pregnant in that year, or at any other period within the compass of our inquiries. The identity of the child, now with the Princess, its parentage, the place and the date of its birth, the time and the circumstances of its being first taken under Her Royal Highness's protection, are all established by such a concurrence both of positive and circumstantial evidence, as can, in our judgment, leave no question on this part of the subject. The child was beyond all doubt, born in the Brownlow-Street Hospital, on the 11th day of July, 1802, of the body of Sophia Austin, and was first brought to the Princess's House in the month of November following. Neither should we be more warranted in expressing any doubt respecting the alleged pregnancy of the

Princess, as stated in the original declarations;—a fact so fully contradicted, and by so many witnesses to whom, if true, it must in various ways have been known, that we cannot think it entitled to the smallest credit. The testimonies on these two points are contained in the annexed depositions and letters. We have not partially abstracted them in this Report, lest, by any unintentional omission, we might weaken their effect; but we humbly offer to Your Majesty this our clear and unanimous judgment upon them, formed on full deliberation, and pronounced without hesitation, on the result of the whole Inquiry.

We do not, however, feel ourselves at liberty, much as we should wish it, to close our Report here. Besides the allegations of the pregnancy and delivery of the Princess, those declarations, on the whole of which Your Majesty has been pleased to command us to inquire and report, contain, as we have already remarked, other particulars respecting the conduct of her Royal Highness, such as must, especially considering her exalted rank and station, necessarily give occasion to very unfavourable interpretations.

From the various depositions and proofs annexed to this Report, particularly from the examinations of Robert Bidgood, William Cole, Frances Lloyd, and Mrs. Lisle, Your Majesty will perceive that several strong circumstances of this description have been positively sworn to by witnesses, who cannot, in our judgment, be suspected of any unfavourable bias, and whose veracity, in this respect, we have seen no ground to question.

On the precise bearing and effect of the facts thus appearing, it is not for us to decide: these we submit to Your Majesty's wisdom: But we conceive it to be our duty to report on this part of the Inquiry, as distinctly as on the former facts: that as on the one hand, the facts of pregnancy and delivery are to our minds satisfactorily disproved, so on the other hand we think, that the circumstances to which we now refer, particularly those stated to have passed between Her Royal Highness and Captain Manby, must be credited until they shall receive some decisive contradiction; and, if true, are justly entitled to the most serious consideration.

We cannot close this Report, without humbly assuring Your Majesty, that it was, on every account, our anxious wish, to have executed this delicate trust, with as little publicity as the nature of the case would possibly allow; and we entreat Your Majesty's permission to express our full persuasion, that if this wish has been disappointed, the failure is not imputable to any thing unnecessarily said or done by us. All which is most humbly submitted to your Majesty.

  (Signed)   ERSKINE,
          SPENCER,
          GRENVILLE,
July 14th, 1806. ELLENBOROUGH.
A true Copy,
 J. Becket.

No. II.

DEPOSITION OF SOPHIA AUSTIN.

I KNOW the child which is now with the Princess of Wales. I am the mother of it. I was delivered of it four years ago the 11th of July next, at Brownlow-street Hospital. I have lain-in there three times. William, who is with the Princess, is the second child I laid-in of there. It was marked in the right hand with red wine. My husband was a laborer in the Dock-yard at Deptford. When peace was proclaimed, a number of the workmen were discharged, and my husband was one who was discharged. I went to the Princess with a petition on a Saturday, to try to get my husband restored. I lived at that time at Deptford, New-Row, No. 7, with a person of the name of Bearblock. He was a milkman. The day I went to the Princess with the petition, was a fortnight before, the 6th of November. Mr. Bennet, a baker in New-street, was our dealer, and I took the child to Mr. Bennet's when I went to receive my husband's wages every week from the time I left the Hospital till I carried the child to the Princess. I knew Mr. Stikeman only by having seen him once before, when I went to apply for a letter to Brownlow-street Hospital. When I went to Montague House, I desired Mr. Stikeman to present my petition. He said they were denied to do such things, but seeing me with a baby he could do no less. He then took the child from me, and was a long time gone. He then brought me back the child, and brought half-a-guinea which the ladies sent me. He said if the child had been younger, he could have got it taken care of for me, but desired that I would come up again. I went up again on the Monday following, and I saw Mr. Stikeman. Mr. Stikeman afterwards came several times to us, and appointed me to take the child to Montague House on the 5th of November, but it rained all day, and I did not take it. Mr. Stikeman came down to me on the Saturday the 6th of November, and I took the child on that day to the Princess's house. The Princess was out. I waited till she returned. She saw the child, and asked its age. I went down into the coffee-room, and they gave me some arrow-root to wean the child; for I was suckling the child at this time, and when I had weaned the child, I was to bring it and leave it with the Princess. I did wean the child, and brought it to the Princess's house on the 15th of November, and left it there, and it has been with the Princess ever since. I saw the child last Whit-Monday, and I swear that it is my child.

SOPHIA AUSTIN.

Sworn at Lord Grenville's House in Downing-street, the seventh day of June, 1806, before us,

ERSKINE,
SPENCER,
GRENVILLE,
ELLENBOROUGH.

A true Copy,
    J. Becket.

No. III.

TESTIMONY OF THE ROYAL PHYSICIANS RESPECTING THE INSANITY OF GEORGE III.

"I should like to give an account of the first consultation we had with Dr. Willis.—The day that I introduced Dr. Willis to the King, I summoned the rest of his Majesty's physicians to a consultation at my house. It was there first settled as a principle, that quiet of body and mind were to be endeavored to be obtained by every means possible; and that every thing should be kept carefully from his Majesty that might tend to prevent this desirable acquisition. It was settled that a regular coercion should be made use of; that every thing should be kept from his Majesty that was likely to excite any emotion; that though his Majesty had not shewn any signs of an intention to injure himself, yet that it was absolutely necessary, considering the sudden impulses to which his distemper subjects people, to put every thing out of the way that could do any mischief. To all this Dr. Willis assented; yet the very next day he put a razor into his Majesty's hand, and a penknife. When I saw the doctor next, I asked him how he could venture to do such a thing? He said, he shuddered at what he had done. As he made use of this expression, I did not think it necessary to say much to him upon the subject. On the 12th of December, as I apprehend, the King took a walk in the garden, and some of the royal children were shewn to him—this produced a considerable emotion, which was accompanied with acts demonstrating that emotion, as I was informed, to the best of my memory, by Mr. Keate.—Notwithstanding this effect of seeing the children, Dr. Willis, the next day, introduced that Person, whose great and amiable qualities, we all know, must necessarily make her the dearest and tenderest object of his Majesty's thoughts—the interview was short—his Majesty was soon afterwards in a great state of irritation; and the strict coercion was, I believe, for the first time, actually applied that night—the blisters were put on that night likewise. The next time that I saw Dr. Willis, I spoke to him upon this subject with some degree of sharpness, because it was contrary to my opinion, and contrary to what had been settled in consultation; for it had been referred, that whatever could be done by deliberation, should be settled by consultation; that the conduct of his Majesty in the interior room, should be left to Dr. Willis's discretion, because it did not admit of deliberation.—I do not know that I convinced the Doctor that his opinion was wrong, but that the act was contrary to what was laid down in consultation could not be denied.—I was always considered, by the highest authority, as the first physician, and therefore thought myself particularly responsible; I thought myself obliged to look into, and to inquire after every thing that related to his Majesty; I did not suppose myself in a different situation upon the arrival of Dr. Willis, and therefore took the liberty of speaking to him with some degree of authority. I remember when his three attendants arrived, I sent for them into the physicians' room, examined them very carefully, particularly as to the temper with which they conducted themselves towards those whom they attended, and spoke to them, as they were strangers to me, in such a manner as to let them know that their conduct would be strictly observed.—My being first physician made me talk to Dr. Willis about every thing that I heard of, that did not appear to me to be quite accurate, and sometimes led to disputes.—I informed the Doctor that he was there in a double capacity—as physician and attendant on his Majesty in the interior room; that I must take my share in directing what related to him in the capacity of physician, though I should not interfere with respect to the conduct of his Majesty in the interior room. Not many days after this transaction I observed a book in his Majesty's hands, which affected me much, and immediately determined me to bring a charge against Dr. Willis, for what I thought bad practice.—I do not mean to bring the story of this book as a fault, because

I believe there was no intention to convey such a book to his Majesty: it was the play of King Lear, not in a volume of Shakspeare, but it was a corrected Lear, by Colman, and mixed with his plays. I can have no reason to think that Dr. Willis could suspect that such a play was in that volume. His Majesty told me that Dr. Willis brought him the book, and Dr. Willis did not deny it, when I spoke to him on the subject.—I do not bring this as a fault, but it was the circumstance that determined me to put in execution what I had been thinking of before, with respect to Dr. Willis; for his Majesty's observation on the book affected me strangely. I carried an account of this to the Prince of Wales, and he desired me, as he had done in every case of difficulty that had happened, from the beginning of the illness, to lay the affair before the Lord Chancellor. The Lord Chancellor went to Kew, I believe; and the result was, when I saw the Lord Chancellor, that the rules of the consultation should be strictly obeyed.—Dr. Willis has, a second time, introduced the same great and amiable Person. I was informed that some degree of irritation came on in the night; but having collected, as I thought, from several small circumstances, that the power of introducing persons to his Majesty was to be left entirely to Dr. Willis, I did not make any complaint about it."

"Can you ascertain the time of the last interview?"——"I cannot."

"What time of day was the first interview?"

"I apprehend the first interview was in the evening—and that the interview happened, not only without consulting his Majesty's physicians collectively, but that Dr. Gisborne, who was in the house that evening, and sitting in the anti-chamber when the introduction took place, was not consulted upon the occasion."

"Do you recollect any conversation you had with Dr. Willis concerning the King's being asleep, or disposed to sleep, at a time when you was going in to his Majesty?"

"I remember a morning when Dr. Willis said his Majesty had had a bad night, which I myself had been acquainted with by asking the page, as I passed by the King's anti-chamber, the door of which I opened as I was going into the physician's room.—In the physician's room I mentioned that I had learnt the King had had a very bad night, but was then fallen asleep.—I sat down, and what discourse passed between me and Dr. Willis then, about the night, I do not know—a few words only.—The Doctor soon went out of the room, and when he returned, said, 'That the King was not sleeping, for that he spoke.'—I got up, the attending physician of the day with me, and walked towards Dr. Willis—we went together through the anti-chamber; when I arrived at the door of his Majesty's bed-room, Dr. Willis said, You may open the door, a circumstance that I do not recollect, ever to have happened to me before—somebody else generally opening the door:—when I opened it, I found that the room was dark—I stepped forwards very slowly; as soon as I had gone the width of the door, I was visible to his Majesty. The door being open, his Majesty immediately addressed himself very pointedly to me, saying, 'I am glad to see you,' and adding his wish to be released from the state he was then in, which was a state of coercion. I hesitated; went one step back to look for Dr. Willis, who was standing very near me. I said something to the Doctor, and he immediately replied, in substance, that if his Majesty complained I might comply with his request. In consequence of which it was done, by my desire. I staid but a short time with his Majesty, and, as I was walking back, I said, 'I had some doubts whether the complying with his Majesty's request was not improper, for he is in a very irritated state.' Dr. Willis said, 'His Majesty will rise presently, and then we shall be able to do without coercion.'"

No. IV.

SPECIMEN OF EDMUND BURKE'S ELOQUENCE ON THE REGENCY BILL.

Mr. BURKE rose, and declared himself astonished that the Bill should be proposed to be read a second time, without the House having heard a syllable as to what the principles of the Bill, as opened and acted upon by the clauses and provisions of the Bill, were. He had, he said, often known the principles upon which a Bill had been ordered to be brought in, either totally lost sight of in the Bill itself, or so violently strained and departed from in the various clauses, that scarcely a single principle upon which the House had resolved to legislate, was to be found in the Bill, or to be found entire. It behoved the House, therefore, at all times, to watch great and important Bills narrowly, and to see that they were not deceived and deluded; and that while they meant and had resolved to pass a Bill for one purpose, they were not induced to pass a Bill, containing provisions to answer a very different purpose. There might possibly, he said, exist some doubts as to the constitutional and legal competency of the character in which they were then proceeding to act as a branch of a perfect legislature; in argument and in debate, he and others had much questioned the validity of the Commission, under the authority of which Parliament had been opened; but admitting for the present that there had been exercised a competent power to make the House a Parliament, and enable them to do the act, upon which they were proceeding, they ought to see what the Bill was, before they went on with it, and therefore, though he meant not to debate the subject at large, he should take the liberty of calling the attention of the House, before they read the Bill a second time, to the extent of its provisions, and the extraordinary manner in which the Resolutions that the two Houses had come to were now attempted to be made use of, and carried into effect. Never surely, said he, was there a time when the people of England and that House were so called on to see what they were doing, and to examine, with every possible degree of prudence and foresight, the serious and important consequences what they were doing might lead to. His Majesty's incapacity to exercise the Royal Authority had been established, to the conviction of the two Houses, in a manner that left all possibility of doubt out of the question; indeed, if the examination of his Majesty's physicians had not taken place, the fact would be too clear to have admitted a dispute, from a great variety of consequences not necessary to be detailed, because they were consequences which they not only saw but felt. The duration of his Majesty's malady, the turns it might take, the disguises it might assume, lay hidden in the secret recesses of the dispositions of Providence. His Majesty was insane, but his malady was not like that of some other persons who were under confinement in houses and places destined for such purposes, intermittent, various, subject to degrees, lucid intervals, and occasional visitations of reason, but his faculties were totally eclipsed; and as Dr. Willis, in the sanguine temper, ungoverned zeal, and impetuous rashness of his mind, could not take upon him to decide what would be the duration of his Majesty's illness, it was not likely that physicians of more moderate minds, of cooler judgments, and of more sober reason, should take upon them to decide the duration of the malady that had struck at the Sovereignty of the Empire, and wounded every thing that was Sovereign, either in the political or natural capacity of the King upon the Throne. Not any thing like a moderate time, therefore, had been promised for the duration of his Majesty's illness; the malady of the Monarch consequently was fixed to no known definite time, and at that moment a Bill was brought in totally to separate and parcel out the Royal Authority, so as to leave only the chance of a Government necessarily so weak and impotent, as to be scarce able to stand at all. All limited power, Mr. Burke said, was from its nature feeble, and the circumstance of its being only temporary and uncertain, rendered it still more deficient in vigor and in efficacy. The first object of the Bill was, he observed, to nominate a person to hold this weak and almost useless Government. The next purpose it avowed its aim to effect, was the raising a power in opposition to that Royal Authority. Those who gave such powers, were clearly to be the masters of them, and there could no doubt remain but that the Bill was drawn with a design to answer the rash ends of the mad and daring ambition of a Right Honorable Gentleman, whose conduct had but too plainly manifested his view, and his intentions. Thus there was a partition of power, in which the Prince was destined to have no other than an *official* character, while all the Palaces, Offices, and Dignities, were given to another. This partition was more odious and offensive than the famous partition treaty relative to the succession, on the death of the last Prince of the House of Austria. It was a partition founded on a most wicked and malicious principle; every thing that was degrading and restrictive, every thing that stamped a suspicion on the character of the Prince, and conveyed a gross affront to his Royal Highness, by holding him out as a person not to be trusted, as a person whom the public ought to suspect, and were likely to be deceived by, was done by what was withheld in the Bill; while, on the other hand, all that was graceful, all that was honorable, all that was calculated to hold up a character as great, virtuous, and meritorious, was given where an opposition was set up to oppose and counteract the executive Government. This Bill affected to give the Royal Authority, and tended to answer the purposes of a faction against that authority. Its real object was to defeat the preferable claim of the Prince of Wales to the Regency, in the very moment that the Claim had been in practice and in effect, found to be irresistible, and to set up what had been termed the *equal* Right of a Subject as paramount to the Prince's Right. Mr. Burke, with great warmth, declaimed upon the purport of the Bill, in the view of which he chose to consider it, and among a variety of other invectives against it, said, the doctrine of divine right, which had been exploded in the House of the Stuarts, was now revived in favor of another House. The present Minister, he understood, had been called an *heaven-born* Minister in another place; they might fairly suppose, therefore, that he had a divine right to take to himself a larger portion of power and of patronage than he chose to leave to the

Prince on the Throne; and when he said the Prince on the Throne, he begged to be understood as alluding to the Prince of Wales, sitting on the Throne in his delegated character, on the behalf, in the name, and as the representative of his father. But if the Minister was already declared by one of his fanatics to be an *heaven-born* Minister, he did not wonder at his considering himself as acting under the influence of a divine right, and that he should go any lengths to secure the power that he aimed at. By the present Bill, all the powers of distributing honors, and even charity, were denied the Regent. There were, Mr. Burke observed, a variety of lesser instances of bounty annexed to the Crown, that the Regent was most invidiously restrained from. There were employed by the Household, painters, architects, poets, historiographers, and many other artists and artificers of different degrees, ranks, orders, and descriptions, to reward whom, the Prince was deprived of every possible opportunity. He was left without a table, without any provision that resembled the shadow of royalty, further than what he had enjoyed as Prince of Wales, from his Majesty's personal bounty. Mr. Burke enlarged upon this topic considerably and with his customary ardor of expression. Though, he trusted, he honored her Majesty as much as any other subject, he did not think she ought to have that patronage. She might be nominated to hold it, but he was confident the exercise of it would devolve into other hands. The Bill was calculated, he said, to eclipse the Royal dignity, and to reduce the Regent to an *official* character, which was a scandal to the nation, and the more so, as coming from those who were thought men of honor, and therefore he should consider it as a wicked, base, and unjust action, not more degrading to the Prince of Wales, than disgraceful to the perpetrators. By the Bill, responsibility was given to the Prince of Wales, who was saddled by having all the onerous duties of Government imposed on him, without having any grateful powers to counterbalance the burthen, while the dignity, splendor, and real distribution of emoluments, were given to the Minister. The Bill meant not only to degrade the Prince of Wales, but the whole House of Brunswick, who were to be *outlawed, excommunicated,* and *attainted* as having forfeited all claim to the confidence of the country!

INDEX.

A

Addison, Joseph, his genius and writings, 68, 84, 85.
American Colonies, origin of difficulties with, 224; first Congress convenes at Philadelphia, 227; conclusion of the revolutionary war, 229.
Anne, Queen, her accession, 2; her death, 18.
Anne, Princess, her marriage to the Duke of Orange, 103.
Anson, Commodore, his successes, 134.
Atterbury, Bishop, plots for the Pretender, 59; his profanity, 90.
Augusta, Dowager Princess of Wales, death of, 225.

B

Birmingham, riots at, 258.
Black Hole, horrors of, 166.
Blenheim, battle of, 3; its results, 5; rejoicing in England, 6.
Bolingbroke, flight to France, 41; his return to England, 68; his intellectual and moral qualities, 71, 72, 73.
Brent, Miss, becomes mistress of George I., 75.
Bonaparte, Napoleon, his hostility to England, 264; military operations of, 265; his autograph letter to George III., 267; his downfall, 278; escapes from Elba, 279; prepares to oppose the coalition, 280; battle of Charleroi, 281; battle of Waterloo, 283.
Brougham, Lord, his birth, 423; enters Parliament, 423; rivalry between him and Canning, 424; qualities of his mind, 424; peculiarities of his eloquence, 425; his defence of Queen Caroline, 372, 426; becomes chancellor, 426; his diversified talents, 427.
Braddock, defeat at Fort Du Quesne, 155.
Brunswick, princes of, 20, 21; Caroline of, 338.

Bute, Lord, his history and character, 181; becomes premier, 191; measures of, 192; signs treaty of Fontainbleau,192; his great unpopularity, 195; he resigns, 196.
Burke, Edmund, his rise, 207; animosity to Warren Hastings, 242; his detestation of the French revolution, 255; his personal qualities, 302; his eloquence, 303.
Byng, Admiral, his trial and execution, 157, 158.
Byron, Lord, his personal history, 434, 435; his writings, 435.

C

Canning, his birth, 418; circumstances of his youth, 419; first speech in Parliament, 420; his principles, 421; his eloquence, 422; enters the Cabinet, 270, 405; retort on Mr. Brougham, 399; his mental qualities, 422; his death, 406.
Campbell, Thomas, his poetical works, 436.
Caroline Queen of George II., her character, 129, 130; last sickness and death, 124-127.
Carteret, Lord, his eloquence, 99; becomes Premier, 140.
Catholics, Roman, prejudices against, 63; Catholic Association, 402; Catholic Relief Bill passed, 409.
Caroline of Brunswick, her marriage, 339; charges against her, 352; travels on the continent, 362; her conduct, 364; second prosecution against her, 364; her return to England, 365; her trial before the House of Lords, 369; her council, 371; her acquittal, 373; her abortive attempt to be crowned, 381; her last sickness, 383; her death, 384; her burial, 387.
Charlotte of Mecklenburg Strelitz, 178; marriage to George III., 179.
Charlotte, Princess, her appearance, 356, deserts her father, 360.
Chatham, Lord. (See Pitt.)

452

INDEX.

Chesterfield, Lord, his character, 98.
Clarence, William Henry, Duke of, 395; his promotions, 395; connection with Mrs. Jordan, 396; his personal qualities, 396.
Clive, Lord, commencement of military career, 164, 165; heroic conduct at Arcot, 165; victory at Plassey, 167.
Corn Laws, proposed repeal of, 404.
Cornwallis, Archbishop, his levity reproved, 319.
Criminal Jurisprudence, efforts to reform, 294.
Culloden, battle of, 145.
Cumberland, Duke of, his character and death, 206.

D

Darby, Miss, mistress of George IV., 326; separate provision made for her, 327.
Denman. Lord, his defence of Queen Caroline, 373.
Dettingen, battle of, 141.
Douglas, Lady, her intrigues against Queen Caroline, 351.
Dowlah. Surajah, cruelty of, 167.
Dupleix, his achievements in India, 163, 164.

E

Egremont, Earl of, succeeds Pitt as Premier, 185.
Emmet, Robert, his insurrection and death, 265, 266.
Eugene, Prince, gallantry at Blenheim, 4.

F

Fitzherbert, Mrs., history of her connection with George IV., 335; her claims as his wife, 337.
Fontainbleau, treaty of, 192; discussions on, 193.
Fontenoy, battle of, 143.
Fox, Henry, enters the cabinet, 159.
Fox. Charles James, rise of, 225; his East India Bill, 239; becomes Premier, 269; his personal qualities, 304; his eloquence, 305; causes of his popularity, 306.
Francis, Sir Philip, author of Junius, 312.
France, war with, 261.
Frederic, Prince of Wales, 94: hostility of his parents, 95; proposals for his marriage, 112; his bride, 114; marriage ceremonies, 114; his death, 148, 149.
French Revolution, effects of, 259, 260.

G

Gay, John, his poetical works, 88.
George I., birth of, 22; suitor of the Princess Anne, 22; becomes elector of Hanover, 23; his marriage, 24; his accession to the British throne, 34; arrival in England, 85; state of the nation, 36, 39; his coronation, 40; his mistresses, 43; journey to Hanover, 44; his death, 80, 81; his character, 81, 82, 83.
George II., birth of, and youth, 91; his marriage, 92; his social habits, 93; his mistresses, 94; his accession, 96; his first Cabinet, 97; his visit to Hanover, 109; takes a new mistress. 110; narrowly escapes shipwreck, 118, 119; buffoonery on the death of his wife, 126, 127; perils at Dettingen, 141; his death, 168; his character, 170; writers during his reign, 171.
George III., birth of, 175; chief incident of his boyhood, 176; connection with Hannah Lightfoot, 176; proposals to marry Charlotte of Mecklenburg Strelitz, 177; his accession, 179; overruled by Lord Bute, 181; his coronation, 189, 190; his first indications of insanity, 204; incidents of his domestic life, 230; attempts to assassinate him, 249, 262; attack of insanity, 251; his recovery, 253; renders thanks in St. Paul's cathedral. 253: another attack of insanity, 263: minute details respecting his insanity, 273, 274, 275; his moral qualities, 320; religion during his reign, 320; his general character, 321.
George IV., birth of, 323; his early education, 324; his personal appearance, 325; his first mistress, 326; removes to Carlton House, 328; becomes enamored with Mrs. Fitzherbert, 328; her history, 329; debts of the Prince, 331; removes to Brighton, 332; proposed marriage with Caroline of Brunswick, 334; difficulties with Mrs. Fitzherbert, 336; his connection with the Marchioness of Hertford, 337; his marriage with Caroline, 339, 341, 342; his enormous debts, 345; his connection with Lady Jersey, 346; his want of principle, 349: his hostility to his wife, 350; intrigues of Lady Douglas, 351; has a commission appointed to prosecute the Princess Caroline, 352; her vindication, 353; he becomes Regent, 356; he becomes King, 376; his coronation, 375; refuses to allow the Queen to be crowned, 381; exultation at his wife's death, 385; his hostility to reform, 407; reasons of his Protestantism, 407; his last illness, 415; his death, 416; his character, 417.
Gibbon, Edward, personal incidents, 315, 316; his historical works. 317.
Goderich, Lord, succeeds Mr. Canning as Premier, 406.
Grafton, Duke of, interview with Pitt, 214; resigns the Premiership, 222; Horace Walpole's opinion of him, 222.
Grenville, George, becomes Premier. 196.
Grey, Charles, Earl, his youth, 431; his parliamentary abilities, 431; his personal qualities, 432.

H

Hanover, origin of house of, 19; treaty of, 66, 67.
Hastings, Warren, his early history, 244, 245; measures of his administration in India, 246; his trial in Westminster Hall, 247; his ultimate acquittal, 243.

INDEX. 453

Hawke, Admiral, great victory, 161.
Hervey, Lord, fate after Caroline's death, 128, 129.
Howard, Mrs., mistress of George II., 108.
Hume, David, 171; his merits as an historian, 317.
Huskisson, Mr., his financial abilities, 398; his great public services, 398.

Nelson, Lord, victory of Trafalgar, 263.
Newcastle, Duke of, his character, 97; becomes Premier, 154.
Newton, Sir Isaac, his genius, 89.
North, Lord, becomes Premier, 223; his personal and political qualities, 299, 300.
Nottingham, Earl of, his bill in Parliament in favor of the Trinity, 60, 61.

I

India, East, British Company, its origin, 162; its charter renewed, 220; vast extension of its power and wealth, 232, 233, outrages perpetrated on the subject natives, 234; influence and power of Hastings, 235.
Ireland, unsettled state of, 243; continued troubles in, 401.

O

O'Connell, Daniel, his abilities and labors, 403.
Orangemen, their aims, 402.
Orange, Prince William of, 2.
Oudenarde, battle of, 12; its results, 13.

J

Jacobite epitaph on Prince Frederic, 150.
Jersey, Lady, mistress of George IV., 346.
Jesuits, order of, their character, 410, 411.
Junius, publication of his letters, 221.

P

Pelham, Henry, his qualities, 152.
Pension Bill, the, 139.
Perceval, Mr., becomes Premier, 356; his assassination, 356.
Pitt, William, his first speech in the House of Commons, 112; rise of his popularity, 151; becomes Prime Minister, 159; immediate results. 160; splendid achievements of his administration, 184; singular disease of, 212, 213; his letters to George III., 216; recovers his health, 218; peculiarities of his eloquence, 297; his personal qualities, 298.
Pitt, William, the Younger, his first appearance in Parliament, 231; he becomes Premier, 240; peculiarities of his eloquence, 241; his admirable measures, 243; his project respecting unclaimed dividends, 257; his death, 269; his intellectual qualities, 306; his patriotism, 307.
Plassey, victory of, 167.
Platen, Countess von, her conduct and character, 27.
Pope, Alexander, his life and writings, 87, 88.
Pragmatic sanction, 64.
Priestly, Joseph, 258.
Prestonpans, battle of, 144.
Pretender, heads the rebellion in Scotland, 45; his defeat, 46; his second rebellion, 55; his victory at Prestonpans, 144; his defeat at Culloden, 145.
Pulteney, William, 69, 102.

K

Kent, Edward Augustus, Duke of, 389; early discipline of, 390; his residence at Gibraltar, 391; his bravery, 392; becomes Governor of Gibraltar, 393; his marriage, 394; his death, 394.
Koenigsmark, family of, 25; Philip von, 26; his connection with the wife of the Elector of Hanover, 28; his assassination, 29.

L

Law, his adventures, 47, 48.
Legge, Mr., becomes Chancellor of the Exchequer, 154.
Lexington, battle of, 228.
Louis XIV., his colossal power, 1; his acquisitions of territory, 2; his losses by the War of the Succession, 13.

M

Macclesfield. Earl of, his impeachment, 67.
Madrid, treaty of, 132.
Malplaquet, battle of, 15; its results, 16.
Marlborough, Duke of, commands at Blenheim, 3; rewards received for his gallantry, 7; Duchess of, 10; loses her influence, 11; the Duke is disgraced, 17.
Masham, Mrs, rise of, 11.
Mississippi, French forts on, 155.
Moore, Thomas, his poetical works, 436.
Murray, Lord, qualities and talents of, 152.

R

Ramillies, battle of, 9; its results, 10.
Reform Bill, its provisions, 413, 414.
Regency, first council of, appointed, 205.
Representation, Parliamentary, efforts to reform, 294.
Riots in Staffordshire and South Wales, 291.
Robertson, William, 171; his qualities as a historian, 318.
Rockingham, Marquis of, becomes Premier, 206; his various measures, 236, 237.

N

Nassau, Rev. Mr., his mission to Rome, 336.

S

Saxe, Marshal, his victory at Fontenoy, 142.
Scott, Sir Walter, his personal history, 432; his various writings, 433; his pecuniary difficulties, 433.
Septennial Parliaments, 106.
Seville, Congress of, 101.
Shelbourne, Earl of, becomes Premier, 237; events during his administration, 238.
Sheridan, R. B., specimen of his eloquence, 256; his history, 309; his talents, 310.
Smith, Adam, his writings, 318.
Spain, preparations for war with, 79; its results, 80; second war declared against, 186; results, 187, 188.
South Sea Bubble, history of, 48, 49, 50.
Stamp Duties, origin of, 203, 204; discussions respecting, 209, 210.
Succession, war of the, 3.
Swift, Jonathan, his life and writings, 85, 86, 87.

T

Tories, doctrines of, 37.
Trafalgar, victory of, 268.
Trinity, controversies concerning, 60, 61.

U

United States, their freedom acknowledged, 237.
Utrecht, treaty of, 17.

V

Vernon, Admiral, his successes, 133.
Versailles, meeting of the States-General at, 254.

W

Walmoden, Madam, 110; her conduct, 115.
Walpole, Robert, his qualities as a statesman, 52, 53, 54; retained as Premier by George II., 97; furious attack on, in Parliament, 134; his final retirement, 137.
Wellington, Lord, victories in the Peninsula, 271; victory at Waterloo, 283.
Wellington, Earl of, becomes Premier, 138.
Wilkes, history and character of, 197, 198; his political agitations, 199; His Essay on Woman, 201; his frequent re-elections to Parliament, 219.
Willis, Dr., physician of George III., 275.
Whigs, doctrines of, 36.
Walpole, Horace, his history and character, 315.
Waterloo, victory of, 283.
Wilberforce, William, efforts against the slave-trade, 292, 428; his unwearied exertions, 429; his personal qualities, 430.
Windham, William, qualities of, 70, 71.

Y

York, Duke of, his death, 404.
Young, Sir George, enters the Cabinet, 237.

Z

Zell, princes of house of, 21; Sophia Dorothea, her imprisonment, 31, 32; her death, 57, 74.